The Cambridge Companion to Harriet Beecher Stowe

The Cambridge Companion to Harriet Beecher Stowe establishes new parameters for both scholarly and classroom discussion of Stowe's writing and life. This collection of specially commissioned essays provides new perspectives on the frequently read classic *Uncle Tom's Cabin*, as well as on topics of perennial interest, such as Stowe's representation of race, her attitude to reform, and her relationship to the American novel. The volume investigates Stowe's impact on the American literary tradition and the novel of social change. Contributions also offer lucid and provocative readings that analyze Stowe's writings through a variety of contexts, including antebellum reform, regionalism, law and the protest novel. Fresh, accessible, and engaged, this is the most up-to-date introduction available to Stowe's work. The volume, which offers a comprehensive chronology of Stowe's life and a helpful guide to further reading, will be of interest to students and teachers alike.

THE CAMBRIDGE
COMPANION TO
HARRIET BEECHER STOWE

EDITED BY

CINDY WEINSTEIN

California Institute of Technology

CAMBRIDGE
UNIVERSITY PRESS

PUBLISHED BY THE PRESS SYNDICATE OF THE UNIVERSITY OF CAMBRIDGE
The Pitt Building, Trumpington Street, Cambridge, United Kingdom

CAMBRIDGE UNIVERSITY PRESS
The Edinburgh Building, Cambridge, CB2 2RU, UK
40 West 20th Street, New York, NY 10011–4211, USA
477 Williamstown Road, Port Melbourne, VIC 3207, Australia
Ruiz de Alarcón 13, 28014 Madrid, Spain
Dock House, The Waterfront, Cape Town 8001, South Africa

http://www.cambridge.org

First published 2004

Printed in the United Kingdom at the University Press, Cambridge

Typeface Sabon 10/13 pt.   *System* LATEX 2$_\varepsilon$ [TB]

A catalogue record for this book is available from the British Library

ISBN 0 521 82592 X hardback
ISBN 0 521 53309 0 paperback

CONTENTS

Notes on contributors   *page* vii
Acknowledgments   x
Chronology   xi

Introduction   1
CINDY WEINSTEIN

1   Stowe and race   15
    SAMUEL OTTER

2   *Uncle Tom's Cabin* and the south   39
    CINDY WEINSTEIN

3   *Uncle Tom's Cabin* and the American Renaissance: the
    sacramental aesthetic of Harriet Beecher Stowe   58
    MICHAEL T. GILMORE

4   Reading and children: *Uncle Tom's Cabin* and *The Pearl
    of Orr's Island*   77
    GILLIAN BROWN

5   Uncle Tom and Harriet Beecher Stowe in England   96
    AUDREY FISCH

6   Staging black insurrection: *Dred* on stage   113
    JUDIE NEWMAN

7   Stowe and regionalism   131
    MARJORIE PRYSE

v

CONTENTS

8   Stowe and the law   154
    GREGG CRANE

9   Harriet Beecher Stowe and the American reform tradition   171
    RONALD G. WALTERS

10 Harriet Beecher Stowe and the dream of the great
    American novel   190
    LAWRENCE BUELL

11 Stowe and the literature of social change   203
    CAROLYN L. KARCHER

12 The afterlife of *Uncle Tom's Cabin*   219
    KENNETH W. WARREN

    Select bibliography   235
    Index   245

NOTES ON CONTRIBUTORS

GILLIAN BROWN is Professor of English and American Studies at the University of Utah. She is the author of *Domestic Individualism: Imagining Self in Nineteenth-Century America* (California, 1990) and *The Consent of the Governed: The Lockean Legacy in Eighteenth-Century American Culture* (Harvard, 2001). She is now working on two books: *In the Name of the Child*, a study of childhood and American literature, and *Books without Borders*, a study of the rise of children's literature.

LAWRENCE BUELL is Powell M. Cabot Professor of American Literature at Harvard University and author, among other books, of *New England Literary Culture: From Revolution Through Renaissance* (Cambridge, 1986) and *Emerson* (Harvard, 2003).

GREGG CRANE is Associate Professor of English at the University of Michigan. He is the author of *Race, Citizenship, and Law in American Literature* (Cambridge, 2002).

AUDREY FISCH is Associate Professor of English and Coordinator of Secondary English Education at New Jersey City University. She is the co-editor of *The Other Mary Shelley: Beyond Frankenstein* (Oxford, 1993) and the author of *American Slaves in Victorian England: Abolitionist Politics in Popular Literature and Culture* (Cambridge, 2000).

MICHAEL T. GILMORE is the Paul Prosswimmer Professor of American Literature at Brandeis University. A contributor to the *Cambridge History of American Literature*, his books include *American Romanticism and the Marketplace* (Chicago, 1985) and *Surface and Depth: The Quest for Legibility in American Culture* (Oxford, 2003).

CAROLYN L. KARCHER is the author of *Shadow over the Promised Land: Slavery, Race, and Violence in Melville's America* (Baton Rouge, 1980) and *The First Woman in the Republic: A Cultural Biography of Lydia Maria*

Child (Duke, 1994). Her other publications include *A Lydia Maria Child Reader* (Duke, 1997) and scholarly editions of Child's *Hobomok and other Writings on Indians* (Rutgers, 1986) and *An Appeal in Favor of that Class of Americans Called Africans* (Massachusetts, 1996) and of Catharine Maria Sedgwick's *Hope Leslie* (Penguin, 1998). She is currently collecting material for an anthology *cum* critical study of nineteenth-century American women's journalism.

JUDIE NEWMAN MA (Edinburgh) 1972, MA Edinburgh (1974), PhD (Cambridge) 1982. Founding fellow of the English Association, Academician, Academy of Social Sciences, Professor of American Studies, University of Nottingham.

SAMUEL OTTER is Associate Professor of English at the University of California, Berkeley. He is the author of *Melville's Anatomies* (California, 1999) and currently is writing a book on race, manners, violence, and freedom between the Constitution and the Civil War, entitled *Philadelphia Stories*.

MARJORIE PRYSE is Professor of English and Women's Studies and Chair of the Department of Women's Studies at the University at Albany, State University of New York. She has written extensively on regionalism in American fiction. Her most recent publication is *Writing out of Place: Regionalism, Women, and American Literary Culture*, co-authored with Judith Fetterley (Illinois, 2003). This critical book, along with the collection, *American Women Regionalists 1850–1910: A Norton Anthology*, co-edited with Judith Fetterley (Norton, 1992), places Stowe early in the tradition of literary regionalism.

RONALD G. WALTERS is Professor of History at the Johns Hopkins University. He is the author of *The Anti-slavery Appeal: American Abolitionism after 1830* (Johns Hopkins, 1976, paperback ed.: W. W. Norton, 1984), and *American Reformers: 1815–1860* (Hill and Wang, 1978, revised ed. 1997). He is also the editor of three books, including *Primers for Prudery: Sexual Advice to Victorian America* (Prentice–Hall, 1974, new ed., with additional material, 2000). At present, he is working on a history of twentieth-century American popular culture.

KENNETH W. WARREN teaches English at the University of Chicago. He is the author of *So Black and Blue: Ralph Ellison and the Occasion of Criticism* (Chicago, 2003) and *Black and White Strangers: Race and American Literary Realism* (Chicago, 1993).

CINDY WEINSTEIN is Associate Professor of Literature at the California Institute of Technology. She is the author of *The Literature of Labor and the Labors of Literature: Allegory in Nineteenth-Century American Fiction* (Cambridge, 1995) and *Family, Kinship, and Sympathy in Nineteenth-Century American Literature* (Cambridge, forthcoming).

ACKNOWLEDGMENTS

It's been my privilege and pleasure to edit this volume. I would like to thank Ray Ryan, editor at Cambridge University Press, for inviting me to take on this project and helping see it to completion.

The contributors of this Companion have given me an experience of intellectual partnership of the best kind. For their intelligence, diligence, enthusiasm, and timeliness, they have my deepest appreciation. Thanks to the Harriet Beecher Stowe Society, the American Literature Association, and the Harriet Beecher Stowe Center in Hartford for the chance to present this project while in progress. Molly Hiro's research assistance has been invaluable. I am grateful to Jean Ensminger, Susan Davis, and Margaret Lindstrom of the Caltech division of humanities and social sciences for providing crucial support. I would also like to thank the following people for advice and encouragement: Jim Astorga, Gregg Crane, William Merrill Decker, Michael Gilmore, Dori Hale, Joan Hedrick, Catherine Jurca, Robert Levine, Samuel Otter, Mac Pigman, Stephen Railton, Eric Sundquist, and John Sutherland.

CHRONOLOGY

1811 Harriet Elizabeth Beecher is born in Litchfield, Connecticut, June 14, seventh of nine children and youngest daughter of Dr. Lyman Beecher, Congregationalist minister, and Roxana Foote Beecher.

1816 Roxana Foote Beecher dies of tuberculosis at 41.

1817 Lyman remarries Harriet Porter of Portland, Maine; they eventually have four children together.

1819 Enters Litchfield Female Academy.

1823 Harriet's oldest sister, Catharine E. Beecher, establishes Hartford Female Seminary.

1824 Moves to Hartford to attend the Female Seminary. Composes her first work, "Can the Immortality of the Soul Be Proved by the Light of Reason?"

1825 First conversion experience.

1827 Begins teaching at the Hartford Female Seminary. Teaches there until 1832, mainly rhetoric and composition.

1832 Lyman Beecher becomes president of the Lane Theological Seminary in Cincinnati and moves the family to this frontier city. Catharine founds the Western Female Institute, and Harriet serves as her chief assistant and faculty member.

1833 Publishes *Primary Geography for Children*, a widely adopted textbook. Begins publishing stories and sketches in Cincinnati's *Western Monthly Magazine*. Visits a student in nearby Kentucky, the only occasion in her life when she witnesses slavery firsthand.

1836 On January 6, marries Calvin Stowe, a widower, clergyman, and faculty member at Lane Theological Seminary. Birth of twin girls, Harriet and Eliza, September 29.

1838 Her son Henry Ellis is born in January.

1839 Begins to publish her stories and sketches – including "Uncle Enoch," "Trials of a Housekeeper," and "Olympiana" – in national periodicals, such as *Godey's Lady's Book* and the *New-York Evangelist*.

1840   After giving birth to Frederick William on May 6, confined to bed for two months.

1842   Passage of the Maine Law, the first set of legal restrictions on the liquor trade.

1843   First collection of stories, *The Mayflower; or, Sketches of Scenes and Characters among the Descendants of the Pilgrims* published by Harper & Brothers in New York. Stowe's brother, George, commits suicide. Georgiana May is born in July, and Stowe is again ill afterwards for some months. Second religious conversion.

1845   An early anti-slavery sketch, "Immediate Emancipation," published in the *New-York Evangelist*.

1846   Takes the Water Cure at Brattleboro, Vermont, where her poor health improves markedly.

1848   Samuel Charles (Charley) is born in January, but dies during the 1849 cholera epidemic in Cincinnati.

1850   Returns to New England when Calvin is appointed to the faculty at Bowdoin College in Brunswick, Maine (his alma mater). Congress debates and then passes the Compromise of 1850; its strengthening of the Fugitive Slave Law is vigorously debated in New England circles. Publishes "The Freeman's Dream: A Parable" in the *National Era*, an abolitionist paper edited by Gamaliel Bailey in Washington, DC. Birth of her last child, Charles Edward, in July.

1851   In June, *Uncle Tom's Cabin* begins serialization in the *National Era*. The novel is printed in 41 installments over the next ten months.

1852   In March, *Uncle Tom's Cabin* published as a book in two volumes by John P. Jewett in Boston and sells 3,000 copies the first day, 300,000 by the end of its first year of publication. In Britain, sales were even more phenomenal: a million and a half the first year alone. The first staged version of *Uncle Tom's Cabin* opens this same year. Calvin leaves Bowdoin to teach at Andover Theological Seminary in Andover, MA, where the Stowe family resides until 1864.

1853   Publishes *A Key to Uncle Tom's Cabin* to defend against critics' charges of *Uncle Tom's Cabin*'s inaccuracies. Frederick Douglass asks for Stowe's support in establishing an industrial school for black men, and Harriet Jacobs requests her assistance in writing the story of her life as a slave, but she declines both appeals. Departs in April for first of three visits to Europe, where she is greeted enthusiastically by readers and fans and meets, among other celebrities, Lady Byron. Presented with the "Affectionate and Christian Address," an anti-slavery petition signed by a half a million British women.

1854   Publishes "An Appeal to the Women of the Free States of America, On the Present Crisis in Our Country" in the *Independent* to rally opposition to the Kansas–Nebraska Act, which was passed a month later. *Sunny Memories of Foreign Lands*, Stowe's account of her European travels, published by Phillips, Sampson of Boston.

1856   *Dred: A Tale of the Great Dismal Swamp*, an anti-slavery novel based, in part, on the Nat Turner slave rebellion, published by Phillips, Sampson in Boston. The novel never approached the popularity of *Uncle Tom's Cabin*. Publishes *The Christian Slave*, a dramatic version of *Uncle Tom's Cabin* that Stowe had written for Mary Webb to perform in England. Second trip to Europe.

1857   Henry Ellis Stowe, her oldest son and a freshman at Dartmouth College, drowns in the Connecticut River.

1859   After its serialization in the *Atlantic Monthly*, Derby and Jackson of New York publish *The Minister's Wooing*, a love story with theological overtones inspired by Stowe's religious crises, especially that provoked by Henry's untimely death. Third trip to Europe.

1861   Civil War begins, and Frederick, the Stowes' alcoholic son, enlists in the Union Army.

1862   *The Pearl of Orr's Island*, a story of New England, and *Agnes of Sorrento*, Stowe's Italian novel, published by Ticknor and Fields in Boston. At her meeting with the President on the occasion of the Emancipation Proclamation, Lincoln is said to have greeted her with "So you're the little woman who wrote the book that started this great war!"

1864   Calvin retires from Andover Seminary, and the Stowes move to Hartford, into "Oakholm," the elaborate house Stowe has built for them there. In 1870, sells the house to ease financial hardships.

1868   Purchases a home in Mandarin, Florida; the Stowes spend their winters here until 1884. Publishes *Men of Our Times*, sketches of famous men, with the Hartford Publishing Company

1869   *Oldtown Folks* published by Fields, Osgood in Boston, the second of Stowe's novels to appear only as a book rather than being serialized first (the other was *Dred*).

1870   *Lady Byron Vindicated*, Stowe's exposé of Byron's incestuous infidelities and defense of the poet's wife, published by Fields, Osgood in Boston. The book is taken up by the women's rights movement, but widely savaged by critics as sensationalist and lewd.

1871 Son Frederick, having struggled with alcoholism for much of his life, disappears and is not heard from again. *Pink and White Tyranny* published in Boston by Roberts Bros. This is the first of three New York "society" novels; the latter two are *My Wife and I* (1871) and its sequel *We and Our Neighbors* (1875). Writes these and other, more ephemeral works as a means of financial support for her family. Tours New England and the west throughout the 1870s, giving lectures and public readings of her works.

1872 *Sam Lawson's Oldtown Fireside Stories* published by J. R. Osgood in Boston. Staunchly defends her brother and celebrated minister Henry Ward Beecher against public charges of committing adultery with the wife of Theodore Tilton (editor of the *Independent*, in which Stowe had published essays). In the trial that follows, Beecher is cleared of all charges, but his reputation is irrevocably damaged by the scandal.

1873 *Palmetto Leaves*, a series of sketches about Florida, published by Osgood and Fields. *Woman in Sacred History*, a collection of stories about Biblical women, published by J. B. Ford & Company.

1878 Last novel, *Poganuc People*, based on her New England childhood, published by Fords, Howard, & Hulbert in New York.

1886 Calvin Stowe dies August 6.

1887 In August, death of daughter Georgiana May after years of illness and morphine addiction.

1889 Suffers decline in health; in an 1893 letter, describes her mental condition as "nomadic." Two biographies appear: an official one authored by her son Charles Edward Stowe, and an unauthorized version by Florine McCray.

1896 Dies of a stroke on July 1 in Hartford, age 85. Publication of *The Writings of Harriet Beecher Stowe*, a complete, sixteen volume collection of her works.

CINDY WEINSTEIN

Introduction

Harriet Beecher Stowe's most famous introduction took place on or around Thanksgiving Day, 1862, when she was introduced to President Abraham Lincoln, who allegedly greeted her with these memorable words, "So you're the little woman who wrote the book that made this great war!" Even if we grant Lincoln's statement its obvious degree of ironic intention, he, nevertheless, makes quite a claim for the impact of *Uncle Tom's Cabin* on American history. One glance at virtually any of Lincoln's speeches reveals that he, like Stowe, believed that the power of words could alter the minds and hearts of individuals. Stowe's faith in the transforming capacity of language makes a great deal of sense, given that she came from a distinguished family of ministers and social activists – in an 1851 letter to Frederick Douglass, she writes, "I am a ministers daughter – a ministers wife & I have had six brothers in the ministry . . . & I certainly ought to know something of the feelings of ministers." Stowe here refers to her father, Lyman Beecher, President of Lane Seminary, her husband, Calvin Stowe, who served at various times as Professor at Lane Seminary, Professor of the Chair of Sacred Literature at Andover Theological Seminary and Professor at Bowdoin College, and her brothers, the most famous of whom was Henry Ward Beecher, head of the prestigious Congregationalist Plymouth Church in Brooklyn and anti-slavery activist. This list, it should be noted, doesn't even mention her influential sisters, Catharine Beecher, founder of the Hartford Female Seminary and author of many tracts, including *A Treatise on Domestic Economy*, and Isabelle Beecher Hooker, whose close ties to Elizabeth Cady Stanton and Susan B. Anthony made Isabelle an important figure in the campaign for women's rights. To what extent Stowe's own words of ministration and protest catapulted the nation toward Civil War is an unanswerable question, but clearly Stowe wanted her novel to bring about great social change and Lincoln thought she had succeeded.[1]

    The Cambridge Companion to Harriet Beecher Stowe takes as its starting point Lincoln's suggestion that Stowe's writing changed the course of history. All of the essays in this volume take the position that *Uncle Tom's Cabin* exerted a momentous impact upon the life of American culture (and continues to do so), but the essays significantly diverge on what to make of Stowe's contribution in terms of her representations of race, gender, region, and nation. His words, therefore, serve not as a statement of truth about *Uncle Tom's Cabin*'s effects, but rather as a provocation to pose a series of questions: How and with what implications might this kind of novelistic influence be possible? How has the history of *Uncle Tom's Cabin* intersected with and, perhaps, changed US literary history? How does its narrative structure, depiction of characters, and ideological positioning produce, on the one hand, readings that champion the novel for its progressive call to action and, on the other, indict the novel for its racist prescription for inaction? How does *Uncle Tom's Cabin* produce such vastly different, indeed contradictory, positions, and how is this rich interpretative vortex made richer by the many theatrical productions, consumer products, and films, inspired by Stowe's novel? We might also ask, how does Stowe's great novelistic achievement fit into her own literary history which spans over six decades? After all, by the time Lincoln and Stowe met, she had already written several other texts, including *A Key to Uncle Tom's Cabin* (1853), her powerful defense of the novel's authenticity; *Dred: A Tale of the Great Swamp* (1856), her second anti-slavery novel and, according to some recent critics, a more devastating attack on slavery than *Uncle Tom's Cabin*; *The Minister's Wooing* (1859), a masterfully crafted novel (and the one most influenced by one of her favorite writers, Nathaniel Hawthorne), with a critique of slavery as it was practiced in eighteenth-century Newport, Rhode Island; *The Pearl of Orr's Island* (1862); and *Agnes of Sorrento* (1862). Although her celebrity status derived from her authorship of *Uncle Tom's Cabin*, the fact is that she not only continued to write about slavery, and in ways that interestingly depart from that novel, but she was beginning to lay the groundwork in her writings of the 1860s for the regionalist fictions of Sarah Orne Jewett, Mary Wilkins Freeman, and many others.

Lincoln's introduction presents us with the Harriet Beecher Stowe who needs no introduction; the woman from Litchfield Connecticut, born in 1811, who wrote *Uncle Tom's Cabin*, the best-selling novel of the nineteenth century. It was first serialized in the *National Era* from June 5, 1851 through April 1, 1852, and published in a two-volume book form by John P. Jewett on March 20, 1852. Two cataclysmic but very different events laid the political and emotional foundation for Stowe's inspiration, which first took shape in her famous vision of "the scene of the death of Uncle Tom . . . as if the crucified, but now risen and glorified Christ, ere speaking to her through the black man, cut and bleeding under the blows of the slave whip". First,

Uncle Tom's Cabin was written as a protest against the Fugitive Slave Law, which was, for many northerners, the most controversial element of the Compromise of 1850 in that it legally mandated them to cooperate in the capture and return of runaway slaves. Second, it was written as a lamentation in response to the death of her infant son, Charley.[2]

It should come as no surprise that a novel produced out of anger and sadness has elicited in the course of its one hundred fifty years in print responses ranging from tears to outrage. The tears were the result of her harrowing and, for many, effective representation of the cruelties of slavery, in particular its devastating impact on slave families. The upset generated by her novel has a more complicated trajectory. Not only were readers devastated by the fact that such brutal scenes were being enacted in slave states, but many readers for very different reasons were outraged by Stowe's depiction of them. Southern whites, in general, objected to Stowe's allegedly false depiction of the peculiar institution, and prominent white abolitionists and African Americans found the stereotypical representation of black characters unpalatable and her seeming endorsement of colonization deplorable. Even Douglass, her staunch supporter, felt called upon to remind Stowe, "the truth is, dear madam, we are *here*, and we are likely to remain." Indeed, the responses to *Uncle Tom's Cabin* provide a medium through which one could construct a history of US black/white relations, one that is, perhaps, framed on the one end by William Lloyd Garrison's attack in March 1852, "is there one law of submission and non-resistance for the black man, and another law of rebellion and conflict for the white man?" and, on the other, with the last words of the epigraph to Richard Wright's *Uncle Tom's Children*, "Uncle Tom is dead!"[3]

The range of responses to the character of Uncle Tom is here startlingly bracketed: from one perspective, the book that carries his name helped to inspire a Civil War and bring about the end of slavery, while from another, Uncle Tom came to stand for, as Wright puts it, "reluctant toleration for the cringing type who knew his place before white folk." A study of the visual images of Uncle Tom, of sundry collectibles, of musical productions, attests to the noxious, racist deployment of Stowe's central character. But Uncle Tom, it should also be recalled, refuses to flog the exhausted slave Lucy, whom he had earlier assisted by adding to her sack of cotton, and refuses to give Legree any information regarding Cassy and Emmeline's plans to escape – an escape that he has encouraged after listening to Cassy's story of unrelenting suffering. All heroic acts of resistance that culminate in his sacrificial death.

Stowe's depiction of the Christ-like Uncle Tom as docile, maternal, and childlike (characteristics, it should be noted, valued dearly by many in the antebellum period), clearly laid the foundation for the deeply racist images that followed. Her racial essentialism, or what historian George Frederickson calls "romantic racialism," provided her with a set of types which she then applied to blacks, southerners, and northerners, and which had, paradoxically, its most tenacious and corrosive effects on the group she was most interested in aiding: African Americans. In examining and assessing the content and form of Stowe's racialism, contemporary critics have been deeply divided as to its racist implications – as divided as the novel's first readers. *Uncle Tom's Cabin* may have been written by Stowe in the early 1850s, but the novel has been written many times over since then. In other words, the life of the novel has been extended and the novel has been transformed, virtually since the moment of its publication, through stage adaptations that often borrowed quite heavily from the minstrel tradition, children's editions that heavily redacted Stowe's text, and anti-Uncle Tom novels that inverted Stowe's characters in order to defend slavery. A representative example of this last is W. L. G. Smith's *Life at the South; or "Uncle Tom's Cabin" as It Is. Being Narratives, Scenes, and Incidents in the Real "Life of the Lowly,"* in which Uncle Tom appears as a "refractory," lazy (the second chapter is entitled, "The Plantation – Uncle Tom's Laziness"), and "stubborn" slave. *Uncle Tom's Cabin*'s rich afterlife makes it both inevitable and necessary that many of the essays that follow take up the question of Stowe's contribution to the representation of race and its continuing legacy in African-American literature, in the literature of social reform, in US legal and political thought, to name just a few areas of cultural production where one can examine the influence of Stowe's novel and its endlessly signifying effects. Although Stowe had confidently written in 1852 to Gamaliel Bailey, her editor at the *National Era*, that "there is no arguing with pictures," her novelistic picture of slavery with "its reverses, changes, and the negro character" has done nothing but inspire debate and dialogue. With that in mind, the complexities of Stowe's contributions to questions of race, gender, popular culture, *et al.* neither go away nor are resolved in the essays that make up this volume – that would not be a rational outcome given the hugely disparate range of responses to her work. Instead, these essays present readers with arguments and analyses that at once sharpen the focus, expand the pictures, and clarify the rich and diverse legacy of Stowe's literary efforts.[4]

But why a *Cambridge Companion to Stowe* now? One reason is that, along with Hawthorne's *The Scarlet Letter* (1850) and Herman Melville's *Moby-Dick* (1851), *Uncle Tom's Cabin* is taught in virtually every American literature undergraduate and graduate survey course, in addition to appearing on the syllabi for classes in American history, women's studies, and African-American studies. The pedagogical centrality of Stowe's novel has significantly increased in the last twenty years as literary critics, in particular, have adopted interpretative approaches (new historicism, feminism, cultural studies) that contextualize literary texts in relation to decisive cultural issues of their time. *Uncle Tom's Cabin* is obviously an exemplary and provocative text to present in this methodological climate. Students are often disarmed by its seeming simplicity and flustered by its apparent lack of a dominant symbol, whether it be an "A," a whale, or a pond. They find the foundational terms of Stowe's symbolic system, which combines Christianity, her culture's most salient belief system, with slavery, her culture's most divisive issue, at once more and less straightforward. More direct, in that what the novel means – end slavery – seems so obvious that students often feel that there is little to say, other than to observe and often complain about Stowe's propagandistic authorial interventions, the repetition of families being separated, or the incessant tears that accompany those separations. At the same time, students find Stowe to be less direct, in that those very methods for conveying her meaning seem irretrievably remote, decidedly abstract, relentlessly sentimental. The capaciousness of *Uncle Tom's Cabin* invites a range of readings that puts it in the same category as *The Scarlet Letter* and *Moby-Dick*. Consequently, a key concern among all of these essays is to provide readers with a number of interpretative options that will help them make sense not only of *Uncle Tom's Cabin*'s aesthetic arrangements and narrative devices, but also of its enormous representational breadth.

This leads us to a second reason for a Stowe Companion. *Uncle Tom's Cabin* has become, in approximately the last twenty years, another leviathan in the canon of American literature. Like *Moby-Dick*, which virtually disappeared from the critical radar screen for over sixty years and then experienced a critical renaissance that has no end in sight, Stowe's novel is now an indispensable text through which to convey the volatility of the antebellum landscape as related to race, gender, politics, aesthetics, region, and class. To be sure, the novels radically differ in a variety of ways, including their focus, style and content, to name three of the most obvious: Aunt Rachel and "Madame Leviathan" are the only female characters in *Moby-Dick* compared to the many women who constitute the center of *Uncle Tom's Cabin*'s plot and politics; the narrative voice in *Uncle Tom's Cabin* is much more consistent and obtrusive than in *Moby-Dick*; and the ideal family to which one aspires in *Moby-Dick* is figured by the orgiastic homosocial union in "A Squeeze of the Hand," whereas happy families in Stowe's novel are orchestrated by mothers, such as Eliza, Aunt Rachel (quite different from Melville's character of that name), and Mrs. Shelby. There are, however, intriguing similarities. Like *Moby-Dick*, *Uncle Tom's Cabin* is a book very much preoccupied with the status of books, the Bible in particular, and their hermeneutic possibilities. Like *Moby-Dick*, *Uncle Tom's Cabin* is deeply invested in critiquing antebellum society, which both Melville and Stowe believe can be better. Like *Moby-Dick*, with its relentless representation of how bodies, human and cetological, are violated and turned into things, *Uncle Tom's Cabin* is determined to end a system that turns men into things (which was, of course, the original subtitle of the novel). And even though one can argue, and influential scholars have, that their critiques of the status quo are ultimately complicit in the structures of power that they strive to undermine, the fact is that *Uncle Tom's Cabin* has borne the particular brunt of contemporary critical disdain.

Stowe's novel has become, in recent years, a critical white whale. And I don't mean as the bearer of interpretative capaciousness, but rather as an object to be spatially isolated (in terms of her career), hermeneutically contained, and thereby classified once and for all. Surely, though, there were reasons why southern readers committed to slavery, for example, were deeply unsettled upon reading the novel. Or why Senator Charles Sumner in his 1852 speech, "Freedom National, Slavery Sectional," invoked *Uncle Tom's Cabin* in his argument against the Fugitive Slave Law. Oddly enough, the woman who was championed by Douglass as having written "a work of marvelous depth and power [to which] nothing could have better suited the moral and humane requirements of the hour," now stands for the racist presumptions of her society. Not only does this position fail to confront fully the historical impact of the novel, it has produced a stalemate in interpretations of Stowe that inevitably places her in the position of the benevolent, though benighted, antebellum woman eager to champion the cause of progressive politics but ideologically paralyzed by her place in time. The reader of *The Companion* is presented with a set of essays and analytical tools that allow him/her to move beyond a critical paradigm in which Stowe can only be either trapped or transcendent. We have instead a multi-dimensional Stowe – progressive, romantic racialist, social reformer, close reader, litigant, Christian, regionalist.[5]

This collection, then, expands our understanding of Stowe's career and her influence in American literature and culture. It presents a heterogeneous and intellectually rich Stowe whose manifold literary productions are best read through as broad a set of contexts as possible, including antebellum reform movements, novels of social protest, eighteenth-century ideals of language, nineteenth-century theories of reading, twentieth-century racial politics, and more. In doing so, the essays illuminate what Jane Tompkins calls the "cultural work" of Stowe's fiction by paying particular attention to *Uncle Tom's Cabin* and to the aesthetic and ideological developments in her career as a whole. As this last suggests, *Uncle Tom's Cabin* stands as the textual centerpiece of the volume – without that novel, clearly there would be no *Companion to Stowe* – but several of the essays examine the critical consequences of interpreting *Uncle Tom's Cabin* as if it were Stowe's only word, and last word, on slavery, religion, and domestic life. A reading of her later works suggests that this isn't the case. For example, the problem of slavery is a matter of much importance to *The Minister's Wooing*. Her abiding attraction to the rituals and romance of Catholicism in *Agnes of Sorrento* is evidence of her dissatisfaction with the aridity and severity of the Calvinist religious forms bequeathed to her by her father. Her defense of Lady Byron in *Lady Byron Vindicated* (1870) registers her ongoing contribution to the debate about women's place in nineteenth-century society. She continued to write well into the 1880s, and although it is difficult to imagine even the most devoted of Stowe readers making a compelling argument for the centrality or literary excellence of a text like *Palmetto Leaves* (1872) or *Poganuc People* (1878), the fact is that many of Stowe's less well known texts are garnering enough interest to warrant republication.

This gets us to the third reason. In 1986, when Eric Sundquist edited *New Essays on Uncle Tom's Cabin*, he prefaced his bibliography with the following statement: "Although the critical literature on *Uncle Tom's Cabin* is slight compared to that on the works of other major writers of the period, a number of recent books and essays have given Stowe and her novel more serious attention." These words – accurate then but inapplicable now, a mere two decades later – were written in the wake of the pioneering work on Stowe that was produced by critics such as Ann Douglas in *The Feminization of American Culture* (1977), Tompkins in *Sensational Designs: The Cultural Work of American Fiction, 1790–1860* (1985), and Philip Fisher in *Hard Facts: Setting and Form in the American Novel* (1985). Several of the essays in this volume discuss the institutional and political conditions leading up to this critical renaissance of *Uncle Tom's Cabin*, which include, perhaps most importantly, the impact of the women's movement and the civil rights movement on feminist literary criticism and African-American studies. It is also important to point out that, although there are examples of literary histories of the antebellum period in which Stowe's novel receives more than adequate treatment, more often than not, *Uncle Tom's Cabin* was consigned to the margins of literary analysis, and in some cases, completely erased. F. O. Matthiessen's *American Renaissance* (1941), Charles Feidelson's *Symbolism and American Literature* (1953), and Richard Chase's *The American Novel and its Tradition* (1957), three key texts in the formation of the canon of antebellum American literature, have virtually nothing to say about the most popular novel written in the antebellum period. The effect of correcting this lacuna has been a critical interest in Stowe that shows no signs of abating. In particular, literary examinations of Stowe's ideal of sympathy, articulated at the conclusion of the novel when she urges her readers to "see to it that *they feel right*," has led to enormous interest in the sentimental writers of Stowe's generation, the "feminine fifties," to invoke Pattee's rather dated phrase. Indeed, the starting point for many contemporary readings of Stowe is the debate between Douglas and Tompkins about the ideological effects of Stowe's novel, with Douglas maintaining that *Uncle Tom's Cabin* demonstrates "the political sense obfuscated or gone rancid" and Tompkins asserting that the novel "represents a monumental effort to reorganize culture from the woman's point of view." Several of the essays in this *Companion*, while engaging the central issues taken up by Douglas and Tompkins, nevertheless depart from their binary approach to Stowe so as to demonstrate the intellectual range and the ideological variability of her cultural work.[6]

There are other important collections, specifically on *Uncle Tom's Cabin*, that have followed in the wake of these foundational analyses of Stowe, including *The Stowe Debate: Rhetorical Strategies in "Uncle Tom's Cabin"* (1994), edited by Mason I. Lowance, Jr., Ellen E. Westbrook, and R. C. De Prospo, and *Approaches to Teaching Stowe's "Uncle Tom's Cabin"* (2000), edited by Elizabeth Ammons and Susan Belasco. *The Cambridge Companion* differs from these volumes in its commitment to representing scholarly essays that embrace Stowe's entire career, many of which analyze elements of *Uncle Tom's Cabin* in relation to that career, as well as its attempt to broaden the conversation by situating the novel with reference to a set of historical contexts that have been heretofore relatively marginalized in examinations of it. These include, for example, the transatlantic aspect of Stowe's celebrity, the appropriation of Stowe's call to sympathy by pro-slavery southern writers, her imbrication in antebellum legal discourse, her fluctuating status as sentimentalist and regionalist, and her place in the tradition of the American novel. It is also worth mentioning that, in addition to the canonical status now accorded to *Uncle Tom's Cabin*, a renewed interest in Stowe's other texts has followed. Undoubtedly, Joan Hedrick's 1994 Pulitzer Prizewinning biography of Stowe has much to do with this resurgence as well. A list of recent publications suffices to prove the point: Penguin's 1999 publication of *The Minister's Wooing*, its 2000 publication of *Dred*, a 1992 edition of *Dred* first published by Ryburn Publishing and then picked up by Edinburgh University Press in 1999, a 1998 third printing of *Poganuc People* by the Stowe–Day Foundation, a 1999 University Press of Florida edition of *Palmetto Leaves*, and Houghton Mifflin's 2001 edition of *The Pearl of Orr's Island*. This flurry of publishing activity bespeaks an interest in Stowe's oeuvre to which this Companion responds.

The essays thus expose its readers to the key issues in the literature written by and about Stowe. They are designed to speak to one another, offering readers a variety of compelling and competing interpretative possibilities. A brief word on their organization before explaining their content is in order. They are arranged so that the earlier essays concentrate, in large measure, on *Uncle Tom's Cabin*, with the middle essays expanding the view of Stowe's career through analyses of *Dred, The Pearl of Orr's Island,* and *Oldtown Folks* (1869), and the later essays widening the contextual scope still further to include examinations of Stowe's impact on debates about the law, reform, and genre, which also include analyses of less read texts, including *The Minister's Wooing, Lady Byron Vindicated* (1870), and *My Wife and I* (1871). The collection is framed by Samuel Otter's and Kenneth W. Warren's essays on race in Stowe's writing. Essays in between, such as Judie Newman's and Ronald G. Walters's, approach the question of race from a more tightly conceived historical perspective. Several essays, my own and Audrey Fisch's, consider Stowe from the point of view of reader response, with Gillian Brown's essay taking up the very issue of reading itself in *Uncle Tom's Cabin* and *The Pearl of Orr's Island*. The essays by Michael T. Gilmore and Lawrence Buell revitalize discussions of Stowe through the relatively absent, but important, vocabulary of aesthetics and genre. Questions of form and narrative are also central to Marjorie Pryse's discussion of Stowe's regionalism and Carolyn L. Karcher's analysis of what she calls the literature of social change and Stowe's essential place in a form of artistic expression that links art and praxis.

Because *Uncle Tom's Cabin* has been such a lightning rod for debates about race in US literature, the Companion begins with Otter's "Stowe and race," which explores how Stowe's novel, and particularly the character of Uncle Tom, has come to signify a tradition of representing African-American identity that must be ruptured. Using contemporary African-American readings of Stowe, which resonate powerfully with Martin Delany's 1853 indictment of Stowe – "she *knows nothing about us*, 'the Free Colored people of the United States,' neither does any other white person" – Otter goes on to suggest that Stowe, shortly after the publication of *Uncle Tom's Cabin*, might very well have understood how Delany reached that conclusion and then revised her next anti-slavery novel, *Dred*, accordingly. Otter proposes that even as contemporary critics have striven to historicize *Uncle Tom's Cabin* through a number of different contexts, race and gender being the most significant, scholars have replicated the antebellum tendency to isolate *Uncle Tom's Cabin* from Stowe's other anti-slavery texts.[7]

That Stowe continued to be a reader and reviser of her own work and ideas means that *Uncle Tom's Cabin* can be productively analyzed in the context of her developing and, as he suggests, changing notions of race. In "*Uncle Tom's Cabin* and the south," I examine how the south's reception of *Uncle Tom's Cabin*, particularly reviews of the novel and the anti-Tom novels that challenged Stowe's representations of slavery, assumed the form of an epistemological debate about evidence and fact. Stowe found herself required to prove the truth of her fiction, which she aims to do in *A Key to Uncle Tom's Cabin*, by demonstrating that pro-slavery expressions of sympathy are inherently fallacious and that anti-slavery expressions of "feeling right" are founded in fact. *A Key*, in other words, picks up where *Uncle Tom's Cabin* left off, and is, indeed, key. Written almost immediately upon the publication of the novel, it transforms our understanding of Stowe's sympathy by riveting it to fact and by insisting that "feeling right," though a necessary first step toward abolishing slavery, is insufficient to accomplish that end, if divorced from acting right.

If *A Key* is Stowe's attempt to ensure that the meaning of her anti-slavery words is not perverted by pro-slavery appropriations of them, Michael T. Gilmore's "*Uncle Tom's Cabin* and the American Renaissance" historicizes Stowe's abiding belief in what he calls "the potentially lethal energy of words." Antebellum fiction, he demonstrates, is marked by a hopeful fascination that language could change the world and a fear that, perhaps, words no longer had the power to do so. Like Stowe, Thoreau, Melville, Hawthorne, Cooper, and Poe have inherited a redoubtable verbal legacy, with the republican rhetoric of the Revolution, on the one hand, and the religious rhetoric of America's founding, on the other, each of which inspires acts of linguistic power and conspires, in some cases, to induce anxieties of linguistic failure. The sacramental aesthetic to which his essay's subtitle refers is the condition of language to which *Uncle Tom's Cabin* and other texts of the American Renaissance aspire; one which closes the gap between aesthetics and acts, between representation and reality. And for Stowe's novel, in particular, one which joins her words and "the Word," or Christ.

Gillian Brown's essay, "Reading and children," similarly takes up the issue of Stowe's ongoing attempt to bridge sacred and secular narrative. Stowe's investment in the child reader (and the reader as child) is crucial both to this operation and the larger project of representing and producing the interiority of children. Through an analysis of Topsy and Eva, and their scenes of reading, interpretation, and conversion in *Uncle Tom's Cabin*, Brown establishes how Stowe models for her audience correct and incorrect, Christian and un-Christian ways of reading. The "issue of irreconcilable readings" gets reenacted, though not resolved, in *The Pearl of Orr's Island* as its two child protagonists – Mara and Moses – are characterized in terms of their relations to texts, especially the Bible and *The Tempest*. Stowe's recognition of hermeneutic divergences (and their basis in racial, gendered, and class identity) spurs her narrative toward its ministerial promise, the deliverance of its readers to a Christian way of life.

The two essays that follow present Stowe's work from the different and extremely important perspective of the transatlantic context. In "Uncle Tom and Harriet Beecher Stowe in England," Audrey Fisch explores why *Uncle Tom's Cabin* was such a hugely popular, though sometimes lamented, phenomenon in England. She contends that the publication of Stowe's novel coincided with a British reading public that was very well positioned to receive Stowe's novel for a number of reasons, including the circulation and popularity of slave narratives, the strength of the British anti-slavery movement, and perhaps most interestingly, the fact that "Tom-mania" functioned to construct a coherent and progressive national identity that could be distracted from its own troubling internal politics. Judie Newman's essay, "Staging black insurrection," approaches Stowe from the vantage point of British reception as well, but establishes the importance of *Dred* in the history of British theatre during the 1850s. She brings to light a previously unknown archive in order to examine the differences between Stowe's novel and British adaptations of it (which widely diverge, often comically so), and to make the case that these adaptations demonstrate a willingness on the part of British audiences, as opposed to US ones, to see African-American violence as a likely outcome of the controversy over slavery. Such an outcome, of course, is one that Stowe evades at the conclusion of *Dred*, while leaving the reader with little sense of how anything but violence could be the logical outcome of the novel. Although British and American adaptations are linked by their often bizarre reimaginings of the text, Newman's essay makes it clear that British audiences were exposed to an interpretation of *Dred* that was closer to the more troubling, more violent undercurrents of Stowe's novel.

Marjorie Pryse's essay, "Stowe and regionalism," asks us to think about Stowe's writing from the point of view of someone deeply invested in and empathetic toward the local cultures of US life, New England in particular: an investment that characterizes her career, from her earliest writings, such as "The Old Meeting-House: Sketch from the Note-Book of an Old Gentleman," published in 1840, to *Palmetto Leaves*, her homage/tour guide to life in northern Florida. From this analytic perspective, *Uncle Tom's Cabin* can be understood as a precursor to Stowe's more traditionally understood regionalist texts, such as *The Minister's Wooing*, *The Pearl of Orr's Island* and *Oldtown Folks*, in that "Stowe's first novel both initiates and reveals the complexity of [her] struggle to understand the relationship between geographical region, national values, and literary form." Regionalism thus becomes an alternative and, according to Pryse, a more radical method of narrative by which Stowe confronts many of the same issues she had explored in her earlier novels of reform, but with greater empathy and effect.

Reform is also the subject of the next two essays, Gregg Crane's, "Stowe and the law," and Ronald G. Walters's, "Harriet Beecher Stowe and the American reform tradition." Crane introduces us to a Stowe whose profound discontent with the laws of the US, especially the Fugitive Slave Law, motivates her to critique them, break them, and hopefully transform them. Based on a theory of "higher law," in which the law would "correspond with the citizenry's moral faith," Stowe's fictions work to make law become a reflection of an ideal and just society. Crane analyzes Stowe's purposeful, persistent and, at times, inconsistent entanglements with the law, from an early short story entitled, "Love versus Law," through *Uncle Tom's Cabin*, *A Key*, *Dred*, and *Lady Byron Vindicated*. On the one hand, she makes a cogent case, in the form of interactions between her fictional characters, on behalf of consensus as the necessary foundation for justice, but on the other she stops short of delegitimizing relations based on status. Walters is similarly interested in the imaginative limits encountered and, in some cases, traversed by Stowe as she attempts to effect reform through popular fiction. The essay first situates Stowe's ideas about reform *vis-à-vis* other movements of the period designed to promote a better society, including temperance, alternative, utopian communities, and, of course, abolitionism. The interpretative interest of Stowe's anti-slavery novels (*The Minister's Wooing* being one of them) lies in her faith that words can reform individuals, a faith that is both promulgated and undermined. Her commitment to moral suasion is accompanied by a profound understanding that suasion itself had been compromised in a society where people were defined as things. And her faith in individual conversion as the foundation for social change ultimately becomes an obstacle to her reformist vision. Unable to portray the liberation of all African Americans, she imagines the emancipation of individual slaves.

Lawrence Buell's "Harriet Beecher Stowe and the dream of the great American novel" anatomizes the workings of Stowe's imagination in *Uncle Tom's Cabin* and *Dred* in terms of her approach to the representation of character, nation, and literary form. Using John W. DeForest's recommendation in 1868 that *Uncle Tom's Cabin* be considered "the great American novel" as a starting point, Buell interrogates exactly what that phrase might mean for a reading of Stowe's text (she didn't conceive of it as a novel, per se). The essay establishes how *Uncle Tom's Cabin* participates in her culture's investments in fiction as embedded in fact – *A Key* being the fullest expression of this attitude – but then demonstrates how Stowe moves beyond this potentially limiting rubric in *Dred*. In her comparative willingness to relinquish the imperative to ground her fiction in actuality, Stowe produces in *Dred* a vision of slavery more gothic, more violent, more effective, perhaps, and, paradoxically, more realist, than *Uncle Tom's Cabin*.

Stowe's relation to genre or, more accurately, genres, is the topic of Carolyn L. Karcher's "Stowe and the literature of social change." Stowe's enormous contribution to a variety of literary genres is here delineated at the same time as her debts to earlier writers are unfolded (some of them quite controversial, as in the case of Josiah Henson, who Delany believed should share Stowe's profits given her seemingly wholesale usage of his story). The characters and structure of *Uncle Tom's Cabin* are analyzed in relation to an array of anti-slavery texts, enabling us to understand better the breadth of Stowe's accomplishment and, perhaps, the reasons for its tremendous success. The Stowe of this essay is not only the most influential writer of all protest literature, whose influence can be found in texts as disparate as Upton Sinclair's *The Jungle* and Rachel Carson's *Silent Spring*, but also a generic innovator who, in *The Minister's Wooing* and *My Wife and I*, played a central role in establishing the prototypes for regional and urban fiction.

Kenneth W. Warren's "The afterlife of *Uncle Tom's Cabin*" presents a broad account of the novel's reception post World War II, and explains both the ideological limitations of Stowe's protest novel, with particular reference to the writings of Richard Wright and James Baldwin, and the essential (and often conflicted) role it has played in the production of contemporary literary criticism of the antebellum period. Warren examines how *Uncle Tom's Cabin* circulates within these separate, yet in several cases overlapping, communities. He explores how, on the one hand, Stowe's text functions as a basic, though fundamentally inaccurate condition of representation against which African-American writers write, while, on the other, the novel played a crucial role in the reformation of the canon of American literature and the formation of scholarly identity, particularly for feminist critics. This account of *Uncle Tom's Cabin* as the well-spring of both intense disapprobation and profound productivity offers a model of reading what has come before and is, appropriately, the last essay in the volume.

NOTES

1. I would like to thank Joan Hedrick for directing me to the proper reference for this story, which is *Harriet Beecher Stowe: The Story of Her Life* (Boston: Houghton Mifflin Co., 1911), 223, written by Stowe's son, Charles Edward, and her grandson, Lyman Beecher. The letter to Douglass, written on July 9, 1851, is reprinted

in Hedrick's *The Oxford Harriet Beecher Stowe Reader* (New York: Oxford University Press, 1999), 60.

2. *Harriet Beecher Stowe: The Story of Her Life*, 145.
3. Quoted in Robert S. Levine, "*Uncle Tom's Cabin* in *Frederick Douglass' Paper*: an analysis of reception" (rept. in Elizabeth Ammons's edition of *Uncle Tom's Cabin* [New York: W. W. Norton & Company, 1994]), 535; *Documents of Upheaval: Selections from William Lloyd Garrison's The Liberator, 1831–1865*, ed. Truman Nelson (New York: Hill and Wang, 1966), 239; Richard Wright, *Uncle Tom's Children: Five Long Stories* (Cleveland and New York: The World Publishing Company, 1936), epigraph on unnumbered page.
4. W. L. G. Smith, *Life at the South* (Buffalo: Jewett, Thomas and Co., 1852), 52, 40. Thomas F. Gossett's *Uncle Tom's Cabin and American Culture* provides a wealth of information on the novel's legacy. He writes about the dramatic adaptations, "Perhaps as many as fifty people would eventually see *Uncle Tom's Cabin*, the play, for every one person who would read the novel" (Dallas: Southern Methodist University Press, 1985), 260. Stowe's letter to Bailey, written on March 9, 1851 from her home in Brunswick, Maine, is reprinted in *The Oxford Harriet Beecher Stowe Reader*, 65.
5. Robert S. Levine, *Martin Delany, Frederick Douglass, and the Politics of Representative Identity* (Chapel Hill: University of North Carolina Press, 1997), 89.
6. Eric J. Sundquist, *New Essays on Uncle Tom's Cabin* (Cambridge: Cambridge University Press, 1986), 198; Leslie Fiedler is one of the most interesting exceptions. Not only does he examine *Uncle Tom's Cabin* in *Love and Death in the American Novel* (originally published 1960), but his return to the novel in *The Inadvertent Epic: From "Uncle Tom's Cabin" to "Roots"* (1980) anticipates several of Tompkins's own strategies in her recovery and recuperation of *Uncle Tom's Cabin*; *Uncle Tom's Cabin*, 385; Ann Douglas, *The Feminization of American Culture* (New York: Avon, 1977), 307; Jane Tompkins, *Sensational Designs: The Cultural Work of American Fiction, 1790–1860* (Oxford: Oxford University Press, 1985), 124.
7. *Martin Delany, Frederick Douglass and the Politics of Representative Identity*, 78.

1

SAMUEL OTTER

Stowe and race

In Robert Alexander's 1992 play, *I Ain't Yo' Uncle: The New Jack Revisionist Uncle Tom's Cabin*, Harriet Beecher Stowe's African-American characters accuse her of creating stereotypes and place her on trial.

George Harris delivers the main charge along with his verdict: "I find the accused – GUILTY!! . . . of writing stuff she couldn't possibly know about. A slave's experience. The black experience . . . my life here in America."[1] To make their case, the characters restage Stowe's story. They alter much of the dialogue, insert scenes, and rewrite their endings.

Restless in Canada, the escaped slave George returns to the United States at the head of the Black Thunder gang, whose mission is to free slaves and kill their masters.

Cassy, whose children have been sold and who has been the prisoner of Simon Legree for five long years (and in Alexander's version, Legree does rape his newest acquisition, the young Emmeline), sees Legree beating Tom, aims a gun at him, and blows him away. This script change is too much for the manful George Harris, who yells "Cut," demands to know "Who said the women get to shoot him?," and summons Harriet, who insists that this is not the ending that she wrote. Cassy responds, powerfully: "You wrote every word of the rage that's in me! You just didn't give me a gun" (88).

Tom, listed in the dramatis personae as "a man with an image problem," is transformed from an aggressively non-violent martyr into a figure resembling the protagonist's grandfather in Ralph Ellison's 1952 novel *Invisible Man*. Tom advises Topsy to follow a policy of strategic acquiescence with Miss Ophelia: "Let her think she's teaching you sumpthin! You'll have her eatin' outcho' hand like a heafer at feeding time" (51). With this scene, in which the irrepressible Tom counsels the young Topsy, Alexander brings the two characters together, which Stowe never does, thus rendering vivid this lacuna in *Uncle Tom's Cabin*.

Topsy herself has become a conjuror (she uses a lock of Eva's hair to cast a fatal spell on her rival) and also a rapper – not a nineteenth-century spirit-rapper but a late-twentieth-century hip-hop artist. After getting her free papers from Miss Ophelia (another scene not represented by Stowe), Topsy doesn't linger for a New England education nor does she end up being baptized or pursuing a missionary career in Africa. Instead, she heads for New York. She is given some of the last, most unsettling words in the play.

Tom is an ironic presence. He comments on the potentially different reactions of audience members to the approaching demise of Little Eva. As he carries her to her chamber, he imagines "white folks" reaching for their handkerchiefs and "bloods" urging, "Drop the bitch." Yet he refuses to cater to his audience, asserting that "This child done all she could to get me my freedom. But y'all can't take credit for what she did" (60). Tom fervently prays that his wounded master St. Clare will survive . . . at least until he finalizes his manumission. At the end of the play, bloodied on the ground, Tom greets George Shelby, who has come to ransom him, with a laconic "You's late" (89). His remark stands as a commentary not only on George Shelby but also on all the sentimental rescuers in literature whose timing is just a bit off.

The satire and racial humor in *I Ain't Yo' Uncle* are cathartic. George, Tom, Cassy, and Topsy express their frustrations, rearrange their types, and seize a fantasy of agency. They are neither victims nor savages, nor children. Alexander writes in a tradition of African-American responses to images that fix and confine, and to the legacy of *Uncle Tom's Cabin* in particular. His literary refugees might be counted among the spectral denizens of Ellison's 1963 essay, "The World and the Jug," who protest the textual impositions: "Prefabricated Negroes are sketched on sheets of paper and superimposed upon the Negro community; then when someone thrusts his head through the page and yells, 'Watch out there, Jack! There're people living under here,' they are shocked and indignant." Alexander's caricatures of stereotypes prefigure the plantation silhouettes of the contemporary artist Kara Walker, who evokes but also ruptures the smooth lines, who accentuates the edge between black figures and white ground. The unruly characters of *I Ain't Yo' Uncle* might be the immediate descendants of Ishmael Reed's antebellum tricksters in his bicentennial parody of slave representations, *Flight to Canada* (1976). In the first section of *Flight*, entitled "Naughty Harriet," Reed rephrases Hugh Auld's concerns about educating his slave Frederick Douglass, from Chapter 6 of Douglass's *Narrative*: "If you teach him how to read, he'll want to know how to write. And this accomplished, he'll be running away with himself. . . . Master Hugh could have taught Harriet Beecher Stowe a thing or two."[2]

Reed's pun conveys the ways in which African Americans under slavery figuratively and literally ran away with themselves. It nicely evokes questions of possession and agency at the center of debates about racial representation in *Uncle Tom's Cabin*. (Such debates hardly ever imagine that the white characters might themselves wish to indict Stowe.) Reed, Alexander, and Walker seek to emancipate Stowe's characters. In the title of another trenchant Ellison essay collected in *Shadow and Act*, they seek to "change the joke and slip the yoke."

The joke, however, is not only on or about Stowe. The characters of *Uncle Tom's Cabin* have been appropriated for book illustrations, newspaper cartoons, posters, toys, dolls, sheet music, and playing cards. They have been conscripted for stage plays, minstrel shows, and movie screens. As Thomas F. Gossett demonstrates in his *Uncle Tom's Cabin and American Culture*, since the publication of the book the characters in their many incarnations have influenced thinking, in America and abroad, about race, region, religion, politics, and gender.[3] Stowe's title character lives on in the language, aged and bent by his circulation. Even – and maybe especially – for those who haven't read a word of Stowe's book, "Uncle Tom" evokes a posture of deference, abjection, or betrayal. Given the prominence of the many "Tom" shows in the nineteenth and twentieth centuries, Alexander's characters appropriately conduct their trial on stage.

Yet, in some ways that Alexander suggests and in some ways that he doesn't, this trial of, by, and for *Uncle Tom*'s characters is more complicated than it seems.

Alexander's Stowe enters her guilty plea too easily. The evidence against her is restricted to her first novel, which was serialized in the *National Era* from June 1851 until April 1852 and then published in two volumes in 1852. There is no mention of the five-hundred-page *Key to Uncle Tom's Cabin*, the documentary defense that Stowe published in 1853 in response to attacks on the novel's veracity; nor of her second anti-slavery novel *Dred*, published in two volumes in 1856. With its melodrama and epitome, *Uncle Tom's Cabin* has invited readers to abstract its characters from their actions and its scenes from their contexts. In both the popular and critical culture, the temptation has been great to stylize Stowe's difficult portrayals and to treat *Uncle Tom's Cabin* as though it can stand for all of her thinking about race in the United States. These temptations, as they used to say in the 1960s, are part of the problem and not part of the solution.

Alexander's African-American characters' primary charge against Stowe – that she writes about an experience "she couldn't possibly know about" – resuscitates one of the earliest complaints, leveled by Martin R. Delany in a sly 1853 letter to Frederick Douglass. "In all due respect and deference to Mrs. Stowe," Delany writes," I beg leave to say, that *she knows nothing about us*, 'the Free Colored people of the United States,' neither does any other white person – and, consequently, can contrive no successful scheme for our elevation; it must be done by ourselves." Although Delany is specifically addressing, and resisting, Douglass's consultation with Stowe about strategies for improving the condition of free blacks, his letter makes clear that his sense of Stowe's lack of knowledge extends to African Americans under slavery and to the representations in *Uncle Tom's Cabin*. In a subsequent letter to Douglass, Delany suggests that Stowe relied heavily on Josiah Henson's 1849 slave narrative – to such an extent that she and her publishers owe him a portion of the profits.[4] In *Flight to Canada*, Reed's narrator amplifies the charge to one of theft (one of the acts that makes his Harriet "naughty"). Reed suggests not financial royalties but literary retribution: "Josiah never would have thought of waging a plot-toting suit against her . . . When you take a man's story, a story that doesn't belong to you, that story will get you" (8–9).

What is the reach and what are the limits of intersubjective and interracial knowledge? Who owns which stories? What are the responsibilities of characters and of readers? What are the bases for the identifications made by writers and readers? What kinds of judgments do we make about works of literature?

These issues lie at the center of Stowe's work and at the center of our twenty-first-century evaluations. They are issues too complicated for the literary courtroom and its verdicts of "guilty" or "innocent," even when delivered (as they often are by critics) with extenuating circumstances of "ambivalence." In another letter to Douglass, Delany pulls back from his charge that Stowe *"knows nothing about us,"* explaining that he meant ironically to suggest her comparative lack of knowledge (April 18, 1853; *Delany Reader* 232–236). Although I may have seemed to be verging on a defense of Stowe, I mean instead to suggest that such a model of interpretation – defend or prosecute – has been part of the problem in interpreting Stowe's writings. With attention to sequence and contexts and to some features in Stowe's writing that have been overlooked, I hope to convey the complexity – the characteristic peculiarity – of her thinking about race.

Uncle Tom's Cabin

Much of the critical attention to questions of race in *Uncle Tom's Cabin* has focused on the prominent figure of Tom.[5] According to Stowe, he "was a large, broad-chested, powerfully-made man, of a full glossy black, and a face whose truly African features were characterized by an expression of grave and steady good sense, united with much kindliness and benevolence."[6] With "the soft, impressible nature of his kindly race, ever yearning toward the simple and the childlike" (127), he is drawn to the young Eva St. Clare, the daughter of his Louisiana master. Like his fellow Africans, he receives the Gospel "with eager docility" (343). While shackled by the slavetrader Haley, he dispenses advice to George Shelby, the son of his Kentucky master, urging him to be deferential to his parents. During the steamboat trip down the Mississippi to be sold by Haley in New Orleans, Tom saves Eva from drowning. After being beaten on the Legree plantation on the Red River, his days clearly numbered, he refuses to use the axe Cassy has provided against Legree or to escape with her and Emmeline, as he earlier refused to flee the Shelby estate with Eliza and her son Harry. Most dramatically and memorably, after suffering punishments that Stowe's narrator redundantly figures as a kind of Crucifixion, Tom tells Legree, who has come to kill him, that his blows will hurt the perpetrator more than his victim and that he would give the last drop of blood in his body if it would save Legree's precious soul. Before dying, he asks George Shelby to give his love to his former master and mistress and "everybody in the place." Quoting *Romans* 8.35, he poses the rhetorical question "Who, – who, – who shall separate us from the love of Christ?" and he exclaims "what a thing 't is to be a Christian!" (363).

The slavetrader Haley seems to get it right when he markets Tom to Augustine St. Clare as "all the moral and Christian virtues bound in black morocco" (129). Tom is less a person than a glossy package, a beautifully bound and stereotyped book of virtues. He is bound in various senses: legally, by slavery; racially, by his skin; theologically, by his Christian destiny; and ideologically, by Stowe. These are the bonds that later writers such as Reed and Alexander have in mind when they seek to liberate Stowe's characters through satire and parody. Tom is not the only character who seems manufactured. Most of the characters in *Uncle Tom's Cabin*, black and white, are not intended to be the realistic portrayals whose absence is lamented by many critics. They are the products of Stowe's uncanny ability in her first novel to give eloquent form to ideas about character and to discern and recast types: the little blonde evangelist, the anguished quadroon, the discontented mulatto, the sensitive (and ultimately ineffective) master, the selfish mistress, the vicious master (from New England), the conscientious spinster (who becomes conscious of her prejudice), and the Christian slave (the darker, the more devout). Stowe makes her arguments through these types. In Stowe's second anti-slavery novel, *Dred*, the arguments will become sharper and the types less clear.

Is the portrait of Tom racist? Racialist? Progressive? Repellent? Heartbreaking? Has Tom been emasculated? Feminized? If feminized, for good or for ill? Part of the answer has to do with what the historian George Frederickson has called Stowe's northern "romantic racialism," her view in

Uncle Tom's Cabin that racial differences were essential and permanent but not hierarchical.[7] Drawing on the arguments of thinkers such as the educator Alexander Kinmont, who lectured in Stowe's Cincinnati in 1837 and 1838, she envisioned a Protestant racial historical plot. At the end of *Uncle Tom's Cabin*, Stowe places this plot in a letter written by George Harris to a friend. Dissatisfied with the prospects of freedom in the United States, Harris argues for an African nation with a Christian destiny, specifically for the colony of Liberia: "To the Anglo-Saxon race has been intrusted the destinies of the world, during its pioneer period of struggle and conflict. To that mission its stern, inflexible, energetic elements, were well adapted; but, as a Christian, I look for another era to arise . . . I trust that the development of Africa is to be essentially a Christian one. If not a dominant and commanding race, they are, at least, an affectionate, magnanimous and forgiving one" (376). While these opinions technically belong to George, they certainly are Stowe's too. They culminate ideas about racial propensities and prospects that appear throughout the book. Charles Johnson, in his introduction to the Oxford University Press sesquicentennial edition of *Uncle Tom's Cabin*, reports, with exasperation, at least fifteen proclamations on the "nature" of blacks.[8]

"Romantic" racialism, I suppose, is preferable to "classical" racism, especially in the context of the vehement racial politics of the 1850s. Stowe's efforts to elevate her African-American characters to leading roles in the next, more truly Christian phase of history should not be dismissed, given the Negrophobia she sought to counter. These advances come with a cost, though.

Stowe portrays Tom as a patient sufferer who embraces his masters. "God bless you, Mas'r," Tom says to St. Clare, with tears in his eyes, when his new owner announces that he has bought him (131). At Legree's plantation, Tom, like Christ, incorporates suffering. He absorbs the blows and will not strike back. He forgives the hands that torture him. He converts the brutal slaves Sambo and Quimbo. He worries about the souls of his tormentors. The scene in which Tom tries to sway Legree continues to stir student readers, even in the early twenty-first century. As she often does, Stowe guides her readers' responses to the scene, providing a surprising surrogate in Legree:

> ". . . Do the worst you can, my troubles'll be over soon; but, if ye don't repent, yours won't *never* end!"
>
> Like a strange snatch of heavenly music, heard in the lull of a tempest, this burst of feeling made a moment's blank pause. Legree stood aghast, and looked at Tom; and there was such a silence, that the tick of the old clock could be heard, measuring, with silent touch, the last moments of mercy and probation to that hardened heart.

It was but a moment. There was one hesitating pause, – one irresolute, relenting thrill, – and the spirit of evil came back, with seven-fold vehemence; and Legree, foaming with rage, smote his victim to the ground. (358)

Quite a pause: in which the hardest of hearts is encouraged to feel, in which Tom is at his most sacrificial, and in which Legree, offered a last chance, proves irredeemable. Scriptwriters, performers, and critics often caricature Tom's behavior in this scene as meek. Yet Stowe is careful to represent his "eager docility" (343) as an active force, an expression of strength through its reserve. He is beaten to death because he refuses to betray Cassy and Emmeline by revealing the details of their escape. His resistance and his plea provoke Legree's blow. In that "moment's blank pause," Stowe invites her readers to identify with Tom (or with Legree), to appreciate the meanings of Tom's suffering, and to be moved. Especially moving is Tom's capacity to turn the other cheek, to take abuse and forgive his abusers. Here, though, is where the picture gets complicated.

Writing in March 1851 to the editor of the *National Era*, the periodical in which *Uncle Tom's Cabin* appeared serially, Stowe described her "graphic manner" of representing slavery: "There is no arguing with *pictures*, and everybody is impressed by them, whether they mean to be or not."[9] What exactly is impressive about the scene of Tom's sacrifice? Certainly the character's nobility, discipline, and faith; but also, one imagines for readers in the past and some in the present, the remarkable spectacle of punishment without consequence. Tom gets beaten, not Legree. If Legree, one of the most revolting villains in nineteenth-century literature can be forgiven (see his memorable introduction in Volume II, Chapter 30), then so too can readers, whether they mean to be or not. In the death of Tom, a gentle child-man, a female man who, beaten again and again, absorbs the blows and refuses to strike back, Stowe has painted a picture that conveys racial injustice and also contains the specter of African-American retribution. Some of the power and durability of this novel, and of its enervated later renditions, may have to do with this fantasy of reprieve. It is a fantasy from which she will retreat while defending the truth of *Uncle Tom's Cabin* in her *Key*.

In a preface to a later edition of *Uncle Tom's Cabin*, Stowe claimed that the death of Tom was the first part of the book she wrote, shortly after she had experienced an overwhelming vision during a communion service of a slave being fatally beaten.[10] Throughout the book, Stowe seeks to contrive an imaginary "communion." She attempts to understand and to communicate to her readers the point of view of African Americans under slavery by using emotional pivots, for example Tom's redemptive suffering or the loss of children by parents. Stowe's narrator associates, but does not equate, the injuries experienced by free and enslaved parents. One can argue with the particular levers Stowe uses to link white and black and writer and reader, or with her manipulation of these levers, but to deny the imaginative attempt to connect would be to deny a central dynamic of nineteenth-century fiction. In *I Ain't Yo' Uncle*, after Harriet pleads guilty to misrepresentation and distortion, Alexander puns on this issue. Cassy announces, "Case dismissed. . . . She tried," and Harriet responds, "But not hard enough!" (89). Cassy may be saying that the case should be dismissed because Harriet has been put to a severe test and that is sufficient, or because she did make an effort even though she only partially succeeded. In *I Ain't Yo' Uncle*, verdicts of guilty or innocent are avoided.

In the character of Miss Ophelia, the most psychologically interesting portrayal in *Uncle Tom's Cabin*, Stowe dramatizes the challenge of identification and reveals her own difficulty in imagining the aftermath of slavery. Ophelia's depth may be due partly to the ways in which she reflects and rearranges her author's character. Like Stowe, Ophelia is a product of New England Calvinism. Stowe was forty when *Uncle Tom's Cabin* began to be serialized; Ophelia is described as "some forty-five years" (136), without Stowe's large family. Like Stowe, Ophelia is conscientious, conscience being "the granite formation" of New England women, according to the narrator (138). Ophelia "thought with great strength within certain narrow limits" (137). She is energetic: "It really was a labor to see her" working, the narrator observes (206). Unlike Stowe, who, according to her husband Calvin, lacked the skills of domestic management, Ophelia is "a living impersonation of order, method, and exactness" (137). Her life is literally compartmentalized: "There she is, sitting now in her state-room, surrounded by a mixed multitude of little and big carpet-bags, boxes, baskets, each containing some separate responsibility which she is tying, binding up, packing, or fastening, with a face of great earnestness" (138). The exaggerations of Ophelia's character often come with a knowing irony. Ophelia is eager for custodianship: her "keen, dark eyes had a peculiarly searching, advised movement, and travelled over everything, as if they were looking for something to take care of" (137). The impressive thing about Ophelia, though, is that her region and her religion define her limits but also press her to exceed them. An "absolute bond-slave of the '*ought*'" (138), she is burdened with a scrupulousness and zeal that haunt her with a sense of deficiency and goad her to improve.

The most difficult limit Ophelia encounters is her racial discomfort, the "sin" of New England "prejudice of caste and color," as Stowe describes it in her analysis of Ophelia in *A Key to Uncle Tom's Cabin*.[11] Stowe incarnates this problem in Topsy, whom her cousin Augustine St. Clare has purchased for her partly as an intellectual joke. Topsy is meant as a test of Ophelia's New England pieties about the duty of educating African Americans under slavery. Ophelia flinches not only at the task but also at the presence of the "heathenish" girl (207). Earlier, arriving at her cousin's New Orleans mansion, Ophelia had been repelled by the sight of Eva kissing Mammy and sitting on Tom's knee. After the Tom incident, St. Clare comments on the distance between the abstract affection of northerners and their personal revulsion for enslaved African Americans. His barbs come with many edges: "You would not have them abused; but you don't want anything to do with them yourselves. You would send them to Africa out of your sight and smell, and then send a missionary or two to do up all the self-denial of elevating them compendiously" (154). Thoughtful, as always, Ophelia admits that her cousin may be right. In a small but telling echo (and critics often miss the small moments in this grandiose book), St. Clare uses words with Ophelia – "You loathe them as you would a snake or a toad" (154) – that Topsy later repeats to Eva. After the little evangelist assures Topsy that Ophelia would love her if Topsy were good, she responds: "No; she can't bar me, 'cause I'm a nigger! – she'd soon have a toad touch her!" (245) It is as though Topsy had overheard St. Clare and Ophelia treating her as a specimen.

Topsy is black, ragged, and tricky. She is less a character than an anarchic force, an anti-Ophelia. Her antics (or they may be tactics) constitute some of the more embarrassing moments in the novel. In *A Key to Uncle Tom's Cabin*, sensing that there was something inadequate about her rendering of Topsy, Stowe provides social background and psychological analysis. She offers retrospective directions for reading. Topsy is the emblematic product of racism, southern and northern. Degraded by a sense of imposed inferiority, "urged on by a kind of secret desperation," she uses her ingenuity to confirm her status (*Key*, 91).

Miss Ophelia recoils from Topsy, but she is also drawn to her. She is drawn from a sense of duty, but also from something more than duty. In *I Ain't Yo' Uncle*, Alexander suggests that this something more has to do with the spinster's desire for a child to love and to mold in her own white image. While Alexander acknowledges that Ophelia's motives are not merely egocentric, he emphasizes the New Englander's self-indulgence and myopia and Topsy's need to liberate herself from this northern bondage. His appraisal of Ophelia seems harsh. In *Uncle Tom's Cabin*, Stowe represents Ophelia as being altered by Topsy's grief after Eva's death. Ophelia assures Topsy that she is capable of loving her, "having learned something of the love of Christ" from Eva. The narrator tells us that Ophelia's voice and her "honest tears" communicated more than her words and that, for the first time, she has an influence over the girl (259).

At the end of *Uncle Tom's Cabin*, we are briefly informed that Ophelia has brought Topsy back to Vermont to live in her house, despite the resistance of the locals, and that she has educated and disciplined her. Baptized and a church member, Topsy is now a missionary in Africa. The limits of Stowe's imagination in *Uncle Tom's Cabin* are vivid here. She can only gesture toward a freedom for Topsy, and this freedom involves her submission and removal. Alexander sharply avoids this homogenized ending for Topsy. In some alarming way, Ophelia and Topsy seem to be the unwitting ancestors of the apparently endless white–black pairings in post-1960s Hollywood movies, in which African Americans (always) teach European Americans to have "soul" and European Americans (sometimes) teach African Americans "discipline." Yet Ophelia and Topsy are not Steve Martin and Queen Latifah in the recent film *Bringing Down the House*. However awkwardly and asymmetrically, Stowe attempts to use her Christianity to extend her understanding and to enlarge the responses of her readers. In the section of the *Key* on Ophelia, Stowe calls for strenuous efforts to break down distinctions and to reform the human heart, citing Paul in *Colossians*, *Galatians*, and *Ephesians* (51–52). The box into which Topsy is placed at the end of *Uncle Tom's Cabin* injures but does not invalidate the larger effort.

Ophelia is at the center of the book. The two chapters that bridge the end of the first and the beginning of the second volume, Chapters XVIII and XIX, are both titled "Miss Ophelia's Experiences and Opinions." In these chapters, Ophelia unsuccessfully tries to systematize Dinah's kitchen and she discusses the condition and future of the United States with her cousin. St. Clare argues that the exploitation of human beings corrupts south and north, the United States and England, and he suggests, partly out of conviction and partly out of ennui, that a day of wrath is at hand in which the masses of the world will rise up against their masters. Balanced against this prophecy is the alternative of what both St. Clare and Ophelia refer to as social "experiment" (203, 215). St. Clare describes how he subdued a defiant slave named Scipio through kindness (a story which sends Eva into a fit of weeping), and Ophelia, in Chapter XX, begins her test of character with Topsy. St. Clare's experiment is one-sided and paternalistic; Ophelia's experiment opens up and then closes down. Stowe will rethink her ideas about revolution and experiment in her next anti-slavery novel, the aptly titled *Dred*.

A Key to Uncle Tom's Cabin

In the last chapter of *Uncle Tom's Cabin*, acknowledging that questions about her story's veracity had arisen during its serial publication, Stowe describes actual parallels for some of the incidents and characters. In

A Key, published in 1853, she responds to the pro-slavery attacks with over five hundred pages of documents and reflections: court records, travel narratives, personal narratives, private and public letters, newspaper stories, slave narratives (including mention of Josiah Henson and excerpts from Frederick Douglass), advertisements for runaway slaves, notices of sale, legal opinions, trial transcripts, congressional records, Biblical passages, sermons, poems, and anecdotes of her own and her family's experiences. *A Key to Uncle Tom's Cabin* is written in the tradition of other anti-slavery compendia such as Theodore Dwight Weld's *American Slavery As It Is* (1839), which Stowe frequently uses as a source. *A Key* is divided into four sections focusing on the characters in *Uncle Tom's Cabin*, slavery law, public opinion, and religion.

More than a collection of documents and a retrospective defense of *Uncle Tom's Cabin*, this book is also a prospective validation of Stowe's 1856 anti-slavery novel *Dred*. *A Key* represents an important stage in her thinking about race and slavery. It is a complicated formal and intellectual work in its own right. At the beginning of *A Key*, Stowe describes *Uncle Tom's Cabin*'s as a "mosaic of facts," emphasizing both its aesthetic and authentic qualities (1). Yet the term "mosaic of facts" seems a more appropriate description of *A Key*, which is a mixture of gloss, evidence, and analysis. Stowe uses techniques of juxtaposition and rhythms of comment, silence, and outrage. The *Key* also seems to turn its author. Across the book, as though the change occurred in writing the book, Stowe finds that her ideas about fact and fiction have altered.[12]

A Key begins as a defense of *Uncle Tom's Cabin* in particular and fiction in general. Stowe concedes that her novel was "a very inadequate representation of slavery," but insists that it was "necessarily" so: "A work which should represent it strictly as it is would be a work which could not be read; and all works which ever mean to give pleasure must draw a veil somewhere, or they cannot succeed" (1). If fiction is to achieve one of its main effects, a giving of pleasure that will move an audience, Stowe argues that it must screen features that might preclude enjoyment and paralyze the reader. This danger is acute when representing the "peculiar" "evil" of slavery (v). In the introduction to Harriet Jacobs's *Incidents in the Life of a Slave Girl* (1861), the writer and abolitionist Lydia Maria Child will invoke the gendered aspects of this narrative "veil." She associates the image with the concealed sexual abuse of African-American women under slavery and insists that the veil be withdrawn.[13] "In fictitious writing," Stowe argues at the start of her *Key*, "it is possible to find refuge from the hard and the terrible, by inventing scenes and characters of a more pleasing nature. No such resource is open in a work of fact; and the subject of this work is one on which the truth, if told at all, must needs be very dreadful" (v). In the ameliorating inventions of *Uncle Tom's Cabin*, Stowe suggests, she provided the safer vantage offered by fiction. Facts, on the other hand – and at the beginning of *A Key* she insists on the difference – offer direct exposure.

Yet the clarity of such distinctions erodes under the weight of evidence that Stowe amasses. She expresses surprise at the expansion of what she originally imagined would be a shorter vindication. *A Key* has "overrun its limits" (v). In an ironic Topsy's revenge, which Robert Alexander or Ishmael Reed might savor, Stowe was confronting an unruly creation that just "grow'd" (*UTC*, 210). The archival horror seems to have both transfixed the author of *Uncle Tom's Cabin* and magnified her response. What had seemed a necessary refuge, a concession to audience sensibilities and to the limits of representation, in *Uncle Tom's Cabin* and at the start of *A Key*, emerges across the pages of *A Key* as evasion and even whitewash. Stowe comes to acknowledge that *A Key*'s "facts make the fiction of *Uncle Tom's Cabin* appear tame in the comparison" (112). When, at the end of the first part of *A Key*, Stowe defends her portrait of the benevolent owner St. Clare largely by reproducing long testimonials from southern readers about her moderateness, she becomes implicated in her own defense.

The turning point in *A Key* is the second part, on the law of slavery. At the center of these chapters are two court cases, *The State v. Mann* (North Carolina, 1829) and *Souther v. The Commonwealth* (Virginia, 1851). The issues, decisions, characters, narratives, and diction in these two cases circulate through *A Key* and reappear three years later in *Dred*.

In *Mann*, the defendant had shot and wounded a female slave, whom he had hired for a year, while she was fleeing his attempt to punish her. The lower court found him guilty, not because his act was cruel and unwarranted but because the right to shoot her belonged only to her master. A higher court overturned this verdict, insisting that the hirer of a slave has all the rights of her master. As Judge Ruffin explained, using words that Stowe could not get out of her mind, "THE POWER OF THE MASTER MUST BE ABSOLUTE, TO RENDER THE SUBMISSION OF THE SLAVE PERFECT" (*Key*, 133). Ruffin advanced a legal and racial perversion of Calvinist doctrine, of the intimate mystery of the all and the nothing summed up in the title of a sermon by the eighteenth-century American theologian Jonathan Edwards, "God Glorified in Man's Dependence." Both the opinion and the doctrine troubled Stowe. In *A Key* and in *Dred*, she decries the "absolute despotism" of slavery that corrupts all who come in contact with the system (*Key*, 233). Judge Ruffin's words are put in the mouth of *Dred*'s Judge Clayton, who delivers them while overturning his lawyer son's conviction of a man who shot his hired slave.[14]

In *Souther*, a case that had been touted to Stowe by her detractors as evidence of the fairness of the slave codes, a master is indicted for the sadistic torture over twelve hours of his slave Sam, who died as a result of his treatment. He is convicted of murder in the second degree and sentenced to five years in prison. Souther (and one imagines that Stowe appreciated the allegorical insinuations of his name) protested his conviction. He argued that he had not intended to kill Sam, that he had believed Sam was pretending to suffer, and that it had been his lawful right as master to discipline his property. The superior court rejected Souther's request for a new trial and expressed its view that he had committed an atrocious act of murder in the first degree, while acknowledging that he could not be tried twice for the same crime. The court also reaffirmed the principle that a master cannot be prosecuted for any punishment short of death inflicted on a slave. Stowe is multiply appalled at these results: that Souther would not have been convicted of the highest degree of murder; that the jury, in mitigating the seriousness of his crime, seemed to have accepted the argument that he did not intend to kill Sam even though he beat, stamped, scalded, burned, and mutilated him; that the higher court's outrage resulted in a mere verbal reprimand; and that this court could tongue-lash murder and confirm the right to torture. For Stowe, the doctrine of despotism in *Mann* and the cruel judgments in *Souther* epitomize the lawful violation of morality that defines the system of slavery. In the last part of *A Key*, on religion, she focuses on the complicity of southern churches and the compromises of their northern counterparts. In *Dred*, she transforms such exposition into satires directed at temporizing clergy (see, for example, Book II, Chapter 18, "The Clerical Conference").

Stowe's close and caustic readings of *Mann*, *Souther*, and other cases in the second part of *A Key* set the stage for her exposure, in the third part, of the diction and syntax of slavery. Here she reprints advertisements for the sale of African Americans and rewards for the return of those who have escaped. The two parts, on law and on public opinion, form the ideological center of the book. At this center, Stowe seeks to understand "practical infidelity," how, at local, state, and national levels, communities have consented to an evil system (246). She describes the situation that preoccupies her: "we can become accustomed to very awful things" (413). Americans "*re-enact* these unjust laws everyday, by their silent permission of them" (479). Stowe opens her readers' eyes to the violence of legal judgments and to the vehemence rippling the pages of their newspapers. Her complex tone of disbelief, sorrow, irony, and outrage and her rhythms of stress and silence resonate with the approach of Hortense Spillers, who scrutinizes William Goodell's *The American Slave Code* (1853) and Daniel Patrick Moynihan's *The Negro Family* (1965) in her influential 1987 essay, "Mama's Baby, Papa's Maybe:

An American Grammar Book."[15] Systems, legal and linguistic, rather than persons, fix Stowe's attention in the two central parts of *A Key*, and so it is not surprising to find her, in the first part, defending her characters as types rather than people. Whether or not Stowe in *Uncle Tom's Cabin* represents "real people" has been a crux for critics. James Baldwin cogently addresses the question in his essay "Everybody's Protest Novel," in which he condemns Stowe for sacrificing "human beings" to "categories."[16] However we evaluate her practice, Stowe in *A Key* stresses her interest in systems, types, and facts. For Stowe, each character, like "each fact," is "a specimen of a class," exemplifying the effects of slavery (298).

By the end of *A Key*, Stowe's opening distinction between fact and fiction has collapsed under the pressures of evidence and interpretation. She moves from defending the factuality of her fiction to explaining that under slavery facts and fiction mingle. Law books have taught Stowe an "awful kind of truth, stranger than fiction, which is all the time evolving, in one form or another, from the workings of this anomalous system" (222; see also 298). In an appendix entitled "Fact v. Figures; or, the Nine Arab Brothers," she reflects on the transformation of her opening terms. Despite the "favourite maxim that '*figures cannot lie*,'" Stowe, personifying the nine Arabic numerals, laments that these characters often do, or are made to, misrepresent. Their "unprecedented power and popularity" in modern republican debate has turned their heads and made them susceptible to lobbying and deceit. Stowe's figures of speech are peculiar here. She turns numbers into living characters, members of "an ancient and most respectable race" (505). She invokes the Arabic inheritance but also the canard of shiftiness, which she almost but does not quite expunge by alluding to the history of colonial manipulation. Embodying the nine Arabic numbers is part of Stowe's effort to bring into relief the dynamic of conversion that for her is the deforming mark of slavery, a system in which human beings are turned into things and things into human beings. Stowe had considered giving *Uncle Tom's Cabin* the subtitle "The Man Who Was a Thing" (a phrase she echoes twice in Chapter 11), and in *A Key* she emphatically draws attention to a Louisiana law that inflicts severe penalties on anyone who mistreats, by cutting or breaking, the spiked iron collar used to subdue a slave (169–170).

With the "nine Arabic brothers," Stowe puns on the concept of "figures." The "nine Arabic brothers" are numbers, bodies, and tropes. The turns of *A Key* have undermined Stowe's confidence in a certain kind of representation. She sarcastically reminds her readers in the appendix that statistics have been used to palliate the carnage of the "Middle Passage" across the Atlantic from Africa to the "New World." She objects to the perverted authority of the famously corrupt state results in the Federal census of 1840, which continued to be used to justify slavery, purportedly demonstrating the incapacity of Africans in America to endure freedom.[17] Facts are figures, and Stowe comes to doubt the value of the truths they convey, enshrined in law and consented to by the public. Pressed into service in the modern United States, the nine Arabic brothers display a "characteristic turn for romancing" (506). Figures *can* and do lie, slavery is supported by romance, and facts become stranger than fiction – *A Key* unlocks this "awful kind of truth" (222). "If state documents are falsified in support of slavery," Stowe asks in the final line of *A Key*, "what confidence can be placed in *any* representations that are made upon the subject?" (508). Herman Melville will ask a similar question four years later in his satiric *The Confidence-Man* (1857), and he will answer it with a profound skepticism about the trustworthiness of figures.

Yet Stowe's response to the fictionality of facts is not Melville's vertiginous irony or his suggestion of the absurd necessity of faith, nor is it inertia or despair at the abyss of signification, nor a placid acceptance that truth is a relative thing. Instead, the "awful truth" that facts are specimens in an anomalous system – fantastic, exotic, perverted, evolving – impels Stowe to expose the truth of slavery: its violation of moral law. Stowe cites especially the injunctions to masters to give unto their servants that which is just and equal (*Colossians* 4.1) and to the multitudes to do unto others as you would have them do unto you (*Matthew* 7.12). *A Key* sharpens her anxieties about the consequences of inaction and about the judgments that will be visited upon the nation. It suggests to her a different rhetorical texture for her next novel, one that incorporates the figurative qualities of facts.

Dred: A Tale of the Great Dismal Swamp: Edward Clayton

In *Dred*, her second anti-slavery novel, Stowe tells the story of three locations: a plantation in North Carolina, another in South Carolina, and a swamp extending along the southeastern coast, where fugitive slaves take refuge and plot. Showing the influence of *A Key to Uncle Tom's Cabin*, Stowe in *Dred* makes explicit use of the historical archive: the cases of *Mann* and *Souther*, the insurrections of Denmark Vesey and Nat Turner in the southern United States and of Toussaint L'Ouverture in Santo Domingo, the violence that followed the 1854 Kansas–Nebraska Act potentially opening these territories to slavery, the beating of the abolitionist Charles Sumner in the United States Senate. *Dred* comes with its own documentary appendices. The novel is more didactic than *Uncle Tom's Cabin*, with fewer set-pieces and more sustained debate about religion, politics, and law. It is also, as we shall see, a book of strange energy.[18]

Canema, a plantation in North Carolina, is presided over by Nina Gordon, who begins as a flighty young woman and develops a sense of moral responsibility under the tutelage of her suitor, Edward Clayton. Along with his sister Anne, Clayton supervises Magnolia Grove, their family plantation in South Carolina. Nina's moral education is cut short when she dies during a cholera epidemic. On the Gordon plantation lives the mulatto Harry, who is the son of his master and a secret brother to Nina. Harry is unfitted to be a slave by his parentage and his education. Aunt Milly also serves at Canema. She is majestic and devout, and she tells Nina her harrowing story of losing fourteen children to slavery and finding rage and religion. When Milly is shot by her temporary employer, Stowe recapitulates the Mann case, which the budding lawyer Edward Clayton argues and wins, only to have his father, a judge, overturn the verdict on appeal. Nina's racist brother Tom plays the Legree role. In the pine woods near the swamp, loyal, steely Old Tiff takes charge of the children of a poor white family after their mother dies. Dred, the visionary slave rebel, inhabits the Great Dismal Swamp. Both he and his domain suffuse the second volume of the novel.

Edward Clayton uses Magnolia Grove to conduct a series of "experiment[s]" to prepare African Americans for freedom (309). *Dred* is part of a wider literary imagining of alternatives to slavery in the decade before the Civil War, including Sarah Josepha Hale's 1853 *Liberia; or, Mr. Peyton's Experiments* and Frank J. Webb's 1857 *The Garies and Their Friends*. Both of these novels respond to Stowe. Clayton is certain that the day of liberation will come, and he insists that enslaved African Americans "be emancipated on the soil" (310). For Clayton and his sister Anne, education is the key to advancement. In *Dred*, Stowe refuses the status quo, the position that slavery is wrong but that nothing can be done about it. Whenever characters voice this opinion, they are condemned. Through the Claytons' "experiments," Stowe tests contemporary efforts at legal reform and gradual emancipation. She is at her paternalist, or maternalist, worst when she describes the entry into the schoolroom of Anne's uniformed, synchronized, hymn-singing *élèves* (314–315). This display is followed a few pages later by the happy Dulcimer's pageant celebrating Clayton's return to the plantation. In these scenes, Stowe offers the bracing spectacle of indoctrination.

Yet Edward is more serious than his sister, and he himself is taught several lessons. Edward hopes that the example of Magnolia Grove will spur emancipation. He insists on teaching his slaves to read and write, despite the resistance of his fellow plantation owners and the threats of Tom Gordon. His firmness leads to his being beaten senseless with a cane by Tom, "after the fashion of the chivalry of South Carolina" as Stowe pointedly notes (493). Here she refers to South Carolina representative Preston Brooks's attack on the anti-slavery Republican senator Charles Sumner in the Senate chamber in May 1856. In addition to this physical education in southern hostility to reform, Clayton receives a legal education about institutional violence in his father's courtroom. Judge Clayton reverses his son's conviction of the employer who shot Milly, using words taken from the mouth of Judge Ruffin: "THE POWER OF THE MASTER MUST BE ABSOLUTE, TO RENDER THE SUBMISSION OF THE SLAVE PERFECT" (353). In an exchange of letters with Harry, now escaped from Canema, Clayton acknowledges the justice of the argument that African Americans under slavery have a right to resist oppression and to declare their independence, but he maintains that they are not yet ready to govern themselves. Clayton's gradualism and paternalism are allied with his racial essentialism, and all three are undermined by the fastidious metaphors in his odd parley with his sister Anne: "The Ethiopian race is a slow-growing plant like the aloe . . . but I hope, some of these days, they'll come into flower; and I think, if they ever do, the blossoming will be gorgeous . . . There is no use in trying to make the negroes into Anglo-Saxons, any more than making a grape-vine into a pear-tree. I train the grape-vine" (328). The horticultural condescension here is peculiar enough, and we might take it as coming straight from Stowe were it not for the ways in which it is contradicted, or at least distanced, by the narrator's quite different account of Dred's extravagant development, which I will take up shortly. Clayton's romantic racialism with a cultivated twist – the difference between grape-vines and pear-trees – is a characterological vestige of the narrative perspective that predominated in *Uncle Tom's Cabin*.

Clayton receives an education in the Swamp, too. Recovering from Tom Gordon's blows in Dred's stronghold, Clayton, like Stowe, becomes "interested in Dred, as a psychological study" (509). The effort to imagine and to represent Dred's perspective is part of Stowe's novelistic experiment in reckoning different points of view, which she defends as an artistic and political necessity (445). Stowe has prepared Clayton and her readers for his encounter with Dred, having associated the two characters earlier in the novel. A friend had remarked, with ironic disapproval, that Clayton was "*Jewish* in his notions," referring to his archaic outrage at his father's legal reasoning, evoking the Hebrew prophets with whom Dred is frequently identified (356). In his own prophetic words to his father, Clayton quotes apocalyptic Latin and translates it to the mid-nineteenth-century United States: "I say repeal the law, if it do uproot the institution . . . 'Fiat justitia ruat coelum'" (358). Clayton resigns from the bar, protesting the law of slavery and of his father. He risks his property and his life in continuing to instruct his slaves.

Of course, Clayton is not Dred. While acknowledging the irresistible force of emancipation, he defends his reformist model as an "escape valve," a way of yielding "gracefully before the growing force of the people" (469–470) – not an unreasonable strategy for one in his position. Disillusioned by the violent resistance to his plans, he buys land in Canada. There, we are told briefly at the end of the novel, he and Anne have moved with their slaves, who now have become tenants. They have established a thriving agricultural community. Clayton relinquishes his idea of emancipation on United States soil. Yet both Clayton and Dred share a moral resoluteness. In this novel, Stowe often arrays her characters and their positions in surprising patterns. As was the case with Ophelia, there is more to Clayton than meets the eye.

In *Dred*, Stowe still finds it difficult to imagine freedom, that is, to depict Africans in the United States living outside the geographical, legal, and psychological confinements of slavery. This absence may define the limits of her literary interest or invention or it may result from her sense of the representational burdens of her conspicuous role as an opponent of slavery. *Uncle Tom's Cabin* and *A Key to Uncle Tom's Cabin* concern themselves with the "peculiar institution" and *Dred* points toward alternatives, but in both novels readers are given only a happily-ever-after glimpse of African-American freedom either in Canada or in the north. In the preface to *A Key*, Stowe tells her readers that she had planned to include a section on "the characteristics and developments of the colored race in various countries and circumstances," but had to omit it because it would not fit in her already expanded volume and would be more appropriate for separate publication (v–vi). Although it is not clear what became of Stowe's materials (she writes that she had transferred them to a friend), in a sense there was a subsequent publication on African "freedom" in America, with a preface by Stowe, a publication that drew upon and also contended with her writings: Frank J. Webb's 1857 novel *The Garies and Their Friends*. In 1855 and 1856, Webb's wife Mary had delivered a version of *Uncle Tom's Cabin* on stage that Stowe prepared expressly for her.[19] Frank Webb's fierce and subtle novel tells the story of the black community in Philadelphia before the Civil War.

Dred: A Tale of the Great Dismal Swamp: Dred

The location specified in Stowe's second anti-slavery novel is not the humble, tidy space of *Uncle Tom's Cabin* but the murky expanse known as the Great Dismal Swamp. It is part of what the narrator describes as "an immense chain of swamps, regions of hopeless disorder, where the abundant growth and vegetation of nature, sucking up its forces from the humid soil, seems to rejoice in a savage exuberance, and bid defiance to all human efforts either to penetrate or subdue" (209). In Stowe's novel, and in the nineteenth century, this "immense chain of swamps" and this "hopeless disorder" provided a sanctuary for African Americans attempting to escape from bondage.[20] In the second volume of *Dred*, the Swamp offers refuge to Harry, his wife Lisette, Tiff and his children, Milly, and Clayton. In her *Key*, Stowe had reprinted Longfellow's 1842 poem, "The Slave in the Dismal Swamp" (162–163). Unlike Longfellow, who depicts a prospect in which the hunted slave crouches like a wild beast, Stowe emphasizes the vitality of the swamp. She links this vitality to "the indefinite stimulating power" of the Bible on the souls of the oppressed (446) and to the "incalculable ardor of growth" of her titular African-American prophet and revolutionary (211).

The Swamp exemplifies "the principle of *growth*": "It is a mysterious and dread condition of existence, which, place it under what impediment or disadvantage you will, is constantly forcing on; and when unnatural pressure hinders it, develops in forms portentous and astonishing" (496). Here the narrator is fascinated with power and how it expresses, propels, and transforms itself. This passage refers to character, landscape, and Scripture. It contains one of the explicit puns in the novel, suggesting the mixture of apprehension and awe – the *dread* – inspired by Dred (see also 209). This law of growth is different from the reserve valued by the narrator of *Uncle Tom's Cabin* or the gradualism of Edward Clayton's gentle aloe and disciplined grape-vine. These "portentous and astonishing" forms do not require and would not suffer cultivation. Clayton himself comes to articulate a version of this transfigured development: "You see, in this day, minds *will grow*. They *are* growing . . . I have seen a rock split in two by the growing of an elm-tree that wanted light and air, and would make its way up through it" (470).

Dred is George Harris, the refractory slave from Stowe's first novel – "a whole volcano of bitter feelings burned in his bosom, and sent streams of fire through his veins . . . He had been able to repress every disrespectful word; but the flashing eye, the gloomy and troubled brow, were part of a natural language that could not be repressed" (*UTC*, 11) – unbound. Dred reacts like George, looks like Tom, and speaks and acts like no one else in Stowe's first anti-slavery novel. Unlike Tom, who forgives his masters, Dred represents the possibility that punishment may be followed by retribution, human and divine. He echoes the warning at the end of *Uncle Tom's Cabin* that the "signs of the times" may portend for the United States a coming "*day of vengeance*," rather than a "day of grace" (*UTC*, 388).

Dred is not merely an abstraction. Stowe gives him a history and a geneal-ogy. He is the fictional son of the actual Denmark Vesey, a freed black slave who was accused of planning a revolt in Charleston, South Carolina, in 1822 and was hanged, along with some thirty-five others, for his affront. Vesey's son Dred, Stowe tells us, was fourteen years old when his father was exe-cuted and he was sold to a distant plantation. Steeped in the Bible and its visions of emancipation and retribution, as was his father, the indomitable Dred killed his overseer and escaped to the Swamp. Stowe ties Dred not only to Vesey but also to the most feared or admired antebellum black insur-gent, Nat Turner. Turner heard voices, discerned signs, and led a series of attacks in Southampton, Virginia, in 1831 that killed eighty-five whites. He was vilified, tried, convicted, and hanged. Stowe confirms her novelistic par-allels between Dred and Turner in the first part of her appendix, where she includes passages from Turner's *Confessions*, as told to Thomas Gray in 1831. The second part of the appendix reprints documents on the Souther case and another case of legally sanctioned violence, both invoked in *Dred* (455–458). The third part contains material on the inaction of churches in the face of slavery. Stowe takes most of the material in the last two parts of the appendix from her *Key*.

Dred is also given a European-American Revolutionary heritage. Through Harry's letter to Clayton, Stowe connects him to George Washington and to the Declaration of Independence (435–436). In the Swamp, under Dred's guidance, Harry recites for the assembled fugitives the story of the Declara-tion, asserting that they have at least as great a right and duty to throw off the government of their oppressors (454–455).

During the course of the novel, Dred is associated with the strength of Hercules (198); with Samson, who destroyed the temple of the Philistines, and himself (210); with Jael, who drove a nail through the head of a sleep-ing enemy general in the book of *Judges* (210); with the prophet Elijah and John the Baptist, who emerge from the wilderness to preach the coming judgment (211); and, most frequently, with the prophet Isaiah, whose por-tentous words he often uses (for examples, see 450, 458–459, 500–501). We are told that Dred "felt himself an instrument of doom in a mightier hand" (447). As critics have recognized, Dred is not a "real" person – but he is also not a stereotype. Nor is he a traditional Old Testament "type," a figure whose meaning is fulfilled in the higher truth of a later New Testament "anti-type." Instead, Stowe suggests that we interpret Dred as a volatile mix of *Prophets* and *Revelation*. Classical hero, African-American and European-American revolutionary, Biblical warrior, and African and Biblical prophet, Dred broods over the book, especially on subsequent readings, "portentous and astonishing." He embodies the "theological terror" that James Baldwin disparagingly identified in *Uncle Tom's Cabin*.[21] Unlike the self-indulgent, superstitious fear of damnation that Baldwin sees in the earlier book, the "theological terror" in *Dred* is moored in the histories of slavery and revolution.

Influenced by the discoveries of *A Key* and by her encounters with African Americans and their history and writings, witnessing the increasingly vicious politics of the 1850s, Stowe in *Dred* tells a different kind of story than she had in *Uncle Tom's Cabin*.[22] In *Dred*'s swamp, facts are saturated with figures and the nation is on the verge of apocalypse. Stowe sustains the ominous possibilities even after Dred is fatally wounded, offstage, while defending his community. In one of the most resonant scenes, placed at the center of the novel, joining passages from *Isaiah*, *Amos*, *Joel*, and *Nahum*, Dred addresses the participants in a camp meeting, prophesying divine judgment and desolation. His auditors do not see any body. Their only sense of presence is a thunderous voice speaking down to them. While it is true, as some have observed, that Stowe dispatches Dred before the novel ends and thus averts the promised revolt, she does not silence him. Stowe may not know what to do with her revolutionary character once she has given him form, lineage, and purpose, but his persistent allure, from the woman who gave us Uncle Tom, is something of a surprise. Stowe's imaginative apprehension is part of the drama that unfolds across the book.

In *I Ain't Yo' Uncle*, Robert Alexander casts a different Dred. His choice is surprising and clarifying. His play ends with the hip-hop Topsy as a prophet of urban rage. She resembles the Topsy described in *A Key*: "quick, active, subtle and ingenious, *apparently* utterly devoid of principle and conscience" (*Key*, 91). The italics are mine but the emphasis is Stowe's. Alexander's Topsy provides a more unyielding kind of comic relief, and maybe no relief at all, compared with Stowe's antic Topsy. Alexander's Topsy announces that she now controls the proceedings. Harriet did not create her. She has a life of her own. She threatens her audience: "I oughta fuck you up! I see the way you look at me when I get on the bus . . . you sit there, scared . . . tensed . . . clutchin' yo' purse . . . hoping I don't sit next to you" (89). She says that she burned down Uncle Tom's condo with him inside: "I love to hear glass break" (90).

Tom gets the last words. He asks the audience if there are any budding Ophelias in the house, giving an edge to one of Stowe's most famous lines: "Any volunteers to take Topsy? Ya'll think she come from nowhere? Do ya 'spects she just growed?" (*Yo' Uncle*, 90; see also *UTC*, 210). Neither a dismissal of *Uncle Tom's Cabin* nor a verdict of guilty or innocent, Alexander's *I Ain't Yo' Uncle* is a knowing, critical appraisal. It is about genealogy, history, and lapses of memory. It is about the uncanny resonance of Stowe.

NOTES

1. Robert Alexander, *I Ain't Yo' Uncle*, in *Colored Contradictions: An Anthology of Contemporary African-American Plays* (New York: Plume, 1996), 25–26.
2. Ralph Ellison, "The World and the Jug," in *Shadow and Act* (New York: Random House, 1964), 123; Annette Dixon, ed., *Kara Walker: Pictures from Another Time* (Ann Arbor: The University of Michigan Museum of Art, 2002); Ishmael Reed, *Flight To Canada* (New York: Random House, 1976), 14; Frederick Douglass, *Narrative of the Life of Frederick Douglass, an American Slave, Written by Himself*, ed. William Andrews and William S. McFeeley (New York: W. W. Norton and Co., 1997), 29.
3. Thomas F. Gossett, *Uncle Tom's Cabin and American Culture* (Dallas: Southern Methodist University Press, 1985). See also Linda Williams, *Playing the Race Card: Melodramas of Black and White from Uncle Tom to O. J. Simpson* (Princeton, NJ: Princeton University Press, 2001); Stephen Best, *The Fugitive's Properties* (Chicago: University of Chicago Press, 2004); and the internet website established by Stephen Railton and the University of Virginia, "*Uncle Tom's Cabin* and American Culture: A Multi-Media Archive" (http://www.iath. virginia.edu/utc).
4. Martin R. Delany to Frederick Douglass, March 20, 1853, April 15, 1853 in *Martin R. Delany: A Documentary Reader*, ed. Robert S. Levine (Chapel Hill: University of North Carolina Press, 2003), 224, 230. On Douglass's and Delany's response to *Uncle Tom's Cabin*, see Robert S. Levine, *Martin Delany, Frederick Douglass, and the Politics of Representative Identity* (Chapel Hill: University of North Carolina Press, 1997), 58–98.
5. Significant essays on Stowe and race include those found in Eric J. Sundquist's collection *New Essays on Uncle Tom's Cabin* (New York: Cambridge University Press, 1986), especially Sundquist's "Introduction," 1–44, Richard Yarborough, "Strategies of black characterization in *Uncle Tom's Cabin* and the early Afro-American novel," 45–84, and Elizabeth Ammons, "Stowe's dream of the mother–savior: *Uncle Tom's Cabin* and American women writers before the 1920s," 155–95; Hortense J. Spillers, "Changing the letter: the yokes, the jokes of discourse; or, Mrs. Stowe, Mr. Reed," in Deborah E. McDowell and Arnold Rampersad, eds., *Slavery and the Literary Imagination* (Baltimore: Johns Hopkins University Press, 1989), 25–61; Christina Zwarg, "Fathering and blackface in *Uncle Tom's Cabin*," *Novel: A Forum on Fiction* 22.3 (Spring 1989), 274–87; Arthur Riss, "Racial essentialism and family values in *Uncle Tom's Cabin*," *American Quarterly* 46.4 (Dec. 1994), 513–44; and Michael J. Meyer, "Toward a rhetoric of equality: reflective and refractive images in Stowe's language," in *The Stowe Debate: Rhetorical Strategies in Uncle Tom's Cabin*, ed. Mason I. Lowance, Jr., Ellen E. Westbrook, and R. C. De Prospo (Amherst: University of Massachusetts Press, 1994), 236–54. For books, see the Stowe chapters in Jane P. Tompkins, *Sensational Designs: The Cultural Work of American fiction, 1790–1860* (New York: Oxford University Press, 1985); Philip Fisher, *Hard Facts: Setting and Form in the American Novel* (Cambridge: Harvard University Press, 1985); Gillian Brown, *Domestic Individualism: Imagining Self in Nineteenth-Century America* (Berkeley: University of California Press, 1990); Lora Romero, *Home Fronts: Domesticity and its Critics in the Antebellum United States* (Durham: Duke

University Press, 1997); and Gregg D. Crane, *Race, Citizenship, and Law in American Literature* (New York: Cambridge University Press, 2002). See also Joan D. Hedrick, *Harriet Beecher Stowe: A Life* (New York: Oxford University Press, 1994).

6. Harriet Beecher Stowe, *Uncle Tom's Cabin*, ed. Elizabeth Ammons (W. W. Norton & Co., Inc., 1994), 18.

7. On "romantic racialism," see George M. Frederickson, *The Black Image in the White Mind* (New York: Harper Collins, 1971), 97–129. Mia Bay analyzes the African-American version, in which "messianic ethnologists" imagined that theirs was the "redeemer race." See *The White Image in the Black Mind: African-American Ideas about White People, 1830–1925* (New York: Oxford University Press, 2000), 38–74.

8. Charles Johnson, "Introduction" to *Uncle Tom's Cabin*, by Harriet Beecher Stowe (New York: Oxford University Press, 2002), ix.

9. Harriet Beecher Stowe to Gamaliel Bailey, March 9, 1851, in *The Oxford Harriet Beecher Stowe Reader*, ed. Joan D. Hedrick (New York: Oxford University Press, 1999), 66.

10. Harriet Beecher Stowe, "Preface" to *Uncle Tom's Cabin; or, Life Among the Lowly; New Edition with Illustrations and a Bibliography of the Work by George Bullen, Together with an Introductory Account of the Work* (Boston: Houghton, Mifflin, and Co., 1880), xi. Her son and biographer, Charles Edward Stowe, retells the story in his *Life of Harriet Beecher Stowe, Compiled from her Letters and Journals* (Boston: Houghton, Mifflin, and Co., 1890), 148–149. In *Uncle Tom's Cabin and American Culture*, Gossett reminds us that Stowe told different stories about the writing of Tom's death scene (91–93).

11. Harriet Beecher Stowe, *A Key to Uncle Tom's Cabin* (rpt. New York: Arno Press and the New York Times, 1969), 51–52.

12. Few critics have treated *A Key to Uncle Tom's Cabin* as more than a footnote to Stowe's first novel. Cindy Weinstein is a notable exception. See her essay "*Uncle Tom's Cabin* and the South" in this volume and also her *Family, Kinship, and Sympathy in Nineteenth-Century American Literature* (Cambridge: Cambridge University Press, 2004).

13. Lydia Maria Child, "Introduction" to *Incidents in the Life of a Slave Girl, Written by Herself*, ed. Jean Fagan Yellin (Cambridge: Harvard University Press, 1987), 4.

14. Harriet Beecher Stowe, *Dred: A Tale of the Great Dismal Swamp*, ed. Robert S. Levine (New York: Penguin Books, 2000), 353.

15. Hortense J. Spillers, "Mama's baby, Papa's maybe: an American grammar book," *Diacritics* 17.2 (Summer 1987), 65–81.

16. James Baldwin, "Everybody's protest novel," in *The Price of the Ticket: Collected Nonfiction, 1948–1985* (New York: St. Martin's/Marek, 1985), 27–33.

17. On the 1840 census, see William Stanton, *The Leopard's Spots: Scientific Attitudes toward Race in America, 1815–59* (Chicago: University of Chicago Press, 1960), 58–66.

18. For recent work on *Dred*, see especially Robert S. Levine, *Martin Delany, Frederick Douglass*, 144–176, and "Introduction" to *Dred: A Tale of the Great Dismal Swamp* (New York: Penguin Books, 2000), ix–xxxv; Judie Newman, "Introduction" to *Dred: A Tale of the Great Dismal Swamp*, by Harriet

Beecher Stowe (Halifax, England: Ryburn Publishing, 1992); Lisa Whitney, "In the shadow of *Uncle Tom's Cabin*: Stowe's vision of slavery from the Great Dismal Swamp," *New England Quarterly* 66.4 (1993), 552–69; and Gregg D. Crane, *Race, Citizenship, and Law*, 56–86.

19. Harriet Beecher Stowe, *The Christian Slave: A Drama, Founded on a Portion of Uncle Tom's Cabin, Dramatised by Harriet Beecher Stowe, Expressly for the Readings of Mrs. Mary E. Webb; Arranged, with a Short Biographical Sketch of the Reader, by F. J. Webb* (London: Sampson Low, Son, and Co., 1856); Frank J. Webb, *The Garies and Their Friends*, intro. Robert Reid-Pharr (Baltimore: The Johns Hopkins University Press, 1997).

20. See David C. Miller, *Dark Eden: The Swamp in Nineteenth-Century American Culture* (Cambridge: Cambridge University Press, 1989), 90–102.

21. Baldwin, "Everybody's protest novel," 30.

22. On Stowe's encounters with African-American literature and vice versa, see Richard Yarborough, "Strategies of black characterization"; Robert B. Stepto, "Sharing the thunder: the literary exchanges of Harriet Beecher Stowe, Henry Bibb, and Frederick Douglass," in Sundquist, ed., *New Essays on Uncle Tom's Cabin*, 135–153; Haryette Mullen, "Runaway tongue: resistant orality in *Uncle Tom's Cabin, Our Nig, Incidents in the Life of a Slave Girl*, and *Beloved*," in *The Culture of Sentiment: Race, Gender, and Sentimentality in Nineteenth-Century America*, ed. Shirley Samuels (New York: Oxford University Press, 1992), 244–264; Eric J. Sundquist, *To Wake the Nations: Race in the Making of American Literature* (Cambridge: The Belknap Press of Harvard University Press, 1993), 101–102, 109–110, and passim; and Levine, *Martin Delany, Frederick Douglass*, 144–176.

2

CINDY WEINSTEIN

Uncle Tom's Cabin and the south

"Read *Uncle Tom's Cabin* again."

These simple words are from Mary Boykin Chesnut's magisterial *Diary* of her life in South Carolina during the Civil War years, and they indicate that she has read *Uncle Tom's Cabin* at least once before. Chesnut frequently invokes Stowe's novel as a discursive foil for her typically positive observations about the institution of slavery, the slaves within it, and the south more generally. She writes, "Topsys I have known – but none that were beauties – or ill-used. Evas are mostly in the heaven of Mrs. Stowe's imagination. People can't love things dirty, ugly, repulsive, simply because they ought, but they can be good to them – at a distance." Despite their great political differences, however, Stowe's imagination seems never far from Chesnut's, who concedes, in one of her most famous lines, that "Mrs. Stowe did not hit the sorest spot. She makes Legree a bachelor" (168).[1]

Chesnut's *Diary* provides an entry point into an analysis of southern responses to *Uncle Tom's Cabin*. That they were deeply hostile comes as no surprise, although the negativity assumed particular discursive forms and strategies which will be the subject of this essay. That Stowe was a woman made the southern counter-assault more complicated in that several reviewers, especially men, felt the need to explain the vehemence of their critique of a novel written by a woman. In an especially rabid review, George Frederick Holmes begins by defending himself against the hypothetical accusation that he lacks chivalry: "the rule that everyone bearing the name and appearance of a lady, should receive the delicate gallantry and considerate tenderness which are due to a lady, is not absolutely without exception." Stowe, though, is no lady, having "wantonly forfeited her privilege of immunity, she has irretrievably lost our regard." Another review in the *Southern Literary Messenger*, most likely written by its founder, John R. Thompson, characterizes her as neither a lady writer nor a female writer, but some terrible hybrid who has abdicated "the high and holy office of maternity" and, therefore, "has placed

herself without the pale of kindly treatment at the hands of Southern criticism." Attacks on Stowe's femininity – from speculations that "her voice is
probably harsh" to her "big, scrawling hand, with the letters all backwards,
avoiding neatness with pains-taking precision" – frequently appear, with one
southern woman referring twice to "the man Harriet" and accusing Stowe
of having "unsexed herself."[2] Southerners, in particular, reviled Stowe for
intervening in the masculine sphere of political activism. She found herself
on the receiving end of a great deal of opprobrium that was directed not
only at anti-slavery activism but feminism as well.

Indeed, readers south of the Mason–Dixon Line had little patience with
what Thompson describes as "her abuse of the Southern States" combined
with an "utter indifference to fact and probability." Although many recent
readers have critiqued *Uncle Tom's Cabin*, in part, on the grounds that it
wasn't abusive enough – that Stowe embraced southern racism as she was
making a case against it – the fact is that the anger generated by her novel
cannot be underestimated. Thompson describes it as a "miserable tissue
of falsehoods and abominations," and Holmes contends that "every fact is
distorted, every incident discolored, in order to awaken rancorous hatred and
malignant jealousies between the citizens of the same republic."[3] Stowe tried
to make *Uncle Tom's Cabin* less a wholesale indictment of the south and more
a critique of the peculiar institution by revealing northern complicity and by
representing virtuous white southern characters, such as Mrs. Shelby and
her son, George, Mrs. Byrd, and Eva. In the preface to *A Key to Uncle Tom's
Cabin*, she writes, "Slavery is not the element which forms the picturesque
and beautiful of Southern life."[4] But as pro-slavery author, Caroline Lee
Hentz, noted: "Slavery is not an outer garment that can be thrown off at
will. . . . It is a dark thread; but as it winds along, it gleams with bright and
silvery lustre, and some of the most beautiful lights and shades of the texture
are owing to the blending of these sable filaments."[5] Here, the beauty of
the south is inextricable from slavery. Stowe's effort to make the blight and
responsibility of slavery a national affair (and unwillingness to acknowledge
anything beautiful about it) had clearly failed. There was no separating the
south from slavery.

Reviews of *Uncle Tom's Cabin*, as well as novelistic responses, repeatedly
call into question Stowe's representation of the "facts and documents upon
which the story is founded," to quote from *A Key*'s subtitle. According to
the *Southern Press Review*, "the system of the South relies on fact – the sentiment of the North flies to fiction." Hentz's *The Planter's Northern Bride*,
the most interesting anti-Uncle Tom novel, to which I shall return, argues on
behalf of "true-hearted Southerners" who have been reviled by Stowe's scur-
rilous, irresponsible portrayal of southern life.[6] This essay goes beyond the

obvious point that southern reviewers were outraged by Stowe's intervention and explains how the debate about *Uncle Tom's Cabin* became an epistemological one about evidence, fact, and truth. Facts, as reviews and *A Key* make clear, were crucial in this controversy because Stowe had argued that if southerners had the facts, they couldn't possibly support slavery. Southern readers responded that Stowe could only be against slavery because she didn't know how the institution worked, because she didn't have the facts. The debate about the facts of slavery is also a debate about what Stowe had famously called "feeling right," or "seeing to your sympathies" at the conclusion of *Uncle Tom's Cabin*.[7] Fact and feeling were mutually implicated in the reception and refutation of the novel, as southerners endeavored to prove that slavery was the result of their right feeling. *A Key*, though marginalized heretofore, is essential to our understanding of Stowe's anti-slavery strategies, because it reveals the bankruptcy of the pro-slavery position not only by proving that its facts are lies, because they are predicated on an absence of sympathy, but that anti-slavery facts are true because they are based on sympathy's presence. Irony, citation, and documentation comprise Stowe's unconventional weaponry as *A Key* invalidates southern feelings and facts and establishes the authenticity of her own. To establish the authenticity of one's evidence was to sanction one's political position (anti or pro-slavery) with the imprimatur of sympathy, one of the most deeply held values in antebellum culture, north and south.

The Real Presence of *Uncle Tom's Cabin*

Uncle Tom's Cabin was a publishing phenomenon, selling "50,000 copies in eight weeks," according to publisher John P. Jewett, and "within eight months [Jewett] issued more than a quarter of a million of copies of it." Although statistics prove its tremendous national popularity, less available is specific information about how successful *Uncle Tom's Cabin* was in the south. Clearly, southerners read it, but on what scale remains undetermined. The *National Anti-Slavery Standard* notes, "we know personally of copies that have found their way to the extreme South, and have heard of single copies being kept in active though secret circulation in a circle of friends." A Boston paper writes, "we learn that large orders for Uncle Tom's Cabin are now beginning to come in from the South. The publishers have just received one order from Vicksburg, Miss., another from New Orleans, another from a bookseller in Georgia." Such evidence, though intriguing, is sketchy. We can begin to get a better sense of the novel's impact on the south by examining how deeply *Uncle Tom's Cabin* established a seemingly inescapable framework through which southern culture was represented.[8]

Uncle Tom's Cabin became the quintessential representation of the south against which writers often felt the need to position themselves. Most obvious are the anti-Tom novels that were written in the wake of Stowe's, for example, *Aunt Phillis's Cabin; or, Southern Life as It Is*; *The Cabin and the Parlor; or Slaves and Masters*; *Life at the South; or, "Uncle Tom's Cabin" as It Is: Being Narratives, Scenes, and Incidents in the Real "Life of the Lowly"*; *"Uncle Tom's Cabin" Contrasted with Buckingham Hall*. *Uncle Tom's Cabin* or its characters, however, don't only appear in texts explicitly written as responses to Stowe's portrayal of slavery or the south. Mary Jane Holmes's *Meadowbrook Farm* has little in common with Stowe's novel, except that her heroine temporarily resides in the south. But during her stay there, this exchange takes place after one character mistakenly refers to another character as Eva: "I done forgot again, and called her Eva. Her name is Evangeline, and we used to call her Eva, until mother read a bad book that had little Eva in it, and then she called her Lina." This seemingly perfunctory intrusion of *Uncle Tom's Cabin* also occurs in *Two Pictures; or, What we Think of Ourselves, and What the World Thinks of Us*, Maria J. McIntosh's 1863 novel, where the main character impatiently reads a "review of 'Uncle Tom,' with its unflattering portraiture of Southern planters." Her husband says "there are two sides to every picture," to which she replies, "True; and I thank God there are – that we are not obliged to see ourselves or each other as the false world sees us."9

As an immediately recognizable metonym for the anti-slavery position, *Uncle Tom's Cabin* frequently figures that other side. I have begun to delineate its embedded literary manifestations, but other discursive arenas – ethnographic material, in particular – registered Stowe's enormous representational power. While southerners busily defended the peculiar institution, in part, on the grounds that they lived in the south and Stowe didn't (had southerners realized just how little Stowe knew about the south – a short stint in Kentucky constituted her first-hand knowledge of slavery – their reviews might have been dismissively rather than defensively scathing), some northerners went south to get what New England clergyman, Nehemiah Adams, called *A South-Side View of Slavery*. His preface states, "if *Uncle Tom's Cabin* is true, there are other things just as true which ought to modify every judgment of slavery as dictated by that book."10 What follows is a fascinating and disturbing defense of slavery, based on a three-month tour, that simultaneously makes two incompatible cases: he argues that the difference between the theory of slavery and its practice makes slavery a beneficent institution at the same time as he claims that the south, not the slaves, is the true victim of (the beneficent institution of) slavery. Adams's rosy view of slavery was countered by C. G. Parsons, a Maine physician, who traveled south and wrote *An Inside View of Slavery: or a Tour Among the Planters*, upon which Stowe gives her blessing: "all unprejudiced, or even prejudiced persons, [should] *read* it." Although their politics are diametrically opposed, Adams and Parsons agree upon one thing – Stowe's portrayal is their shared point of departure against which their observations are measured. The most intriguing use of Stowe in an ethnographic text, however, occurs in Frederick Law Olmsted's *A Journey in the Seaboard Slave States*, volume three of his De Tocqueville-like inquiry into the economic and affective states of the Union. While in Louisiana, a passenger mistakenly believes that Olmsted is reading *Uncle Tom's Cabin*, a mistake which Olmsted parlays into a debate about the abolitionist's accusation that "cruelty [is] a necessity of Slavery." Olmsted's argument hinges on "narrating the Red River episode" where Emmeline senses the horrors that await her with Legree. The passenger tries to refute Olmsted (and Stowe), but with little success: "I said this story cor-roborated the truthfulness of *Uncle Tom's Cabin*."[11] Here, Olmsted uses a chapter from Stowe as reliable evidence against his opponent; that is, he grants Stowe's fiction a degree of truth-telling that he is unwilling to give to a first-hand account of slavery. This exchange registers how Stowe's characters could be deployed as a litmus test for the truthfulness of an actual person. Olmsted's real-life antagonist failed. No wonder defenders of slavery felt compelled to undermine the "facts" of *Uncle Tom's Cabin*. But as we have begun to see, the truthfulness of Stowe's representation of slavery seemed to transcend the question of whether it was fact or fiction, even as she tried to vindicate herself (and her novel) on the grounds that every character, scene, and event had some basis in fact.

The Southern Heart

When Stowe urged her readers to "feel right," she assumed that a position against slavery had to follow. She was wrong, according to many southerners (and northern supporters of slavery like Adams), who "looked to their sym-pathies in these matters" and were convinced that slavery expressed their sympathy for African Americans. Many argued that masters, not slaves, deserved sympathy given the burdens of caring for slaves who had been inherited, like it or not, and the unfair assault that Stowe had launched against southern character. Louisa J. McCord's 1853 review of *Uncle Tom's Cabin* begins with this tableau of self-pity: "Truly it would seem that the labour of Sisyphus is laid upon us, the slaveholders of these southern United States." Mary Eastman's *Aunt Phillis's Cabin* denounces Stowe, "In what an attitude, O Planters of the South, has Mrs. Stowe taken your likenesses!" And Caroline Rush's *The North and South, or, Slavery and its Contrasts*.

A Tale of Real Life begins with an extended reply to Stowe in which Rush claims, "I would never refuse to do a kind action for a person because that person happened to be black, but I would far rather relieve the suffering of my own colour, because I believe they stand far more in need of relief, and are far less apt to be relieved."[12] In arguing against Stowe, defenders of slavery adopted various strategies. They maintained the greater suffering of whites over blacks in order to redirect the circuits of sympathy toward masters, toward northern white workers, toward the British factory workers, toward anyone *but* slaves. They also argued that one of the master's primary duties, in contrast to the purely economic function of factory owners, was the proper dispensation of sympathy toward his slaves.

Sympathy was a key term in the antebellum lexicon, as literary critics and historians have shown, and the debate about *Uncle Tom's Cabin* (as well as the novel itself) underscores this point. Not only does the word appear throughout the novel, but the act of extending or withholding sympathy functions as one of the most reliable indicators of a person's character. Sympathy is one of the hallmarks of the narrator's style (she writes, "we forbear, out of sympathy to our readers" [78]), as well as one of the defining features, according to Stowe, of "the negro [who is] sympathetic" (291). In contrast to the "real sympathy" (84) that is registered when Aunt Chloe and Mrs. Shelby mourn Tom's departure, Maria responds to Prue's relentless tale of suffering, "I don't feel a particle of sympathy for such cases" (202). Eva's response to Prue's story – "these things *sink into my heart*" (204) – stands as a counter-image to Maria's callousness.

Stowe's attack on slavery was so effective, so blistering because she argued that slavery was only possible in the absence of sympathy. She had not just misrepresented the south, but, worse, she had impugned the region's sympathies, its collective heart. From Stowe's perspective, the precondition of slavery was the legalized refusal to acknowledge that slaves had feelings and the legalized inability of (potentially sympathetic) masters to do anything about it, whether teaching them how to read, allowing them to marry, or freeing them. Defenders of slavery, therefore, found themselves not only defending their facts but their feelings. That southerners had feelings at all was something that many felt required proof, especially when advertisements for the novel included pronouncements such as "he who can read this greatest of all American Tales unmoved, must have been very successful in hardening his heart," or "these volumes will be read South as well as North, and find response in every honest heart." Thompson thus identifies himself as having a "willing heart," before critiquing Stowe's American tale. McCord contends that "Southern hearts and Southern souls can beat high," and Adams argues that "southern hearts and consciences . . . were no more insensible than mine" (69).[13]

The most eloquent defense of the southern heart, however, is *The Planter's Northern Bride*. Much has been written about the many anti-Tom novels, although it is often conceded that their attempts at refuting Stowe fall considerably short of the mark. "A more remarkable instance of asinine pretension than the announcement of this insipid volume as the counterpart to 'Uncle Tom's Cabin' has never fallen under our notice" is the verdict on W. L. G. Smith's *Life at the South; or, "Uncle Tom's Cabin" As It Is.* That these words appeared in Douglass's *Paper* is expected; however, even southern reviewers expressed displeasure with such efforts. Combining literary sensibility with misogyny, Holmes laments "all the replies to *Uncle Tom's Cabin* which have hitherto been attempted under the form of corresponding fiction, usually, we are sorry to say, by weak and incompetent persons."[14] Hentz is anything but weak and incompetent, and the power of her reply lies in understanding that *Uncle Tom's Cabin* is a direct attack on sympathy as it is practiced in and upon the south. Hentz limits the rabid diatribes of most anti-Uncle Tom literature and concentrates instead on finding a "Northern heart [which will] respond to our earnest appeal" (10–11). Hentz's recovery of the southern heart establishes the south's prolific capacities for sympathy (as giver and receiver), and the allegedly satisfying arrangements of the slave family. She upholds the integrity of slave families by not acknowledging their separations and by insisting that children don't necessarily love most their biological family, especially their birth mother. This could not be more different from Stowe.[15]

"I grant that some of these tales of cruelty are true . . . But, generally speaking, they are nothing but gross fabrications, invented to enlist the sympathies of credulous fanatics" (195). So declares the hero, Russell Moreland, after reading abolitionist tracts meant to "enlist the sympathies" of readers. Because these "tales of cruelty" can take place anywhere, anytime, the southerner Moreland believes that it is wrong to assign them a particular cause, like slavery, when their occurrences are infrequent and primarily fictitious. They are "tales," "fabrications" designed to elicit an anti-slavery response. Sympathy, in the hands of "credulous fanatics" (that is, abolitionists), is extremely dangerous, as Hentz's abolitionists mistake these "gross fabrications" for the truth, thereby destroying southern families, slaves, and, as if that weren't bad enough, the national body politic. Moreland wishes to direct sympathy to the proper targets, including slave-owners, white northern workers, blacks who have been duped into thinking they want freedom, and the south, which has been persecuted by "the thorns of prejudice" (31).

For Hentz, a transplanted northerner, *Uncle Tom's Cabin* was the most potent of these "fabrications." During her residence in the south, she "never *witnessed* one scene of cruelty or oppression, never beheld a chain or a manacle" (5). She claims to have been "delighted and affected by their [the slaves'] humble devotion to their master's family, their child-like, affectionate reliance on their care and protection, and above all, with their genuine cheerfulness and contentment" (6–7). Hentz contends that slaves do not require sympathy because their economic, spiritual, and affective needs are wholly cared for by their masters. Economic considerations pervade the spousal and parental relations of the novel's white families, while the economic transactions at the heart of slavery are erased. Because Hentz believes that slaves are free of economic concerns and don't require sympathy, which is a required emotion only when there is a material lack.

The novel's frame is the love story between Moreland and Eulalia, who, though a northerner, is "a tropic flower, born to be nurtured beneath milder skies" (148). Moreland has journeyed northward to eradicate memories of a bad first marriage, when he encounters Eula whom he courts and marries. To counter the objections of Eula's abolitionist father, Hastings, Moreland convinces him of the national consequences of their union. When Eula departs for the south, where the rest of the novel takes place, Hastings explains his change of mind: "I believe Providence has a mission for you to perform . . . you will be a golden link of union between the divided interests of humanity" (136). Their marriage clearly functions as an allegory of sectional conflict and reunion.

This reunion will be accomplished by eradicating northern prejudice, which is why Eula must venture southward to see that "there is no such thing as irresponsible power at the South" (204). Through Eula's encounters with plantation life, Hentz presents and dismisses abolitionist stereotypes. That slavery breeds an unregulated system of labor is countered by "the systematic arrangement of everything. The hours of labour were all regulated – the tasks for those hours appointed" (341). In answering the charge that slavery meant relentless labor, Eula is informed that slaves "did not do as much work in one week as a white servant will accomplish in one day" (184). Lastly, the belief that slavery legalizes unregulated passions within slaveholders is offset by Moreland's statement, "I would sooner give my right hand to the flames than make it the instrument of cruelty and oppression to them [the slaves]" (303). Here, the vulnerability of the master's white body supersedes the violation of black, enslaved bodies.

The most pernicious northern prejudice is the fiction of southern prejudice. Hentz explains that slavery is not based on prejudice, but is a system inflicted upon masters: "We are not responsible for it, though we are for the duties it involves, the heaviest perhaps ever imposed upon man" (82). In fact, Eula must become a slave-owner to be cured of racism. Her abolitionist upbringing has perverted her instinctive understanding of the difference and superiority of white over black into an unnatural fear and "repugnance to the African race." Moreland admonishes her, "You must struggle with this from the first, and it will surely be overcome. It is of unnatural birth – born of prejudice and circumstance" (201). Only in the sympathetic south where this repugnance to the African race doesn't exist can Eula be freed from northern prejudice.

Eula overcomes her prejudice once she realizes that the slaves do not require the sympathy she assumed they needed: "I never dreamed that slavery could present an aspect so tender and affectionate" (333). One resident, however, does need her sympathy, and that is Effie, Moreland's child with his first wife, Claudia. Effie is Hentz's Topsy-figure, undisciplined and unloved. Moreland says, "make her like yourself, Eulalia, all that is lovely and good, and I will forget she ever had another mother" (217). Effie responds fully to her stepmother's love. So fully that when Claudia takes Effie from her home, claiming, "She is mine! I will not give her up! Has not the mother a right to her own child?" (368) Effie pleads with Claudia, "Take me to my dear, sweet, other mamma!" and asks her, "How came I to have two mammas?" (466). Eula recovers Effie, but the complexities of this narrative strand are multiple. Effie is virtually kidnapped by her biological mother who exclaims, "'I *will* have the child! . . .' snatching Effie with frantic violence from her arms and rushing to the door" (370). When the narrator ponders, "Had not the mother purchased her child by the pains and sorrows of maternity, and could any legal decision annul the great law of God, which makes the child a mother's almost life-bought property?" (369), the answers are no and yes. The mother has not purchased her child through the pain of labor (that was no guarantee for slave mothers), and legal decisions can annul the great law of God (the slave code). A child, then, is not a mother's almost life-bought property.

That the narrator imagines this relationship economically, figuring the child in terms of property and inquiring about its/her price, is revealing. Effie occupies the position of slave with Claudia and Eula arguing over the maternal right of ownership. In response to Claudia's "She is mine," Eula cries, "This child is *mine* – committed to my guardianship by the father, who has abjured your maternal right!" (370). Biological attachments are less compelling than non-consanguineous ones, and Effie easily shifts her attachments from birth mother to stepmother. She asks Eula, "She isn't my mamma, is she? . . . Make her go away – I don't love her" (369), surely a model for a slave child who must establish an alternative maternal bond in the absence of a biological one. Effie's family drama validates slavery's creation of new parental relations while displacing (and effacing) that very drama taking place in the slave family.

From Stowe's perspective, a reunion with the biological mother is every child's, particularly every slave child's, dream. It is Effie's worst nightmare, and she becomes a slave once Claudia gets her back: "Advertisements [are] inserted in every paper, with offers of munificent reward" (432). Whereas the sanctity of the mother–child bond is what should prevent the practice of slavery in Stowe, the flexibility of this relationship in Hentz (children can have deeper attachments to second mammas) undergirds the structure of slavery and provides a defense for it. Effie, prototype for the slave, is most free when she is with her newly constructed family. Her kidnapping mimics and inverts the structure of slavery whereby children are taken from their mothers by perniciously suggesting that the separation between children and biological mothers is a salvific one.

Strategic appropriations like this pervade Hentz's text; to wit, Crissy's flight from slavery. Crissy is the slave of Ildegarte, the sister of Moreland with whom she lives. When "Ilde" travels west with her consumptive husband, Richard, Crissy accompanies them. There, she encounters Mr. and Mrs. Softly, evil abolitionists who seduce her with fantasies of freedom and effect her escape when Ilde needs her most – during Richard's agonizing death. According to Hentz, Crissy has no thoughts about freedom except to fear it: "She glanced from one side to the other, with a vague dread of being pounced upon and carried off [by abolitionists]" (250). Indeed, when the Softlys finally do "exert [their] influence upon her" (270), her escape is designated "the abduction of Crissy" (357–358). Hentz's abolitionists act like Stowe's slave-owners, and the guardians of freedom are indistinguishable from the keepers of slavery. Questioning the Softlys' abolitionism, the narrator asks, "What, but the carrying out of a fixed, inflexible purpose, at any cost, at any sacrifice; the triumph of an indomitable will?" (281). Their desire to free her cancels out Crissy's will to be a slave. It is the abolitionists, not the slaveholders, who undermine Crissy's agency: "Thus beset, day after day, poor Crissy grew weak and impotent, till she became a passive tool in their soft, insinuating hands" (271). Crissy's freedom leads to an enslavement greater than any she has ever known. In a passage reminiscent of Harriet Jacobs's sequestration, Crissy finds herself in a "room [that] was unplastered, not even lathed, and when she looked up she knew by the slanting rafters overhead that she had been sleeping in a garret . . . Chill, shivering sensations went creeping up and down her back" (378–379). Instead of desiring freedom, though, Crissy fondly recalls her mistress: "how kind and sympathizing she was in sickness! How often her soft, white hand, had bathed the negro's aching brow" (379).

Because freedom, not slavery, produces suffering, sympathy for Crissy can only be articulated at the moment of her liberation. We should rejoice when Crissy "come[s] back" to "the fold" (399) of Moreland's plantation because "however glorious freedom was in itself, it had proved to her the only slavery she had ever known" (392). Crissy's situation as a potentially free person is dire, but worse off is Ilde, from whom the Softlys have stolen "a *friend*, in the hour of extremest need" (359). Ilde's need for sympathy during Richard's death supercedes Crissy's need for freedom, which according to Hentz is no need at all, but one manufactured by the Softlys for the "gratification of prejudice and intolerance" (281). The union is threatened not by southern racism but by northern prejudice, with its "fiery fanaticism" and frantic zeal, which, reckless of all consequences, was spreading through the land (272). Abolitionism, not slavery, is the "dark spot" (459) which endeavors "to destroy our liberties and rights" (407) and ends up enslaving the south. Just as Hentz's abolitionists are as heartless as the slaveholders in an anti-slavery text, so too a slave's acquisition of freedom condemns her to the worst slavery imaginable. This is why so many slaves who become free beg to be re-enslaved. Judy, who has escaped one of the few abusive slave-owners, implores Eula and Moreland to buy her. Exhausted by her freedom and its responsibilities, she asserts, "'I belongs to a mighty mean missus, just now, honey – dat's my own ugly, black self. I'm tired of being my own missus, dat I am'" (290–291). It would seem that self-ownership is a version of slavery far worse than the one in the south, leaving freed slaves desperate to return to slavery.

That northern workers and free blacks had harder lives than slaves was a staple of pro-slavery discourse: "There was the bondage of poverty, whose iron chains are heard clanking in every region of God's earth, whose dark links are wrought in the forge of human suffering, eating slowly into the quivering flesh, till they reach and dry up the life-blood of the heart" (27). Nancy, a white worker, is dying of consumption due to over-work. The solution? Slavery. "She thought of her days of servitude, her waning health, her anxious fears and torturing apprehensions of future want, and it seemed to her the mere exemption from such far-reaching solicitudes must be a blessing. She thought, too, of the soft, mild atmosphere that flowed around those children of toil, and wished she could breathe its balm" (52). The iron chains of poverty destroying the lives of northern workers seem far more palpable than any chains one might have read about in abolitionist texts. They are, Hentz contends, "mere figures of speech" (51).

Hentz, like Moreland, works to make slavery "a figure of rhetoric" (105) as she defends slavery against abolitionist depictions so as to quash what she sees as the false distinctions made between freedom and slavery. Those distinctions don't hold because abolitionist texts are "fabrications" and hers is truthful, and because she has redefined freedom as slavery and slavery as freedom: "Even *bondage*, which at a distance had seemed so dark and threatening, lightened up as they approached it, like the mist of their valley, and receded from their view" (576). Her polemic aims to make bondage recede from view so that it looks like something else, so that it can be called freedom. The chains, the family separations, the unrelenting labor, all of the alleged "facts" of slavery become merely discursive strategies in the abolitionist artillery. She takes these allegedly sectional and peculiar "facts" and argues for their applicability in the north. "The anathema of prejudice" (552) does not allude to race relations, but to the conflict between abolitionists and slave-owners. And slavery is not slavery but freedom, and freedom is not freedom but slavery. In creating sectional differences where none need exist, Hentz maintains that Stowe constructs a south far more enslaved by northern prejudice and far more in need of sympathy than any slave could ever be. Sympathy, in Hentz's text, functions to erase the differences between north and south, between freedom and slavery. One difference won't be erased because, for Hentz and for Moreland, "inequality is one of Nature's laws" (305). She believes that black is black and white is white, and it is the insistence upon and hierarchization of this difference that produces the real facts of slavery. And so, for Stowe, the need for sympathy.

Reading *A Key*

A Key is an irate and ironic critique of critiques of *Uncle Tom's Cabin* which aims to prove the mutual exclusivity of being both pro-slavery and sympathetic. Stowe examines court cases, legal statutes, newspaper articles, and fictions proffered by defenders of slavery and argues for their unreliability (in more generous moments) or their mendacity (in less patient ones). It is an archeological discovery of facts that confirms that "the slave code of America is a case of elegant surgical instruments for the work of dissecting the living human heart" (82). Hentz's "southern heart" is not a functioning organ. And if hearts have been dissected, not only can they not feel, but they cannot "feel right." Because defenders of slavery specialize in the art of euphemism or their "endless variety of specifications and synonyms" (113), Stowe pierces through their fraudulent language to get to the brutal facts of slavery and to prove that pro-slavery facts are lies. Indeed, the exposure of euphemism acts as the spur to her narrative. She deploys pro-slavery euphemism and linguistic manipulation as evidence which begins to prove that the facts supporting the argument in favor of slavery are fallacious. "Feeling right" *has* to produce an anti-slavery stance because the facts of the pro-slavery position are predicated upon the absence of feelings.

Stowe's interventions require the reader to wonder, if people like Hentz, McCord, and Thompson don't know the meaning of words, if the differences between "nominal bondage" and "bondage" don't matter, how can one trust them, their facts, their feelings? Stowe exploits the strategy of "anti-Tom novels" that attempt to extinguish the differences between freedom and slavery in order to defend slavery on both its evidentiary and sympathetic merits. She exposes this tactical maneuver as a perversion of facts, and she does so through her use of irony, citation, and hermeneutic expertise. Stowe is unapologetically ubiquitous in *A Key*, inserting herself through punctuation, such as capitalization, italics, or quotation marks, as a way to establish the insincerity of pro-slavery terminology. Although it is a compendium of citation, she has to call attention to the places where she is not: "The following is quoted without comment" (188), or "The italics are the writers" (197). Furthermore, to make implausible the pro-slavery counter-assertion that her version of the facts is fiction, she demonstrates how defenses of slavery – legal, religious, or novelistic – instantiate the "deadening of sensibility" (203), the "gradual deterioration of the moral sense" (206). "The numbness of public sentiment" (83) makes it impossible for defenders of slavery to recognize the difference between fact and fiction, truth and lies, freedom and slavery. And not to know or not to acknowledge these differences (Stowe alternates between these two poles) is the clearest sign of that "awful paralysis of the moral sense" (128). Stowe's sympathy is validated because she has the facts to prove such categorical distinctions, the most important being that a person is not a thing.[16]

A Key records Stowe's own rereading of *Uncle Tom's Cabin* in the context of southern responses, and it is a devastating counter-attack. The text's insatiable appetite for various discourses, whether novels, poetry, newspapers, personal correspondence, the Bible, statistics, or the law demonstrates that the ideology of slavery is not limited to any genre but rather inhabits discourse itself. To the extent that *A Key* is a "mosaic of facts" (5), its generic hybridity underscores and undermines the ubiquitous facts of pro-slavery discourse, which are, from Stowe's point of view, lies. Its opening chapter characterizes *Uncle Tom's Cabin* as an "arrangement of real incidents – of actions really performed, of words and expressions really uttered" (5). By way of contrast, Stowe quotes J. Thornton Randolph's *The Cabin and Parlor*, which maintains that slave families are separated in "*novels*," but not "in real life, except in rare cases." She then asks the question that had been asked of her book, "Are these representations true?" (133). Stowe's answer is a resounding no, and her critique proceeds by reproducing advertisements for "NEGROES WANTED" (139) and "NEGROES FOR SALE" (135) Stowe's rage at such mendacity is evident, and expressions of southern benevolence are juxtaposed with advertisements describing slaves with missing teeth or toes. She intersperses searing readings of the perfidious language of "indefinite terms" (142) used to describe slaves for sale, such as *"selected"* (142) "assortment" (142) and "lots" (142), all of which help Stowe prove that *Uncle Tom's Cabin* is true and *The Cabin and Parlor* is false.

Although *A Key* concerns itself with many texts written in response to *Uncle Tom's Cabin*, Stowe uses slave law as evidence of the institution's most "glaring facts" (133). Her relentless exposure of its barbarity begins by taking on Thompson, who cites slave law to prove that Eliza's escape with Henry could not have happened because Louisiana Law prohibited separating children under ten from their mothers. He also quotes a portion of the Crimes and Offenses section of Louisiana's *Code Noir*, a set of imported French laws considered by some to protect more adequately than most the rights of slaves, in order to demonstrate "the utter falsity" of St. Clare's statement that "he who goes furthest and does the worst only uses within limits the power that the law gives him."[17]

Stowe warms up to Thompson's challenge by reproducing a barrage of citations from sources, including court cases and legal treatises, documenting the physical abuse of slaves. She then sets her critical sights on "the following most remarkable provision of the *Code Noir*: the offending person 'shall be deemed responsible and guilty' unless that person 'can prove the contrary by means of good and sufficient evidence, or can clear himself by his own oath.'" Stowe responds with disgust to this law, calling it a "specimen of utter legislative nonsense" (88). In answer to Thompson's contention that benevolent statutes make impossible the Eliza/Henry narrative, Stowe quotes the section of the *Code Noir* that Thompson had quoted, and sarcastically comments, "What a charming freshness of nature is suggested by this assertion! A thing could not have happened in a certain state, because there is a law against it!" (92). Stowe sabotages Thompson's use of law as evidence of slavery's humanity by her use of irony. Hardly a page of *A Key* goes by without Stowe italicizing, underlining, capitalizing, or putting in quotation marks words whose meanings she believes have been perverted in defense of slavery. The statutes, she argues, are fictions which Thompson, in his "amiable ignorance and unsophisticated innocence" (92), has mistaken for facts. Defenders of slavery can't produce reliable evidence because they don't or won't know the difference between fiction and fact. Under the best of circumstances they err; under the worst, they lie.

This mishandling of evidence is precisely what Stowe was accused of. Her position is precarious. In order to defend her fiction in terms of the accuracy of its anti-slavery facts, she must prove that pro-slavery facts are lies, and anti-slavery fictions (*Uncle Tom's Cabin*) are truths. She accomplishes this difficult task by undermining the reliability of particular sites of fact and fiction (newspapers, the law, church resolutions), as they operate in defenses of slavery, not fact and fiction themselves, thereby maintaining the functionality of these categories for her anti-slavery appeal. Thus, Stowe's running commentary, which surrounds her citation of documents of the slave trade, deploys the language of literary analysis in order to illustrate that the facts of slavery as presented in pro-slavery sources must be interpreted because defenders of slavery know no "scorn of dissimulation, that straightforward determination not to call a bad thing by a good name" (79). Her reproduction of rewards offered for runaways begins, "Let us open the chapter" (176). The cruelties of Mississippi slave law "are a romance of themselves" (114). She reproduces an advertisement for a "negro woman and two children" who have fled Mr. Ricks of North Carolina: "I burnt her with a hot iron, on the left side of her face. I tried to make the letter M" (109). Stowe scathingly observes, "It is charming to notice the *naïf* betrayal of literary pride on the part of Mr. Ricks." Stowe's application of the "literary" accomplishes two seemingly mutually exclusive desiderata: she defends *Uncle Tom's Cabin* on the grounds that in the very vicinity of advertisements such as these, "a hundred such scenes as those described in 'Uncle Tom' may have been acting" (136), while the palpable irony with which she deploys those literary terms signals that she is in full control of the differences between fiction and fact. Thus, only sentences after implying an interpenetration of locations in her novel and life in South Carolina, she authoritatively distinguishes between them, "This is not novel-writing – *this* is fact" (137).

But isn't Stowe being "far from straightforward," playing an anti-slavery version of a pro-slavery game? She calls things and people what she clearly believes they are not, referring to slavery as "the good trade" (140), "the blessed trade" (141), or describing one slave trader as "judicious" (140) and another as "a man of humanity" (142). What distinguishes Stowe from her antagonists is the irony which exposes their necessary and pernicious euphemisms, and guarantees the authenticity of her not-so-humble "humbl[e] inquiries" (138) and words. Irony, a tonal feature absent from Hentz and the countless pro-slavery documents Stowe assembles, becomes the unambiguous sign of Stowe's truthfulness. Not a page of *A Key* goes by that doesn't pit Stowe's irony against her opponent's reckless unconcern for the truth. Stowe cites an advertisement for the purchase of 5,000 slaves which boasts, "Families never separated." She responds, "If a man offers him a wife without her husband, Mr. John Denning won't buy her. O, no! His five thousand are all unbroken families. . . . This is a comfort to reflect upon, certainly" (142). Elsewhere, she "humbly inquire[s] what '*assorted A No. 1 Negroes*' means" (138). The advertisements include no irony, just half-lies and half-truths designed to convey information to slave traders *and* to obfuscate the family separations, to make them "recede from their view" (576), to invoke Hentz. Stowe's irony, however, is present in her "respectful" (139) inquiries, as well as her use of italics (nothing in the advertisement is italicized) which registers her suspicion, indeed certainty, that "assorted" means broken families. She wonders, "We hear a lot of field men and women. Where are their children?" Her ironic citation of their unironic words exposes the facticity of their facts – "Families, of course, never separated!" (139) – and the authenticity of her own.

A Key is a hermeneutic *tour de force* whose indictment of slavery begins and ends with demonstrating the difference between fact and fiction, between the true and false meaning of words. Stowe's commentary on the 1851 *Souther v. Commonwealth* case in which Sam, a Virginia slave, died after being tortured, centers on its language: "If this be murder in the *second degree*, in Virginia, one might earnestly pray to be murdered in the first degree, to begin with," and "as he preferred to spend *twelve hours* in killing him by torture, under the name of '*chastisement*,' that, says the verdict, is murder in the second degree" (81). Stowe quotes the Bible, "inasmuch as ye have done it unto *one of the least* of these, ye have done it unto me," reminding them of the second coming at which "Every one of these words shall rise up, living and burning, as accusing angels to witness against thee" (170). The perversion of words is the perversion of the Word or Christ himself. Irony aside, her faith in Christ, she believes, ultimately ensures the truthfulness of her words.

Like *Uncle Tom's Cabin*, *A Key* demands religious renewal as an essential means of combating the linguistic, religious, and political corruption wrought by slavery. And, like the novel, sympathy is key. When Stowe asks "What can any individual do?" (385) a pro-slavery response is not what she has in mind. *A Key* aims to demonstrate that defenses of slavery in the name of sympathy are unsupportable. Whereas earlier she answered her question with, "They can see to it that *they feel right*" (385), only a year later the question and answer have changed. In *A Key*, she asks, "What is to be done?" and answers, "the whole American church, of all denominations, should unitedly come up, not *in form*, but *in fact* . . . to seek the ENTIRE ABOLITION OF SLAVERY" (250). Individuals and feelings matter – she refers to the "human heart as that very dangerous and most illogical agitator" (104) – but as one element in the anti-slavery movement. *A Key* demands group action not in the form of church resolutions, but in fact, as in breaking the laws of slavery through church activism. She concedes that "Although the sentiment of honorable men and the voice of Christian charity does everywhere protest against what it *feels* to be inhumanity, yet the popular sentiment engendered by the system must *necessarily* fall deplorably short of giving anything like sufficient protection to the rights of the slave" (132). Elsewhere, she notes, "all the kindest feelings and intentions of the master" do nothing to obviate the "absolute despotism of the slave-law" (115). Stowe is profoundly aware that for some "feeling right" is not the equivalent of being anti-slavery and so she revises and reinforces the terms of her first call to action.

The revision looks like this – "to *mean* well is not enough" (217). This rich statement expresses Stowe's sense that "meaning well" as in "feeling right" comprises one part of the anti-slavery crusade. Her formulation resonates with the imperative to "mean *well*," (my emphasis) especially since *A Key* is about validating the truthful or Christian meaning of words rather than the perverse significations attributed to them through slavery, "or whatever the trade pleases to term them" (209). Let us recall that Stowe admonishes readers to "see, then, to your sympathies in this matter!" (385). Many did just that and, armed with their own "remarkable facts," they found that their sympathies resided with slave-owning southerners. Stowe's brilliant performance in *A Key* aims to make such a finding impossible.

As in *Uncle Tom's Cabin*, sympathy remains the originary condition for anti-slavery action just as the lack of sympathy is the condition for pro-slavery inaction. *A Key* reclaims the radical powers of sympathy, not with the hope that "an atmosphere of sympathetic influence encircles every human being" (385) – defenders of slavery had proven incapable of registering that point – but on the basis of her presentation of "hard facts," to invoke the work of Philip Fisher, such as judicial decisions, legislative actions, and the published activities of the slave trade. Realizing that seeing to one's sympathies is no easy task and unwilling to take a chance that her readers' sympathies will be led astray by "the shams and sophistry wherewith slavery has been defended" (36), Stowe shows her readers exactly what to see and how to see it. She establishes the rightness of her sympathies by asserting their foundation in facts, facts which she proves by reading the evidence presented in defenses of slavery against itself. She, then, deploys those defenses as evidence of their own disingenuousness, which then becomes evidence of the unfeelingness at the core of pro-slavery belief.

Southern responses to *Uncle Tom's Cabin* demanded that Stowe recuperate sympathy for the anti-slavery cause, which she does in *A Key*. One can only imagine that like Chesnut, Stowe was forced to "read *Uncle Tom's Cabin* again." Stowe's rereading of her novel in light of pro-slavery appropriations of her call to "feel right" provides us with an important model for reevaluating our understanding of sympathy to include kinds of affect and modes of expression not usually associated with sympathy, such as irony, citation, and facts. To read irony and fact as an expression of sympathy as deep as tears, to read Hentz's discursive erasure of the differences between freedom and slavery as her most profound expression of a lack of sympathy is to begin to use the expanded repertoire of sympathy that Stowe provides in *A Key*. These texts encourage, indeed require us to think through sympathy in the antebellum years as well as our own.

NOTES

1. Mary Boykin Chesnut, *Mary Chesnut's Civil War*, ed. C. Vann Woodward (New Haven: Yale University Press, 1981), 307–308.
2. George Frederick Holmes, *Southern Literary Messenger*, December 1852; John R. Thompson, *Southern Literary Messenger*, October 1852; Thompson, *Southern Literary Messenger*, January 1853; reprinted in *The Liberator*, March 4, 1853. There is some dispute about the identities of the October and December reviewers in the *Southern Literary Messenger*. Elizabeth Ammons's Norton Critical Edition of *Uncle Tom's Cabin* identifies Holmes as the author of the October review, whereas Stephen Railton's comprehensive *Uncle Tom's Cabin* website – *www.iath.virginia.edu/utc* – indicates that Thompson "probably" wrote the October review and Holmes the December review. Although I'm using Railton's identifications and am grateful for his assistance with this matter, it's difficult to establish with absolute certitude – neither essay was signed – who wrote which review.
3. Thompson, *Southern Literary Messenger*, October 1852; Thompson, *Southern Literary Messenger*, January 1853; Holmes, *Southern Literary Messenger*, December 1852.
4. Harriet Beecher Stowe, *A Key to Uncle Tom's Cabin; Presenting the Original Facts and Documents upon which the Story is Founded, together with Corroborative Statements Verifying the Truth of the Work* (Boston: John P. Jewett, 1853), iii. All further quotations from *A Key* will be from this edition and will be incorporated into the text.
5. Caroline Lee Hentz, *Marcus Warland; or, The Long Moss Spring. A Tale of the South* (Philadelphia: A. Hart, late Carey & Hunt, 1852), 18.
6. *Southern Press Review*, unsigned, 1852; Caroline Lee Hentz, *The Planter's Northern Bride* (Chapel Hill: University of North Carolina Press, 1970; originally published 1854), 302. All further quotations from Hentz will be from this edition and will be incorporated into the text.
7. Harriet Beecher Stowe, *Uncle Tom's Cabin*, ed. Elizabeth Ammons (New York: W. W. Norton & Co., 1994), 385. All further quotations from *Uncle Tom's Cabin* will be from this edition and will be incorporated into the text.

8. Jewett and Co. advertisement in *The New York Independent*, May 20, 1852; Frederick Douglass's *Paper*, March 11, 1853; *The National Anti-Slavery Standard*, November 4, 1852; Douglass's *Paper*, March 11, 1853. These materials can be found at *www.iath.virginia.edu/utc*, Stephen Railton's excellent website, "*Uncle Tom's Cabin* and American Culture: A Multi-Media Archive."

9. Mary Jane Holmes, *Meadowbrook Farm* (New York: Miller, Orton, and Company, 1857), 185. Maria J. McIntosh, *Two Pictures; or What We Think of Ourselves, and What the World Thinks of Us* (New York: D. Appleton and Company, 1863), 547. McIntosh wrote her explicity anti-Tom novel ten years earlier – *The Lofty and the Lowly; or, Good in All and None All-Good*. Also see Marion Stephens's *Hagar the Martyr; or, Passion and Reality. A Tale of the North and South* (New York: W. P. Fetridge & Co., 1854), in which an extremely minor character – an editor – has this to say about his latest book review: "I'm writing it up famously . . . Uncle Tom's Cabin will be distanced altogether; besides, the work itself is a thousand times superior to Uncle Tom" (192).

10. Nehemiah Adams, *A South-Side View of Slavery* (Boston: Ticknor and Fields, 1860; originally published 1854), 167; C. G. Parsons, *An Inside View of Slavery* (Boston: John P. Jewett, 1855), xi.

11. Frederick Law Olmsted, *A Journey in the Seaboard Slave States, with Remarks on their Economy* (New York: Dix and Edwards, 1856), 618, 619.

12. Louisa J. McCord, "Uncle Tom's Cabin," in *Southern Quarterly Review* 23 (January 1853), 81; Mrs. Mary E. Eastman, *Aunt Phillis's Cabin; or, Southern Life as It Is* (Philadelphia: Lippincott, Grambo & Co. 1852), 268; Caroline E. Rush, *The North and South, or, Slavery and its Contrasts. A Tale of Real Life* (Philadelphia: Crissy and Markley, 1852), 14.

13. Jewett and Co. advertisement in *The New York Independent*, May 20, 1852; *Southern Literary Messenger*, January 1853; McCord, "Uncle Tom's Cabin," in *Southern Quarterly Review* 23 (January 1853), 110.

14. Frederick Douglass's *Paper*, October 22, 1852; George Frederick Holmes, *Southern Literary Messenger*, December 1852.

15. See Elizabeth Moss, *Domestic Novelists in the Old South: Defenders of Southern Culture* (Baton Rouge: Louisiana State University Press, 1992), who similarly maintains that "Hentz's excellent mimicry of Stowe's style and skillful manipulation of the northern novelist's message lent Hentz's interpretation a freshness and vigor that distinguished it from the spate of replies issued by less talented southern writers" (112).

16. The serial version of *Uncle Tom's Cabin* had as its subtitle, "Or, the Man that was a Thing," as opposed to the novel's subtitle, "Life among the Lowly."

17. Thompson, *Southern Literary Messenger*, October 1852.

3

MICHAEL T. GILMORE

Uncle Tom's Cabin and the American Renaissance: the sacramental aesthetic of Harriet Beecher Stowe

I

When discussing *Uncle Tom's Cabin* in relation to the American Renaissance, it is customary – or perhaps obligatory – to marshal the differences between Stowe's great work and the masterpieces, say, of Hawthorne and Melville, a move that invariably begins with the same enumeration but proceeds to radically polarized conclusions. The male-authored classics of the 1850s, goes the argument, are marked by philosophical probing, stylistic density, subtle characterization, and self-reflexive irony. Stowe's novel, on the other hand, is stocked with two-dimensional characters, written in a straightforward, undistinguished prose, and rife with sentimental situations intended to reduce readers to tears rather than taxing their intellects. Having established this contrast, the critic, depending on his or her perspective, then construes the undeniable differences as either a tribute to Stowe's political agenda or a reproof of her aesthetic shortcomings. The second judgment, more common a generation ago, would pronounce the author of *Uncle Tom's Cabin* an effective agitator but an infinitely less accomplished writer than her contemporaries. The first judgment, now pretty much the standard one, acclaims her as a novelist of "sentimental power" who sought not textual complexity but societal change, and whose narrative was supremely calculated to achieve that objective.[1]

This essay will suggest that the venerable itemization and antithesis summarized above is precisely the wrong way to go about the discussion. It is wrong because it scants the degree to which both Stowe *and* the American Renaissance artists shared a common preoccupation with the authority of writing. There were two reasons for this. First, all of them, from Poe to Thoreau to Hawthorne to "the little lady who made this big war" (as Lincoln is supposed to have said), were haunted by the previous century's seemingly effortless integration of "poetry and policy," or language and action.[2] Their native literary forebears were not first and foremost specialized craftsmen of the word, distilling their thoughts into high art for a select audience, but statesmen and ministers who used writing, quite literally, to transform the world. For these predecessors, the discursive was not an end in itself but a tool to accomplish other objectives. Stowe and the romantics never ceased sparring with this notion of literary efficacy.

Second, the Revolutionary era's understanding of utterance did not simply disappear with the new century. It went into temporary dormancy and then was revitalized in the crucible of the slavery crisis. The twenty-five year period beginning in 1835–36 – the moment when Emerson mutated from a preacher to a writer – saw repeated assaults by the "Slave Power" on free inquiry. Measures, often violent, to censor abolitionist agitation as seditious and "incendiary" (the preferred adjective) brought home the potentially lethal energy of words to all the antebellum authors, including those, like Hawthorne, who were themselves alarmed by the threat that anti-slavery oratory posed to the Union. The litany of provocations would have to include the impounding of the mails by southern postmasters, a palpably illegal policy that erected an "intellectual blockade" along the Mason–Dixon Line; the "gag rule" nullifying the right to petition; the mobbing of abolitionist lecturers; the caning of Charles Sumner on the floor of the US Senate; and the attempts by southern legislators and their allies to roll back anti-slavery state laws as unconstitutional.[3]

The contemporary novelist Phillip Roth, in comparing the artist's situation in democracies with that in the former Soviet bloc, has said that in the West "everything goes and nothing matters," whereas in the East "nothing goes and everything matters."[4] The free states of the pre-Civil War north were not, to be sure, embryonic tyrannies. But the south *was* a thoroughly repressive society, where freedom of speech and the press had been virtually extinguished, and northern writers, living in close proximity to an expanding slavocracy, knew that all language, not just that advocating abolition, could have the weight of deeds. The term applied to the era's literature, "American Renaissance," is doubly apt: it captures the high quality of the works composed during those years and also their revival of the eighteenth-century paradigm.

In the space of a brief essay, there is obviously not room to develop these claims in detail. So I will simply note two especially influential models of linguistic agency: the republican or libertarian and the Biblical. Thomas Jefferson's Declaration of Independence is exemplary of the first strain. A piece of writing antithetical to W. H. Auden's modernist credo, "poetry makes nothing happen," the Declaration altered the course of history by calling a nation into being. Cast the net still further back in time and one might arguably invoke the Bible itself as the textual cornerstone of American history. The dream of a Christian commonwealth – "we shall be as a city upon a hill," as John Winthrop famously said in his *Arbella* sermon, paraphrasing the gospel of St. Matthew – inspired the original Puritan migration and the settlement of New England. The Bible offers western civilization's clearest illustration of the inseparability of language and events, not simply in its power to convert readers to Christianity, and so to reform their lives, but in its equating of divine speech with the act of creation: "And God said, Let there be light: and there was light." So reads the Book of Genesis in the King James version conned by American Protestants; and the power of words had enduring resonance in a nation with an identifiable origin, a recoverable "genesis" of its own. The two traditions converged in 1776 when the deist Jefferson said, "Let there be the United States," and there was the United States.

Both rhetorical strains, the religious and the revolutionary, persisted into the antebellum years. Abraham Lincoln, for example, regularly appealed to the Founders' legacy when he resisted the efforts of slaveholders to spread their labor system, and with it their suppression of civil liberties, into the territories. He exhorted his countrymen not to let the enemies of freedom force them "to unsay what Washington said, and undo what Washington did."[5] For Stowe, the more vibrant verbal inheritance was devotional. The drama of what the text can do, a mystery exemplified for her by the Scriptures, cast its spell over this novice author as she produced her nation-changing novel in a burst of outrage against the Fugitive Slave Law. That legislation, by requiring northerners to return runaways without either the writ of habeas corpus or the right to trial by jury, obliterated the line between the sections and, as Frederick Douglass put it, turned New York into a second Virginia.

II

Before looking more closely at the recurrence of the word–action dynamic in the traditional romantic canon, I want to turn to a crucial scene from *Uncle Tom's Cabin*, the one in which Stowe's novel ponders its capacity for intervention in history. The moment occurs in Chapter IX, "In Which It Appears that a Senator Is But a Man." Eliza has told her harrowing story of flight over the Ohio River, and now Senator Bird must decide whether to help the fugitive or uphold his oath as a state official and return her to captivity. The senator, a master at political "eloquence," has previously persuaded his colleagues, as well as himself, that patriotism requires obedience to the law. But "then," says Stowe, his idea of a fugitive was only an idea of the letters that spell the word, – or, at the most, the image of a little newspaper picture of a man with a stick and bundle, with "Ran away from the subscriber" under it. The magic of the real presence of distress, – the imploring human eye, the frail trembling human hand, the despairing appeal of helpless agony, – these he had never tried.

Confronted with the reality of a frantic mother and her terrified child, Senator Bird does "penance" for his political sinning and defies the law to lead Eliza and Harry to safety (77).[6]

The "magic of . . . real presence" is the ideal toward which all representation in Stowe's narrative strives. The living person is the antonym both of "dead letters" (Melville's phrase from "Bartleby, the Scrivener" [1853]), the black marks on the page that convey only the idea of a fugitive, and of empty images, newspaper drawings that flatten the runaway into a series of lines and visual contrasts. Real presence alone can awaken readers or listeners out of their sleep of law and custom and rouse them to act in the name of conscience.

To say this much is merely to pose the problem, however, not to solve it. Stowe after all is providing a verbal approximation of Eliza's escape from bondage. The technology of print cannot literally place the physical mother and child before us. It cannot supply the unmediated fact of Eliza's being there, the "trembling" hand and "imploring" eye that overcome Senator Bird's scruples. As Stowe often states, she regards the ocular as an especially affecting rhetorical strategy. In a preview of the cinema's mass appeal, her style aspires to the vividness of "moving picture[s]" (124). But, again, this is to frame the dilemma, not to indicate an exit from it. What causes the image rendered in language to come alive, to transcend the inertia of the newspaper cartoon and attain the "*living dramatic reality*" (382) that can change hearts and minds? How can a textual proxy duplicate the alchemy of presence? How can it galvanize readers to purge the land of slavery?

Political oratory, Stowe makes clear, has no prospect of sparking the needed renovation. It has been too debased by politicians. For Stowe, politics has devolved into the craft of self-promotion. (The senator's harangue in the state legislature did him no honor, as Mrs. Bird points out.) The story Eliza relates to the Birds is but one of three renditions of her experience included in *Uncle Tom's Cabin*, and we are invited to evaluate the other two for their rhetorical effectiveness – to ask whether those second-hand versions can even begin to approach the transformative pressure of Eliza's own words, delivered in person, on the senator. A second account comes from Black Sam, the Shelbys' factotum who is dispatched to help Haley recover his property. The role Sam plays is purely instrumental, calculated to advance his own standing with his mistress and narrated so as to advertise his oratorical skills. Stowe calls him "an electioneering politician," and he rehearses the day's adventures to the assembled slaves "with all kinds of ornament and varnishing which might be necessary to heighten its effect." When Andy objects to the self-congratulatory speech, reminding Sam that he originally intended to apprehend Eliza, the old slave sniffs that "Dat ar was conscience." And it was conscience, too, when he realized that Mrs. Shelby didn't want the runaway caught, and changed course in order to obstruct the chase. Sam's "principled" credo is a burlesque of every antebellum lawmaker, Stowe implies. He defends his consistency by explaining, "I'm persistent in wantin' to get up which ary side my larder is; don't you see, all on yer?" (65–66). It is Thoreau's Daniel Webster, from "Resistance to Civil Government" (1849), in blackface: his "truth is not Truth, but consistency, or a consistent expediency."[7]

Not all political rhetoric in the novel is subjected to this kind of parody. Stowe herself invokes the republican–revolutionary tradition on behalf of George Harris, although she also suggests that secular nationalism has been so sullied by hypocrisy and legal obfuscation that it can no longer, on its own, inspire heroism among white people. She suspects that "Liberty! – electric word!" has become, to "the men and women of America," nothing more "than a name – a rhetorical flourish" (332). Canada, not the United States, is in 1852 the "shores of refuge" (372) for those seeking emancipation, and George, who delivers a stirring "declaration of independence" to his pursuers (172), eventually elects to abandon the New World altogether and return to Africa. Moreover, those who shield the Harris family are invariably devout Christians like the Quaker network around the Hallidays. For such individuals, abolition has roots in religious faith, and to deprive someone of liberty is above all to commit a crime against God. A Christianized vocabulary, not a political one, has moved them to risk their welfare for the bondsman.

Which brings us to the third representation of Eliza's escape, the one inscribed by Stowe herself. This is the first version in order of appearance, and it is addressed to us, the readers of *Uncle Tom's Cabin*. It may come as a surprise to realize that the actual flight across the Ohio, along with Eva's death perhaps the novel's best-known scene, comprises just a single paragraph. (The previous paragraph tracks the pursuit to the water's edge, with the trader Haley after his quarry "like a hound after a deer," and records Eliza's wild leap "over the turbid current by the shore, on to the raft of ice beyond.") The description is graphic, its kinetic energy conveyed by dashes, by the "ing" endings of the verbs – "stumbling – leaping – slipping – springing upwards again!" – and by the sudden change of tense to the present in the clause, "Her shoes are gone . . ." (52). Stowe relates the entire incident in three moderately sized sentences, and it takes less time to scan than Eliza must have needed to make her dash across the ice. Brief as it is, the moment is indelible, and though we, the novel's readers, are not standing on the Kentucky shore, watching the fugitive bound to freedom, we almost feel as though we are. Something approaching "real presence" has been achieved; and was achieved even more powerfully for Stowe's contemporaries, who so relished the episode that they insisted on seeing it regularly reproduced on stage for the next half century.[8]

The breathless quality of the writing is part of it, but only part. For Stowe, what lifts the scene out of the category of lifeless words is the Biblical and eucharistic resonances. Eliza's escape is an unmistakable echo of the passage out of Egypt. Her miraculous crossing of the frozen river, with the slave catchers at her heels, commemorates the parting of the Red Sea for the fleeing Israelites. The scene's original telling in Chapter VII, "The Mother's Struggle," is already a retelling, Stowe's imitation of, and variation on, God's deliverance of His chosen people. The vivifying spark inheres in the scriptural source, the authentic Word whose lessons for the present too many antebellum Christians, according to *Uncle Tom's Cabin*, have refused to heed.

For Jews, the release from bondage is remembered in the Passover feast; for Christians, salvation from sin is celebrated in the Lord's Supper, the consuming of bread and wine in memory of Christ's death. For well over a thousand years, Catholics described that sacrament as the "real presence." They believed that at the moment of communion, the elements were quite literally "transubstantiated" into the body and blood of the Savior. Protestantism is a history of disagreement with this doctrine. As Emerson observed, in the sermon in which he resigned from the pulpit, "The famous question of the Real Presence was the main controversy between the Church of England and the Church of Rome."[9] The disputes are too technical to canvass here, but the key point is that for "post-Calvinists" like Stowe, the Supper was a sort of hybrid: neither merely symbolical nor the actual physical substance of the crucified God. Jesus was indeed there when worshipers received the sacraments; He suffused the rite, not as a figure of flesh and blood, but as a living spirit.

Stowe had her first intimation of the story of *Uncle Tom's Cabin* in a pew in the First Parish Church in Brunswick, Maine, while she watched the celebration of the Eucharist. The "real but spiritual presence" (the formula that descends from Calvin) of the suffering Christ in the bread and wine kindled in her mind the image of a bleeding slave, and when she reached home after services, she jotted down her vision.[10] The rite was her model for the abolitionist narrative she went on to write over the next year, the impetus for her own effort to create a text of "real presence" that would, as an *imitatio Dei*, bring to life the letters on the page. Stowe knew that she could not produce the physical Eliza for her readers. The Lord's Supper, and the Bible, assured her that she didn't have to. She could simulate – no, she could tap into and capture – the spiritual reality that infused the ordinance and the Word and that, after eighteen hundred years, still had the power "to stir up the soul from its depths, and rouse, as with trumpet call, [enough] courage, energy, and enthusiasm" to remake the world (101).

III

It is remarkable how often one encounters scenes of self-conscious verbal display in classic American literature. Speeches, sermons, and stories within stories abound, and we are constantly being asked to weigh their impact on surrogate listeners and readers. There is no preordained attitude that governs these episodes. Some writers brood with horrified fascination on the verbal's fatal consequences; others perceive a diminution of language's (and the writer's) prestige and search for ways to resurrect that faded glory. Still other authors oscillate between exalting writing's efficacy and despairing over the suppression of utterance under a regime of censorship. What falls across all these pages is the shadow of a social order in which the linguistic flirted with omnipotence.

The fixation emerges as early as Cooper and the western, roughly a decade before the slavery quarrel and thus evidence of a subterranean continuity antedating that rhetorical renewal. In *The Last of the Mohicans* (1826), the renegade Indian Magua uses verbal cunning to gain authority over the Hurons and cajole them into waging war against the Delawares and British. On repeated occasions, this Satan-like villain manipulates his followers with dramatic delivery, changes of tone, flattery, gesture, and calculated obscurity. Cooper channels into Magua all his misgivings about the dangers of eloquence in the hands of a demagogic leader:

> The orator, or the politician, who can produce such a state of things, is commonly popular with his contemporaries, however he may be treated by posterity. All perceived that more was meant than was uttered, and each one believed that the hidden meaning was precisely such as his own faculties enabled him to understand, or his own wishes led him to anticipate.[11]

Demagogues are not the only ones, Cooper knows, for whom language is power. The many references in the text to the "speech" or "words" of Kill-deer, Hawkeye's unerringly accurate rifle, establish an equation between speaking and destroying that recoils back upon the hero and, through him, upon Cooper as the author of the novel. Cooper understood that westward expansion involved semantic as well as physical dispossession, and he was uneasily aware of his own complicity in the civilizational process. The opening pages of *The Last of the Mohicans* note that the narrative's celebrated sheet of water has been an ongoing site of verbal struggle. "Lac du Saint Sacrament" to the French, it became Lake George to the English and has retained that title under American rule because of George Washington's exploits in the area; the effect has been to rob the natives of their "right to perpetuate the original appellation of 'Horican.'" The theft is the novelist's too, a fact he apologized for after a quarter century. The "Author's Preface" of 1850 acknowledges that the *real* Indian name for the lake was "too unpronounceable" for American readers, and Horican, the title Cooper restored with so much fanfare, was in actuality a cognomen of his own invention. To make amends for this act of verbal usurpation, he guiltily concludes the Introduction by "relieving" his "conscience by the confession."[12]

Perhaps it is not to be wondered at that the western, a genre implicated in the depopulating of the wilderness, should betray a troubled consciousness of verbal malfeasance. Less expected is the case of Edgar Allan Poe, the fantasist whose stories are set in either a vaguely delineated Europe or a "nowhere" that seems wholly detached from American realities. These alien milieus paradoxically hold the key to Poe's investment in "The Power of Words" (the title of a tale of 1845). The hermetically sealed worlds of his fiction are decontextualized houses of art, earmarked for destruction by a repressed linguistic praxis that hovers just offstage, poised to reassert its authority.

Consider "The Fall of the House of Usher" (1839), a text bristling with dynasties, palaces, and aristocratic titles. Roderick Usher, the protagonist, is a sequestered connoisseur of the arts – he refuses to venture from his home – who has converted his ancestral residence into a private version of the museum. Musical instruments, artworks, furniture, tapestries, books, and manuscripts of Usher's own composition lie scattered about in profuse disarray. These objects have no apparent connection to the world outside the mansion's walls; they resemble the precious artifacts culled from throughout the globe and displayed without regard for function in national collections such as the Louvre or the British Museum (both creations of the eighteenth century, roughly a century before their American counterparts). Usher's "haunted palace" – his phrase, from a poem he recites for the narrator – memorializes aesthetic self-enclosure. It would seem to be a place where poetry makes nothing happen.[13]

Yet this palace of art turns out to be haunted by the memory of the letter's agency, and the tale climaxes in the revenge of writing on its dispossession.

The unnamed narrator is reading aloud to Usher during a stormy night not long after the two of them have buried the protagonist's twin sister, the lady Madeline, in the house's underground vault. Ordinarily, a narrative is subordinate to events; it transcribes something that has already occurred in fact or imagination. (The use of the past tense in storytelling honors this dependency – action first, and then the record or account of action – and the convention of the blind bard, a tradition going back to Homer, originates it. The bard, wielder of words, can't act because he can't see; the hero performs great deeds, and the poet subsequently sings of them.) But in Poe's fiction, the text being read by the narrator is no passive copy: it reverses the customary sequence of cause and effect. The "Mad Trist" (the title of the story within the story) tells of the slaying of a dragon by a knight named Ethelred. Each time the narrator relates one of Ethelred's violent exploits, the incident produces an echo in the commotion of Madeline's subterranean struggles. The "dragon's unnatural shriek as described by the romancer," to cite a single example, is immediately followed by the "unusual screaming or grating sound" of Madeline's bursting out of her tomb.[14] The reading of the interior narrative precedes events occurring in the mansion and even appears to be the catalyst for them. Reality takes its cue from language. A work of literature sets in motion the chain of horrors culminating in the destruction of the House of Usher.

Thus does Poe strive to arrest the drift of art toward its final resting place in the museum/mausoleum, modernity's monument to the separation of the aesthetic from worldly practice. The collapse of the Usher art palace simultaneously prophesies and enacts the word's return from the graveyard of self-referential impotence. Poe's story renders vicariously the impact of his terrifying narratives on their consumers. The reader–narrator, our representative in the text, reacts to the catastrophe his reading has unleashed by fleeing "aghast" from the mansion as it dissolves into the tarn. Poe always emphasized the production of effect as the goal of his writing, and here he gives us a fictional analogue to the shock and fear that real readers experience from their immersion in his gothic tales. And a reader whose hair stands on end from fright is a reader but one degree separated from being moved to action.

Hawthorne and Melville, like Poe, regularly fashioned images of audience response to verbal mastery. Hawthorne uses a number of such scenes to structure his masterwork, *The Scarlet Letter*. The electrifying speaker in each case is the Reverend Arthur Dimmesdale, and the question that worries the novelist is whether linguistic expertise can be harnessed for truth, or whether it must, Magua-like, invariably misuse its influence for selfish purposes. For Hawthorne, a man averse by temperament to moral passion, the religious–revolutionary legacy, as well as its reawakening in the present, was less a noble endowment than a powder keg. Dimmesdale, Hester's secret lover, is a thoroughly compromised figure who possesses an extraordinary "power of experiencing and communicating emotion." This gift, the "Tongue of Flame" (an attestation hinting at explosive danger), rivets the community. Welded by language into "one accord of sympathy," the people of New England worship their pastor as "the mouth-piece of Heaven's messages of wisdom, and rebuke, and love."[15]

The problem, of course, is that verbal versatility in Hawthorne's book seems indistinguishable from turpitude, and that the Puritans, besotted by eloquence, have given their reverence to a hypocrite. Nor does the concluding scaffold scene, where Dimmesdale makes an ambiguous public confession, untangle the dilemma. Neither we, as readers, nor the multitude, as physically present auditors, can ever be quite certain if the clergyman has really admitted his guilt or simply deployed his great skill with words to obfuscate his sinfulness.

Hawthorne reminds us that in the seventeenth century, artful speakers like his minister could aspire to the highest positions in the land. "Even political power . . . ," he says, "was within the grasp of a successful priest." If comparable prestige, in the nineteenth century, no longer accrued to the clergy, did it lie within the reach of writers like Hawthorne himself, practitioners – to quote again from *The Scarlet Letter* – of "the profession, at that era, in which intellectual ability displayed itself far more than in political life?"[16] This question, too, the book leaves unanswered, though it is worth noting that Dimmesdale, Hawthorne's conflicted self-portrait as wordsmith, has the sentimental novelist's intuitive understanding of emotions and is described as more tremulous and feminine than any woman in the story, including Hester Prynne. Two years later, when Stowe realized the dream of literary activism, she did so in a narrative that toppled "political power" with tears and religious sentiment.

Melville's Ahab is another mesmerizing and morally problematic orator, and in *Moby-Dick* (1851) the link to national roots is again made explicit, not in setting this time but in the emphasis on the captain's longevity. "Old man" Ahab, as he is endlessly referred to, is a latter-day Founding Father, a return of revolutionary fervor in the colorless and commercialized present. He would rid the world of "all evil" in the figure of Moby-Dick, and he inflames the *Pequod*'s crew with a combination of Shakespearean rhetoric and demagogic stage tricks. Ahab represents a diabolic force, and Melville doesn't pretend otherwise, but he also gives the captain his due as a tarnished but charismatic leader. Even the skeptical Ishmael vibrates to Ahab's speeches and is swept up in the hunt for the white whale. Not even the apocalyptic final chapters, in which the American ship of state plunges to destruction, can altogether banish the sense of regret over the defeat of heroic oratory.

In later works, especially the short stories, Melville regards language as fallen under a prohibition and depleted of originating power. Bartleby the scrivener's refusal to copy can be seen as a reluctance on his creator's part to indite words without consequences. The failure of literary authority oppresses "Benito Cereno" (1855) as much as does the curse of chattel bondage. Babo's concocted narrative almost wins freedom for the slaves aboard the *San Dominick*. But in the end his made-up story succumbs to the superior might of the whites, and, once he is captured, recognizing that his, the slave's, viewpoint will get no hearing from those in power, he refuses to testify before the tribunal that sentences him to death. Babo's silence mourns the futility of the linguistic, and there are no more despairing lines in the whole of antebellum literature than those in which Melville appears to concur: "Seeing all was over, he uttered no sound, and could not be forced to. His aspect seemed to say, since I cannot do deeds, I will not speak words."[17]

A glance at Thoreau's "Resistance to Civil Government" (or "Civil Disobedience," the more common title) will conclude this severely abbreviated overview of the American Renaissance.[18] Thoreau's piece marks a return to verbal self-assurance after the darkly pessimistic odysseys of Hawthorne and Melville. An imaginary interlocutor poses the standard question: why bother to protest against this overwhelming force, the millions of men and women who are indifferent to slavery and the war with Mexico? What hope is there of change against such odds? In response, Thoreau elaborates a contrast between the power of truth, as enunciated in speech, and the brute power of the state, which always, he insists, acts upon men's bodies and not their minds. He argues that persuasion will inevitably prevail against "superior physical strength," and he throws down his gauntlet to the government: "Let us see who is the strongest. What force has a multitude? They only can force me who obey a higher law than I. They force me to become like themselves."[19]

Like Poe, his nominal opposite, Thoreau inserts an interpolated narrative into his essay in order to test the greater effectiveness of language. This section, which he calls "My Prisons," describes the night he spent in jail for refusing to pay his poll tax. The three or four pages *prove* that authorship can best the state, because the embedded history takes what the authorities did to Thoreau – punishing him by depriving him of freedom – and turns that physical confinement into a polemic, a fragment of writing that will convince others of the government's moral bankruptcy and so stir them to defy its power. "My Prisons" doubles the act of resistance to an unjust polity: the first time, Thoreau withheld his tax; the second, he uses words to vanquish blind compulsion.

Thoreau goes on to contend for a conception of speech as action that leads him to revise the ancient idea of the bard or author as secondary copier. He imagines a Homer who is simultaneously Achilles or Odysseus, a poet whose lays are weapons. After criticizing Webster as a failed legislator, someone who stands too deeply within the government to "speak with authority about it," he offers himself as an alternative, a writer who governs through language and not the statute book. Today's politicians, Thoreau says, cannot move society because they "have no resting-place without it." Only a person who does not hold office, who sees the state's inadequacies clearly because he observes them from afar, can have the moral and verbal leverage to precipitate a reformation in his countrymen. Such a writer–legislator would be a hero for the ages:

> There are orators, politicians, and eloquent men, by the thousand; but the speaker has not yet opened his mouth to speak, who is capable of settling the much-vexed questions of the day. We love eloquence for its own sake, and not for any truth which it may utter, or any heroism it may inspire.[20]

"Resistance to Civil Government" went unread in Thoreau's lifetime. He was wrong about himself, about his ability to overthrow the status quo with his pen. About Stowe and *Uncle Tom's Cabin*, he was prophetic. His words heralded the words that helped to inspire the heroism of Union sacrifice.

IV

Without presence, no salvation, no healing, and no transformative action can occur. Stowe reiterates this premise throughout *Uncle Tom's Cabin*. George Harris, like his wife Eliza, is the subject of a newspaper advertisement promising a reward for the capture of a runaway. The empty words are obliterated by the "real presence" of the fugitive himself, who, disguised as a Spanish gentleman, reveals his true identity to the manufacturer Wilson. George's passionate self-defense – "delivered with tears, and flashing eyes, and despairing gestures" (97) – persuades his otherwise pro-slavery but good-natured former employer to switch allegiances. Deeply moved by the black man's plight, Wilson breaks down and cries and offers George a wad of bills to aid him in his flight.

Then there is the education of Miss Ophelia. As St. Clare points out, northerners recoil from physical proximity to blacks even as they reproach the south for the wrongs of slavery. You would send them all to Africa, "out of your sight and smell" (154), he tells his cousin. Topsy's unruly antics around Ophelia stem from the same perception: she rightly senses that the Vermonter can't bear to touch her. Eva softens the hearts of both her aunt and the black child and in doing so lives up to her nickname of "The Little Evangelist" (the title of Chapter xxv, where the incident takes place). Laying her "little thin, white hand on Topsy's shoulder," she assures the slave girl that she loves her – loves her as Jesus does, precisely because she is black and friendless. The effect on Topsy is instantaneous – "a ray of real belief" penetrates her soul, and she vows to reform – and Ophelia learns a lesson that enables her to overcome her prejudice. "[I]f we want to give sight to the blind," St. Clare summarizes for Stowe, "we must be willing to do as Christ did, – call them to us, and *put our hands on them*" (italics in the original; 246). Fastidious distance leaves the heart untouched; nothing less than being fully there, as the Savior was for the suffering and infirm, can make a difference.

But presence, as we have seen, doesn't have to be corporeal. It is possible to be present without being visible in the flesh, just as the risen Christ is immanent spiritually but not materially in the Eucharist. Or, perhaps better yet, just as He is present in the Word and in the life around us, discernible not by the five senses but by the insight that comes from faith. Stowe is contemptuous of the notion that things lack reality unless they can be physically seen and heard. To her, such literalism betrays an utter poverty of imagination, like that shown by the servants who misinterpret the parental reactions to Eva's death. These people are "the slave of their eye and ear" (260); they foolishly assume that Marie suffers more than St. Clare because his eyes remain dry while she makes a great show of sobbing and complaining.

The indispensable book of spiritual presence, and the template for Stowe's story, is the Bible. To those who attend to that ancient volume, the letters on the page pulsate with life; they undergo a categorical sea change similar to that which overtakes the signifier "runaway" when one comes into contact with the real human being, the woman Eliza or her husband George. Eva, her health failing, faces death without misgiving because of her immersion in the sacred text:

> In that book which she and her simple old friend had read so much together, she had seen and taken to her young heart the image of one who loved the little child; and, as she gazed and mused, He had ceased to be an image and a picture of the distant past, and come to be a living, all-surrounding reality.
>
> (239)

When, on her deathbed, St. Clare asks his daughter how she can love someone she has never set eyes on, Eva has her answer ready. "That makes no difference," she replies; "I believe him, and in a few days I shall *see* him" (253).

Eva is Stowe's exemplary reader, the standard to be emulated by the ante-bellum audience. She opens herself to the salvational narrative and is not only transfigured as a consequence but perceives divinity where others are incapable of sight. Indeed, Eva internalizes every affecting story she reads or is told about, including those she encounters at second hand like Tom's history of Prue and St. Clare's recollection of Scipio, the slave who nursed him back to health from cholera and then died of the disease himself. Eva rejects her father's suggestion that she ought not to hear such things, because they impress her much too deeply. We must allow these "sad stories" to "sink into our hearts," she says more than once, because only by listening to them without reserve can we truly empathize with the "pain and sorrow" of their victims (188–189, 204, 241).

The dynamic of reception is double-sided, then: the text must appropriate the spiritual truth of the Scriptures, and the reader must be prepared to accept that truth with his or her entire being. Taken together, these two desiderata impart spiritual life to the rite of narrative incorporation. The parallel to the Protestant Lord's Supper holds firm: in Reformed sects, as opposed to the Catholic Church, the miracle of the sacrament is never independent of the parishioner. For the bread and wine to be effective, communicants must take the Savior into their souls. The ordinance can do nothing with a congregant whose heart is closed against it, any more than the story of Prue, or Uncle Tom, or Jesus Christ can move a Haley or a Simon Legree to repentance. How one responds to the story is what separates the sheep from the goats.[21]

That Eva expires, as it were, from too much sensitivity to others' suffering, does not mean that the novel's internal narratives issue in stasis or inaction. On the contrary. The stories are a crucifixion for the child-heroine, and Eva's fate is one of two cases of sacrificial death that have a profound and lasting effect on survivors and are presented by Stowe as fictional imitations of Christ. Topsy and Ophelia, whose awakenings were cited above, are never the same after watching the heroine die. The older woman, having "learnt something of the love of Christ" from Eva, tells Topsy that she loves her, and no longer shrinks from her charge's touch. "From that hour," according to Stowe, "she acquired an influence over the mind of the destitute child that she never lost" (259). Even the cynical St. Clare starts to change. He studies his daughter's Bible with growing seriousness and announces a resolve to free his slaves before his life is cut short in a brawl. But no one experiences Eva's example more intensely than Uncle Tom, for whom her goodness proves contagious. Inheriting the mantle of *imitatio*, the eponymous hero evolves into that cliché of literary criticism, a black Christ-figure. What interests us here is how Stowe conceives this metamorphosis as molding response to the text. Tom becomes the fulcrum or relay through whom invisible presence flows on its passage from the Scriptures to her readership.

Tom's accession to preternatural sight and hearing begins in earnest immediately following Eva's death. St. Clare reads aloud to his servant from the gospel of St. John, and the two men have this exchange:

> "Tom," said his master, "this is all *real* to you!"
> "I can jest fairly *see* it, Mas'r," said Tom.
> "I wish I had your eyes, Tom."
> "I wish, to the dear Lord, Mas'r had!"
>
> (263)

On Legree's plantation, Tom's certainty in the reality of the unseen will be tested, in what amounts to a rewriting of Frederick Douglass's "dark night of the soul," the episode from the *Narrative* (1845) where the overseer Covey almost breaks the great abolitionist. But the moral desert of Red River also witnesses the definitive intervention of the divine on behalf of the oppressed. The Savior, in this novel, does not confine His outreach to Holy Writ; He makes Himself resplendently manifest to Uncle Tom as real but non-material being.

Stowe's most explicit rejoinder to the problem of bodily non-appearance, the quandary raised by Eliza's personal plea to the Birds, comes in Chapter XXXVIII, "The Victory." The moment has been thoroughly prepared for. A recurrent theme in this last quarter of the novel has been, precisely, absence or apparent emptiness. When Tom reads his Bible to Legree's slaves, they refuse to credit the words because they cannot imagine that God is there in Red River. They are versions of the skeptical reader–auditor for whom the verbal, being powerless to reproduce presence, cannot bring about conviction. "The Lord never visits these parts," says Cassy; and when Tom, his spirit almost crushed, cries out to Jesus, she tells him not to bother: "There's no use calling on the Lord, – he never hears . . . there isn't any God, I believe" (306, 312). Even Stowe, appalled by the misery on Legree's farm, wonders, "Is God HERE?" (302). But this section also abounds in hints of an approaching revelation. At one point, Tom's hopes are strengthened by an "invisible voice" (293); at another, he has a dream of Eva reading to him from the Scriptures. The intimations culminate at the lowest moment of Tom's ordeal, when God's silence seems complete and Legree taunts him with the failure of his religion.

The dejected hero suddenly has a vision of the crucified Jesus; and as he gazes "in awe and wonder," the thorns change into "rays of glory," and a voice assures him of salvation. Is the apparition real? Stowe, anticipating readerly disbelief, musters "psychologists" to justify the incident. According to these unnamed experts, the "affections" can grow so strong "that they press into their service the outward senses, and make them give tangible shape to the inward imagining." And who, Stowe adds, can doubt that "an all-pervading Spirit" can do this with human capabilities (339–340)? (One psychologist whom Stowe foreshadows is William James, particularly his merger of pragmatism and religious faith. In *The Varieties of Religious Experience* [1902] and "The Will to Believe" [1896], James argued that truth comes into existence because of one's willingness to believe it. "[F]*aith in a fact can help create the fact*," he wrote, supplying the italics for incredulous modern readers.[22])

The scene is a watershed for Uncle Tom and the climactic instant in his creator's sacramental aesthetic. With "an ever-present Saviour" in his heart (341), the protagonist turns his mind entirely to heaven, and he becomes a source of redemption for the other slaves. To Cassy, "this lowly missionary" breathes "Holy Writ" (343); his sufferings convert even Sambo and Quimbo, Legree's most degraded henchmen, who relieve his agony with a cup of water, as Jesus was succored on the cross. Here "real but spiritual presence" emigrates from the Bible, through spectral visitations, to the "man that was a thing" (the novel's original subtitle) whom Stowe pictured being whipped while communion was celebrated in her family church. And from Tom, spiritual being radiates outward to members of the reading public. If the novel has taught these readers to "*feel right*," "in harmony with the sympathies of Christ" (385), they will give "tangible shape" to their imagining of Stowe's hero. They will experience him as unforgettably present as Eliza was to Senator Bird and the Almighty was in Tom's vision, as real as Jesus proved to be when Tom was murdered, and Sambo and Quimbo felt divinity "a standin' by you so, all this night!" (359). Transformed by their encounter with invisible presence, the novel's readers, again like Senator Bird, will no longer allow themselves to be lulled by dead letters but instead, energized by faith, help to cast out the sin of slavery from America.

V

Not everyone will hear and "follow me," as Tom, copying the Savior, pleads with the slaves at Red River (363). Stowe, whose imagination had room for a Simon Legree, could not have been more mindful of this fact. Her Christ is a God of love; but He is a good deal more than that: He is a God of wrath and vengeance, too. Her novel, which teems with apocalyptic references to the Last Judgment, incorporates an alternative mode of storytelling that makes greater use of fear than belief. Cassy, playing on Legree's superstitions with singular "words and language," (348) persuades the villain that spirits inhabit the upper regions of his house. She and Emmeline then hide out in the garret while awaiting their moment to flee. In Chapter XLII, "An Authentic Ghost Story," she masterminds a spectral visitation of her own, the complement and opposite of Tom's exultant revelation. A ghostly white figure assaults Legree's "spiritual eyes" (365) as he lies half awake in bed, and the vision so fills him with terror that he absolutely refuses to search the garret, thus allowing the two women to make good their escape. The threat of damnation lurks in the background of this staged act of spooking.[23]

It is an efficacious fiction, as potent in its way as the eucharistic narratives of Eva and Uncle Tom. Stowe's "ghost story" is another reminder of her connection to writers with whom she appears to share little, such as her fellow Gothicist Poe (who was, of course, an opponent on the slavery issue).[24] To turn back to "The Fall of the House of Usher" is to invite some last thoughts on the interrelations between the author of *Uncle Tom's Cabin*, the American Renaissance, and the theme of literature's agency. One might suggest that Stowe's text realizes the promise of Poe's cataclysmic ending – that her novel's role, however minor, in instigating the Civil War levels the palace of self-reflexive art. Add to this the fact that Usher's house, with its "barely perceptible" fissure extending from the roof to the "sullen waters of the tarn," dovetails with contemporaneous images of the Union. Lincoln's trope, taken from St. Mark, was the most celebrated. The future president described the nation as half-slave and half-free and declared that a house divided against itself cannot stand. *Uncle Tom's Cabin* is the work of literature that fulfilled that prediction as well.

NOTES

1. The phrase "sentimental power" comes from Jane Tompkins, *Sensational Designs: The Cultural Work of American Fiction, 1790–1860* (New York: Oxford University Press, 1985). Tompkins's pro-Stowe argument did as much as anyone's to change the way present-day readers interpret the contrast.
2. The Lincoln quote, endlessly circulated, is probably apocryphal. I take the terms "poetry and policy" from Allen Grossman, "The poetics of union in Whitman and Lincoln: an inquiry toward the relationship of art and policy," in *The American Renaissance Reconsidered*, ed. by Walter Benn Michaels and Donald E. Pease (Baltimore: The Johns Hopkins University Press, 1985), 183–208.
3. Many scholars have written on the antebellum south's war on intellectual freedom. Several noteworthy titles are Clement Eaton, *Freedom of Thought in the Old South* (Durham, NC: Duke University Press, 1940); Russel B. Nye, *Fettered Freedom: Civil Liberties and the Slavery Controversy* (East Lansing: Michigan State University Press, 1949); and William Lee Miller, *Arguing About Slavery: John Quincy Adams and the Great Battle in the United States Congress* (New York: Alfred A. Knopf, 1996).

4. Phillip Roth, *Reading Myself and Others* (New York: Vintage International, 2001), 145.

5. From the Address at New York's Cooper Institute (February 27, 1860), in Lincoln, *Great Speeches* (New York: Dover Publications, 1991), 51.

6. All quotations refer to Elizabeth Ammons's Norton edition of *Uncle Tom's Cabin* (New York, 1994); page numbers are given in the text. The quoted passage has been analyzed in some detail by Catharine E. O'Connell, "'The magic of the real presence of distress': sentimentality and competing rhetorics of authority," in Mason I. Lowance, Jr., Ellen E. Westbrook, and R. C. De Prospo, eds., *The Stowe Debate: Rhetorical Strategies in "Uncle Tom's Cabin"* (Amherst: University of Massachusetts Press, 1994), 13–36. Another relevant discussion of "real presence" in Stowe's novel is Marianne Noble, *The Masochistic Pleasures of Sentimental Literature* (Princeton: Princeton University Press, 2000), 126–146. Noble also links the term to Calvinism, but her interest is in God's love as affliction and the erotic ecstasy of sentimental "wounding."

   I am mindful that the relation between writing and presence occupies a central place in deconstructive criticism. The standard work on this subject is Jacques Derrida, *Of Grammatology*, trans. Gayatri Chakravorty Spivak (Baltimore: The Johns Hopkins University Press, 1976). In this essay my goal is practical rather than theoretical: I am trying to historicize the discussion of verbal presence by developing its filiations, in the American nineteenth century, with the Protestant sacrament of communion.

7. In Thoreau, *Reform Papers*, ed. Wendell Glick (Princeton: Princeton University Press, 1973), 87.

8. See Joan D. Hedrick, *Harriet Beecher Stowe: A Life* (New York: Oxford University Press, 1994), 213–214.

9. Emerson, "The Lord's Supper," (1832) in *Selected Prose and Poetry*, ed. Reginald L. Cook (New York: Holt, Rinehart and Winston, 1950), 89. The scholarship on this subject is vast; a venerable and still useful example is Alexander Barclay, *The Protestant Doctrine of the Lord's Supper: A Study in the Eucharistic Teaching of Luther, Zwingli and Calvin* (Glasgow: Jackson, Wylie and Co., 1927).

10. The experience is related in Hedrick, *Harriet Beecher Stowe*, 155–156.

11. Cooper, *The Last of the Mohicans: A Narrative of 1757* (New York: Signet Classic, 1962), 334–335.

12. Ibid., 12, viii.

13. On the stripping away of context in the museum, see Philip Fisher, *Making and Effacing Art: Modern American Art in a Culture of Museums* (New York: Oxford University Press, 1991), esp. 3–29. I published an earlier version of my analysis of "Usher" in "Words and things in antebellum American literature: notes toward an interpretation," in John Hazel Smith, ed., *Brandeis Essays in Literature* (Waltham, MA: Brandeis University Press, 1983), 85–99.

14. "The Fall of the House of Usher," in *The Complete Tales and Poems of Edgar Allan Poe* (New York: Modern Library, 1938), 245.

15. Norton Critical Edition of *The Scarlet Letter*, ed. Sculley Bradley *et al.* (New York: W. W. Norton, 1978), 103–105, 53.

16. Ibid., 169.

17. In *Great Short Works of Herman Melville*, ed. Warner Berthoff (New York: Harper and Row, 1969), 315.

18. I do not include Emerson in my discussion, in part because his idea of literature as advocacy has gotten so much recognition lately. Readers should consult the following studies: Len Gougeon, *Virtue's Hero: Emerson, Antislavery, and Reform* (Athens: University of Georgia Press, 1990); Albert J. Von Frank, *The Trials of Anthony Burns: Freedom and Slavery in Emerson's Boston* (Cambridge, MA: Harvard University Press, 1998); and Gregg D. Crane, *Race, Citizenship, and Law in American Literature* (Cambridge: Cambridge University Press, 2002).

19. *Reform Papers*, 81.

20. Ibid., 86–88.

21. I am not implying that Stowe endorsed her father's anti-Catholicism. Lyman Beecher was the author of an anti-immigrant tract, *A Plea for the West* (1835), but Harriet makes St. Clare's mother a devout Catholic and says that Cassy received religious training from nuns. My argument is the perhaps self-evident one that *Uncle Tom's Cabin* is the product of a Protestant sensibility.

22. In *The Will to Believe and Other Essays on Popular Philosophy* (New York: Dover Publications, 1956), 25.

23. The pioneering study of this phenomenon in *Uncle Tom's Cabin* is Karen Halttunen, "Gothic imagination and social reform: the haunted houses of Lyman Beecher, Henry Ward Beecher, and Harriet Beecher Stowe," in Eric J. Sundquist, ed., *New Essays on "Uncle Tom's Cabin"* (Cambridge: Cambridge University Press, 1986), 107–134. On the eschatological dimension in Stowe's novel, see Helen Petter Westra, "Confronting Antichrist: the influence of Jonathan Edwards's millennial vision," in Lowance *et al.*, *The Stowe Debate*, 141–158.

24. On Stowe and Poe, see two essays collected in Shawn Rosenheim and Stephen Rachman, eds., *The American Face of Edgar Allan Poe* (Baltimore: The Johns Hopkins University Press, 1995): Jonathan Elmer, "Terminate or liquidate? Poe, sensationalism, and the sentimental tradition," 91–120; and Eva Cherniavsky, "Revivification and utopian time: Poe versus Stowe," 121–138.

4

GILLIAN BROWN

Reading and children: *Uncle Tom's Cabin* and *The Pearl of Orr's Island*

People have always noticed that representations affect them, and have variously explained, classified, evaluated, justified, regulated, and enjoyed this phenomenon. Whereas Plato banned poets from his republic in order to restrict influences upon the citizenry, Aristotle formulated his theory of catharsis to legitimate the effects of art upon persons. Noting that drama consistently produces in audiences certain effects – fear, pity, admiration, awe, superiority, affinity, belief, skepticism, compassion, and relief – Aristotle identified these responses as official aims of art, formalizing what audiences feel as the standard moral effects achieved by art.

Since the late seventeenth century, when mass print culture provided greater numbers of persons with the regular affective experience of literature, the novel became another focal point in the ongoing debate and discourse about the effects of representation. Even more than drama and poetry, the novel seemed to demand the reader's sentiments, through the staged direct address of epistolarity, or through the differently but equally contrived direct address of apostrophe to reader. Thus, when Harriet Beecher Stowe famously enjoins readers of *Uncle Tom's Cabin* to "feel right," she is writing in an ancient tradition to which modern sentimentalism has contributed its affective techniques, upholding longstanding assumptions about reader response. No less than Aristotle assuming that tragedy arouses terror and pity in audiences, Stowe relies on the sentimental novel to produce sympathy in readers, an abolitionist sympathy for the plight of slaves in mid-nineteenth-century America.

Yet not all readers of the best-selling *Uncle Tom's Cabin* became abolitionists. Neither Aristotelian poetics nor sentimental procedures can produce uniform responses or predict all possible responses. A reader might sympathize with slaves, put down the book *Uncle Tom's Cabin*, and think no more about the subject. Because the reader is not the object of sympathy or the character with whom she identifies, she can stop sympathizing at any point during or after reading the book. Or the sympathizing reader may translate her feeling into something else; you can channel sympathy into rituals and charitable gestures and donations rather than act upon it.[1] You could name your daughter Eva or smile at a slave or denounce the south without doing anything to abolish slavery. This limit of sympathy understandably has always generated criticism about the performance of Stowe's novel and the role of sentiment in political solutions.

Other criticism of the novel has stemmed from what might be considered its sentimental failure with some readers, readers not moved to feel as Stowe intended. *Uncle Tom's Cabin*, despite its enormous immediate popularity and acclaim, generated unsympathetic and antipathetic readings as well as tears. Slavery apologists labeled Stowe's portrait of slavery inaccurate and wrote counterviews of happy plantation life. African Americans objected to the racist portrayal of slaves as obedient, cunning, and childlike. After the novel's publication, Stowe found herself not so much surrounded by right-feeling people as under fire from critics concerning the accuracy of her presentation of life among the lowly. This surprising effect of sympathy – that it didn't work with every reader – led Stowe both to lecture tours and to writing *A Key to Uncle Tom's Cabin*, in which she copiously documented her characterizations of slaves, compiling and reprinting newspaper articles, bills of sale, advertisements for runaway slaves, and testimonies of slaves.[2]

To take on this evidentiary project, what we might call the supplement to tears, Stowe had to put aside the novel she had just begun, *The Pearl of Orr's Island: A Story of the Coast of Maine*, the story of an orphaned girl and boy growing up in a tightly knit shipping community. After touring Europe for *Uncle Tom's Cabin*, writing another anti-slavery novel (*Dred*, 1856) and a different New England novel (*The Minister's Wooing*, 1859), and beginning an Italian novel (*Agnes of Sorrento*, 1862), Stowe finally returned to and completed *The Pearl of Orr's Island* (1862).[3] While Stowe's long hiatus in writing the novel and her New England focus seem to distance it from *Uncle Tom's Cabin*, *The Pearl of Orr's Island* importantly continues Stowe's exploration of different ways of reading and of the sometimes tragic consequences that follow when people cannot reconcile their different readings of the world.

In this novel, Stowe explores the very problem that *Uncle Tom's Cabin* posed: the radical variability of reading despite directing literary conventions, a variability that Stowe suggests is set in human psyches. In *Uncle Tom's Cabin* itself, Stowe had already disapprovingly displayed the incommensurability among different Christian readings of the Bible with respect to slavery. Clearly the southern minister who justifies American slavery by finding examples of slavery in the Bible provokes Stowe's ire as he pleases Marie St. Clare's complacent racism. The project of making people feel right, then, involves, making people read rightly. This is a more difficult task than generating sympathy because readers so easily get bored, lose attention, or attend to other matters. Each reader varies in countless ways; the reader's individuality is a constant challenge to the novelist who would achieve a desired effect – a uniform sentiment which proceeds to action.

The lesson Stowe learned from the reception of *Uncle Tom's Cabin* is one she already anticipated in the novel itself where she regularly depicts people arguing about slavery (besides conflicting views of the Bible, she describes arguments between Mr. and Mrs. Shelby, Senator and Mrs. Bird, the women on the steamship taking Tom south, Ophelia and St. Clare, St. Clare and his brother, St. Clare and his wife, George Harris and his employer, herself and the reader). Stowe continued to consider the issue of irreconcilable readings in *The Pearl of Orr's Island*. In this novel, two orphaned children, Moses and Mara, grow up in the same household, beginning as and remaining very different types of persons, seeing the world in incompatible ways. Bound by experience and life-long love, they nevertheless cannot be happy together. In this "story of the coast of Maine" removed from the slavery controversy, Stowe focuses on the difficulty of negotiating deep-seated variant and contradictory views, the phenomenon at the heart of any political change.

In this sense *The Pearl of Orr's Island* truly is a sequel to *Uncle Tom's Cabin*, extending Stowe's interest in the fact of diverse readings coupled with her belief in right reading. Stowe dramatizes the individuality of reading most memorably in scenes of children reading, which serve as a template for the case study of Mara and Moses to which she next turned. Thus, to see where *The Pearl of Orr's Island* begins, we must start with Eva and Topsy reading.

Eva and Topsy Reading

Though only "a child," Eva "was a beautiful reader – a fine musical ear, a quick poetic fancy, and an instinctive sympathy with what is grand and noble, made her such a reader of the Bible, as Tom had never before heard." Her reading to Tom leads her to love "the majestic book," especially "the Revelations and Prophecies" that "spoke of a glory to be revealed" (224).[4] Reading is revelation for Eva, "a pillar of inspiration," as in the ideal of Protestant Bible study. When she reads aloud to Tom, she sees the images described by the words she recites. As soon as she reads the line "And I saw a sea of glass, mingled with fire," Eva points to the "glassy water" of Lake Pontchartrain "which, as it rose and fell, reflected the golden glow of the sky." Sure of her reference, Eva declares "There's a 'sea of glass, mingled with fire'" (226). Eva's certainty about seeing what she reads extends to other forms of sacred words so that when Tom sings a Methodist hymn about the

New Jerusalem, Eva immediately locates it in the clouds "like great gates of pearl" above them (227).

Stowe credits Eva's eager literalization of the read and spoken word as divine inspiration, showing the child prophesying her own death and entry into heaven. Eva's credibility follows from her status as a pious sentimental heroine; the conventional death of such heroines marks their superiority to this world. The message of the vivid sentimental death scene is that Eva thinks and feels right. Stowe takes the occasion for deepest sympathy, the death of a beloved child, to promote the Christian truths that this child reads and speaks. To assent to Eva's reading of the Bible and the world, it seems that the reader must share her Christian view or convert to it.[5] Or, if not actually converting, the reader must grant validity to the Christian narrative within the novel: that is to say, accept the sentimental portrait of Eva and her death within the logic that the novel sustains. Since not all sympathetic readers of *Uncle Tom's Cabin* share Stowe's religious beliefs, the effect of the book depends more on Stowe's successful use of sentimental conventions than on her proselytizing.

This is not in any way to scant Stowe's religious convictions and intentions, but to underscore the shrewd formal choices she made in composing her story. Though popular dramas based on the novel and much discussion of it have foregrounded Eva's evangelicalism and exemplary death,[6] Eva exits in the middle of the book, leaving the reader to follow the fates of Tom and all the other characters. Even as the deaths of St. Clare and Tom recapitulate the Christian narrative of Eva's passage into heaven, Stowe busies the reader with the lives and worldly futures of everyone who knew Tom or Eva. Stowe significantly undergirds and supplements the sentimental narrative of Eva with other narratives, furnishing readers with events that don't necessarily represent Christian values, such as the horrific abuses of slavery and the hopelessness of slaves that leads to suicide and infanticide. Alongside Eva, Stowe sets Topsy, who presents another type of reading, an experiential rather than prophetic mode.[7]

Topsy, like Tom, learns to read only because her mistress believes it is a Christian duty to educate slaves. To believe in this duty, as Miss Ophelia and Mrs. Shelby do, is to recognize and respect the souls of slaves despite the prevailing legal and customary denial of literacy to African Americans. Thus the details of Topsy's learning to read register the Christian doctrine of the importance of God's word as they simultaneously reveal the failure of Christian history that slavery epitomizes. At first, Topsy dramatically demonstrates her alienation from the Christian narrative that Miss Ophelia would have her learn and believe. As instructed (and Topsy is a very quick study), she recites a catechism: "Our first parents, being left to the freedom of their own will, fell from the state wherein they were created" (218). Instead of accepting this statement, Topsy immediately questions and parodies it on the basis of her own experience. "Please, Missis," she asks Ophelia, "was dat ar state Kintuck? . . . I used to hear Mas'r tell how we came down from Kintuck" (218). Putting the word state in the geographical context that her life in slavery has taught her, Topsy translates the Christian story within her own frame of reference, showing how the understanding of words depends upon the experience the reader draws on for her associations. Whereas Eva instantly finds evidence for Biblical representations, Topsy hits on the different applications and significations that words can bear.

Amusing St. Clare and exasperating Ophelia, Topsy "would oddly transpose some important words, and persist in the mistake, in spite of every effort to the contrary" (218). But, as her identification of state with Kentucky manifests, Topsy doesn't really make a mistake in her reading; her understanding makes perfect sense from the perspective of a slave child for whom the usual assumptions about parents, family, and genealogy cannot operate. As Topsy posits, she "never was born" and "never had no father nor mother, nor nothin'. I was raised by a speculator" (209). She has every reason to think so. Topsy's reading therefore carries weight even as it lacks the divine inspiration of Eva's reading. In a sense, Topsy's reading appears even more credible than Eva's, because her juxtapositions and interpretations resonate so strongly with familiar instances of children making striking or comic formulations as they learn to read. In her question about the state of Kentucky, Topsy conflates the political and spiritual meanings of state, not realizing that Ophelia wants her to confine the meaning of state to the catechism text – to recite the word as it appears without questioning it. As Topsy reads across context, she shows how conventions shape meaning even as she reveals ignorance of the Christian conventions presented to her. The fact that the McGuffey primers from which so many nineteenth-century American children learned to read rely on the association of words with pictures and the oral repetition of these associations reflects the process of matching word to object or concept, the cognitive feat children attempt to accomplish.[8] Memorization wouldn't be necessary if children could immediately understand language and its contextual usage. Standard nineteenth-century pedagogical procedure required children to recite pages of primers, catechisms, and readers, so that they thereby learned such conventions as pronunciation and tone. While such a method might appear narrow-minded or unimaginative, it assumes the capability of children to connect words with context and custom.[9]

Because *Uncle Tom's Cabin* is the key abolitionist novel in United States history, and because its characterizations of slave-owners and slaves have produced the indelible (and controversial) figures of Uncle Tom, Little Eva, Topsy, and Simon Legree, we tend to overlook Stowe's contribution to the representation of children, her recognition of their intelligence, interiority, and feeling.[10] From the 1830s onward, a popular set of child characters emerged in American literature (for adults as well as children): Jacob Abbott's Rollo, Nathaniel Hawthorne's Pearl, Mary Mapes Dodge's Hans Brinker, Susan Warner's Ellen Montgomery, Martha Finley's Elsie Dinsmore, Horatio Alger's heroic boys, Louisa May Alcott's little women and little men. Children's lives under slavery became well known through slave narratives by Frederick Douglass and Harriet Jacobs. American readers also enthusiastically followed the exploits of Dickens's many child characters. In tandem with a new religious emphasis on the goodness and innate spirituality of children and new educational theories highlighting children's intellectual and aesthetic capacities, fiction promoted the distinctiveness of children.[11] Eva and Topsy clearly reflect and contribute to the increasing appreciation for the particularities of childhood. Though Stowe underscores the racist treatment of Topsy by noting "St. Clare took the same kind of amusement in the child that a man might in the tricks of a parrot or a pointer" (218), she also makes Topsy a far more recognizably human child than Eva. Besides indicating the marks of slavery, Topsy's distinctive reading displays the marks of childhood that characterize beloved figures of young readers such as Jo March and Tom Sawyer – like them, she is willful, charming, trying, endearing, disobedient, entertaining, clever, imaginative, and memorable. Like them, she appears in rich psychological detail as a distinctive personality. "I'se so wicked!" Topsy gleefully declares (217), assured and ready like Maurice Sendak's Max to go and preside where the wild things are.

The individuality of Topsy, however, lies in her exemplification of childhood under slavery. Just as Topsy's idiosyncratic reading employs, as it reflects, the conventionality of meaning, Topsy's particular experience evokes the institution of slavery: the racist and socio-economic formation of her very self. Stowe explains in *A Key to Uncle Tom's Cabin* that she designed Topsy to stand "as the representative of a large class of children who are growing up under the institution of slavery – quick, active, subtle, and ingenious, apparently utterly devoid of principle and conscience, keenly penetrating, by an instinct which exists in the childish mind, the degradation of their condition, and the utter hopelessness of rising above it."[12] In *Uncle Tom's Cabin*, Topsy describes this state of mind as she tells Eva why it makes no sense for her to try to do good. "Couldn't never be nothin' but a nigger, if I was ever so good . . . There can't nobody love niggers, and niggers can't do nothin'!" (245). Her sense of hopelessness starkly contrasts with, as it overshadows, the liveliness and resourcefulness that Topsy exercises in the St. Clare

household. This sophisticated awareness of the slave's state of mind anticipates Du Bois's later articulation of the double consciousness of African-
American experience: how a degraded and enslaved race internalizes its
despised status, reflecting its hateful condition with collective self-hatred.[13]

Topsy is thus a forerunner of complex psychological portraits such as
Nella Larsen's Clare and Richard Wright's Bigger Thomas. But Topsy's story,
as Stowe tells it, serves not to illuminate the environmental and individual
experiences that make up her life, but to fulfill Eva's evangelical mission. The
slavegirl's ultimate conversion helps to depict a socially engaged operation of
Christianity in which blacks as well as whites live as God's beloved children,
all entitled to the same rights and responsibilities. An unloved child, Topsy
elicits sympathy and occasions the passionately charitable feeling that Eva
models for readers of *Uncle Tom's Cabin*. "O, Topsy, poor child, I love
you!" Eva declares. "I love you, because you haven't had any father, or
mother, or friends; – because you've been a poor, abused child!" (245). Eva's
"Christ-like" ministrations to the slavegirl (246), presented as the rescue of
a suffering child, immediately imbue Topsy with "a ray of real belief, a ray
of heavenly love" and with the desire "to be good" so that you, too, "can go
to Heaven at last, and be an angel forever, just as if you were white" (246).
Stowe thus identifies evangelicalism with eternal equality, albeit an equality
conferred only "at last" in another existence.

Under the aegis of the Christian narrative of the novel, Topsy's maturation,
rather than her childhood, defines her. After Eva, and subsequently, Ophelia
and God supply the love that Topsy so sorely lacks, she no longer manifests
her childish traits. Indeed, Topsy, who accompanies Ophelia back to New
England, becomes as evangelical as Eva:

> At the age of womanhood, she was, by her own request, baptized, and became a
> member of the Christian church in the place; and showed so much intelligence,
> activity, and zeal, and desire to do good in the world, that she was at last
> recommended, and approved as a missionary to one of the stations in Africa;
> and we have heard that the same activity and ingenuity, which, when a child
> made her so multiform and restless in her developments, is now employed, in
> a safer and wholesomer manner, in teaching the children of her own country.
>
> (377)

Topsy now teaches the correct Christian account of the words she once
so illuminatingly and entertainingly misconstrued. Like Eva, she reads and
feels rightly. Eva's path to heaven and happiness appears more accessible
through Topsy's experience because Topsy proves what Eva preaches: that
God provides for all his children. But Topsy's commitment to Christianity
carries no abolitionist fervor nor any program of equal rights. She performs

the Lord's work in what Stowe calls "her own country" (377), somewhere in Africa, far removed from the United States. Stowe similarly relocates former slave George Harris and his family in the new Liberian nation, which he hopes "shall roll the tide of civilization and Christianity along its shores, and plant there mighty republics, that, growing with the rapidity of tropical vegetation, shall be for all coming ages" (375). Following this vision of African-American repatriation, Stowe closes her novel by appealing to white Americans to do their Christian duty against slavery and its enduring evil effects lest they be held accountable by "that stronger law, by which injustice and cruelty shall bring on nations the wrath of Almighty God!" (388). Though all persons importantly figure in the Christianization of the world, reformation of the United States appears to depend on the separatist plan of removing African Americans.[14]

Thus, Topsy's reformation – and the fact that Stowe presents the religious and social conversion of the slavegirl rather than of the slave-owner – makes the Christian narrative unconvincing or unsatisfying for its very embrace of two such different children, for its simple erasure of racial difference and racist history. For the non-believing or skeptical reader, Topsy's conversion, instead of strengthening the sentimental impact of the novel, seems an obvious sentimental convention, a formal plot device that doesn't achieve Stowe's intended effect (the conversion of whites). Topsy's mischief and initial unusual literary associations remain so memorable that her conversion disappoints readers who sympathize with her precisely because of her endearing independent childish ways. (The domestication and marriage of another beloved child heroine, Jo March, similarly disappoints many readers.) When Topsy becomes an unquestioning reader of the Bible, her initial misreading of Christian history appears merely a childish utterance, rather than a trenchant albeit unwitting description of the historical connections between Christianity, racism, and slavery. The very characteristics of children that Topsy so vividly exhibits fade with her maturation. Along with her antics, Topsy herself seems to recede as Stowe relocates her in Africa.

The racist implications of the conclusion to *Uncle Tom's Cabin* certainly qualify the novel's status as great reform literature. Yet I would maintain that the novel's powerful anti-slavery message remains strong precisely because Stowe repeatedly emphasizes the capacity for human change. Besides Topsy's conversion, the slave-catcher Tom Loker changes his profession and mind, the slave-owner Shelby's son George emancipates all the family slaves, and the most hardened slaves on Legree's plantation ask Uncle Tom to tell them about Jesus. Because Stowe portrays Topsy in far more psychological detail than these other players in the plot, Topsy's depth of character, anchored in the familiarity and pathos of her childishness, creates expectations beyond the Christian sentimental narrative. Topsy's character requires another story, a narrative honoring the breadth and depth of her understanding of the world. While such fictional narratives come after *Uncle Tom's Cabin* and after the Civil War, in the great African-American novels such as *Contending Forces*, *Passing*, *Native Son*, and *Beloved*, we might say Stowe helps initiate the literary tradition.

Uncle Tom's Cabin demonstrates that the representation of racial character, especially when embedded in childhood, reveals the integrality of personality with social conditions – the imbrication of biology with sociology that the category of race so strongly signifies. Thus Topsy affects readers with lasting impressions about childhood and race that exceed or contradict the neatness of the Christian conversion story. Put another way, the reformation and relocation of Topsy epitomizes the limit of sentimental sympathy. Topsy effectively gets into the reader's skin as she draws the interest and concern of Eva, St. Clare, and Ophelia. As Francis Spufford usefully points out, "this kind of vicarious experience can be very powerful," especially in helping "nicely brought up white children learn to imagine what it is like to be on the receiving end of racism."[15]

But no one gets into Topsy's skin, for "to understand somebody else's life as it feels to the person living it, you have to imagine you being them, a far harder task, for it refuses sympathy's speedy, magical wiring-together of two nervous systems." Sympathy can powerfully connect a reader with a character, but cannot represent how a character fully experiences his or her situation. For a reader to get a sense of this independent reality, Spufford recommends that "you empty yourself so far as you can, and you try to subdue yourself to the material of another life, to have the horizons another life has, to enter into its separate density, which can seem as hard, at times, as for water to enter a block of solid close-grained wood."[16] The difficulty readers encounter in entering into a separate density appears in the persistence of racism in *Uncle Tom's Cabin* and registers in the distance at which Topsy's fate places her. Eva's conversion of Topsy, to be sure, significantly changes Ophelia, causing her to overcome her physical repulsion to black skin. Though Ophelia's embrace of Topsy importantly figures the change in white attitudes that Stowe attempts to produce, Topsy's future lies outside white society. Stowe takes us only as far with Topsy as sympathy will go.[17]

The fundamental individuality of persons and the consequent differences between them – the formidable obstacles to sympathy – not surprisingly preoccupy Stowe in writing her next novel. In *The Pearl of Orr's Island*, she takes the psychological features of her characters so seriously that their lives follow invariable patterns that divide them despite their desires and efforts to conform to each other. Against this problem, which appears most dramatically in the different ways characters respond to narratives, Stowe sets all imaginative operations, which can valuably work like Biblical narrative to extend readers into elevated states of mind. Rather than disregarding differences among individuals, Stowe here presents an account of reading as so basic and general a Christian activity that we can be ecumenical about the inevitable variety within reading even as we witness the irresolution and unhappiness generated by the different perspectives of persons.

Mara and Moses Reading

In *The Pearl of Orr's Island*, the psychological traits of people figure so significantly that they appear in their physiognomy. Stowe accordingly describes an old man with "a face deeply lined with the furrows of shrewd thought and anxious care" and a young woman with a mouth "delicately formed, with a certain sad quiet in its lines, which indicated a habitually repressed and sensitive nature" (1). The forms of individuals, etched into their faces, bespeak not their experiences but their natures from birth. The novel focuses on three children, the unrelated orphans Mara and Moses Pennel who grow up together under the care of Mara's grandparents, and their neighbor Sally Kittridge. Aunt Roxy and Aunt Ruey, the community needlewomen and nurses, provide a choral commentary throughout the novel that defends the particularity of children and their needs. Noting "all children ain't alike" (37), Roxy insists "there's reason in all things and there's difference in children" (59). From the start, Stowe underscores the distinctive looks and personalities of the three different children which govern their lives.

Between the two girls, "never was there a more marked contrast of nature. The one [Sally] seemed a perfect type of well-developed childish health and vigor, good solid flesh and bones, with glowing skin, brilliant eyes, shining teeth, well-knit supple limbs, – vigorously and healthily beautiful; while the other [Mara] appeared one of those aerial mixtures of cloud and fire, whose radiance seems scarcely earthly" (37). Their looks correspond to their different personalities. While Sally is a practical, energetic, capable, and easygoing girl, Mara from babyhood is a child "with ways and manners so still and singular as often to remind the neighbors she was not like other children" (27). She has "one of those sensitive, excitable natures, on which every external influence acts with immediate power"(36). Her malleability makes her a medium not just of Sally's and Moses's moods but of beings from beyond this world. As a baby, "her eyes always look so kind o' wishful" (28), as if she were longing for her dead mother. Her timorousness and helplessness further manifest her unearthly nature, her dependence on "the utmost stretch of indulgence and kindness" (13).

Moses, by contrast, behaves with utter independence, with a "fiery, iras-cible spirit" (56) that Stowe characterizes as "a perfect miniature of proud manliness" (81). "A vigorous, well-made, handsome child, with brilliant eyes and teeth" (56), Moses differs from Mara and Sally in being "a little wretch" (104), "a self-willed little elf" (101). He almost immediately forgets his dead mother and quickly adapts to his new familial situation with Mara and her grandparents. Stowe attributes the boy's strong will and temper not only to his sex but also to his foreignness, to his Spanish heritage and thus Catholic background.[18] To the Orr Islanders, Moses notably shows no signs of "a babe of grace" (75). During family Bible reading, at which Mara sits composedly, he stares "with his great, black, irreverent eyes" and laughs "in the most inappropriate manner" during psalm-singing (75).

This disrespectful behavior marks Moses's fundamental difference from the Bible-minded Protestant community that adopts him, naming and bap-tizing the boy Moses because he came to them from the water. The pious and generous people of Orr's Island honor and live by the Bible, giving their children Biblical names such as Moses, Mara, and Sarah and habitu-ally finding references for their lives in Biblical stories. As Stowe comments, "New England, in her earlier days, founding her institutions on the Hebrew Scriptures, bred better Jews than Moses could, because she read Moses with the amendments of Christ" (122). From the Orr's Islanders' reverence for and dependence upon the Bible, Stowe mounts a defense of the Old and New Testaments of the Bible as the universal all-purpose sacred text:

> We hear sometimes in these days that the Bible is no more inspired of God than many other books of historic and poetic merit. It is a fact, however, that the Bible answers a strange and wholly exceptional purpose by thousands of firesides on all shores of the earth; and till some other book can be found to do the same thing, it will not be surprising if a belief of its Divine origin be one of the ineffaceable ideas of the popular mind. It will be a long while before a translation from Homer or a chapter in the Koran, or any of the beauties of Shakespeare, will be read in a stormy night on Orr's Island with the same sense of a Divine presence as the Psalms of David, or the prayer of Moses, the man of God.
>
> (43–44)

The very fact that Stowe mentions other great books and the possibility of some other book doing the same thing for thousands of people suggests that the Bible could be supplanted. Homer, the Koran, and Shakespeare already claim wide readership. On Orr's Island, children must learn the Bible and value it above all books, but their literary education includes Latin and Greek literature as important fundamentals and supplements to religious training. As might be expected, Moses struggles in learning to read all these books, while Mara excels. Sally, in training for housekeeping, capably learns the basics of reading, and thinks little about it. All three children grow up hearing the fanciful stories told by Captain Kittridge, Sally's father. A retired sailor, the captain can find a correlative story for any event or narrative: "there was no species of experience, finny, fishy, or aquatic, – no legend of strange and unaccountable incident of fire and flood, – no romance of foreign scenery and productions, to which his tongue was not competent" (31). The captain's yarns significantly evoke several Biblical episodes – the miraculous experiences of Jonah, Lot, and Noah. Stowe interestedly accompanies her defense of the Bible with a defense of the captain's fictions, observing that "works of fiction, as we all know, if only well gotten up, have always their advantages in the hearts of listeners over plain, homely truth" (31). She carefully notes that despite "the Captain's disposition to romancing and embroidery . . . in all real, matter-of-fact transactions, as between man and man, his word was as good as another's, and he was held to be honest and just in his dealings" (67). Stowe even credits Captain Kittridge with "a rude poetic and artistic faculty" (67) through which "the bounds between the real and unreal become foggier than the banks of Newfoundland" (68).

Throughout the novel, Stowe includes stories of the passage between these realms: besides Captain Kittridge's tales, old women tell of deathbed apparitions, Mara dreams of future events, and the children play hard at imaginary adventures which they closely enact.[19] Fiction thus plays a powerful role in life on Orr's Island, operating alongside the Bible to furnish narratives through which people find connections with their actual experience. Individual psychology, of course, affects the way different people identify with stories. All three children love hearing the captain's stories. As they listen to a tale about mermen and mermaids, Sally curiously wonders if the shining shoe-buckles worn by the merman described by her father might really be diamonds. Moses, a stickler for narrative details, wants to know how the merman got out of his ship anchored at the bottom of the sea with the anchor blocking the front door. Mara gets so enthralled with such romances that she worries about the strange dangers her grandfather and Moses might encounter on their sailings. She lives "on that shadowy boundary between the dreamland of childhood and the real land of life; so all things looked to her quite possible." After the captain tells her about friendly white bears on icebergs, "gentle white bears, with warm, soft fur, and pearl and gold saddles, walked through her dreams" (133).

Mara has some reason to value imaginary narratives. When only a few years old, she has a prophetic dream: she sees a beautiful woman who hands her a little black-eyed boy, saying "Take him, Mara, he is a playmate for you" (50). The next day, when she is playing with Sally and Captain Kittridge in a cove, they find the body of a shipwrecked woman who, miraculously, holds in her arms a still live little boy. Mara immediately recognizes him as the "pitty boy" of her dream and "seemed to appropriate him in feminine fashion, as a chosen idol and graven image" (56). Stowe's characterization of Mara's relation to Moses clearly indicates the impropriety of this love.[20] Yet Stowe initially endorses Mara's prophetic capacity, speculating that "it may be that our present faculties have among them a rudimentary one, like the germs of wings in the chrysalis, by which the spiritual world becomes sometimes an object of perception; there may be natures in which the walls of the material are so fine and translucent that the spiritual is seen through them as through a glass darkly" (57). The natures of some persons may enable them to see divine operations. For such persons, imaginary narratives furnished by dreams, stories, history, play, and daydreaming open pathways to the spiritual, thus supplementing and contributing to the purpose of Biblical narrative.

The problem with the affinity of fictional forms with the Bible, however, is that readers can conflate the earthly with the divine. Mara's dream leads her not only to invest in a boy psychologically unsuitable to her temperament, but to regard him as her destiny, the supreme object of her love and care. Her intensive reading of Roman history, Aesop's fables, and the Bible causes her to muse

> on the things that she read till her little mind became a tabernacle of solemn, quaint, dreamy forms, where old Judean kings and prophets, and Roman senators and warriors, marched in and out in shadowy rounds. She invented long dramas and conversations in which they performed imaginary parts, and it would not have appeared to the child in the least degree surprising either to have met an angel in the woods, or to have formed an intimacy with some talking wolf or bear, such as she read of in Aesop's Fables (134–135)

By mixing and equating all fictions and narratives, Mara exemplifies both Stowe's ideal Christian reader, who finds divine revelation in all forms, and Stowe's recognition of the mistaken reader, who makes the wrong connections.

Recapitulating in Mara the different models of reading exhibited by Eva and Topsy, Stowe presents Mara's life as the story of a girl who learns to distinguish between the earthly and divine and to value the latter over the former. In this sense, Mara's experience, more than Moses's, works as a conversion narrative. Here Stowe depicts a child's maturation that remains consistent with her psychology: always more "aerial" than earthly, Mara simply has to find the correct object of adoration. In keeping with Stowe's effort in this novel to show the congruence of reading fiction with reading Scripture,

Mara's doubts about Moses begin with her reading of *The Tempest*. The play enchants her; the story of an enchanted island reminds her of Captain Kittridge's sea stories while the characters strike her as "very probable" because they correspond to her experience (135). She fancies Caliban "with a face much like that of a huge skate-fish she had once seen drawn ashore in one of her grandfather's nets; and then there was the beautiful young Prince Ferdinand, much like what Moses would be when he was grown up – and how glad she would be to pile up his wood for him, if any old enchanter should set him to work!" (135). The song "Full fathom five thy father lies" recalls her finding Moses on the beach after the shipwreck (and after her dream) and makes her wonder if Moses's father "were lying fathoms deep with sea-nymphs ringing his knell, and whether Moses ever thought about him" (137).

When Mara reads the story of *The Tempest* to Moses while he is building a ship, she is shocked by his response, or rather, non-response.

> He listened with interest, though without any of the extreme feeling which Mara had thought possible, and even interrupted her once in the middle of the celebrated – "Full fathom five thy father lies," by asking her to hold up the mast a minute, while he drove in a peg to make it rake a little more. He was, evidently, thinking of no drowned father, and dreaming of no possible sea-caves, but acutely busy in fashioning a present reality; and yet he liked to hear Mara read, and, when she had done, told her that he thought it was a pretty – quite a pretty story, with such a total absence of recognition that the story had any affinities with his own history, that Mara was quite astonished.
>
> (175–176)

That night while Mara lies awake thinking about Moses, he lies thinking about "a new way of disposing a pulley for raising a sail" (176). Stowe thus marks the gulf between the two as a conflict in reader response that stems from the nature of each child. With Mara's recognition of the incompatibility between Moses and herself, Stowe stopped work on *The Pearl of Orr's Island*, announcing that the story will resume ten years later in the lives of the characters.

In completing the novel, Stowe simply unfolded the logical, yet protracted, consequences of Mara's realization about Moses: the impossibility of these two living happily in intimacy. Even though Moses is just as in love with Mara as she is with him, his love is "egotistic, exacting, tyrannical, and capricious" (199). Mara's reticence about her feelings causes Moses to find comfort in the attentions of Sally while Mara suffers in silence. This divergence from the love story between Mara and Moses operates as a prediction of what follows. Mara and Moses finally become engaged, Mara becomes ill and dies, Moses and Sally ultimately marry. As the novel moves to a classic sentimental death scene, Mara divests herself of her feelings for Moses, telling Sally she has "given him up to his Saviour and my Saviour" (369). Having relinquished a false idol, Mara now thinks that "perhaps our Father saw that I could not have the strength to live with him and keep my faith. I should be drawn by him earthward instead of drawing him heavenward" (368). Now Mara thinks and speaks purely within Christian narrative, maintaining a clear distinction between earth and heaven, and a preference for the latter. She accordingly can tell Moses that "in all that was deepest and dearest to me, I was alone. You did not come near to me, nor touch me where I feel most deeply" (395–396).

Mara's development into a confident Christian reader who, like Eva, sees visions of Jesus and eternity, leads her out of this world, where the occasions for mistaken readings and judgments abound. Stowe calls the chapter that depicts Mara's spiritual clairvoyance about her impending death "The Victory." In *Uncle Tom's Cabin*, Stowe uses the same title for the chapter in which Tom dies; in *The Pearl of Orr's Island*, victory refers not to the actual passage into heaven, but to the moment of Christian enlightenment in which Mara feels "happy" (358) to "be forever with the Lord" (359). Mara shares this moment with her grandparents and Aunt Roxy and Aunt Ruey, who honor it by reading the Bible. Thus Stowe reaffirms the primacy of the Bible. Yet she continues to supplement it with other imaginative narratives. After Mara dies, her grandfather Zephaniah dreams he was looking on the seashore for his lost pearl, for Mara, the child who has seemed to enter his life like a "pearl washed ashore by a mighty, uprooting tempest" (27). In the dream, he sees the pearl on the sand, but before he reaches it, he sees Jesus, who picks up the pearl and places it on his forehead, where "it shone like a star" as he "rose in the air, and melted in the clouds" (402). Mara's beloved images from *The Tempest* merge into the vision of heavenly ascension; her grandfather's dream subsumes the Shakespearean representation of marvelous events on earth, like the production of pearls, into Christian narrative, which pairs pearls with the gates of heaven.

Before closing the novel, Stowe supplies another story, the romantic ending for Moses and Sally. Four years after Mara's death, Moses proposes to Sally, saying "We are as different as if we were each another person. We have been trained in another life, – educated by a great sorrow" (406). Their wedding, the novel's hopeful view of human nature eventually conforming to the Christian principles of conversion and transcendence, requires the scriptural confirmation of the novel's final words. Stowe concludes with the quotation "He turneth the shadow of death into morning" (407). The novel thereby asserts a divine design in both Mara's death and the subsequent marriage between Moses and Sally.

By careful narrative resolution, Stowe reconciles secular and religious representations, earthly and spiritual aspirations. The narrative functions ritualistically, performing by literary fiat the reformative process – or training, to use Moses's word – necessary to change persons. Earlier in the novel, Stowe stresses how "education is in many cases nothing more than a blind struggle of parents and guardians with the evolutions of some strong, predetermined character, individual, obstinate, unreceptive, and seeking by an inevitable law of its being to develop itself and gain free expression in its own way" (189). This description aptly applies to Moses, whose actual religious conversion never occurs in the novel (despite his claim to be a different person), but appears a future possibility. Given that Moses so vividly exemplifies the rigidity of human character, the prospect of his attaining Christian transcendence appears more a sentimental formal production than the psychological possibility of spiritual growth that Mara exhibits.

Moses's improbable change highlights the narrative maneuvers through which Stowe would train her readers. The coherence of *The Pearl of Orr's Island* depends upon the reader accepting novelistic conventions while fully understanding the fictionality of novelistic accounts of life. In following this novel's resolution of the abiding contradiction between fictive life and actual life, readers encounter Stowe's technique, the work behind the scenes presented for their consideration. Like the repeated addresses to readers in *Uncle Tom's Cabin* stressing the reality of Stowe's fictional scenes, the insistent assertions of divine design in *The Pearl of Orr's Island* remind readers that they are reading: that they are following a narrative design. Both novels attempt to affect readers by accentuating the act of reading not only in depictions of children reading but also in appeals to readers' consciousnesses of their own reading. Reading these books involves not only following the paths that Stowe's children take in their reading but also following the movements of our own reading under Stowe's direction.

To make readers see possible resolutions made available by formal procedures of narrative, Stowe uses three primary representational modes of sentimental novels: description of interior experience, promotion of individual and social reformation, and report on suffering.[21] Absorbing readers in the plights of Eva, Topsy, Mara, and Moses, Stowe asks readers to accept the fates that she allots these characters as readily as they get invested in the characters. She thus challenges her readers to believe in characters' conversions even though, or perhaps precisely because, alterations in human character appear extraordinary events. In others words, Stowe enjoins readers to find within conventions such as sentimental resolutions patterns for changing their minds or other minds. The risk to her project is that she cannot determine whether readers will change or what direction any change will take. Because children simultaneously display individuality and development, they epitomize the coexistence of variability with custom. Yet the volatility of children also demonstrates the fragility of this co-existence, the conflicts that inevitably erupt when individuals strongly disagree.

Ten years after the publication of *Uncle Tom's Cabin*, *The Pearl of Orr's Island* reveals Stowe still working to reconcile human differences through Christianity, even as Civil War battles raged. Whether or not readers harken to her spiritual message – and many obviously do not – Stowe in these novels effectively demonstrates the vital stakes in reading for everyone.

NOTES

1. Discourse about the limits of sympathy emerges in tandem with the sentimental novel, most famously in Adam Smith, *The Theory of Moral Sentiments* (1759), ed. D. D. Raphael and A. L. Macfie (Indianapolis: Liberty Classics, 1982), 9–66.

2. Harriet Beecher Stowe, *A Key to Uncle Tom's Cabin* (Boston: John P. Jewett, 1853). The threat of a lawsuit also prompted Stowe to get her defense of *Uncle Tom's Cabin* in print as soon as possible. For an exposition of how *A Key* reiterates, clarifies, and extends the argument of *Uncle Tom's Cabin*, see Cindy Weinstein's essay in this volume.

3. On the history of Stowe's work on the novel, see Joan D. Hedrick, "Foreword," *The Pearl of Orr's Island: A Story of the Coast of Maine* (Boston and New York: Houghton Mifflin, 2001), vii–xvi.

4. Page numbers refer to Elizabeth Ammons's edition of *Uncle Tom's Cabin* (New York: Norton, 1994) and are incorporated in the text.

5. This missionary intention is exactly what Jane Tompkins asserts is the "sentimental power" of the novel. See "Sentimental power: *Uncle Tom's Cabin* and the politics of literary history," in *Sensational Designs: The Cultural Work of American Fiction, 1790–1860* (New York: Oxford University Press, 1985). A painting of Eva reading the Bible and pointing to the lake as the reference that she has just read quite appropriately appears on the cover of Tompkins's book.

6. On the (ongoing) afterlife of *Uncle Tom's Cabin* in theatre, song, film, and other forms, see the remarkably thorough website instituted by Professor Stephen Railton of the University of Virginia: www.iath.virginia.edu/utc. Ann Douglas famously treats the death of Little Eva and the long-lasting cultural memory of this scene in *The Feminization of American Culture* (New York: Avon, 1977), 1–13.

7. In *Dred*, Stowe's second abolitionist novel, she attributes the prophetic mode of reading to African Americans, whom she describes as resembling the early Christians. White Christians have to learn to read the Bible properly.

8. See, for example, William H. McGuffey, *McGuffey's Eclectic Primer* (Cincinnati: Truman and Smith, 1836; rpt. Milford, MI: Mott Media, Inc., 1982). Interestingly, the publisher initially approached Stowe's older sister Catharine Beecher who recommended McGuffey as editor for the series. On McGuffey and his books, see

Charles Carpenter, *History of American Schoolbooks* (Philadelphia: University of Pennsylvania Press, 1963), 79–92.

9. My view differs from that of Walter Ong, who sees oral reading as distinct from reading for comprehension. Whereas Ong finds the nineteenth-century predilection for oral performances as a mark of nostalgia for prior oral traditions, I think the educational encounter with rules of speaking engages children in their contemporary social world. See Walter Ong, *Orality and Literacy: The Technologizing of the Word* (London and New York: Routledge, 1988), 115–116.

10. From the beginning of her publishing career in the 1830s, Stowe wrote sketches and stories for and about children which appeared in juvenile periodicals. In 1867, these pieces were collected in the volume *Stories and Sketches for the Very Young*. See *The Writings of Harriet Beecher Stowe*, Riverside Edition, Vol. XVI (Boston: Houghton Mifflin, 1896).

11. On the emergence of this new account of childhood, see Bernard Wishy, *The Child and the Republic: The Dawn of Modern American Child Nurture* (Philadelphia: University of Pennsylvania Press, 1968). On nineteenth-century American literary representations of children, see Gillian Avery, *Behold the Child: American Children and Their Books, 1621–1922* (Baltimore: The Johns Hopkins University Press, 1994).

12. Harriet Beecher Stowe, *A Key to Uncle Tom's Cabin*, 50.

13. W. E. B. DuBois, *The Souls of Black Folk* (New York: Penguin, 1989), 5.

14. For a closely related exposition of the disturbing plot closures in *Uncle Tom's Cabin*, see my chapter "Sentimental possession," in *Domestic Individualism: Imagining Self in Nineteenth-Century America* (Berkeley: University of California Press,1990), 39–60. On the imperialist aspects of Stowe's Christian vision, see Amy Kaplan, "Manifest domesticity," in *The Futures of American Studies* ed. Donald E. Pease and Robyn Wiegman (Durham and London: Duke University Press, 2002), 111–130.

15. In a wonderful book on the relation of children to reading, Francis Spufford makes this observation when discussing Atticus's famous advice to his daughter Scout in *To Kill a Mocking-Bird*: "You'll never understand someone until you get into their skin and walk around in it." Quoted in *The Child That Books Built: A Life in Reading* (New York: Metropolitan Books, 2002), 130–132.

16. Spufford, 131.

17. In a recent talk on *Uncle Tom's Cabin*, *To Kill a Mockingbird*, and *Native Son*, Eric Sundquist usefully notes how pathology, a psychological category, effectively replaces sympathy, a social manner, in the novelistic tradition of representing African Americans. I am arguing that Stowe makes the same change in focus when writing *The Pearl of Orr's Island*.

18. Moses's ethnicity disappears almost as soon as the Pennels adopt him, as if Stowe did not want to complicate her presentation of child character with issues of difference other than psychological ones.

19. This prominence of stories in people's lives, especially in the lives of children, also notably figures in *Oldtown Folks*, the novel Stowe published in 1869.

20. Joan D. Hedrick argues that Stowe presents the differences between Mara and Moses as a study of gender and the limits it places upon women. See "Foreword," *The Pearl of Orr's Island*, vii–xv. While I agree that Stowe in

this novel underscores gender differences, she views them as stemming from sexual differences, which themselves only biologically augment and accentuate fundamental temperamental differences among individuals. It is worth noting that Stowe begins the novel with a description of how the two girls, Mara and Sally, differ from each other.

21. For an exposition of Stowe's sentimental literary technique, see Philip Fisher, "Making a thing into a man: the sentimental novel and slavery," *Hard Facts: Setting and Form in the American Novel* (New York: Oxford University Press, 1985), 87–127.

5

AUDREY FISCH

Uncle Tom and Harriet Beecher Stowe in England

Shortly after the US publication of *Uncle Tom's Cabin* on March 20, 1852, and following the publication of the novel in serial form, an employee at the New York publishing house of Putnam's mailed a two-volume set of *Uncle Tom's Cabin* to a contact in England. With no transatlantic copyright law to hinder them, British publishers began to bring out their own editions of the novel as early as July 8, 1852. And after "lying dormant on the bookshelves for several weeks," the novel "exploded into favour."[1] Various British periodicals record the momentous nature of the success of *Uncle Tom's Cabin*: the *Morning Chronicle* writes "of illustrated editions, and newspaper printed editions, and editions in parts and numbers," concluding that *Uncle Tom's Cabin* is "the book of the day" and its "circulation . . . a thing unparalleled in bookselling annals."[2] The *Eclectic Review* records the novel's "marvellous popularity": "its sale has vastly exceeded that of any other work in any other age or country"; *Blackwood's Edinburgh Magazine* describes the sale of *Uncle Tom's Cabin* as "the most marvellous literary phenomenon that the world has witnessed."[3]

Stowe's successes in America were relatively small compared with what she achieved in England where sales of the novel are estimated to have reached a million and a half by the end of the first year of publication. England embraced the novel, its author, and its characters as it had no other text or author ever before. What was it about *Uncle Tom's Cabin* that resonated so powerfully with readers across the Atlantic? What did scenes of Kentucky farms and New Orleans slave markets mean to English factory workers and fashionable ladies? What, more broadly, did *Uncle Tom's Cabin* and its unparalleled commercial success mean for British literary history and for British cultural politics?[4] Stowe's relation to England and the success of *Uncle Tom's Cabin* is a fascinating and relatively unexplored topic. While Stowe's novel is generally studied in a variety of contexts, from the ideological work the novel performs as sentimental fiction to its relationship with the genre of slave narratives, few students consider the novel in this transatlantic context.

An important starting place in studying the phenomenon of Uncle Tom in England is a consideration of the ways in which *Uncle Tom's Cabin* enters into the context of the British-centered international anti-slavery movement. Within the British abolitionist movement, the abolitionist campaign of the eighteenth and early nineteenth centuries developed popular British anti-slavery sentiment and culminated in the abolition of the slave trade (1807) and colonial slavery (1833/1838). Writing from this movement includes the narratives of Olaudah Equiano (1789), Ottobah Cugoano (1787), and Mary Prince (1831), perhaps the best known British slave narratives, and over the decades between Equiano's narratives and Stowe's novel, "roughly one dozen major and minor narratives" were published in Britain, "all going through multiple editions." These were "the precursors to *Uncle Tom's Cabin*," paving the way for the novel's success.[5]

More broadly, the British public had been fed a steady diet of writing about slavery and the slave trade in the decades before Stowe's novel. Recent work in British Romanticism has suggested that "The African presence . . . shaped the British Romantic imagination."[6] New readings of major canonical writers consider the theme of slavery in works such as John Keats' "Lamia," William Wordsworth's "The Mad Mother," Mary Shelley's *Frankenstein*, and William Blake's "Daughters of Albion." Indeed, Debbie Lee suggests that major Romantic writers sought to take up the issue of slavery "in more oblique" ways because "the topic had been made so explicit for so long" (28). That "explicit" writing on slavery includes the popular and well known works of ex-slaves like Equiano and Phillis Wheatley as well as the anti-slavery tracts of leaders in the anti-slavery movement like William Clarkson, John Newton, and William Wilberforce and the popular poetry and ballads of anti-slavery writers such as Robert Southey, Anna Laetitia Barbauld, Hannah More, William Cowper, and Amelia Alderson Opie. In other words, by the time Stowe's novel reached England, the British reading public had been reading about slavery regularly for several decades, and anti-slavery sentiment was becoming central to British national identity.

In thinking about this reading material of stories and poems about slavery, it is important to understand a number of aspects of the early Victorian reading public. The steam press, advances in papermaking and binding, new devices for typesetting and illustration, as well as changes in the stamp tax all made reading material suddenly affordable, and railroads spread these materials quickly across the nation. These advances reached their peak in the forties and fifties, just around the time of the publication of *Uncle Tom's Cabin*, with the origination of cheap weekly papers produced for the middle class and "a still larger, less sophisticated readership."[7] Meanwhile, the century witnessed a rapid expansion of the reading public, with vast increases in literacy and leisure among the newly emerging industrial middle class and working class and among women of all classes.[8]

Culturally, however, the nation had yet to adjust to these changes. This same period marks increasingly shrill concerns about education, moral taste, and literary consumption. Many periodicals "represented attempts by upper-class enterprises to provide useful and agreeable instruction for the new working-class reading public."[9] Indeed, there was an ongoing battle between those who wanted to use the new medium "to win [and open] the minds of the common people" and those who wanted "stories designed to persuade the laboring class to remain loyal and docile."[10] Richard Altick describes the widespread fear among the Victorian elite that "making the 'lower ranks' of society literate would breed all sorts of disorder and debauchery," and Louis James records the concern that the new "*reading* population" was "particularly *susceptible* to such an influence as that of the press" (first emphasis original, second emphasis added).[11] Women were considered particularly vulnerable new readers, their hearts and minds open to potential elevation or debasement, depending on the reading material they encountered.

Slave narratives and the literature of slavery generally, like the lecture tours and shows associated with the abolitionist movement, were an odd and appealing genre in this uncertain new world of Victorian culture. The politically acceptable mantle of abolitionism served as a nearly untouchable vehicle under which Victorian readers could consume thrilling tales with titillating details of torture, murder, and sexual violence that might otherwise have been deemed pornographic or unrespectable for these readers. Because these tales evoked the morally acceptable rhetoric of Christianity and aligned themselves with the Christian odyssey tradition of Bunyan's *The Pilgrim's Progress* (Blackett, 26), they were also both comfortingly familiar to Victorian readers and generally acceptable to the moral censors and arbiters of the day. Without delimiting the appeal of the literature of slavery for Victorians, then, it's clear that this genre allowed readers unique access to material that may have been appealing for any number of reasons.

The contradictory nature of the balancing act the literature of slavery performed in the developing world of respectable Victorian culture is best illustrated by a peculiar example. In a letter between two English abolitionists, one describes his censorship of Frederick Douglass's narrative:

I could not circulate it among my friends and especially among ladies (young ones particularly) until I had erased all the paragraphs after the statement that Covey intended the woman to be bought for a "*breeder*." The minutia following, that [Covey] . . . shut him [a male slave] up with the woman every night for a year, and that the result was twins, are unnecessary and disgusting . . . [such sections would offend] English taste.[12]

The censorship J. B. Estlin describes in his letter actually consists of five sentences marked out with Xs. That Estlin would feel no concern over any other passage in Douglass's narrative, including, for example, the discussion, shortly before the "breeder" section, of a master who "Tie[s] up a lame young woman, and whip[s] her with a heavy cowskin upon her naked shoulders, causing the warm red blood to drip," underlines how uniquely the slave narrative and related texts about slavery were able to negotiate the tricky territory of respectability in the Victorian period.[13] Thus at a time when serious prohibitions still functioned to restrict access to violent or salacious material, the genre of slave tales could be widely circulated without fear of offending good taste.

It is into this world of new readers and uncertain and emerging standards of taste that *Uncle Tom's Cabin* entered with those pirated 1852 editions, produced on cheap paper and in cheap editions, that quickly and easily found their way to the vast numbers of new and relatively uneducated readers. The fact that Stowe's novel sold more copies than any other book in the era besides the Bible and *Pilgrim's Progress* is just the beginning of the story.

Uncle Tom's Cabin was not just an immensely popular novel; it was, as *Blackwood's Edinburgh Magazine* put it, a "literary phenomenon." The *Spectator* coined one name for the unprecedented phenomenon of commercialization of *Uncle Tom's Cabin*: "Tom-mania."[14] The American journal *Putnam's Magazine* coined another: "Uncle Tomitudes."[15]

Douglas A. Lorimer describes how the "extraordinary enthusiasm for Uncle Tom could not be satisfied by [a] simple reading of the novel":

Publishers, shopkeepers, and enterprising manufacturers soon set out to capitalize on this "Uncle Tom-mania" . . . Songbooks appeared with fulsome illustrations of famous passages in the novel. Wallpaper depicting Uncle Tom and Topsy in characteristic poses, or Eliza and Harry's famous escape, began to cover nursery walls. Uncle Tom mementos and ornaments cluttered curio shops, and Topsy dolls won the tender care and affection of little English Evas.[16]

Marcus Wood records more of the "fragmentations and adaptations" of the novel:

There was abolition stationery with envelopes featuring illustrative cycles composed of all the most popular scenes; there were *Uncle Tom's Cabin* jigsaw puzzles and even board and card games in which players represented characters from the novel and had to decide how to act at key moments in the plot.[17]

Harry Birdoff adds:

All along the London streets the wagons of retail shops rumbled on, carrying Tom's face on placards, and named after him were a great variety of articles: "Uncle Tom's pure unadulterated coffee," "Uncle Tom's improved flagelots," "Uncle Tom china," "Uncle Tom's paletot," "Uncle Tom's new and second-hand clothing," "Uncle Tom's shrinkable woolen stockings" . . . Named after the humble abode of Uncle Tom were many creameries and eating places, pastry shops, dry-goods emporiums, and cameo shops.[18]

Children's editions of the novel were also widespread, with most focusing on Topsy. These editions encouraged white English children to respond to Topsy through humor and religion. Children could be entertained by Topsy's antics, learn to "pity the poor little black Africans," and absorb the larger message of "political and economic colonisation of Africa [for] the enlightenment of the black heathen by the Christian Saxon" (Wood, 194). Most children's editions read and are illustrated like missionary tracts (Wood, 191).

John Cassell, the publishing entrepreneur, secured the world-famous George Cruikshank to illustrate his pirated edition of *Uncle Tom's Cabin*. Later, in 1853, Cruikshank's *The Uncle Tom's Cabin Almanack or Abolitionist Memento* was published with twenty-seven illustrations for those who wished the everyday use of "an inseparable companion" to have "a daily lesson about and to bear a daily witness" to the abolitionist cause. Both works reflect "the tensions and collusions between anti-slavery sentiment and the rapidly evolving forms of Victorian racism which inflect much of the English assimilation of the book" (Wood, 173–174). As Jan Marsh writes, Cruikshank's "visual vocabulary for depicting people of African ancestry came virtually unchanged from the earlier satiric tradition of political and social caricature and proved grotesquely inappropriate to a tale of tragic and heroic suffering," although this disparity between the visual text and the message of the novel is unlikely to have struck Victorians who would have shared Cruikshank's prejudices and stereotypes.[19]

Panoramas (giant narrative paintings with frames describing various poignant moments from the novel) and fine art productions by British artists, as well as the variety of illustrations of the novel in circulation, such as Cruikshank's, brought *Uncle Tom's Cabin* to the Victorian public as a visual as well as literary text. Jan Marsh notes early images such as Louisa

Corbaux's lithograph *Eva and Topsy* (1852) and three academy exhibits, F. S. Cary's *The Escape of Eliza*, G. P. Manley's *Uncle Tom and Cassy*, and Anna E. Blunden's *"Love"* (with Topsy kneeling before Eva) (38). Marsh remarks on the irony of Edwin Landseer's *Uncle Tom and His Wife for Sale*, in which his "shallow" knowledge of the story is evidenced by his ignorance of the central pathos-inducing fact of the novel: that only Tom is sold, thus separating him from his wife (39). The point, regardless, is that knowledge of Stowe's novel was both widespread and superficial. Like the children's books and Cruikshank's illustrations, and like Uncle Tom coffee and china, Uncle Tom became an icon and, ironically, an icon detached from his original, political meaning.

Theatrical productions of the novel were also widespread. Stowe herself wrote a monologue entitled "The Christian Slave" for Mary E. Webb, the daughter of a fugitive slave, who performed both in England and America, including a dramatic reading in London for the Duchess of Sutherland. The first dramatic version of *Uncle Tom's Cabin* to be staged was *Uncle Tom's Cabin: or, the Negro Slave* at the Standard on September 8, 1852. By December 1852, eleven different dramatizations competed on the English stage (Birdoff, 144) including versions at the Standard, the Royal Olympic, the Surrey and the Victoria.[20] By Christmas of that same year, four Uncle Tom pantomimes had appeared. English theatrical productions of the play were well known for their drastic revisions of Stowe's original text. In one London version, Tom is a dashing hero "who performs acrobatic feats and daredevil horseback rides" and is able to escape from the Legree plantation "on a race horse."[21] Hazel Waters argues that *Uncle Tom's Cabin* was well suited to the stage because of its "naturalistic dialogue" and its strong melodramatic situations" (31), but she notes the odd and contradictory connections between these stage versions with their "minstrelised vision of the Black" in Victorian popular culture and earlier theatrical denunciations of slavery in productions of Aphra Behn's *Oroonoko* (39).

Consumption by Victorians of "Uncle Tom" in his various commercial forms ranged across classes, ages, and genders, but it was nearly universal. The *Nonconformist* remarked that *Uncle Tom's Cabin* "is in voracious demand among all classes – the book peeps out from the apron, lies beside the workman at his bench, and is found on every drawing-room table";[22] "In the palace, the mansion, and the cottage, it has rivetted attention. The sons of toil as well as the children of opulence have wept over its pages" (*Eclectic Review*, 720). Of course there were differences in who could buy what: the working-class man probably enjoyed "Tom" in the form of cheap and accessible showings of circulating panoramas while the woman of leisure enjoyed him in her more sedate and cultured daily almanack.

As Stephen A. Hirsch notes, other "public preoccupations" had been "commercialized" before Uncle Tom: an American woman could wear her Jenny Lind slippers while cooking at her Jenny Lind stove and play from her Jenny Lind Songbooks while her husband visited the Jenny Lind Saloon. In the US as well, Uncle Tom's commercialism was "as unprecedented in size as it was in sales": Uncle Tom "became, in his various forms, the most frequently sold slave in American history."[23] From the pantomimes, the magic lantern shows, and songs, including eight "Tom-songs" by the English songwriter Charles Jeffries (Hirsch, 316), as well as the dramas and paintings, however, it isn't clear what exactly the British were buying in Uncle Tom. How can Stowe's commercial success be understood?

An article from the *Hartford Courant* on the occasion of the 150th anniversary of the publication of *Uncle Tom's Cabin* calls Stowe the "Victorian Oprah."[24] This characterization strikes me as slightly wrong. Yes, Stowe was one of the more influential and popular figures of the 19th century, but as a woman she probably could not have been an independent and self-motivated businesswoman propelling forward her empire. In any case, the merchandising and commercialization of Uncle Tom was outside of Stowe's control; unlike Madonna or Britney Spears (or the marketing teams behind these icons of merchandising in contemporary American popular culture), Stowe's success seemed to generate itself.[25] As one reviewer noted, the novel spread like a "disease": "The Uncle Tom epidemic still rages with unabated virulence. No country is secure from its attack. The United States, Great Britain, and, by the latest accounts, Germany and France, have yielded to its irresistible influence" (quoted in Hirsch, 303).

It was precisely this self-generating success that so frightened many Victorian intellectuals and characterized much of the critical reception of Stowe and *Uncle Tom's Cabin* in England. For many Victorian writers, the permeation of Victorian culture by "Uncle Tom" was "notorious" (720), as the *Eclectic Review* termed it. It was as if these writers asked themselves the same question – what did Stowe's success mean – and were frightened by their inability to answer it. Clearly, the unprecedented commercialization of the novel gave Stowe's text unparalleled power, and this made many feel that the novel itself was somehow dangerous or even degenerate. In this sense, the novel acquired a set of meanings derived as much from the words on Stowe's pages as from English reaction to and anxieties triggered by the enormous phenomenon of "Tom-mania."

The most important review of *Uncle Tom's Cabin* appeared in *The Times* on Friday, September 3, 1852.[26] It exemplifies a specific hysterical English reaction to Stowe's novel and defined the terms of debate on which much further discussion of the text would depend.

The review begins with an immediate comment on "Tom-mania." *The Times* concedes that *Uncle Tom's Cabin* is a "decided hit" but notes with disdain its financial excesses: "the authoress has already received from her publishers the sum of '$10,300 as her copy-right premium on three months' sales of the work, – we believe the largest sum of money ever received by any author, either American or European, from the sales of a single work in so short a period of time.'"

Having suggested that something is amiss with this fantastically successful novel, *The Times* engages in fairly straightforward misogyny: "Able as she is, Mrs. Stowe . . . will suffer in the minds of the judicious from the female error. With so good a cause it is a pity that her honest zeal should have out-run discretion." Stowe and her work, in other words, are indiscreet, an error that results from her gender. The review continues with a strategically back-handed compliment: "With the instinct of [a] beginner the clever authoress takes the shortest road to her purpose, and strikes at the convictions of her readers by assailing their hearts . . . Who shall deny to a true woman the use of her true weapons?" Inevitably, the woman writer uses the weapons of her gender, such as "assailing the hearts" of her readers, yet with the equation of "woman writer" and "erring beginner" neatly in place, *The Times* is "content to warn the unsuspecting reader." Reader beware: this inappropriately commercial novel is built out of the indiscretion of women and their female weapons.

A series of similar jabs at Stowe's credibility and at *Uncle Tom's Cabin* generally laces the review. The notice denies the political efficacy of the novel and belittles and denigrates Stowe's portrayal of the condition and plight of blacks in American slavery. Moreover, the review plays on the historical charge of hypocritical concern on the part of middle- and upper-class English for the plight of West Indian blacks at the expense of England's laboring poor, England's "white slaves," in order to undermine English sympathy for the cause of abolitionism. The longstanding conflict between "white slaves" and black slaves was central to the British abolitionist movement: British abolitionists were regularly charged with neglecting the "more important" claims of white Englishmen and women at home while hypocritically focusing on the condition of black slaves.[27]

Having dismissed the novel, however, what's remarkable about *The Times*'s review is how the review's author goes on to write despairingly of the dangers posed by *Uncle Tom's Cabin*. After all, "Tom-mania" is already well underway, and thus *The Times*'s crushing review is peculiarly impotent. Perhaps for this very reason, *The Times* stresses the dangerous manner in which *Uncle Tom's Cabin* works on and corrupts its readers. In particular, the review worries about the susceptibility to Stowe's wiles of readers whose "better natures" may be undeveloped because of their lack of education or culture:

> What becomes of the judgment . . . if the intellect be weak and the heart be strong? We are not ignorant of the mode in which great morals are enforced at our minor theatres, and of the means there taken to impress the imagination and to instruct the intellect by help of the domestic melodrama . . . It is very easy to educe startling lessons from a dramatic work, as it is easy enough for an artist to delineate fear by painting a man with staring eyes, open mouth, and hair on end. Truth, however, demands more delicate dealing, and art that would interpret Truth must watch the harmonies of Nature, which charms not by great "effect," but by her blended sympathy and grace, by her logical and unforced developments. Did we know nothing of the subject treated by Mrs. Stowe, we confess that we should hesitate before accepting much of her coin as sterling metal.

On the one hand, *The Times* has made its case that Stowe ought not to be paid attention to, that her work is unlikely to make a difference, and that it fails to convince. In other words, the review seems pretty confident that Stowe's false metals are not likely to be mistaken for "sterling," that is, good, sound English coin. On the other hand, the notice here concedes that Stowe's novel "educe[s] startling lessons" and may, like melodrama, "enforce" by "impress[ing] the imagination" and "instruct[ing] the intellect." While it ought to be ignored, *The Times* despairs that Stowe's novel will and has already achieved success and locates the source of that success in those with "weak intellects" and "strong hearts," clearly an allusion to working-class and female readers. *The Times* writes: "Its very popularity constitutes its greatest difficulty. It will keep ill-blood at boiling point [*sic*], and irritate instead of pacifying those whose proceedings Mrs. Stowe is anxious to influence on behalf of humanity." Indeed, the female-authored novel succeeds in making its male and female readers "excitable," subject to the tempers and irritations of the blood, infecting them, as it were, with the hysteria customarily associated with women. The problem, for *The Times*, is not so much with *Uncle Tom's Cabin* but with the existence of vulnerable readers who not only could but clearly were already being duped by this "clever authoress." "Tom-mania," then, reveals for *The Times* both the inability of the British reading public to discern "truth" and the moral weakening Stowe's melodrama has effected on the nation.

This debate about *Uncle Tom's Cabin*, posed in terms of the disposition and quality of the Victorian reader, the function of popular literature, and the results for Victorian society of improper readers and literature, continued beyond the coterie of *The Times* and its readers. While many periodicals sided with *The Times*, another set of reactions to *Uncle Tom's Cabin* and "Tom-mania" emerged, which allowed the Victorian elite to celebrate rather than mourn Stowe's success.

A review in the *Eclectic Review* turns away from *The Times*'s anxiety about the power of Stowe's novel and follows in a long tradition of using British anti-slavery sentiment and British abolitionist successes as markers of British national stature in order to applaud Stowe's success precisely for what that success indicates about the state of Victorian society.

Abolition was frequently invoked as a testament of British national superiority. Slavery was identified by many writers as a blot on the national character and a stain on the national conscience, and indeed much of the argument against slavery was cast in terms of slavery's effects on the English, and not necessarily in terms of its effects on the slaves. More broadly, the British anti-slavery movement of the eighteenth and early nineteenth century depended on reworking and delinking the negative associations between England and slavery. The famous lines from William Cowper's poem "On Slavery" are perhaps the most well known and the most telling example of this phenomenon. Cowper writes:

> We have no slaves at home – then why abroad?
> And they themselves, once ferried o'er the wave
> That parts us, are emancipate and loosed.
> Slaves cannot breathe in England, if their lungs
> Receive our air, that moment they are free,
> They touch our country and their shackles fall.
> That's noble, and bespeaks a nation proud.
> (lines 39–45)[28]

Cowper's words here, which celebrate the British love for freedom and the proud nobility of the nation, reference the 1772 trial of the slave James Somerset in which Lord Mansfield ruled that slavery was legally unsupported within England and that therefore Somerset, who had been brought to England by his owner, could not be forced to return to the colonies. While this judgment was obviously inspiring to Cowper, and meant freedom to Somerset, its implications were quite limited. Mary Prince, for example, was repeatedly taunted while in England by her owners who cajoled her to leave their house and take her freedom, all the while underlining the dangers such a choice would hold for Prince: "If she goes the people will rob her, and then turn her adrift."[29] Prince writes that, while she knew she was free in England, she "did not know where to go, or how to get my living; and therefore, I did not like to leave the house" (50). When Prince eventually does leave her owners and seek her freedom in England, that freedom means a peculiar version of liberty, since Prince is unable to return to Antigua and to her husband, although she is now able to choose to work for abolitionists instead of her slaveowners. These less laudatory complications of the Somerset decision, not surprisingly, are not allowed to interfere with Cowper's poetic creation of the image of a proud and noble nation.

The review of *Uncle Tom's Cabin* in the *Eclectic Review* follows directly in the tradition of Cowper's poem. With a modicum of British humility and a sense of British responsibility and culpability on the subject of American slavery, the reviewer writes:

> We never recur to the subject of American slavery without pain . . . . As the friends of humanity, we grieve over the wrong done to many of our species; as Englishmen, we are humbled at the part our country has acted in locating slavery in some of the States; and, as Christians, we sorrow in very bitterness of heart at the dishonor done to our holy faith. (717–718)

Mortification at the British role in "locating" or creating American slavery is swiftly transformed, however, by the reviewer's identification of "Englishmen" as "the friends of humanity" and as true "Christians," those who are capable of discerning the purity of "our holy faith" and its pollution through slavery.

The review continues, moving beyond British responsibility for "locating" slavery in the United States and focusing on the "special" relationship between England and the young American republic.

> We rejoice rather that the Anglo-Saxon spirit was sufficiently ripe on the other side of the Atlantic to wrest from the feeble hands of English statesmen a supremacy of which they were unworthy, and which they so little understood. Our feelings towards the American states is that of brotherhood. Attached ourselves to a monarchical government, we cheerfully recognize the many noble features of their republican constitution. We admire their energy, their intelligence, their self-reliance, – nay, we sympathize somewhat with the proud, defiant air with which they stand before the older communities of Europe . . . we are rendered jealous for the good name of America. (718)

An open-minded, sympathetic England looks to its revolutionary brother with pride, this passage seems to suggest, not with bitterness or in ill judgment. American energy and spirit stem from Anglo-Saxon roots, an inheritance shared by their English brothers. The emphasis, however, is on the quality of English good will and cheerfulness for recognizing and being unthreatened by America's republican constitution in contrast to the monarchical government of England.

America, however, is not a "new sanctuary, provided in the providence of God," for freedom (718). American society is, in fact, a pariah because of "the one foul blot which rests on the escutcheon of America": slavery (718). The misguided Americans who belittle the "foul blot" or who try to blame England for its existence only reveal instead their own inferiority:

> Call it what they may; palliate its enormity as they please; discourse however fluently on the limits of federal legislation, or fling back passionately on our people, as they are accustomed to do, the charge of originating the system; the thing itself remains – a hideous, misshapen monster. (718)

Whether or not England originated slavery in America, it is only to the national detriment of the United States that it remains. "Outraged humanity cries shame on the abettors of such a system, and leaves them no alternative but to abandon its atrocities, or to write themselves outcasts from the virtuous and true-hearted of their race" (738). The *Eclectic Review*, finally, celebrates Stowe's novel and its enormous cultural power because the British embrace of Uncle Tom makes clear that the British are "the virtuous and true-hearted of their race." If "Tom-mania" is frightening for *The Times*, it is, for the *Eclectic Review*, reassuring in cementing British superiority.

British superiority was very much in need of reassurance, especially at the initial moment of "Tom-mania" in 1852. The discrepancy between the British monarchical system and American democracy was only one potential threat to the British self-image of enlightened world leader. The eighteen-fifties found Britain anxious to forget on the one hand the devastation of the "Hungry Forties" in which poverty wreaked havoc on the British poor and on the other hand the unresolved political conflicts of Chartism, the working-class movement for universal male suffrage and political reform. These reforms were not achieved, however, and Chartism was by 1852 "merely a residue."[30] Its decline has been attributed to a number of factors, including police action and restrictions by the British legal system. The Newport Rising, for example, illustrates both these effects, with 22 Chartists killed by the police and three protesters sentenced to death for their participation in the political protest. In any case, by the 50s, a better economic climate and increasing industrial stability also account for a decline in working-class agitation. The disturbances of Chartism and the threat they posed to British national identity, however, continued to linger into the more prosperous 50s and found their voice in the industrial novels written by many Victorians including Dickens, Eliot, Bronte, and Gaskell.

It is not surprising, then, that Uncle Tom would figure into this ideological equation. We've seen, after all, *The Times* referencing the long-standing charge that abolitionists callously turned their attention to the plight of blacks at the expense of the poor and politically disenfranchised at home. Reviews of Stowe's novel regularly invoked this comparison between England's "white slaves" and America's black slaves. In considering the ways in which Uncle Tom may have entered into this politically charged territory for Victorians, I want to turn to a little-known fictional response to Stowe's novel, the anonymously published *Uncle Tom in England*.[31] Generally, I've focused here on reactions to Uncle Tom in the periodical press, in part because those writers were responsible for setting and shaping the terms of debate around *Uncle Tom's Cabin*. But an examination of this odd fictional response to Stowe, a novel with perhaps average sales and passing attention from the periodicals of the day, underlines what may have been potentially transgressive for Victorians about Stowe's novel.

While Stowe's novel sends its free blacks back to Africa, *Uncle Tom in England* endorses "amalgamation" (123) in Canada as well as missionary work in Africa, but it is most important for the work it does in imagining a political union between Chartism and abolitionism. The novel invents a new Tom and takes him and a variety of new characters, along with Stowe's George Harris and Emmeline, through the twists and turns of its plot, to England, where the fugitive slaves meet Chartists and discuss the shared plight of "white slaves and black slaves" (123).

In the hands of the unknown author of *Uncle Tom in England*, however, both Chartism and abolitionism are drained of their radical nature and represented as peaceful movements, unthreatening to the social and political status quo. First, Victorian readers are instructed to reject the unresolved struggles of Chartism as the irrational work of a small band of drunk, wife-beating illiterates who don't really represent the movement. Next, these readers are assured that the abolitionist movement and the real Chartism are structured on the principle of self-improvement, not revolution. For the slave and the working-class man, the obstacle to liberty is not the institutions of slavery or legal barriers such as the 1845 General Enclosure Act, which allowed the wealthy to enclose and deny peasant use of previously common land. The obstacle to freedom for both lies within the self. If the slave and the working man educate themselves and practice self-governance and seek moral improvement, the novel insists that the "gates of liberty will fly open of their own accord" (40). The novel even presents us with a Chartist who argues that the campaign to abolish American slavery must take precedence over Chartism: "a very important step to reform in our kingdom would be the abolition of slavery by the republic of America" (115). In other words, readers of *Uncle Tom in England* are rather absurdly presented with the idea that the oppressed of both nations can defeat their enemies through self-improvement and that Chartists are willing patiently to put aside their claims in support of their black brothers. *Uncle Tom in England* seems to have been written to address and defuse the frightening question of what would happen if Chartists and fugitive slaves were to get together and link their causes. That this novel was written, published, and achieved even a modicum of success suggests "Tom-mania" raised this fearful possibility of political alliance for more than just one anonymous novelist.

In 1853, Harriet Beecher Stowe traveled to England "for what would now be called a publicity tour" (Marsh, 38), and her visit was marked by a dynamic quite similar to that provoked by her novel. While British women presented Stowe with gifts and attention at every turn, most remarkable were the "Penny Offering" and "An Affectionate and Christian Address of Many Thousands of Women of Great Britain and Ireland to Their Sisters the Women of the United States of America." Since Stowe had received no royalties from the British sales of her pirated novel, the idea of the "Penny Offering" was for each reader to contribute one penny to the author; in all, Stowe was presented with $20,000. The "Christian Address," meanwhile, contained a detailed petition protesting slavery's "outrages on the Christian family," particularly laws that "deny in effect to the slave the sanctity of marriage" and the practice of denying to slaves "education in the truths of the Gospel and the ordinances of Christianity"; the petition was signed by over a half million women, filling "twenty-six thick volumes."[32] Yet while the people embraced Stowe with their attention, affection, and money, the press continued to complain that she was financially irresponsible and that her work neglected the plight of England's own "white slaves." In particular, Stowe's patron, the Duchess of Sutherland, was accused of evicting her poor tenants from her Scottish estates and setting the blankets of an old woman's bed on fire when she refused to leave (Wilson, 365). And Stowe herself was accused of exploiting London's distressed needlewomen, using for her dressmaking women who worked "sixteen hours a day, six days a week, for pitiful wages" (Wilson, 383). Both charges reflect the same kinds of attempt to respond to and control a woman whose popularity and appeal were seemingly unlimited and uncontrollable.

If nearly everyone in mid-Victorian England was consuming Uncle Tom, both as a character and as a fitting decoration for their wallpaper, this embrace was not just about sympathy for Tom or Topsy or Eva. Without foreclosing the possibility of genuine connection with and legitimate concern for the plight of American slaves on the part of Victorian readers, it's clear that much of the reaction to *Uncle Tom's Cabin* went beyond Stowe and Uncle Tom. The reviewers' attempts to fix the way in which Stowe's text was read and to control interpretations of *Uncle Tom's Cabin* may serve best as a testament to the transgressive power of "Tom-mania." In the end, "Tom-mania" may have threatened to disturb and disrupt but was also used to shore up British national identity.[33]

NOTES

I am grateful to Cindy Weinstein for her help with this essay.

1. Robert Forrest Wilson, *Crusader in Crinoline: The Life of Harriet Beecher Stowe* (Philadelphia: J. B. Lippincott Company, 1941), 302.

2. "Uncle Tom's Cabin," *The Morning Chronicle* (September 16, 1852), 3.

3. Review of *Uncle Tom's Cabin, The Eclectic Review* (December 1852), 720–721; "Uncle Tom's Cabin," *Blackwood's Edinburgh Magazine* (October 1853, vol. 74, no. 256), 393.

4. For a discussion of the relation between American abolition generally and Victorian culture, see Audrey Fisch, *American Slaves in Victorian England: Abolitionist Politics in Popular Literature and Culture* (Cambridge: Cambridge University Press, 2000).

5. R. J. M. Blackett, *Building an Antislavery Wall: Black Americans in the Atlantic Abolitionist Movement, 1830–1860* (Ithaca: Cornell University Press, 1983), 198.

6. Debbie Lee, *Slavery and the Romantic Imagination* (Philadelphia: University of Pennsylvania Press, 2002), 6. See also Helen Thomas, *Romanticism and Slave Narratives: Transatlantic Testimonies* (Cambridge: Cambridge University Press, 2000).

7. Richard Altick, *Victorian People and Ideas* (New York: W.W. Norton and Company, 1973), 67.

8. Altick writes that "it is impossible to distinguish cause from effect" in terms of the expansion of the reading public, on the one hand, and the advances which made "the printed word both cheaper and more readily accessible than it had ever been before" (64).

9. Mary Hamer, *Writing by the Numbers: Trollope's Serial Fiction* (Cambridge: Cambridge University Press, 1987), 15.

10. Richard Altick, *The English Common Reader: A Social History of the Mass Reading Public, 1800–1900* (Chicago: University of Chicago Press, 1957), 68–69.

11. Louis James, *English Popular Literature: 1819–1851* (New York: Columbia University Press, 1976), 18.

12. J. B. Estlin, letter to J. Otis, Bristol, November 5, 1845 (American Anti-Slavery Society Papers, MsA 9.2 vol. 21), 87–88.

13. Frederick Douglass, *Narrative of the Life of Frederick Douglass, an American Slave* (New York: Penguin, 1982), 98–99.

14. "The Theatres," *The Spectator* (December 4, 1852, no. 1275), 1160.

15. Quoted in Stephen A. Hirsch, "Uncle Tomitudes: the popular reaction to *Uncle Tom's Cabin*," *Studies in the American Renaissance* (1978), 305.

16. Douglas A. Lorimer, *Colour, Class, and the Victorians: English Attitudes to the Negro in the Mid-Nineteenth Century* (London: Leicester University Press, 1978), 85.

17. Marcus Wood, *Blind Memory: Visual Representations of Slavery in England and America, 1780–1865* (New York: Routledge, 2000), 146–147.

18. Harry Birdoff, *The World's Greatest Hit: "Uncle Tom's Cabin"* (New York: S. F. Vanni, 1947), 144–145.

19. Jan Marsh, "From slave cabin to Windsor Castle: Josiah Henson and 'Uncle Tom' in Britain," *19th Century Studies* (vol. 16, 2002), 38.

20. Hazel Waters, "Putting on 'Uncle Tom' on the Victorian stage," *Race and Class* (vol. 42, no. 3, 2001), 31.

21. Thomas F. Gossett, *Uncle Tom's Cabin and American Culture* (Dallas, Texas: Southern Methodist University Press, 1985), 282.

22. "Uncle Tom's Cabin," *The Nonconformist* (September 8, 1852), 708.

23. Hirsch, 311. Hirsch writes about the proliferation of Tom paraphernalia in England *and* the U.S.

24. Kendra Hamilton, "The strange career of Uncle Tom," *Black Issues in Higher Education* (vol. 19, issue 8, June 6, 2002), 22.

25. Although Stowe was not an independent businesswoman, she may have fanned the flames of her success by traveling to England on a sort of "publicity tour" (Marsh, 38) in 1853. But as Joan Hedrick writes, Stowe's was a "retired and womanly species of self-promotion." She "*used* modesty . . . as an efficient means to community action that would ultimately redound to her credit." Hedrick cites, for example, Stowe's reluctance about large public meetings, which were held in her honor in Glasgow, Edinburgh, Dundee and London, and Stowe's conventional behavior at these meetings, where she sat quietly while her husband read her speeches or speeches of his own. Hedrick also recounts Stowe's now famous response to Eliza Cabot Follen, a writer of children's stories, that "I am a little bit of a woman. . . . Very modest." *Harriet Beecher Stowe: A Life* (New York: Oxford University Press, 1994), 238–240.

26. "Uncle Tom's Cabin," *The Times* (September 3, 1852), 5.

27. The comparison between England's white slaves and America's black slaves was being deployed in the United States as well, most famously by George Fitzhugh in *Cannibals All! Or Slaves without Masters* (Cambridge, MA: Harvard University Press, 1960). In this 1856 text, Fitzhugh argues in favor of the paternal structure of slavery and criticizes British abolitionists: "What vile hypocrisy to shed crocodile tears over the happy negro, and boast of British Liberty, which is daily and hourly consuming, by poverty, and cold, and foul air and water, and downright starvation, the lives of ten millions of your white brethren and neighbors!" (186).

28. William Cowper, "On slavery," in Duncan Wu, ed., *Romanticism* (Malden, MA: Blackwell, 1994), 9–10.

29. Mary Prince, *The History of Mary Prince, a West Indian Slave*, in William L. Andrews and Henry Louis Gates Jr., eds., *The Civitas Anthology of American Slave Narratives* (Washington, Civitas, 2000), 51.

30. G. D. H. Cole, *Chartist Portraits* (London: Macmillan, 1941), 22.

31. Anonymous, *Uncle Tom in England; Or, A Proof that Black's White* (London: Houlston and Stoneman, 1852).
32. Hedrick, 245.
33. The question of how England's embrace of Tom-mania translated or failed to translate into an active anti-slavery position when it came to the American Civil War has fascinated historians and has received a resurgence of attention in recent years. See D. G. Wright, "Bradford and the American Civil War," *The Journal of British Studies*, 8.2 (1969), 69–85 and "Leeds politics and the American Civil War," *Northern History*, 9, 1974 (96–122); Mary Ellison, *Support for Secession* (Chicago: University of Chicago Press, 1972), and Wendy F. Hamand, "'No voice from England': Mrs. Stowe, Mr. Lincoln, and the British in the Civil War," *The New England Quarterly*, 31.1, March 1988, 3–24.

6

JUDIE NEWMAN

Staging black insurrection: *Dred* on stage

Discussing the 1924 film version of *Uncle Tom's Cabin*, Linda Williams comments that it is memorable for its staging of an unprecedented moment of black-on-white violence. In the film Cassy steals Legree's gun, to protect Emmeline against rape. But although she holds the gun to Legree's head she is unable to shoot. Later a black male slave picks up the gun and stalks Legree.

> These two moments in which black hands hold guns to white human targets are unprecedented in the Tom tradition. . . . Until this moment interracial violence has been pictured exclusively as that of white masters abusing black slaves. This second instance, which culminates in the male slave actually shooting Legree, is especially striking.[1]

Most stage versions of *Uncle Tom's Cabin* did avenge Tom with Legree's death, but usually at the hands of George Shelby, a white male. Even George Harris raises a gun against slave-catchers only in defence of his family. The violence in the film scene is not just directed at foiling masters by escape, but at avenging the violence committed against the slave. As Williams notes, the spectacle of righteous black revenge was considered so deeply incendiary that some prints of the film omit the scene.

Let us compare Williams's comment with the following scene.

> Harry draws out a bowie knife, exclaims "Brother, thus I thank you." Raises it to strike, when Dred suddenly appears at back followed by Jim. He raises his rifle at the moment, exclaims "Fatal rifle now for your last shot." Fires and shoots Gordon. Phillips, unpaginated

Dred is black, Tom Gordon white and the half-brother of Harry, a mulatto slave. The scene occurs in the Victoria Theatre, London, adaptation of Stowe's other abolitionist novel, *Dred: A Tale of the Great Dismal Swamp*.[2] In John Brougham's adaptation Dred shoots Tom dead, with the cry "Vengeance is mine, saith the Lord. I will repay" (Brougham, 38). At Astley's

Amphitheatre, London, and in the juvenile versions, Dred shoots Tom dead. In both Suter's and Conway's versions, Dred shoots Tom who disappears into quicksand. At the Surrey Theatre, London, Tiff, a black slave, saves the day with his pistols and Dred shoots Tom dead in a general melée. At the Britannia Saloon, London, not one but two black characters accomplish the killing. Tom is about to shoot Harry when two shots ring out and he falls dead, simultaneously targeted by Dred, up a tree, and Tomtit, who emerges to reveal that "I too had a pop at him" (29). In short, in every extant dramatic version of *Dred* a black kills a white. Although Harry often threatens his white half-brother, it is always the all-black characters who kill. Vengeance is frequently invoked. Tiff and Tomtit, the former a feminized docile slave who functions as a comic mother figure to the orphaned Cripps children, the latter a male Topsy (memorably portrayed by Cordelia Howard, a famous child actress), also locate violence in potentially female hands, with Tiff often in female garb, and Tomtit played by a girl. The actors may have been white, but the available evidence indicates that Dred, Tiff and Tomtit were played in blackface. Closer examination of the adaptations of *Dred* reveals a wealth of material, hitherto unknown, which provides a more complex understanding of the possibilities of portraying black agency in public in the immediate antebellum period. The adaptations demonstrate that Stowe's own readership was much more prepared to envisage violent solutions on stage than has been thought.

Reams have been written about the dramatic adaptations of *Uncle Tom's Cabin*, but published critical commentary on *Dred* as a drama hardly runs to a dozen pages.[3] Until the 1990s, with the novel itself out of print, any discussion of Stowe's abolitionist writing was almost entirely confined to *Uncle Tom's Cabin*. Inevitably this exacerbated the misleading view of Stowe as a propagator of the stereotypical image of the docile, passive slave as a traitor to his race (the "Uncle Tom" of popular parlance), and encouraged critics to see Stowe as a well-meaning, but fundamentally paternalist white, whose views reflected romantic racialism and the early abolitionist belief in "colonization", the transportation of American black citizens "back" to Africa. The awareness that Stowe's second abolitionist novel focused on slave insurrection and white mobocracy, dismantling the economic case against slavery, while ruthlessly dissecting the institutional roles of the Law and the Church, has led to a contemporary reassessment of Stowe's reputation, allowing for the emergence of a much more radical, less conciliatory writer. Although insurrection is forestalled in the novel, the rhetoric of the central rebel, Dred, is unashamedly vengeful and inflammatory and the rising tide of violence carries all the black characters to freedom (albeit, for reasons of fictional realism, in Canada) by the close of the action.

Readers of Dred have from the beginning debated why Stowe aborted the insurrection, and why she killed off her heroine and destroyed the romantic plot. The dramatic adaptations demonstrate just how astute Stowe was in making these choices. In the novel Stowe's strategy was to counter the stereotype of the passive black male (the "Uncle Tom") with an active, strong hero, but at the same time to avoid the risk of demonizing the black hero as a brute, by demonstrating that the violence of the slave south emanated from whites (in lynch mob scenes) rather than from insurrectionary blacks. On stage, the British adaptors maintain the image of the strong, violent black hero, but thus play into the stereotype of the violent black. In America, productions tone down the effect of the killing by leaving most of the slaves in the south, by providing them with northern protectors and by moving the initiative to white characters. As a result the plays are less likely to confirm the "black brute" stereotype – but diminish black agency. Strengthening the courtship plot between the heroine Nina and her reformist suitor, Edward Clayton, American adaptors allow her to marry and safeguard her slaves. Instead of dying in a cholera epidemic, Nina survives as a benevolent southern protector, quite the reverse of Stowe's novel which relies for its horror on the fact that at the close of the action Tom Gordon is alive and still holds slaves in his power. Unhampered by censorship, American adaptors offer moral uplift and the consolations of religion.

American and British adaptations varied considerably, in their differing emphases on black and female agency, and in their respective support for violent resistance as opposed to gradual reform. Productions ranged from the supposedly improving "museum" show, to popular melodrama, burlesque, "penny dreadful", equestrian spectacle and children's theatre, with the hero successively transformed from messianic prophet of doom, to violent insurrectionist, noble pacifist, trick rider, cardboard puppet, and, in one case, villainous Jewish moneylender. There are at least four separately authored American adaptations, seventeen British, one Russian, and a Bulgarian translation. Eight printed versions of the play exist; others survive only in grimly illegible manuscripts, in summary on the playbills of the time, or in stray references. Selling to large numbers in a successful run meant that their influence was considerable. In New York, Purdy's held 2,500 people, the Bowery 3,000; in London the Victoria held 2,000 in the gallery alone. Frederick Phillips's adaptation ran initially for 41 nights, Conway's for 31. In Britain, the play was a sure thing for actor-managers. Phillips (forced to close after staging Italian opera) reopened with *Dred* and saved his financial bacon. The dramatic adaptations were quite clearly understood as at least as important to the abolitionist cause as the novel itself. As one contemporary reviewer commented,

> Whatever may be Mrs Beecher Stowe's private opinion of theatrical represen-
> tations, there can be no doubt that to them she is indebted for much of the
> popularity which she enjoys; and if she is really earnest in the cause of Negro
> emancipation, she should hail as fellow labourers those who so vividly rep-
> resent her views to thousands of English people through the medium of the
> drama.   *Era*, October 26, 1856

What were the differences between the national adaptations? Essentially, American versions appear to have been politically conservative, as opposed to the more forthright British stage. In America women characters (unless singing) exist only to faint or die, but in Britain they may actually save the day. British versions use the play as a vehicle for anti-American sentiments; American versions use it to cater to northern interests. All American versions add comic attorneys and Yankees, misogyny, happy endings, direct manifes-tations of God's will, and moral or educational instruction. The British are more enthusiastic about displays of flagellation than of education. Where adaptations of *Uncle Tom's Cabin*, contaminated by the tradition of black-face minstrelsy, came to focus on the more passive and inherently racist fictional elements, featuring a kindly (and almost geriatric) Uncle Tom, and happy plantation "darkies", and almost entirely discounting female agency, British dramatizations of *Dred* often did just the reverse, in some cases even putting Stowe's projected insurrection into action.

To the modern reader *Dred* may not seem an ideal candidate for dra-matic adaptation, and the anonymous reviewer for *The Times* was similarly doubtful:

> Whatever impression may be made upon any given reader by Mrs Stowe's last
> novel – whether he weeps or yawns, sympathises or disbelieves – the last thing
> he will dream of will be the possibility of using the story he has just perused
> as the plot of a drama producible on the English Stage.

Dred "with his mouth perpetually overflowing with Scriptural phraseology, scarcely utters six lines which would be tolerable if spoken within the walls of a theatre"; the cholera was "a Nemesis that does not readily wear a pic-turesque form"; Nina's "lively rattle" was too garrulous; and there were insuperable difficulties to staging a camp meeting and a Presbyterian con-ference. The plot lines of the novel include: a courtship plot in which Nina Gordon chooses Edward Clayton from other suitors; the death of Nina and her uncle John from cholera, half way through the action; a planned slave insurrection led by Dred, renegade son of Denmark Vesey; satirical por-trayals of the American clergy; a camp meeting attended by slave drivers; a fiendish villain, Nina's brother Tom, in what John Wayne would have called the "dog heavy" role; attempts by Harry (Tom's slave half-brother) to buy his freedom, thwarted by Tom (coincidentally intent on the sexual possession of Harry's wife Lisette); the re-enslavement by Tom of Harry's freed sister Cora, who murders her children to save them from slavery and is condemned to death; two courtroom dramas concerning the assault of the slave Milly by her master; Edward Clayton's Utopian experiment at Magnolia Grove with a school, public baths and trial by jury for slaves; a "poor white" sub-plot heavily based on the temperance novel involving the drunken Cripps, his tragic wife, Old Tiff their slave, two orphan children and Polly Skinflint, Cripps's second, rum-soaked partner; and finally shipwreck with miraculous preservation and translation of almost all the good characters to Canada. Something for all the family was offered here.

None the less, adaptations were almost immediate. The novel was published on August 22, 1856 in both Britain and America. By the end of the year more than a dozen adaptations had reached the stage. Only one production had any association with Stowe, who neither attended nor profited from any of them. C. W. Taylor produced a version at Purdy's National Theatre which was, according to an advertisement in the *New York Tribune*, September 12, 1856, sanctioned by Stowe and prepared from the page proofs of the novel. First in the field in London was H. Young at the Victoria, a theatre known for its lower-class audiences and its large capacity. Considerable liberties were taken with the plot. Nina, married to her cousin Harry, with a child, is unaware of his slave origins. Both are committed opponents of slavery and as the play opens Harry has bought an estate on free soil, and plans to leave Carolina forever. Tom Gordon has overthrown his uncle's will to prevent Harry's manumission and tracks Harry down. The play illustrates the risks of demonizing slave characters, when affirming black agency. Milly, Harry's free black mother, appears to Nina in the swamp, muffled in a long dark cloak. Nina's companion, Livy Ray, promptly assumes she is the devil. When Milly reveals herself, Nina asks "Dark mysterious woman, why do you seek me?" (30). Darkness and blackness are fully elided in a gothic iden-tification of blackness with evil which is almost Hawthornesque. The play emphasizes black agency, directly raising the accusation of black passivity only to counter it. Dred invokes the example of Native-American resistance.

> These tyrants tried to make slaves of the Indians, but they burst their bonds quickly and paid them shot for shot. But Africans are slaves because they will be slaves.
>
> (36)

When Hannibal objects that they are unarmed, Dred opens the door of his loghut to reveal a fully stocked armory. In Act One a desperate conflict between slaves and pursuers leads to the siege of the loghut, and a general melée presided over by Dred on the roof, proclaiming

You have raised the fire that you cannot quench. You will all be swallowed by sword and fire. Fire. Vengeance. Vengeance is to come.   (44)

With the wood in apocalyptic flames, the cabin door opens to reveal a further conflagration amidst "the crackling and falling of burning trees" (44) as the characters freeze into a tableau. The melodramatic mode continues into the second act with Tom Gordon offering to trade Harry's freedom for Nina's virtue, but Dred swaps the revolutionary for the trickster mode, appearing somewhat improbably as a slave trader ("large hat so as practically to conceal his features" 52), and setting Harry free. All is not yet over, however, since the full spectacular possibilities of the swamp remain to be exploited. The stage direction is detailed.

> The front of the stage represents the island portion. Across the stage there is a barricade of Cat-Briars and wild vine. Right and left are stunted trees and the dark vegetation of the morass. Beyond the barrier is the lagoon and at the extreme back, the sinking swamp formed by tussocks or mounds of turf.   (70)

When Tom's party reaches the hideout, the sinking swamp gives way and swallows them up. Notwithstanding the best efforts of Dred and the swamp, Harry is apprehended and the play ends with a courtroom drama. Despite Clayton's spirited defence of both Harry and "the whole oppressed race" (95), Harry is condemned to die within the hour. Faithfully repeating the main satirical points made in the novel's courtroom scenes, the judge proclaims that "We must support the master as his power must be absolute" (92) and informs Harry that "The African race are foredoomed" (94). Harry's reply is forthright in its challenge to racial definitions.

> But I am not of the African race. I am Colonel Gordon's son. Look at my hair, my eyes. I am not darker than my brother who stands there thirsting for my blood. My language is the same as yours.   (94)

In a surprising twist, the day is saved by Milly who reveals herself as Tom's mother, not Harry's. In their infancy Milly, the wetnurse for both children, had swapped them in the cradle. Dr. Butler identifies Harry as the rightful heir by a birthmark shaped like a bunch of grapes (presumably referring to the grapes of wrath). Dred, dying, foresees the inevitability of sectional conflict.

> There's a storm rising in the South, a dreadful struggle will take place in the great nation. The Union will be rent, like her flag of stars and stripes. The stripes of the South may triumph for a while over the lacerated hearts of the poor Negro slave, but in their turn they will fade before the bright stars of the North.   (102)

The British were not disinterested and were as keen on promoting their own national superiority as abolitionism. The pun on stripes (whipping) had made its appearance earlier in the play as part of a pro-British, anti-American rhetoric when Jim tells Hannibal, who has been flogged,

> You allars supported de stars and de stripes and at last you get him belly full
> of de stars and de stripes. (35)

A similar attack on American notions of liberty emerges with the criminalization of American Independence when Tom tells Clayton that "We will have niggers, 'tis our right" (47).

> Clayton: Who gave you that right?
> Tom: Why the Constitution of the Glorious Union to be sure. The finest
> government in the world. (47)

(Cue hissing and booing from the patriotic British pit.) The British delight in their naval triumphs, and hence in nautical melodrama, also influences the play. Scene Seven opens at Magnolia Grove, now incongruously situated on the ocean shore with "Open Sea at back," where "the Nigger minstrels" appear with banjos, tambourines and stirring chorus. Even minstrelsy gives way to the gathering storm in the south, however. Thunder breaks up the dancing. Clayton comments (ominously, since Tiff and the orphans are at sea in a small boat named the *Liberator*) that the cloud has burst and the sea is rising. The *Liberator*, named for the flagship periodical of the American abolitionist cause, is not much help here to the unfortunate slaves, and makes its appearance only to sink. Tiff makes it to shore by brute force. In short, Clayton's gradualism and the verbiage of the abolitionist cause are roundly defeated, and the black characters carry the day by physical strength. Power is unambiguously vested in the black slaves.

Importantly, the ability to take control of events includes the women characters. If somewhat sinister, Milly is a genuinely interesting character, torn between saving her son and telling the truth. At the end she saves Harry purely of her own moral volition. When Mark Twain borrowed this element of the plot for his *Pudd'nhead Wilson*, lifting the swapped babies, the cloaked disguises, and the sharp young lawyer from dramatic versions of the tale, he transformed Milly into Roxy but saved the falsely enslaved character by male, white intervention.[4] Twain also allows for the possibility that Tom is a cowardly villain because of his black blood, whereas the Victoria's cast of heroic blacks undermines biological determinism. On the other hand, in this adaptation, as opposed to Stowe's idealized maternity, mothers, whether biological or adopted, are just plain dangerous. Polly Cripps is not remotely comic and attempts to sell the white Cripps orphans into slavery.

The next London adaptation, at the Britannia Saloon, is credited to Mrs. Denvil, and as the subtitle indicates, marks the beginning of a growing interest in Tiff and the "poor white" characters. As the only woman to adapt the play, Mrs. Denvil none the less offered a depiction of slavery which was not for the fainthearted, and emphasized women's sufferings and sexual exploitation. Jack Benton, a slave dealer, is seen with a coffle of slaves, including Cora Gordon, unrepentant over her infanticide. Dred taunts Harry for his inability to protect his wife:

> Women always like the master better than the slave. I am a freeman. You are
> a slave. . . . No man whips me. (23)

In case the audience had missed the point, the following scene depicts Hark, a slave who refused to betray his fellows, flayed alive, with whips, wooden shingles and boiling water. The final tableau shows the rebels posed beside a huge flaming pine tree, the sign of insurrection. The overall effect, in a house apparently crowded to excess, was summed up by the reviewer for the *Era* (October 5, 1856, p. 11, col. 1) who thundered that the play was

> calculated to show the debasing nature of slavery as still practised in an enlightened age in North Carolina.

Not all London productions resisted the lure of minstrelsy, however, which reduced active black characters to clownish stereotypes. At the Queen's, W. E. Suter started the action three months after Nina's death, on her 21st birthday when she should have opened sealed papers from her father, guaranteeing Harry's freedom. Tomtit finally discovers the lost papers which reveal Harry as the rightful heir to the plantation. Violence is again prevalent, and not limited to the males. Katy, a slave, pushes Tom around, Tiff is lashed onstage by his master, but rescued by Dred, who promptly flogs Cripps. Even the Cripps orphans join in ("children belabor Jim with bamboos," 21). But Suter's play is deeply marked by racism, leaves mixed-race Harry a happy slave-owner, makes no case for emancipation, and is heavily orientalist. The printed version notes Dred's costume as involving a feathered cap, moccasins and a leopard-skin pouch, a curious mixture of Native American and African, while the plantation house is Indian, furnished with "matting, ottomans, skins." It includes a stereotypical blackface exchange of malapropisms between the slaves Jim and Katy. Katy resents Jim's "resulting" speech and threatens to "infect" someone else and Jim gets "seriously defended" (12). They are reconciled when he describes her as a stellar "consternation" and they look forward to a grand "sore-eye" (soirée). The pair sing duets, one of which includes this verse from Jim:

> Him is black, oo is brown,
> Both am nobby figger,
> And no doubt, our first born
> Will be a piebald nigger.
>
> (28)

Although the play does involve calls for liberty, it is notable that all those prepared to fight say so in standard English. The more passive slaves use dialect. The stage directions stress the spectacular with "every resource of scenic and mechanical effect introduced to give due effect to the novel and harrowing catastrophe" (iv). Hark fares no less well than at the Britannia; he plunges headlong into the swamp and disappears. Suter essentially staged the Victorian equivalent of a disaster movie, the main point of which was, as the play proclaimed at the start, "Destruction of the Villain Gordon" (iv). The interest was in rewarding individual virtue and punishing vice, rather than in abolishing slavery.

Frederick Phillips's adaptation, performed at the Surrey, was much more faithful to the novel. Dred is closer to Stowe's visionary hero and makes his initial entrance, leaning on his rifle and soliloquizing to the moonlight.

> Fair moonlight, how I love you. You are free. I contemplate your beauty and am lost in wonder at your pale and shining rays. I look to earth and lovely as it is the reptile Man has blurred and blotted all.   (n.p.)

Dred is neither demon nor brute, and a firm Christian, if a rather muscular one. He informs Clayton that

> nature hath assigned two sovereign remedies for human grief, religion, surest, finest best. Strength to the weak and to the wounded balm, and strenuous action next.

Once in strenuous action, he is unstoppable:

> He fires. A man falls. He knocks two others down with his clubbed rifle. Seizes Tom Gordon. Throws him in the air. He falls heavily, and lays stunned. While doing this the others rise and are about to stab him, as he giving a turn stands pistol in hand over the body.

When Tom Gordon buys Cora, he puts her and her children to work in the fields, and orders Jake to whip her. Cora's (offstage) screams are halted by Dred, who kills Jake, ties up Cripps and Tom, and escapes, returning in the next scene to knock Tom out and rescue Harry and Lisette in their turn.

Unusually, despite the violence, the Surrey production engages with religious issues. In general the British stage avoided religious material because of the draconian censorship laws. By the Theatres Act of 1843, the Lord

Chamberlain had an unlimited power of veto. Scripture was considered unsuitable for the stage, as were all sacred invocations, references to God, Lord, heaven, angels, and any direct quotation from the Bible. The Bible could not be used as a stage property, and it was a serious offense to bring ministers of the Christian religion into contempt, effectively preventing any actor appearing on stage as a clergyman. It is not surprising, therefore, that the British productions remove all reference to the lengthy scenes in Stowe's novel which feature self-serving clergymen – or even heroic abolitionist clergymen. The scenes in the novel in which Tiff learns to read from the Bible, or where characters exchange different Biblical quotations to prove or disprove the rightness of slavery, and the entire camp meeting sequence, were a lost cause to British adaptors. Dred's Biblical rhetoric was also a risk on stage. The Surrey playscript is unusually religious. Stowe left Dred's final destination uncertain, merely stating: "that splendid frame . . . was now to be resolved again into the eternal elements" (636). The Surrey had fewer doubts of his salvation and sent him straight to heaven. *The Times* (October 22, 1856, p. 7, col. 5) noted that "We are informed by a transparency at the end of the piece that the soul of the sable hero is on its road to the realms of bliss." The Examiner of plays promptly demanded large cuts. In one production Mrs. Cripps expires awkwardly invoking "him that they told me had a glory round his head." Dred loses many of his most impassioned pleas for vengeance, and almost all his references to Samson, Gideon, the goad of Shamgar, and the weapon of Jael. References to debauchery were more acceptable. When Lawyer Jekyl informs Harry that slavery is "a great missionary enterprise for civilising and Christianising the degraded" Harry rebuts him, citing "those plantations where nobody is anybody's husband or wife in particular." Tom is clearly established as a sexual predator, who orders his men to take Lisette "into my chamber and tie her down hand and foot." When Harry begs him to "kill her rather" he rejoins, "I mean to, afterwards." This was too much for the Birmingham production which substitutes the instruction to "take her into the barn and tie her up." It is censorship, however, which has preserved the "lost" American version by C. W. Taylor. The Theatres Act forced all theatres to deposit their plays for official licensing, and most of the manuscripts are now in the British Library. The play was performed in London in 1857, and the manuscript survives. In the manuscript the date 1856 is crossed out and replaced by 1857, suggesting that the copy had served in America already.

As Suter's play demonstrates, the possibility of causing offense on racial grounds was not a concern for the censor. Phillips' play also drew on the tradition of minstrelsy. Act Two begins with a slave chorus suggesting the happy plantation myth:

> Happy Nigger, Massa kind,
> Grateful darkies, massa good
> Here him shackles neber find
> Nor lash to spill der nigger's blood

and ends with "a grand negro ballet." Tiff, even armed with pistols, remains a figure of fun, exaggerated on stage by the famous comic actor, Henry Widdicomb. The *Times* reviewer commented

> That Mr Widdicomb in this part would elicit the frequent roars of his audience might be expected, but his occasional touches of pathos deserve especial commendation.

Tomtit and Pompey (a house slave) were equally comic, described by the *Era* (October 16, 1856, p. 11, col. 27) as "amusing specimens of the Jim Crow style of nigger."

The manuscript gives no hint of costume or setting, but two other "productions" by Green and Webb provide the information. Both were designed as juvenile drama to be played in "Toy" theatres. Green features scenes which are only staged in the Surrey production (Cora in the field with her children, baskets of cotton on their backs). Webb credits the play to the Surrey on the title page. The "book" of the play is necessarily much abbreviated but even for children, *le vice anglais* was in evidence: the play maintains the flogging of Cora. Dred dies calling for liberty and vengeance, but Scene 17 portrays him with one arm raised to heaven with eight winged angels about to carry him there. The young producer was instructed to make this scene transparent. The Toy theatre designers were the video pirates of their day, rushing to popular shows to sketch costumes and scenery, and the available evidence suggests that they offered accurate representations of the theatre productions of the 1850s.[5] Costumes show detailed observation; scenery was copied from actual backcloths. The scenes were sold as printed sheets, "ha'penny plain and tuppence coloured" which children pasted on card, mounting the characters on slides which were pushed across the model theatre stage. Dred is shown with a rifle, pistol, powder horn, hunting knife, plumed cap and a skin cloak, and in the manner of swashbuckling men in tights, shows a lot of leg. Tiff wears comically patched clothing and spectacles and pulls a ramshackle baby carriage, to all effects and purposes, a clown. Tiff, Old Hundred, Tomtit, Milly and Dred are portrayed as black, and Milly and Tiff have Negroid features. Slaves are shown in dancing poses with banjos and bones. Unfortunately the indigenous Toy theatre tradition in America does not emerge until 1870, so the British material offers the only evidence available of actual productions.

The extent to which a novel about slavery could be briskly translated from race to class oppression was demonstrated in a burlesque in rhyming couplets at the Bower Saloon, London. The scene opens in a miserable garret to the "Song of the Shirt," with Lucy lamenting how hard she has to work in the garment industry for Solomon Dred, owner of a loan office. Stowe's Messianic avenger has become an anti-Semitic stereotype. Solomon Dred addresses the workers as "you infernal niggers" (n.p.) but there is little connection to American slavery. Dred does some obscure plotting near a swamp, and is foiled by Tiff, who restores an inheritance to his orphans, and invites all to "Ole Tiff's Dredful Party," as the play closes with dancing. The existence of the burlesque demonstrates how swiftly *Dred* had passed into the popular mind; the story was familiar enough to be parodied in a "spoof." The Bower Saloon revived it in August 1859, advertising

> Great attraction for this week! Dred! Dred! Dred! The celebrated swamp scene in which will be introduced Mr Cox's much admired electric light.

Dred was also popular in London on horseback. In the equestrian version at Astley's Amphitheatre every opportunity was taken to bring horses and carriages into the action. The theatre had a conventional stage, plus a sawdust arena in place of the pit, and maintained a stud of circus horses.

American productions of the play are less interested in spectacle and horsemanship and generally more improving. More attention is paid to marital relations than to slavery, with plots focused upon courtship, amply bearing out Jeffrey Mason's contention that all American melodrama centers on a threat to the family unit – or some future family unit.[6] The comic lawyer, happy ending, courtship plot and political conservatism are the mark of the American adaptations. The Boston Museum production survives only in a playbill, which indicates a hefty comic role for Uncle John, played by the famous comic actor William Warren; a comic "solilokum" from a black character; melodramatic motherhood ("Thy Mother is Avenged") and an extended shipwreck scene. Act Five took place in Canada.

C. W. Taylor's version was performed at Purdy's National Theatre. The surviving playbill refers to the fortieth and last representation, a very successful run. The cast list introduces a new character, Peter Tidmarsh, a village attorney, and a happy ending. Little Cordelia Howard starred as Tom Tit, her father as Clayton and her mother as Milly. Cordelia, usually advertised as "The Youthful Wonder Generally Called the Child of Nature," an infant prodigy excelling as Little Eva, was costumed in ragged breeches, blacked up, with her golden curls covered with a horsehair wig. Purdy's National Theatre was advertised as the Temple of the Moral Drama (Birdoff, 76), the lobby adorned with scriptural texts and a picture of Purdy holding a

Bible. Purdy had managed to transform a low dive into a haunt of the middle classes and their pastors, entirely by performing a long run of *Uncle Tom's Cabin*, with matinees for the genteel. The Howards also performed the play in London at the Marylebone Theatre on February 16, 1857. The cast lists for the American and British performances are almost identical, including Abe Pineapple and Peter Tidmarsh, distinctive characters invented for this version. The only difference appears to be that the character of Tiff (played in America by the author of the play) disappears, and is replaced by Milly who looks after the Cripps children in his stead. As usual, Dred kills Tom Gordon ("to glut my vengeance," n.p.) and dies. There is no sign at all of a planned insurrection. Indeed when Tidmarsh assumes that a group of Gordon slaves are up to no good ("some conspiracy – some design against the state") the slaves are actually "on a bender" to the local grog shop, financed by Tom. The implication is that once slaves are left to their own devices they will be drunk and lazy. Only supervision by whites or near-whites will keep the plantation functioning efficiently. Although a slave, Harry warns others that it is only because of their previous good behavior that he has restricted himself to "kind remonstrance rather than the penalty of the lash." This scene may reassure northern audiences that the mass of slaves are under firm control, but it removes Stowe's emphasis on their energy and industry. The battle in the swamp seems to have little to do with slavery or even with blacks; the runaway slaves cry "death to the palefaces" as they launch their attack. More attention is paid to marital relations than to slavery, with the plot focused upon Nina's simultaneous engagement to "three masculine bipeds," Uncle John Gordon's comically henpecked relation to his wife, and the possibility of Anne Clayton marrying Frank Russell. The play ends in rhyming couplets from the main characters, and a wedding.

The other two versions of the play survive in print. H. J. Conway's, performed at Barnum's American Museum, starred General Tom Thumb (famous for his diminutive stature) as Tomtit. The major focus was no longer black agency, but education, with the possibility of insurrection discounted in favor of gradualism, thus entirely reversing Stowe's arguments and depoliticizing the novel. The emphasis shifts from race to gender and class, with the lower classes outwitting feudal aristocrats, and men pitted against women. The cast list includes Uncle John Gordon, "a specimen of the old Virginia gentleman and like many other gentlemen under petticoat government" (2), and Cipher Cute, a droll Yankee lawyer, probably influenced by Penetrate Partyside in Conway's, or Gumption Cute in Aiken's version of *Uncle Tom*. The opening establishes the main problem of the south as female rule. John Gordon has threatened to whip a slave but his wife, a "downright dragon"

(5) vetoes it. Cuff, a lazy slave, refuses to work until Milly seizes him by the ear. When Tiff is introduced, examining the old clothes which Cripps has bought, the emphasis is less on Cripps squandering money, than on the inherent silliness of women's clothing. Tiff, considering a hooped skirt, wonders if it is a fishing net or an eel pot. Feeling around inside the skirt he concludes in favor of a fish trap. Ribald on stage, the scene probably draws upon the minstrel tradition of cross-dressing. To do his laundry, Tiff wears the skirt as an apron, and is comically mistaken for a woman. The dramatic stage thus quite reversed Stowe's emphasis on women's power. By the end of Scene Four one might be forgiven for assuming that the problem of the south was an absence of dominant males. The play satirizes the south and promotes sectional conflict, with Cipher Cute eventually saving the day. Clearly what the female south needed was the guiding hand of a strong northern male. Female and black agency is largely discounted; the white northern man wins a victory for his own class and ethnic group.

American plays had few problems with religion. In Conway's play God is a strong offstage presence. When Harry prays "Father in heaven, whil'st thou art angry, let thy fiery bolt fall" (31), a thunderbolt obediently strikes the window. Brougham does satirise the clergy (Father Bonnie, as in the novel, recruiting for both converts and a new slave cook simultaneously), and Dred's Biblical rhetoric culminates when he calls down clouds to darken the swamp and hide the fugitives. As a result however, everything marks Dred as atypical as compared to other slaves, more a superhuman entity than a human being. When he invokes God's judgment, a tree on stage is struck by lightning and the foliage disappears, leaving the naked trunk blasted. With God so manifestly on his side, it is hardly surprising that political action hangs fire. Nina is left to speak the final words which would not be out of place in Father Bonnie's mouth:

> May we so profit by the teachings of the time gone by, as to make beautiful the records of our future lives. (Brougham, 43)

These pious platitudes exemplify a play concerned with the salvation (moral or physical) of white characters by white characters. Political or legal initiatives are subordinate to Biblical judgments and, despite the satire on the Church, slavery is left to God to abolish.

Comedy was much to the fore in America. John Brougham's production starred T. D. Rice, the originator of the comic black slave role, as Tiff, with Uncle John prominent in the role of cantankerous old curmudgeon (played by Brougham); comic antics from Tomtit; and more stage business with secondhand bonnets. The scene in which Nina is beset by three suitors is played up (Nina unforgettably described as an "ante-nuptial Bluebeard," 25).

Lisette and Tomtit sing a duet to a banjo and the entire cast, apparently oblivious to Harry's flight to the swamp, take themselves off to a camp meeting, entertained en route in full minstrel mode by "The Magnolia Grove Troubadours." Dred hires a schooner to get everyone to freedom but the shipwreck which ensues involves his replacement as hero by a white character named Harry Dreadnaught, who shoves out a lifeboat and saves the day. Tiff is assumed drowned but bobs up again interrupting his own obituary:

> Nina: Nobly and unselfishly he yielded up his life, that we should not be
> perilled.
> Tiff: Bress the Lor', not yet. (43)

It is a tribute to American audiences that this production was a complete failure and ran for less than two weeks, even when twinned with *Pocahontas*.

The performance of Conway's play at Barnum's, an example of supposedly cultured theatre, produced a more educational emphasis. Act Two opens with Anne Clayton's schoolchildren singing

> The blessings of education
> Make us happy on Mas'r's plantation
> And carry freedom throughout a nation.
> (17)

Later Clayton stages a scene involving the schoolchildren positioned either side of the Goddess of Liberty on a pedestal, and a transparency lettered

> Education
> Leads to Present Amelioration
> and Ultimate
> Liberty

Harry has the last word. "When education is fully carried into effect, we shall need no more Dreds to protect fugitive slaves – nor read more tales of the Great Dismal Swamp" (48). In this play, nobody is going to Canada; indeed nobody is going anywhere except to school.

It is easy to underestimate the value of the melodramatic form, and it is perhaps unsurprising that so few critics have examined the dramatisations of *Dred*. Elaine Hadley argues that

> the absence of the melodramatic mode from the record of cultural formation
> in the nineteenth century results in a distorted analysis of the period that has
> overemphasized the dominance and internal consistency of, for example, the
> private sphere, the free market, and the bourgeois nuclear family[7]

as opposed to the melodramatic emphasis on visibility, the gestural and public representation. Stowe's fiction has repeatedly been read as a prime example of privatised, domestic, sentimental writing, with the effect that critics have neglected the more public concerns of *Dred*. But the current could flow the other way and in the adaptations of *Dred* Stowe's novel reached the public sphere, expressing to differing effect in its various performances the relations between America and Britain, North and South, communities of nation, race, gender and class. Lincoln may have addressed Stowe as "the little lady who made this big war" but her dramatic adaptors also played their part.

List of adaptations

Anon., *Dred*. October 27, November 1, 3, 12, 14, 17, 1856. Theatre Royal Sheffield. Two playbills in Sheffield Central Library.

Anon., *Dred, A Tale of the Dismal Swamp. An Equestrian Drama*. November 15, 1856. Astley's Royal Amphitheatre, London. BL Add. MS 52962 (U).

Anon., *Dred: A Tale of the Dismal Swamp*. November 21–28, 1856. Theatre Royal, Nottingham.

Anon., *Dred*. December 1(–6?), 1856, Theatre Royal, Newcastle Upon Tyne, and December 8–10, New Lyceum Theatre, Sunderland. (Possibly by Sydney Davis).

Anon., *Dred*. September 15, 1857. Theatre Royal, Dundee.

Anon., *Dred*. April 24, 1865. Grecian, London.

Anon., *Dred, Or the Dismal Swamp*. October 30–31, and November 1, 1873, Theatre Royal, Hull.

Anon., *Dred, Or The Dismal Swamp*. February 23, 1882, Beverley.

Banks, Walter, *Dred*. November 11, 1872. Prince of Wales, Wolverhampton.

Brougham, John, *Dred: A Tale of the Dismal Swamp*. September 29, 1856, Brougham's, New York. French's American Drama. The Acting Edition, no. 145. New York, 1856.

Brushtein, Aleksandra Yakovlevna, *Khizhina diadi Toma*. Moskva: Gos.izd-vo "Iskusstvo", 1948. *Chicho Tomovata Kolina*. Piesa v tri deistvii. Sofia, Bulgaria: Prevela El. Kostova, 1948.

Chute, James Henry, *Dred*. November 13, 1856, Theatre Royal, Bristol. November 13; March 3–4, 1858, Swansea; and in Bath.

Conway, H. J. *Dred, A Tale of the Great Dismal Swamp*. October 16–November 22, 1856, Barnum's, New York. New York: J. W. Amerman, 1856.

Cowell, William, *Dred! Or -The Dismal Swamp*. n.d. Boston Museum. Broadside. John R. Hartman Center for Sales, Advertising and Marketing History, Duke University Library.

Denvil, Mrs., *Dred, A Tale of the Dismal Swamp; Or, Poor Uncle Tiff*. September 29–30, October 5–11, 13–18, 20–25, 1856. Britannia Saloon, Hoxton, London. BL Add. MS 52962 (H).

Green, J. K., *Dred: The Freeman of the Dismal Swamp*. London: Green's Juvenile Drama, 1856.

Phillips, Frederick Laurence and J. Colman, *Dred. A Tale of the Great Dismal Swamp*. October 10–15, November 24–29, December 1–5, 1856. Surrey Theatre, London. BL Add. MS 52961 (N). Also produced April 20–22 and 25, 1857,

Theatre Royal, Birmingham. Birmingham City Archives. Box 4. Nos 104–109; January 4, 12–17, and February 5, 1857, October 4, 1875 at Theatre Royal, Hull.

Seaman, William, *Dred*. London: G. Purkess, n.d. Purkess's Penny Pictorial Plays No. 26.

Suter, William E., *Dred; Or, The Freeman of the Great Dismal Swamp*. November 1, 3–8, 10–15, 17–18, 20–22, 1856, June 20, 23, 26, 1857, Queen's Theatre, London, and at the Saint John Dramatic Lyceum, Canada, August 20, 1861, and the Pavilion Theatre 1876. *Dred: A Tale of the Dismal Swamp*. London: Lacy's Acting Edition of Plays, vol. 57. [1863?].

Taylor, C. W., *Dred, A Tale of the Dismal Swamp*. September 22–October 25, 1856, Purdy's National Theatre, New York. February 16, 1857, Marylebone Theatre, London; November 30–December 3, 1858, April 2, 1860, Bowery, New York. BL Add. MS 52964 (X).

Townsend, W., *Dred, A Burlesque in One Act*. October 16, 1856, Bower Saloon, Stangate, London. BL Add. MS 52961 (P).

Webb, W., *Dred; Or, The Freeman of the Great Dismal Swamp*. Webb's Juvenile Drama, London: W. Webb, 1856.

Young, H., *Dred! A Tale of the Great Dismal Swamp*. October 27, 1856, October 20, 22, 1858. Victoria Theatre, London. BL Add. MS 52962 (G).

NOTES

I am grateful to the British Academy for research funding which enabled the first version of this essay to be delivered at the American Literature Association Conference, 2003.

1. Linda Williams, *Playing the Race Card: Melodramas of Black and White from Uncle Tom to O. J. Simpson* (Princeton: Princeton University Press, 2001), 92.

2. Harriet Beecher Stowe, *Dred: A Tale of the Great Dismal Swamp*, edited by Judie Newman. (Edinburgh University Press, 1992, rpt. 1998. First published by Philips, Sampson and Company, Boston, 1856).

3. There is almost no published critical material on adaptations of *Dred*. Two theses are relevant. Hazel Waters, "How Oroonoko became Jim Crow: the black presence on the English stage from the late eighteenth to the mid-nineteenth century" (Ph.D, University of London, 2002) argues that the black figure on the British stage was originally a fearsome, avenging figure, but diminished in ferocity following the advent of T. D. Rice. Dred, while something of a return to the figure of the black avenger, could not dislodge the ubiquitous "Jim Crow" image. Jennifer Workman Pitcock, "Imaginary bonds: anti-slavery dramas on the New York stage, 1853–1861" (Ph.D, University of Kentucky, 2002) considers the Conway, Brougham, and Suter versions on the New York stage as catering to the need to reassure northern audiences worried about the consequences of abolition. In printed sources there is a page on the Brougham adaptation in Alfonso Sherman, "Little known black heroes in antebellum drama," *Speech Teacher* 19 (1970), 130–137; two pages on the Conway, Brougham and Taylor versions in Monroe Lippmann, "Uncle Tom and his poor relations: American slavery plays," *Southern Speech Journal*, 28 (Spring 1968), 183–197, and scattered references in Harry Birdoff, *The World's Greatest Hit: "Uncle Tom's Cabin"* (New York:

S. F. Vanni, 1947), and in various works of theatre history. Bluford Adams, *E Pluribus Barnum: The Great Showman and the Making of US Popular Culture* (Minneapolis: University of Minnesota Press, 1997) offers details of the Conway production. H. Philip Bolton, *Women Writers Dramatized: A Calendar of Performances from Narrative Works published in English to 1900* (London: Mansell, 2000), is invaluable in cataloguing productions, describing plays and supplying cast lists and other details.

4. Judie Newman, "Was Tom white? Stowe's *Dred* and Twain's *Pudd'nhead Wilson*," in *Slavery and Abolition* 20: 2 (August 1999), 125–136.

5. George Speaight, *The History of the English Toy Theatre* (London: Studio Vista, 1969). For examples of toy theatre sheets, and demonstrations, I am grateful to Barry Clarke of the London Toy Theatre Museum.

6. Jeffery Mason, *Melodrama and the Myth of America* (Bloomington: Indiana University Press, 1993).

7. Elaine Hadley, *Melodramatic Tactics: Theatricalized Dissent in the English Marketplace, 1800–1885* (Stanford: Stanford University Press, 1995), 10.

7

MARJORIE PRYSE

Stowe and regionalism

Before readers can begin to address the general question of Harriet Beecher Stowe's relation to regionalism, the category itself requires an introduction. Certainly Stowe wrote "regional" fiction throughout her writing life, even in *Uncle Tom's Cabin*, if in using that adjective we mean to highlight the way she locates her fiction in geographical places. However, literary regionalism from its origins in the nineteenth century does more than name place; it also locates the social and cultural perspectives of the regional characters who live and speak in its pages in ways these characters would recognize as their own, and it does so without holding them up to ridicule or allowing them to serve as yardsticks of the queer which then enable readers outside the place or from urban centers to assert the measure of their own normality.

Critics and literary historians have described a variety of fictional modes that depicted regional characters in the nineteenth century. The "humorists of the Old Southwest" began writing as early as 1831 for the sporting magazine, *Spirit of the Times*, in imitation of Washington Irving's "The Legend of Sleepy Hollow."[1] However, in the works of these humorists, written for an audience of "the wealthy slaveholding sportsmen and their friends and allies,"[2] narrators encourage readers to derive "humor" from cruelty to characters in the tales, especially to white women, Negroes, lower-class white men, and sometimes animals, especially horses. While regionalism may contain elements of humor, which we find as early as the young Harriet Beecher's first significant fiction, her 1834 "A New England sketch" (later renamed "Uncle Lot"), Stowe is clearly suggesting an alternative to the kind of literary regional material characteristic of the "humorists of the Old Southwest." In Stowe's work, and later in the work of regionalists more generally, regional characters receive respectful and even empathic treatment, and narrators do not earn humor at their characters' expense.

Students familiar with "The Legend of Sleepy Hollow" may wonder how Stowe could read this sketch of the headless horseman, considered by critics to be one of the earliest American short stories and often the subject of schoolchildren's most enduring Halloween memories, as a story that turns cruelty into humor. However, if we read Stowe's "Uncle Lot," we can see that Irving's sketch and its imitators clearly disturbed Stowe's sense of the cultural and moral direction toward which she believed the new country, in the 1830s, was moving. Stowe herself writes in imitation of Irving in order to change the outcome of that tale and in order to subvert the legend that would install Brom Bones and the hypermasculinity he represents rather than the more effeminate Ichabod Crane as a prototype for the American hero.[3] Although Irving allows Brom Bones to run Ichabod Crane out of town, Stowe brings Irving's schoolmaster back to serve as a model for her own schoolmaster, James Benton, in "Uncle Lot."

Both Ichabod Crane and James Benton are Yankees and newcomers to their villages, make themselves at home "in all the chimney-corners of the region" (6),[4] keep the "sunny side of the old ladies" (7), and believe themselves to be singers and storytellers. However, Stowe's hero does not lose to his "adversary," Stowe's title character Uncle Lot. On the contrary, Stowe describes Uncle Lot, unlike Brom Bones, as a "chestnut burr, abounding with briers without and with substantial goodness within" (8). With a focus on character instead of plot that becomes characteristic of regionalist fiction, the process by which Uncle Lot comes to reveal his goodness requires the insight and empathy of the young James Benton, for whom "the rough exterior and latent kindness of Uncle Lot were quite a spirit-stirring study" (14). James becomes a tactful observer or "reader" of Uncle Lot and Stowe's sketch records James's efforts at empathic relationship with the old man, in the process becoming a minister, marrying Lot's daughter, and becoming, in effect, both Uncle Lot's adopted son and Stowe's new American hero. Beginning with "Uncle Lot" and continuing throughout her regionalist fiction, Stowe portrays "latent kindness" as a man's attribute, together with numerous qualities that are often expected of women but conventionally denied to masculinity, qualities such as empathy, spirituality, an interest in human relationships, and a capacity for acknowledging these qualities.

Late in her career, Stowe would choose to rewrite another Irving story, this time "Rip Van Winkle," in creating her memorable storyteller Sam Lawson, who appears in the novel *Oldtown Folks* (1869)[5] as well as the sketches collected in *Sam Lawson's Oldtown Fireside Stories* (1872). As I will show later in this essay, Sam Lawson, like James Benton, also revises Stowe's construction of American masculinity to include empathy. However, by the time Stowe returns to Irving in her creation of Sam Lawson, the Civil War has been fought and won and the editors of the *Atlantic Monthly* and other publications have identified "local color" literature as a kind of "regional realism" that might help bind the Union together again. "Local color" could seem to reduce the fear of sectional and regional differences by making "colorful" characters humorous to readers outside the region. While the transcription of local speech as literary dialect becomes a feature of regional writing in its various forms, dialect in "local color" contributes to the humor of the fiction, for "local color," like its antecedents in the writers of the "Old Southwest," derives its humor from an urban outsider's view – a view often, by the end of the nineteenth century, defined as an educated, middle- or upper-class, assimilated Anglo-Saxon reader. Instead of looking and/or laughing with its characters, "local color" encourages readers to look and laugh at them. In creating Sam Lawson, Stowe articulates the critical question of the role of the regional in American literature: does regional writing serve the purposes of national unification, minimizing regional differences as merely "local color," or does it keep alive alternative values and stories that may challenge the fiction of Union?

Stowe struggles throughout her career with her own relationship to this question. In foregrounding her relationship to regionalism, we can frame the terms of her question by seeing her both as the writer of *Uncle Tom's Cabin*, a regional outsider who, for all her moral and political persuasion, nevertheless represents the lives of both white southern slave-owners and black slaves from the perspective of northern nationalism and Christian sentimentalism, and as the writer of *The Pearl of Orr's Island*, *The Minister's Wooing*, *Oldtown Folks*, and *Oldtown Fireside Stories*, a regional insider who attempts a more empathic representation of New England regional life, even if she also writes, in some of her New England fictions, from the perspective of that same nationalism and sentimentalism. One of the clearest descriptions of regionalism from the perspective of a writer who wants to claim "the regional motive" as his own appears a century later than Stowe, in the writing of Kentucky poet and essayist Wendell Berry.[6] Describing himself as writing "in the neighborhood of the word 'regional,'" Berry distances himself both from "a 'regionalism' based upon pride, which behaves like nationalism" and "a 'regionalism' based upon condescension, which specializes in the quaint and the eccentric and the picturesque, and which behaves in general like an exploitive industry" (63). Berry wants to write about his relationship to place without stereotyping the life of a region (64). "The regionalism that I adhere to could be defined simply as *local life aware of itself* . . . The motive of such regionalism is the awareness that local life is intricately dependent, for its quality but also for its continuance, upon local knowledge" (67).[7] In evaluating Stowe's relation to regionalism, we can see her struggle to write an alternative regional fiction that will not replicate either the cruelty of the "humorists of the Old Southwest," the nationalism of a regionalism "based on pride," or the commodification of regional differences for the entertainment of northern, urban audiences characteristic of "local color," but which has no other form to imitate. In short, her struggles contribute to inventing a new form of regional writing which Judith Fetterley and I have traced in our anthology, *American Women Regionalists*, and discussed at length in *Writing out of Place: Regionalism, Women, and American Literary Culture*.[8]

Among the formal features of much of Stowe's fiction, readers will recognize the distinguishing mark of the regionalist text, namely, the ways such a text shifts the reader's perception away from the urban center and instead moves the reader inside the region. Instead of looking and laughing *at* rural, poor, and disenfranchised regional people, readers find themselves drawn in to see *with* regional people. As Fetterley and I have written, regionalists differentiate themselves from local colorists "primarily in their desire not to hold up regional characters to potential ridicule by eastern urban readers but rather to present regional experience from within, so as to engage the reader's sympathy and identification" (*American Women Regionalists*, xii). Through empathic narration, a thematics that often recovers women's authority and provides an alternative to patriarchal values, an emphasis on character over plot and recognition of regional characters in particular as psychologically complex, the inclusion of dialect as the way characters speak rather than as a mark of their queerness, and a focus on elements of plot that move readers outside conventional stories of heroism and romance, regionalist texts diversify their readers' repertory of cultural scripts for both men's and women's lives. Stowe makes it clear that regionalism could serve as a literary vehicle for social and cultural change.

Uncle Tom's Cabin, Stowe's first novel, both initiates and reveals the complexity of Stowe's struggle to understand the relationship between geographical region, national values, and literary form.[9] The anti-slavery nation she envisions in *Uncle Tom's Cabin* proposes the same qualities for Tom's heroism that she first outlines in "Uncle Lot." In some ways, a reader might be inclined to view *Uncle Tom's Cabin* as regionalist fiction. In the novel, Stowe attempts to move her northern readers into the lives of slaves living in the plantation south; she makes an explicit appeal in the novel for "northern men, northern mothers, northern Christians" to "see to it that *they feel right*" (*UTC*, 385), to ensure their sympathies in the matter of human slavery; and Uncle Tom, like James Benton, is a feminized male, a Christ-like character who embraces the forgiveness of the New Testament God. However, as other critics have observed, Stowe reserves psychological complexity for her mixed-blood slave characters and black dialect for her full-blood and illiterate slave characters.[10] In fact, Stowe imposes a perspective on a region she does not know from lived experience. As St. Clare chastises his northern cousin Miss Ophelia, "O! come, come, . . . what do you know about us?" (153). While this does not detract from the power of a novel that continues to bring readers to tears in our own time, it does underscore the limitations of the novel's regionalist elements.

Although early in the novel, in Stowe's description of Aunt Chloe's kitchen, the reader may find just a hint of the New England kitchens that appear in her later novels – notably, Grandmother Badger's kitchen in *Oldtown Folks* – and Stowe is clearly writing about a region she knows from her years in Cincinnati when she describes Senator Bird's carriage transporting Eliza over the Ohio mud that "the rejoicing native calleth" a road (77), she is incapable of conveying a sense of Kentucky or any location further south because she chooses to write from a perspective that remains outside the region. In an interesting foreshadowing of the New England storyteller Sam Lawson's role in Grandmother Badger's kitchen, the slave Sam in Aunt Chloe's kitchen in *Uncle Tom's Cabin* proves his ability to "speechify," to turn his "hour of glory" in helping Eliza escape into "the story of the day" (64, 75), and, in a "local color" commentary on Uncle Tom's own Christian ministry, gives his kitchen of listeners a "pathetic benediction": "'Niggers! all on yer . . . I give yer my blessin'; go to bed now, and be good boys'" (67). Fragmentary moments in which Stowe seems to rely on elements of New England life and humor that she has not yet even written – even her description of Miss Ophelia St. Clare as the New England woman of faculty who comes into the St. Clare household and immediately takes charge – seem to suggest that Stowe would prefer, if she could, to write from experience. Crossing sectional lines and writing a northern nationalist novel for a sectional readership, she writes a powerful but hardly regionalist novel.

Both in *Uncle Tom's Cabin* and in her later regionalist novels and sketches, Stowe approached issues that were controversial, although, as we will see, it was finally easier for her to imagine men and women who escaped slavery than men and women who would be able to move beyond the gender conventions of her time. Critics, biographers, and historians have documented the impact Stowe made with her unabashedly abolitionist novel in the decade preceding the outbreak of the Civil War. Yet Stowe's willingness to raise questions of gender affected the development of American fiction in ways that are also controversial, if less well known. In one of the most unforgettable descriptions of Stowe's effect on American literature, James M. Cox describes Stowe with some regret as the writer who "killed" the "southwest humorists" (591, 593), although for Cox, it is not her regionalist fictions, which Cox terms "local-color stories" that reflect her "genial domestic sketching power, her commonsense realism, [and] her ear for language" (591), that did so, but rather *Uncle Tom's Cabin*.[11] In that novel, "Mrs. Stowe changes everything with devastating suddenness. She begins her novel not with a bear hunt but with a man hunt; for the horse trading of southwest humor she substitutes the slave trade" (Cox, 591, 592). Cox perceives, and laments, that Stowe writes a different kind of literature than that of the "humorists of the Old Southwest," and he describes Simon Legree from *Uncle Tom's Cabin* as "another fierce figure who seems to have stepped right out of southwest humor to become her immortal villain" (592). Cox may be forgetting the humor of the Sam and Andy sequence early in the novel – although I would argue that while the novel itself demonstrates a different moral tone from the "humorists of the Old Southwest," the "humor" of the Sam and Andy sequence may be more "genial" yet still more closely resembles post-Civil War "local color" fiction than regionalism in its caricatures of the slaves. As Richard Yarborough writes, "the blacks she uses to supply much of the humor in *Uncle Tom's Cabin* owe a great deal to the darky figures who capered across minstrel stages and white imaginations in the antebellum years. The black pranksters Sam and Andy, for instance . . . ultimately seem little more than bumptious, giggling, outsized adolescents" (47). Yet however "genial" her approach, Stowe's regionalism even more than *Uncle Tom's Cabin* shows her differences from the "humorists," whether or not keeping Ichabod Crane alive as a model for American manhood can be said to have "killed" them. It is because Stowe also turns her prodigious moral intelligence on gender – on the ways in which children are taught values, character traits, and a sense of their place in society that encourages them to become masculine men and submissive women – that her regionalist writing cannot avoid becoming controversial, if ultimately covert in its appeals.

Stowe's biographers and critics have almost universally agreed on one point, namely, that when she tried to begin a new novel after publishing *Uncle Tom's Cabin*, she retreated from national politics to the landscape and lives of people on the Maine coast near where she had lived for two years when her husband, Calvin, had taught theology at Bowdoin College. However, although she began *The Pearl of Orr's Island* in 1852, she did not finish it for a decade.[12] The primary difficulty Stowe had in completing the novel is due to its depiction of gender inequality in nineteenth-century America and her problem imagining how her society might resolve this inequality.[13] Hedrick describes *The Pearl of Orr's Island* as "Stowe's story of what it meant to a young girl to grow up in a society that prescribed sharply curtailed possibilities for women" and writes that "its structural flaws point toward a deep fissure in American republican ideals" (297). To the extent that Stowe resolves her novel's structural flaws, she does so by developing its regionalism. It is as if regionalism allows her to turn her attention away from questions of heroism and nation and thereby to raise the question of gender inequality because she will not appear to be taking up those "larger," putatively masculine questions. Although *Uncle Tom's Cabin*, as numerous critics have argued, portrays a feminized hero in Uncle Tom, the context for women's participation in the national debate over slavery remains limited to one of influence over men – "If the mothers of the free states had all felt as they should . . . the sons of the free states would not have connived at the extension of slavery, in our national body" (*UTC*, 384).

Regionalism in *The Pearl of Orr's Island* makes the novel one of Stowe's most significant accomplishments after *Uncle Tom's Cabin*, ranking with *The Minister's Wooing* and *Oldtown Folks* but even more successful than these in portraying the complexity of regional characters.[14] From the opening chapters of *Pearl*, Stowe asks her readers to shift their center of perception to a particular location "[o]n the road to the Kennebec, below the town of Bath, in the State of Maine" (*Pearl*, 3), "[d]own near the end of Orr's Island, facing the open ocean" to a "brown house of the kind that the natives call 'lean-to' or 'linter'" (5). Her story begins with the "wreck of a home-bound ship just entering the harbor" (4) and she guides her reader into her scene: "Let us enter the dark front-door. We feel our way to the right . . ." (5) and end up in the "best room" with the body of a young man who has just been drowned.[15] Upstairs, the young man's widow has gone into labor and delivers Mara Lincoln, but dies in childbirth, leaving Mara to be raised by her grandparents, Zephaniah and Mary Pennel; working women of the region, Aunts Roxy and Ruey Toothacre; and their kindly friend, Captain Kittridge. The novel's plot concerns the bringing up of Mara and, soon, of Moses, who washes up on the shores of Orr's Island in the arms of his dead mother, also the victim of a shipwreck, in a scene reminiscent of Shakespeare's *The Tempest*, a copy of which Mara will discover later in a barrel in her grandmother's garret and which she discusses with Captain Kittridge. However, it is not plot but rather character, in particular the characters Aunts Roxy and Ruey and Captain Kittridge, that mark *Pearl's* regionalism from its opening scenes.

Roxy and Ruey establish the novel's perspective as one rooted in the region. In a place where most of the men make their living by going to sea, regionalism becomes centered at home and in the home as metonymic for the local; even when Moses leaves home to go to sea, the novel itself "stays home" in the region, with Mara. Stowe establishes this perspective in her initial characterization of Roxy and Ruey, who "were not people of the dreamy kind, and consequently were not gazing off to sea, but attending to very terrestrial matters that in all cases somebody must attend to" (19). Stowe describes these women as "two brisk old bodies of the feminine gender and singular number" and who "were of that class of females who might be denominated, in the Old Testament language, 'cunning women,' – that is, gifted with an infinite diversity of practical 'faculty,' which made them an essential requisite in every family for miles and miles around" (20). They are "Aunt" Roxy and Ruey by their universal usefulness; "[t]hey are nobody's aunts in particular, but aunts to human nature generally" (20). Between the two, Aunt Roxy receives Stowe's focus. "Her mind on all subjects was made up, and she spoke generally as one having authority; and *who should*, if she should not? Was she not a sort of priestess and sibyl in all the most awful straits and mysteries of life?" (21).

Consulted by all, Miss Roxy becomes the "master-spirit" (21, 22) – except that, by the conventions of patriarchal culture, it is not Aunt Roxy but Reverend Sewell who is invested with both religious and cultural authority and who takes charge of Moses's education, encouraging Mara to recite Latin lessons with Moses only because, in Stowe's prescient depiction of the value of coeducation for boys, "[i]t is better for him to have company" (184). Despite his admiration for Mara's intelligence, Reverend Sewell cannot imagine a world in which gender would not predetermine and limit a girl's social role and her future. As he tells Captain Kittridge in a scene in which the captain has praised Mara's reading ability, "That child thinks too much, and feels too much, and knows too much for her years!" If she were a boy, he continues, you could send her on a sea-voyage and she could develop her body instead of her mind. "'But she's a woman,' he said, with a sigh, 'and they are all alike. We can't do much for them, but let them come up as they will and make the best of it'" (167). Despite Reverend Sewell's well-meaning paternalism and genuine affection for Mara, he brings to the story the force of conventional society's attitudes towards gender – the force that Fetterley argues (in "Only a Story")[16] Stowe cannot finally resist and thus, the second half of the novel portrays Mara's self-sacrificial love for Moses, her constancy while he is away for three years on a long voyage to China, her numerous attempts to improve his character, her decision to marry him – and finally, Stowe's intervention in this romance. Stowe will finally not allow Mara to marry Moses, even if she must die instead. As Roxy says when she objects to the engagement of Moses and Mara, "'I a'n't one of the sort that wants to be a-usin' up girls for the salvation of fellers'" (352).

Aunt Roxy may not actually be able to intervene in the conventions of gender, but her presence in Stowe's text keeps open an alternative perspective to that of Reverend Sewell. Thus, Aunt Roxy becomes the visible manifestation of the alternative spirituality Mara develops throughout the novel and underscores the novel's thematics of the recovery of maternal values despite the killing effects of patriarchal culture on Mara herself. By the end of the novel, when the motherless Mara feels herself to be dying, she is astounded when the "hard-visaged" Roxy covers her "worn, stony visage with her checked apron" and "sobbed aloud" (372). When Mara asks Roxy if she loves her, the woman answers, "Love ye, child? . . . yes, I love ye like my life" (373). Mara tells her friend Sally Kittridge, "No mother could be kinder" (392), and on her deathbed, she tells Roxy she loves her. The novel's end fulfills Mara's vision of heaven, for as she tells Moses, "God has always been to me not so much like a father as like a dear and tender mother" (348).

The alternative power of Stowe's novel and her regionalist critique lie in Mara's mother-centered spirituality. Because Aunt Roxy is not really a priestess or a sibyl, there is no outward way to "worship" a maternal God, at least in Calvinist New England, and so Mara develops an inward sensibility, keeping her thoughts to herself. For Stowe, Mara's inward development marks her moral superiority to Moses. For the reader, it also creates another drama in the novel, one in which Mara's inner thoughts and feelings exist in a place that is itself "region" to the larger world of Orr's Island. Later, regionalist writer and friend of Stowe, Celia Thaxter, in *Among the Isles of Shoals* (1873) would write about the regions of the few acres of rock in the Atlantic Ocean on which she grew up, thereby demonstrating that no place is too small to have its own regions.[17] In *Pearl*, Stowe identifies regionalism in part as a literary and cultural site that underscores the contrast between the external conventions of gender that limit Mara's actions and the inner freedom that seems to allow Mara to develop as she will.

Through this contrast, Stowe develops empathic narration and identifies morally superior characters as those who, like Captain Kittridge and Aunt Roxy, are able to see and encourage Mara's inward development. Captain Kittridge anticipates Stowe's later invention of her storyteller Sam Lawson, as the Pennels frequently call upon Kittridge for his stories that are "marketable fireside commodities" (32); and the man nurtures Mara's imagination by taking literature – *The Tempest* – as "jist like" history (151). Not by coincidence, both Aunt Roxy and Captain Kittridge are also the two whose speech reflects the inflections of Orr's Island, thus marking the use of dialect in regionalism very early in Stowe not as a quaint source of humor, as it would become in local-color writing, but rather as an indication of which characters Mara can trust, and which characters Stowe entrusts, along with Mara, with her novel's critique. In part by virtue of their influence, Mara becomes a controversial character – one who speaks the discourse of religious and patriarchal society but who, in her inner thoughts, "speaks" in language that Stowe's society cannot and would not want to "hear." Mara's spoken language and behavior may conform, but her inner thoughts do not, and with Aunt Roxy and Captain Kittridge, at various points in the novel, she becomes free to utter those thoughts as well. For example, when Captain Kittridge tries to explain to her, after she has transformed Orr's Island in her imagination into Shakespeare's mythical island in *The Tempest*, that he has seen a production of the play but that his wife and other church-going people find theatres filled with "middlin' sight o' bad things," Mara replies, "I am sorry they are bad . . . I want to see them" (154).

Mara's inner world includes empathy for Moses, which she learns in part by virtue of the contrast between her love for and treatment of him, and his for her. Although Moses develops a certain amount of self-knowledge, telling Mara, "there are a class of feelings that you have that I have not and cannot have," he also tells her that his wife must be "one of the sort of women who pray" because he associates the ability to pray with comfort for himself: "I need to be loved a great deal, and it is only that kind who pray who know how to love *really*" (347). Stowe informs the reader that Moses's feelings for Mara are entirely narcissistic, for "in his secret heart he said, 'Some of this intensity, this devotion, which went upward to heaven, will be mine one day. She will worship me'" (348). That Moses realizes Mara's love for him at the end of the novel does not finally suggest insight on his part. From their earliest childhood, Stowe writes about Moses that "his life was in the outward and present, not in the inward and reflective" (161). In this novel, the development of the "inward and reflective" character in Mara that reflects the empathy and encouragement of regional characters Aunt Roxy and Captain Kittridge shifts the center of moral authority to the region; recovers Roxy, not the minister, as an earthly embodiment of a maternal God; and indeed has as its unconventional plot, instead of the happy ending in romance in which Moses finally gets the wife he wants, "only a story" in which Stowe works, in Fetterley's words, "to bring Moses down" ("Only a Story," 124) as a way of finally bringing him up.

The Pearl of Orr's Island is often grouped with the novels that immediately preceded and followed it, *The Minister's Wooing* and *Oldtown Folks*, as those works in which Stowe writes most successfully about New England. However, close examination of the three indicates that while New England may function as a region capable of further development in *The Pearl of Orr's Island*, it takes on an historical and nostalgic function in the other two. Indeed, New England in both *The Minister's Wooing* and *Oldtown Folks* more accurately represents a stage in the development of the nation than a regionalist critique of the nation's masculine values. The nation New England represents is the moral north of *Uncle Tom's Cabin*, not the patriarchal society that limits women's education in *The Pearl of Orr's Island*. As Horace Holyoke, the narrator of *Oldtown Folks*, informs the reader in his "Preface," "North, South, East, and West have been populated largely from New England, so that the seed-bed of New England was the seed-bed of this great American Republic, and of all that is likely to come of it" (3). The kitchens of the Widow Scudder in *The Minister's Wooing* and of Grandmother Badger in *Oldtown Folks* are central to the thematics of both novels, but represent the region's past. The narrator in *The Minister's Wooing* describes "that kitchen of the olden times, the old, clean, roomy New England kitchen!" (*MW*, 17) and Horace links his grandmother's kitchen in *Oldtown Folks* with that moment in which New England becomes the nation.[18] Horace recalls overhearing as a child a conversation in that kitchen between his grandfather and Major Broad about the Constitution of the United States, "recently presented for acceptance in a Convention of the State of Massachusetts." His grandfather states, "We're in an unsettled condition now; we don't know fairly where we are. If we accept this Constitution, we shall be a nation, – we shall have something to go to work on" (71). Echoing Rip Van Winkle's confusion when he comes down from the mountain after his twenty-year sleep, Horace's grandfather offers becoming a nation as a solution to resolve that "unsettled condition."

Furthermore, in *The Minister's Wooing*, Stowe subordinates the development of her regional characters and their wisdom as regionals to a critique of Calvinist theology, even though, as critics have argued, that critique also provides an alternative to patriarchal values. Comparing the book to *Uncle Tom's Cabin*, Hedrick writes, "Stowe drew on the values and experience of a women's culture to pose a radically democratic alternative to feudal and clerical structures" (279), and "[r]eal spiritual power is clearly lodged in women characters" (278) such as Miss Prissy, the dressmaker, and Candace, who offers the grieving Mrs. Marvyn comfort when the minister, Dr. Hopkins, has failed to do so.[19] Thus the novel "forces a re-evaluation of white, male systems of thought" and "depicts women and blacks as instruments of salvation history" (279). Susan K. Harris suggests, further, that a "female imaginary" is the "sexual/spiritual core" of *The Minister's Wooing*, and that this imaginary "is accessible to readers willing to shift their focus from the major, or androcentric, plot or plots, to the minor, women-centered plot" (180–181).[20] Harris's description of how readers locate this imaginary – they become capable of "viewing the major from the minor plot" (191) – in effect describes a methodology readers may use to trace evidence of regionalism itself in Stowe's work.

At the same time, Stowe's treatment of New England in *The Minister's Wooing*, with its appeal to the "fastidious moderns" (*MW*, 15) Stowe sees as her readers, serves to contain the radical domestic ideas that Stowe would try again to explore in *The Pearl of Orr's Island*. No character in *The Minister's Wooing* explicitly critiques gender the way the novel's women characters end by critiquing Calvinism, and the values and wisdom of regional characters do not contribute to the development of any character the way Miss Roxy and Captain Kittridge do to Mara Lincoln's development in *Pearl*. Although in her New England novels, as Dorothy Berkson writes, Stowe envisions a "new society" that "will be communal, anti-materialistic, non-competitive, racially tolerant, and essentially classless" (245–246), Stowe implies in *The Minister's Wooing* that her critique of Calvinism represents her own vision rather than that of the region.[21] Indeed, Stowe refers to the small seaport town of Newport that serves as the site for her novel as "the region of religious faith" (*MW*, 425) and tosses off any need to characterize the region in detail with an oblique reference to "The Legend of Sleepy Hollow," depicting the table set at the quilting to celebrate the engagement between Mary Scudder and the minister as "that plenitude of provision which the immortal description of Washington Irving has saved us the trouble of recapitulating in detail" (459).

When Stowe returned to New England once again after *The Pearl of Orr's Island*, she tried to write "the novel she thought to be the culmination of her career" (Hedrick, 334). Although critics have debated whether or not *Oldtown Folks* succeeds as a novel, this book continues to show Stowe's interest in regionalism as a literary form, but arguably less in her descriptions of Oldtown and Oldtown customs and more in her construction of the character of Sam Lawson. When she chooses to invent the "far less engaging" and "passive" (Hedrick, 333) Horace Holyoke as narrator, rather than allowing Sam Lawson to tell her story, she demonstrates her initial ambivalence towards Sam, vacillating between putting him forward as a regionalist storyteller and allowing other characters to caricature him as a stock figure of local color. From the later vantagepoint of *Oldtown Fireside Stories*, one might argue that, had Stowe chosen Sam Lawson as her narrator of the novel rather than only of numerous inset narratives included within it, the book might have been both more critically successful and more clearly a regionalist fiction.

Stowe introduces Sam Lawson early in *Oldtown Folks* as the only character who perceives that the narrator, Horace, whose father has just died, may need "looking after" (*OF*, 30). "Wal naow, Horace, don't ye cry so. Why, I'm railly concerned for ye," Sam says as he enters the novel (30), and Horace writes, "Nobody but Sam would have thought of poking through the high grass and clover on our back lot to look me up, as I lay sobbing under the old apple-tree . . ." (31). From his first appearance in Stowe's work, Sam Lawson marks the presence of regionalism by speaking in dialect and expressing empathy for Horace. In Horace's description, Sam resembles a composite of Irving's Rip Van Winkle and Ichabod Crane. Like Ichabod, Sam is "an expert in psalmody, having in his youth been the pride of the village singing-school" (36). Like Rip, Sam is the "village do-nothing" – except that he alone seems to spend time with "all 'us boys' in the village," "always on hand to go fishing with us on Saturday afternoons" (31). A "soft-hearted old body," he breaks the necks of the fish rather than watch them flop. "'Why, lordy massy, boys,' he would say, 'I can't bear to see no kind o' critter in torment. These 'ere pouts ain't to blame for bein' fish, and ye ought to put 'em out of their misery. Fish hes their rights as well as any on us'" (31). The scene reminds the reader of Mara Lincoln's response in *The Pearl of Orr's Island* when she tells Moses she wishes she could go to sea like him. When Moses mocks her, saying "What can girls do at sea? you never like to catch fish – it always makes you cry to see 'em flop," Mara replies, "Oh, yes, poor fish! . . . I can't help feeling sorry when they gasp so" (*Pearl*, 136).

As a man, Sam Lawson reflects the values of Stowe's regionalist heroine – even though, at the same time, Stowe suggests that his wife, Hepsy, like Dame Van Winkle, has cause for complaint. "Poor Hepsy was herself quite as essentially a do-something, – an early-rising, bustling, driving, neat, effi-cient, capable little body" (*OF*, 34) who is forced to find ways to feed her six children while married to a "do-nothing." Stowe presents the village opinion that Hepsy, like Dame, is a scold, thereby exonerating Sam from his respon-sibilities just as Irving does, but at the same time, making certain that her reader understands that she is creating a new, feminized Rip Van Winkle, and that her approach to telling regional stories valorizes an Ichabod Crane rather than a Brom Bones in her construction of male heroes.

At the same time, Stowe chooses Horace Holyoke, not Sam Lawson, as her narrator. In *Oldtown Folks*, although Stowe reveals her commitment to regionalism, she keeps Sam Lawson in check, containing his sphere at the fireside corner in Grandmother Badger's kitchen and his role as the Saturday companion of the local boys, thereby marginalizing his influence. She also allows other characters in the novel to ridicule Sam Lawson. For example, when Horace's Uncle Bill, the "wit and buffoon of the family" (59), is home from Harvard college, he describes Oldtown folks as "queer" and reports that he needs to "study" them "so that I can give representations of nature in our club at Cambridge" (61). Citing Sam Lawson in particular, it appears that he intends to entertain his college friends with a bit of Oldtown "local color," or what another character, Mehitable Rossiter, calls giving representations of "Oldtown curiosities" (65). Later, when the young Tina Percival visits Cloudland for the first time with the young Horace and her brother Harry, she writes back to Miss Mehitable that they have acted plays on the trip: "We agreed with each other that we'd give a set of Oldtown representations, and see if Uncle Jacob would know who they were and so Harry was Sam Lawson and I was Hepsy . . ." (348). Tina's letters suggest local color – later she adds to her letters marginal caricatures of Oldtown characters (423) – and the three do enact "a farce called 'Our Folks,'" in which the three young people portray Sam and Hepsy Lawson and another do-nothing character, Uncle Fliakim, "and exhort them how to get along and manage their affairs more prosperously" (418). Stowe's uses of Sam Lawson as both the source of humorous stories and the object of Tina's humor appear to reflect her own ambivalence concerning regionalism's power – not ambivalence concerning its literary value, but rather its power to command the attention of reviewers, who were men. Perhaps Stowe's own lifelong attempts to compete with men, first for her father's attention in the world of Beecher sons, later for editorial support from the editors of the *Atlantic Monthly*, where, from the beginning, "women were not full-fledged members of the *Atlantic* club" (Hedrick, 289), and finally, in her attempts to promote *Oldtown Folks* and to keep her reputation alive (cf. Hedrick, 346–347), led her to make artistic decisions that ultimately worked against her own literary ambitions. Even so, Sam's is the last voice the reader hears in *Oldtown Folks* and Stowe gives him central position as narrator for the selections she included in *Oldtown Fireside Stories*, thereby suggesting that if she had not been harried by her fear of public opinion, she would have been able to create Sam Lawson, like Captain Kittridge or Aunt Roxy, in straightforward fashion as a regionalist character instead of allowing Harry and Tina ultimately to present Sam as a local-color caricature.

Critics have paid very little attention to *Oldtown Fireside Stories*, describing the book as a "sequel" to and a "single *opus*" with *Oldtown Folks*;[22] as a book that "exploited the lucrative market for New England nostalgia" (Hedrick, 347); and as "local color sketches."[23] While the reasons for this neglect may be understandable – Stowe's novels have only achieved a critical revival since about 1980, with renewed attention first to *Uncle Tom's Cabin* – understanding Sam Lawson's strengths requires distinguishing between local color and regionalism, a distinction that itself is quite recent. The best and only full discussion of the volume appeared in 1954. Charles H. Foster's description underscores Stowe's regionalist elements in her creation of Sam Lawson.[24] Describing the book as "a good deal more than postscript or appendix to *Oldtown Folks*," Foster credits Stowe for "the indigenous note readers of 1869 [when the first of the sketches, "The Widow's Bandbox," appeared in the *Atlantic*] were beginning to discover in Mark Twain" (204). Sam Lawson tells his stories in what Horace Holyoke, who exists in the sketches only to provide a frame narrator and a listener's response to Sam, terms his "vernacular grammar" (*OFS*, 139), thereby calling attention to Stowe's own awareness of the care with which she writes in Sam's New England village dialect.[25] Foster describes Stowe as bringing an "essentially new attitude" to the tradition of Down East humor that is marked by an "affectionate respect for village characters and village ways" and describes her as "laughing *with*, not *at* her people" (205). Instead of imagining a Yankee spokesman, "she became the Yankee spokesman" (205), so that Sam Lawson in many ways demonstrates Stowe's most successful attempt to give over storytelling to a narrator character, thinking "not *for*, but *with* Sam" (206). These are ingredients of regionalism, beginning with Stowe's shift in the center of the narrator's perception, writing from inside the region rather than looking in from outside.

Sam Lawson continues the empathic identification in *Oldtown Fireside Stories* that we have already seen in his response to Horace in *Oldtown Folks*. However, in *Oldtown Fireside Stories*, empathy for the poor includes critique of the rich. Sam sets up his own affinity with the poor in "Captain Kidd's Money," complaining, "even poor workin' industrious folks like me finds it's hard gettin' along when there's so many mouths to feed. Lordy massy! there don't never seem to be no end on't" (109). Instead of ridiculing Mother Hokum, he empathizes with her when she criticizes the parson: "I like to see a parson with his silk stockin's and great gold-headed cane, a lollopin' on his carriage behind his fat, prancin' hosses, comin' to meetin' to preach to us poor folks not to want to be rich! How'd he like it to have forty-'leven children, and nothin' to put onto 'em or into 'em, I wonder?" (113–114).[26] Sam continues his humorous but pointed critiques of Parson Lothrop, whom he describes in "The Ghost in the Cap'n Brown House" as "a master hand to slick things over" (153), and of ministers in general. In "Mis' Elderkin's Pitcher," Sam tells his listeners about Parson Lothrop that "since he married a rich wife he never hed no occasion to worry about temporal matters. Folks allers preaches better on the vanity o' riches when they's in tol'able easy circumstances. Ye see, when folks is pestered and worried to pay their bills, and don't know where the next dollar's to come from, it's a great temptation to be kind o' valooin' riches, and mebbe envyin' those that's got 'em; whereas when one's accounts all pays themselves, and the money comes jest when its wanted regular, a body feels sort o' composed like, and able to take the right view o' things, like Parson Lothrop" (136).

In some ways, Sam's portrait of parsons in *Oldtown Fireside Stories* gives Stowe's readers our first unobstructed view of patriarchal power since *The Pearl of Orr's Island*, and it confirms the reading of *The Minister's Wooing* that presents the minister as "a comic character, a bumbling male in female space" (Harris, 190). In "The Minister's Housekeeper," perhaps the most humorous sketch in the collection, Sam's cousin Huldy becomes housekeeper for Parson Carryl after the death of his wife. When the parson decides to "be instructin' and guidin' and helpin' of her" and to "come out of his study, and want to tew 'round and see to things" (62, 63), he proves himself to be uninstructed in the ways of barnyard animals. When the parson's hen-turkey is found killed and there is no hen left to set the eggs, the parson decides that he can make the tom-turkey do the job. "He *shall* set on eggs, and hatch 'em too" (64). Despite his efforts, with Huldy trying not to laugh, the parson does not succeed in getting the tom-turkey to sit on the eggs. Sam's interpretation of the event is that "parsons is men, like the rest of us, and the doctor had got his spunk up," and that this explains the parson's anger when the stone he has placed on the tom's back to keep him sitting falls off the turkey and smashes the eggs. "'I'll have him killed,' said the parson: 'we won't have such a critter 'round'" (67). When he does not do so, but rather yields household authority to Huldy and ends by making her his wife, Sam manages to turn his story about parsons into a story about men and to suggest an alternative masculinity.

Furthermore, Sam Lawson suggests another source of authority than that of ministers. Although readers will recognize in *Oldtown Fireside Stories* some of the stereotyping of Indians and African Americans that characterizes other Stowe fictions, Stowe also suggests, as she does with Miss Prissy and Candace in *The Minister's Wooing*, that there are other sources of knowledge than theology and the men who write sermons. In the process, she creates sympathetic portraits of Indians and African-American characters that counter such stereotyping. For example, the Indian Ketury in "The Ghost in the Mill" is considered a witch by the members of Parson Lothrop's Oldtown congregation – "at least, she knew consid'able more'n she ought to know," says Sam (16), – but the characters in Sam's sketch take her seriously, and rightly so, since she manages to get a dead man's ghost to come down from a chimney, which leads to the solving of an old murder in the village. Primus King, the black man who agrees to help dig in "Captain Kidd's Money," insists on being paid in advance – "[y]e see, Primus was up to 'em," Sam tells the boys (115); and Primus is indeed prescient, for when the men fail to gain any treasure from their large hole in the ground, Primus, having already been paid, can leave them to complete the work. "'Wal,' says Primus, 'I didn't engage to fill up no holes;' and he put his spade on his shoulder and trudged off" (121).

In "The Ghost in the Cap'n Brown House," Sam adds ship-masters to his list of the rich: "Now, there ain't no knowin' 'bout these 'ere old ship-masters, where they's ben, or what they's ben a doin', or how they got their money" (141). Although Stowe stops short of anticipating a critique of colonialism, the story does contrast Quassia, "an old black Guinea nigger-woman" who does the captain's work (142), with the two Christian white women, Cinthy who is frightened by what she thinks is a woman's ghost in the house, and

Aunt Sally Dickerson, who claims to have seen the captain and Quassia sending a real woman off in a coach in the middle of the night. Sam ends his story ambiguously – "Aunt Sally's clear she didn't dream, and then agin Cinthy's clear *she* didn't dream; but which on 'em was awake, or which on 'em was asleep, is what ain't settled in Oldtown yet" (159). However, earlier he has revealed that "the story got round that there was a woman kep' private in Cap'n Brown's house, and that he brought her from furrin parts" (152). Although the story's ending leaves the existence of this woman uncertain, it seems clear that there really is a woman "kep' private," one who keeps the keys to all of the closets in the captain's house, who does know exactly what the town would like to know, and who even knows how ship-masters make their money – but who keeps that knowledge to herself. Quassia knows even more than Sam does, especially "how foolish white folks is" (146), and in a covert way, that is Sam's point.

In the final sketch in the original collection, "How to Fight the Devil," Sam himself shows up the knowledge of "some o' these 'ere modern ministers that come down from Cambridge college" (that is, Harvard). These ministers say "there ain't no devil, and the reason on't is, 'cause there can't be none." But Sam knows the devil exists, and he takes the boys up to Devil's Den to prove it. "[T]hese 'ere fellers is so sort o' green! – they don't mean no harm, but they don't know nothin' about nobody that does," Sam tells them, as he introduces the story of "how old Sarah Bunganuck fit the Devil" (195). Sarah, "one of the converted Injuns," has a small plot of land "right alongside o' Old Black Hoss John's white-birch wood-lot" (195). Old Black Hoss John is a mean-spirited, stingy man, "as nippin' as a black frost" (196), who accuses old Sarah of being a thief, "when everybody knew that she was a regerlar church-member, and as decent an old critter as there was goin'" (196). Standing up for Sarah's right to gather huckleberries and chestnuts and to cut white-birch brush for brooms, Sam ends his collection (and Stowe hers) with Black Hoss's attempt to frighten Sarah, in front of a hidden audience of his friends, by jumping out from the brush one moonlit night when she is gathering brush. "'Woman, don't yer know who I be?' 'No,' says she quite quiet, 'I don't know who yer be.' 'Wal, I'm the Devil,' sez he. 'Ye be?' says old Sarah. 'Poor old critter, how I pity ye!' and she never gin him another word . . ." (199). It takes an alternative storyteller to tell stories that challenge theology or any other patriarchal structure. When Stowe writes regionalism, she becomes like Sam.

Sam Lawson becomes Stowe's most successful regionalist narrator and she seems to have indicated this late in life when, after she stopped writing but began to give public readings of her work in public libraries and churches in Massachusetts, she chose to read Sam Lawson's stories (Hedrick, 392). Sam allows Stowe to poke fun at ministers while ostensibly making Sam himself the object of her humor. Sam Lawson's stories are also humorous, but he does not achieve his own humor at others' expense. Rather, he includes himself in the general realm of human inadequacy and finds alternative authority in Indians, African Americans, and some white men and women who are poor, orphaned, or working class. Neither does Sam Lawson judge his characters. For example, "The Widow's Bandbox" derives its plot from the discovery of the presence of a transvestite on board a revolutionary war sloop, a "widow" who turns out to be a British sailor in disguise. While Sam unmasks the plot, he does not make fun of the cross-dressed man but rather defends the captain who agreed to help the "widow." He says, "Folks 'll have to answer for wus things at the last day than tryin' to do a kindness to a poor widder, now, I tell *you* . . . [I]t's my humble opinion, that the best sort o' folks is the easiest took in, 'specially by the women. I reely don't think I should a done a bit better myself" (102). Stowe combines a regionalist sensibility with an anti-patriarchal perspective, leavened by the humor she achieves as a result of Sam's ostensible willingness to play the part of "the village do-nothing" she names him in *Oldtown Folks*.

Yet Sam Lawson's need to make a living in *Oldtown Fireside Stories* makes it possible for the reader to take seriously what at first glance might seem only humorous critique. Sam clearly derives some of his own and his family's sustenance through the stories he tells, and indeed, his profession is that of storyteller; as Stowe/Horace opens the collection by acknowledging, "In those days," when "we had no magazines and daily papers, . . . no the- atre, no opera, ... chimney-corner story-telling became an art and an accomplishment" (*OFS*, 1–2). Sam almost always "earns" something for his stories, whether it is "a warm seat at the hearth-stone" (3), "a mug o' cider and some cold victuals" (82), or as often, the exchange of labor with Horace and his brother, who call Sam "our mentor" (178). In one sketch, for example, the boys do Sam's work of "hatchelling" flax in the barn while he talks; in others, they pick blueberries, huckleberries, or catch fish for Sam while he rests against a tree – all of which ostensibly confirms Sam's status as "do-nothing" but which actually reveals the most important way he works. In *Oldtown Folks*, it is also clear that Sam's storytelling is his livelihood, for at Thanksgiving, he returns home from Grandmother Badger's kitchen with a turkey, as well as mince and pumpkin pies, what Stowe calls a "yearly part of his family programme" (*OF*, 290).

Stowe's creation of Sam Lawson and the ways she uses humor to distract her readers while managing to write sketches that shift the center of percep- tion to marginal and socio-economically disenfranchised characters marks regionalism as a literary model for her successors. Critics do not appear to have noticed that Sam Lawson and his narrative method in *Oldtown Fireside Stories* may have served as a prototype for Charles Chesnutt's Uncle Julius and his own way of telling a story in his 1899 collection, *The Conjure Woman*, which appeared seven years later. Although unlike *Oldtown Fireside Stories*, which records a history of a time that has passed, *The Conjure Woman* addresses the more recent legacy of slavery and the ongoing problems of reconstruction, like Sam, Chesnutt's Uncle Julius has developed complex strategies for survival; storytelling serves both as his livelihood and the means by which he attempts to interrupt the operations of power.[27] Like Stowe's, however, Chesnutt's alternative story is accessible only to readers willing, in Harris's words, to "shift their focus" and read Chesnutt the way Annie listens to Uncle Julius's stories.

Foster may have first suggested that Stowe uses this technique, what he calls "the happy device of the framework depicting the scene and the storyteller and making a vivid contrast with the story itself" (205). In any event, such a contrast, whether we understand it as shifting the center of the reader's perception or, in works with regionalist elements, "viewing the major from the minor plot" (Harris, 191), finally marks the difference between regionalism and writing that reinforces conventional understanding of regional life. Stowe anticipates her successors and gives them narrative strategies for continuing the work of developing literary perspectives from the regions, writers like Thaxter or Sarah Orne Jewett, who claimed to have read *The Pearl of Orr's Island* "in my thirteenth or fourteenth year."[28] Stowe made possible a heterogeneous set of alternatives that would allow writers as geographically disparate as Connecticut's Rose Terry Cooke, Tennessee's Mary Noailles Murfree, New Orleans writers Kate Chopin, Grace King, and Alice Dunbar-Nelson, Seattle's Sui Sin Far, the Dakota Zitkala-Ša, and the California desert's Mary Austin, in addition to Jewett, Thaxter, and Chesnutt, among others,[29] to invent fictions that keep alive alternative masculinities, to enlarge the range of plots acceptable for women's lives, to advocate on behalf of the poor and socially disenfranchised, and to continue to understand the relationship between gender, race, class, and regional life. Stowe's Captain Kittridge in *The Pearl of Orr's Island* may offer the most convincing rationale for regionalism when he tells Mara, "as long as folks *is* folks, why, they will be *folksy*" (*Pearl*, 154). It was Stowe's contribution to the development of regionalism that she resisted turning at least some of her "folks" into folklore or into local color and instead insisted that the voices of her "folksy" characters – Captain Kittridge and Aunt Roxy in *The Pearl of Orr's Island*, Miss Prissy and Candace in *The Minister's Wooing*, and above all, Sam Lawson in *Oldtown Folks* and *Oldtown Fireside Stories* – continue to be heard in an emerging democracy.

Near the end of the last sketch in *Oldtown Fireside Stories*, Sam Lawson defends Sarah Bunganuck's picking of huckleberries "and them 'ere wild things that's the Lord's, grow on whose land they will, and is free to all." Recalling Sam's own berrypicking and fishing throughout his volume, his eloquence on behalf of Sarah marks Sam's recognition that in Sarah's rights lie his own. He tells the boys, "I've hearn 'em tell that, over in the old country, the poor was kept under so, that they couldn't shoot a bird, nor ketch a fish, nor gather no nuts, nor do nothin' to keep from starvin', 'cause the quality folks they thought they owned every thing . . . We never hed no sech doin's this side of the water, thank the Lord!" (197). Those critics who have called Stowe's work "nostalgic" may have misread the ironies apparent in Sam's "thank the Lord," or her sense that the nation's future depends on the protection of the Sarahs, the Sams, and the guarantee that there would be "no sech doin's this side of the water." She offers regionalism as one narrative strategy among others in her repertory to help readers become willing to "shift their focus" and emulate, rather than dismiss or laugh at, "folksy" regional voices.

NOTES

1. For examples of "humor of the Old Southwest," today's readers may recall the work of writers such as Augustus Baldwin Longstreet (*Georgia Scenes*, 1835), Johnson Jones Hooper (*Some Adventures of Captain Simon Suggs*, 1845), or George Washington Harris's Sut Lovingood yarns (which first appeared in the mid-1850s). Hennig Cohen and William B. Dillingham make the point about the influence of "The Legend of Sleepy Hollow" in *Humor of The Old Southwest* (Boston: Houghton Mifflin, 1964), xvi.

2. Norris W. Yates, *William T. Porter and the Spirit of the Times: A Study of the Big Bear School of Humor* (Baton Rouge: Louisiana State University Press, 1957), 17.

3. For a full discussion of the relationship between Stowe's "Uncle Lot," Washington Irving, and the "humorists of the Old Southwest," see Marjorie Pryse, "Origins of literary regionalism: gender in Irving, Stowe, and Longstreet," *Breaking Boundaries: New Perspectives on Regional Writing*, ed. Sherrie A. Inness and Diana Royer (Iowa City: University of Iowa Press, 1997), 17–37; see also Judith Fetterley and Marjorie Pryse, *Writing out of Place: Regionalism, Women, and American Literary Culture* (Champaign, IL: University of Illinois Press, 2003), esp. chapter 3.

4. "Uncle Lot" is included in Judith Fetterley and Marjorie Pryse, *American Women Regionalists 1850–1910: A Norton Anthology* (New York: W. W. Norton, 1992), 4–24. Page references to this sketch appear in parentheses. We also include in this anthology additional selections from Stowe's regionalism: chapters 4 and 5 introducing Aunts Roxy and Ruey from *The Pearl of Orr's Island*; Horace Holyoke's "Preface" and the chapter introducing "The Village Do-Nothing," Sam Lawson, from *Oldtown Folks*; and "The Minister's Housekeeper" from *Oldtown Fireside Stories*.

5. Harriet Beecher Stowe, *Oldtown Folks* (New Brunswick, NJ: Rutgers University Press, 1987).
6. Wendell Berry, *A Continuous Harmony: Essays Cultural and Agricultural* (New York: Harcourt Brace Jovanovich, 1972).
7. As a late-twentieth-century southern writer, Berry's understanding of regionalism contrasts with the use of the term by southerners earlier in the century. The Southern Agrarians wrote an anti-modern "regionalism," proposing in their 1930 manifesto, *I'll Take My Stand*, that the future of the south lay in its agrarian past. The vision of the Agrarians and of southern critics such as Robert Penn Warren and Cleanth Brooks "is based on conservative values rooted in the ownership of land and its cultivation, naturalizes physical geography to define regions, and in particular seeks to justify the South's continuing cultural and economic autonomy" (Fetterley and Pryse, *Writing out of Place*, 4). The term "regionalism" more explicitly appeared in the work of southern social scientists, particularly sociologist Howard W. Odum, who believed they could make a "factual reinventory" of the south (Daniel T. Rodgers, "Regionalism and the burdens of progress," *Region, Race, and Reconstruction: Essays in Honor of C. Vann Woodward*, ed. J. Morgan Kousser and James M. McPherson [New York: Oxford University Press, 1982], 3–26, at 4). "Realism was the Regionalists' initial battle cry" as "a set of big, encyclopedic, regional inventories" that emerged from the University of North Carolina's sociology department (5). Neither literary nor sociological regionalism, as a reemergent southern sectionalism, survived these particular movements, and Berry is clearly redefining regionalism against these traditions. Both in *American Women Regionalists* and in *Writing out of Place*, Fetterley and I include and discuss southern writers who preceded the Agrarians and who much more closely resemble Berry in their understanding of literary regionalism.
8. Although Stowe has no other American form to imitate, she does have Irish and English predecessors. As Josephine Donovan observes in *New England Local Color Literature: A Women's Tradition* (New York: Frederick Ungar Publishing Co., 1983), English writer Jessica Mitford's series of sketches of local life in a provincial English town, *Our Village* (1824–32), uses the format of a narrator who takes walks with her dog, a greyhound named Mayflower (23). As Donovan notes, the title of Stowe's first published collection, *The Mayflower*, in which the story "Uncle Lot" appears, may partly have represented Stowe's tribute to Mitford. Donovan also mentions Irish writer Maria Edgeworth as "one of the first authentically local color writers" (23). For further discussion of Edgeworth, Mitford, and the other early American writers (John Neal, James Kirke Paulding, Lydia Huntley Sigourney, Caroline Kirkland, Catharine Sedgwick, and Emily Chubbuck Judson [aka Fanny Forester]) who contributed to the development of early regionalism, see *Writing out of Place*, Chapter 3. Readers may be curious about the title of Donovan's book, *New England Local Color Literature*, and why I am citing Donovan while making a distinction between "local color" and regionalism. In 1983, when Donovan published her book, no-one had yet begun to make critical distinctions among various modes of regional writing, or to use these distinctions as a framework for understanding the sometimes conflicting impulses of a writer like Stowe.
9. Harriet Beecher Stowe, *Uncle Tom's Cabin*, A Norton Critical Edition, ed. Elizabeth Ammons (New York: W. W. Norton, 1994).

10. For a discussion of Stowe's endorsement of racial stereotypes, see in particular Richard Yarborough, "Strategies of black characterization in *Uncle Tom's Cabin* and the early Afro-American novel," in Eric J. Sundquist, ed., *New Essays on Uncle Tom's Cabin* (Cambridge: Cambridge University Press, 1986), 45–84.

11. James M. Cox, "Humor and America: the southwestern bear hunt, Mrs. Stowe, and Mark Twain," *Sewanee Review* 83 (1975), 573–601.

12. When she did return to the novel again in January, 1861, she wrote it in serial installments for the weekly magazine, the *Independent*, at the same time as she was planning to write another serialized novel, *Agnes of Sorrento*, for the *Atlantic*. Joan D. Hedrick argues in *Harriet Beecher Stowe: A Life* (New York: Oxford University Press, 1994) that Stowe could not keep two novels going at the same time and that *Pearl* in particular "demanded that she thread her way through psychically perilous waters" (299) because the book "is as close as Stowe ever came to writing a fictionalized autobiography" (297), and that this explains why, in April of 1861, she suspended serialization of the novel and did not return to it until December.

13. Judith Fetterley makes the claim in *Provisions: A Reader from 19th-Century American Women* (Bloomington: Indiana University Press, 1985) for Stowe's willingness to take up controversial subjects in her regionalist fiction. She writes, although "no text exists that I know of that addresses the oppression of women as *Uncle Tom's Cabin* addresses the oppression of black people, . . . [the] text that comes the closest is *The Pearl of Orr's Island*" (12).

14. Harriet Beecher Stowe, *The Pearl of Orr's Island* (Hartford, CT: The Stowe–Day Foundation, 1979).

15. What a contrast this opening creates with the opening sentence of *Uncle Tom's Cabin*, in which "two gentlemen were sitting alone over their wine, in a well-furnished dining parlor, in the town of P —, in Kentucky" (1), a sentence that represents the extent of Stowe's specificity in that novel.

16. Judith Fetterley, "'Only a story, not a romance': Harriet Beecher Stowe's *The Pearl of Orr's Island*," *The (other) American Traditions: Nineteenth-Century Women Writers*, ed. Joyce W. Warren (New Brunswick, NJ: Rutgers University Press, 1993), 108–125.

17. See Fetterley and Pryse, *Writing out of Place*, for further discussions of Thaxter; see also Judith Fetterley, "Theorizing regionalism: Celia Thaxter's *Among the Isles of Shoals*," *Breaking Boundaries: New Perspectives on Women's Regional Writing*, ed. Sherrie A. Inness and Diana Royer (Iowa City: University of Iowa Press, 1997), 38–53.

18. Harriet Beecher Stowe, *The Minister's Wooing* (Hartford, CT: The Stowe–Day Foundation, 1978).

19. For an interesting discussion of Miss Prissy, see Nancy Lusignan Schultz, "The artist's craftiness: Miss Prissy in *The Minister's Wooing*," *Studies in American Fiction* 20.1 (Spring 1992), 33–44.

20. Susan K. Harris, "The female imaginary in Harriet Beecher Stowe's *The Minister's Wooing*," *New England Quarterly* 66.2 (1993), 170–198.

21. Dorothy Berkson, "Millennial politics and the feminine fiction of Harriet Beecher Stowe," *Critical Essays on Harriet Beecher Stowe*, ed. Elizabeth Ammons (Boston: G. K. Hall, 1980), 245–258.

22. Robert Forrest Wilson, *Crusader in Crinoline: The Life of Harriet Beecher Stowe* (Philadelphia: Lippincott, 1941), 501.

23. John Adams, *Harriet Beecher Stowe* (New York: Twayne, 1989), 65.

24. Charles H. Foster, *The Rungless Ladder: Harriet Beecher Stowe and New England Puritanism* (Durham, NC: Duke University Press, 1954).

25. In my discussion of the following stories, I am quoting parenthetically from the more readily available 1967 Gregg Press reprint of the 1892 Houghton Mifflin edition of *Sam Lawson's Oldtown Fireside Stories*, although for the purposes of this discussion, I will limit myself to the first 199 pages of the collection, which reproduces the first edition of the volume, titled in 1872 *Oldtown Fireside Stories*. Later editions, including 1892, add five additional stories, three of which are narrated by Horace Holyoke. Only two of these additional stories resemble those in the first edition ("Tom Toothacre's Ghost Story" and "The Parson's Horse-Race").

26. For ease in reading, I have dropped here the third set of quotation marks (and elsewhere the second set) that is technically necessary to indicate that I am quoting Sam when he is quoting another character. This technicality results from the fact that Stowe already marks all of Sam's narrative with quotation marks in order to emphasize the oral quality of his storytelling and the fact that he has listeners, always including Horace Holyoke, the collection's ostensible narrator.

27. For a discussion of Chesnutt and this collection in particular as regionalism, see Fetterley and Pryse, *Writing out of Place*, esp. 17–26.

28. Sarah Orne Jewett, *Letters of Sarah Orne Jewett*, ed. Annie Fields (Boston: Houghton Mifflin, 1911), 47.

29. Karen Kilcup Oakes, for example, cites *Oldtown Folks* as an influence on Sarah P. McLean Green's 1881 novel *Cape Cod Folks*. See "I like a woman to be a woman: theorizing gender in the humor of Stowe and Greene," *Studies in American Humor* 4.3 (1996), 14–38.

8

GREGG CRANE

Stowe and the law

In its frequent and overt legal engagements, Harriet Beecher Stowe's work would seem to offer a perfect subject for scholars examining the connections between law and literature. *Uncle Tom's Cabin* (1852), *A Key to Uncle Tom's Cabin* (1853), and *Dred: A Tale of the Great Dismal Swamp* (1856) advance an anti-slavery conception of American law. In *Lady Byron Vindicated* (1870), Stowe argues for women's rights, gender equality in marriage, and a more fully contractual conception of marriage in which the duties of both spouses are reciprocal and interdependent. However, with a few notable exceptions, such as Brook Thomas's *Cross-Examinations of Law and Literature*, scholars have not focused on Stowe's legal preoccupations – how the law influenced Stowe or how Stowe may have influenced American jurisprudence. Stowe scholarship has tended to focus on gender, religion, and sentiment to the exclusion or neglect of the jurisprudential aspects of her writing. Many critics seem to share James M. Cox's view of Stowe as writing "against the law" out of what he calls her "essentially sentimental determination to choose the religion of love over the religion of judgment." Such accounts take at face value Stowe's characterizations of sentiment as a feminine and sympathetic alternative to law, which is masculine and more concerned with commercial and material self-interest than salvation.[1]

Stowe, however, does not present this antithesis as final or inevitable. Instead, her stories work toward a merger of sentiment and law. Consider, for example, an early story, "Love versus Law."[2] The story begins with the attempt by Deacon Enos to buy a piece of property from Squire Jones. Not being as forthright as the good deacon, Squire Jones takes Enos's money but does not provide a deed to the property. Jones subsequently dies, and his oldest daughter brusquely denies the good deacon's claim to the land. Though saddened by the moral error of Squire Jones and his eldest daughter, Enos refuses to "go to law" to assert his right to the property. As he explains to a litigious neighbor, Uncle Jaw, "it is better to give up one's rights than to quarrel" ("Love," 70–71). Unmoved by such benevolence, Uncle Jaw tenaciously pursues his own separate legal dispute with Squire Jones's daughters. To bring about an end to the conflict between Uncle Jaw and Squire Jones's eldest daughter, Deacon Enos engineers the courtship and marriage of Uncle Jaw's only son and Squire Jones's youngest daughter ("Love," 69–72).

At first blush, the story's allegorical significance seems plain. Tender-hearted Deacon Enos embodies the feminized and pious alternative of love to combative Uncle Jaw's incarnation of law as the tool of hard-driving, masculine self-interest. To focus solely on the dichotomy presented by the story's title, characters, and plot line, however, is to miss the interdependence between love and law recommended in the story's denouement. To achieve the goals of love and sympathy, Deacon Enos can and must use the law. In addition to having the bride and groom and a preacher assembled at his house, Enos arranges to have some respected lawyers there as well. He uses his strong legal claim against Squire Jones's estate to strike a bargain with Jaw. Enos will relinquish his right of action against Squire Jones's estate if Jaw will permit the marriage of his son to Susan Jones. This marriage unites the quarreling families and represents a happy resolution to the threat posed to the community by litigious conflict and self-interest. It is also a union brought about by the marriage of love and law – the benevolence of Deacon Enos wedded to the skills of the lawyer. The story's happy ending indicates how the forms of law (including the threat of litigation and other lawyerly negotiation tactics) may, if motivated by fellow feeling, help to create a just and compassionate community.

Stowe found great drama in the spectacle of a decent person adeptly using legal procedure to advance the cause of justice. Her portrait of Abraham Lincoln's legal skills provides a telling nineteenth-century precursor to Harper Lee's depiction of Atticus Finch in *To Kill A Mockingbird* (1960):

> The prosecutor, sure of his prey, made only a short and formal argument [at the trial's conclusion]. Mr. Lincoln followed for the defence. He began slowly, calmly, carefully. He took hold of the heart of the evidence for the state – that of the chief witness. He pointed out first one discrepancy, and then another, and then another. He came at last to that part of the evidence where this principal witness had sworn positively that he had been enabled by the light of the moon to see the prisoner give the fatal blow with a slung shot; and taking up the almanac he showed that at the hour sworn to on the night sworn to *the moon had not risen*; that the whole of this evidence was a perjury.[3]

The thrill of Lincoln's closing argument like that of Atticus Finch's demon-stration that Tom Robinson could not have raped and throttled Mayella Ewell comes from the hopeful prospect that, using elementary logic and legal procedure, the good-hearted and clear-headed advocate will be able to reveal the truth despite his opponent's superior resources or the community's prejudice. Such scenes present the rule of law as romantic adventure: the attorney-hero seeks not only to defend the innocent but also to make the law embody standards different from and better than the majority's will and outlook.

Though an amateur, Stowe was herself an accomplished advocate. When her depictions of slavery in *Uncle Tom's Cabin* were challenged as fantastic and grossly exaggerated, Stowe produced *A Key To Uncle Tom's Cabin*, a devastating compendium of documentary evidence drawn from southern judicial opinions and newspapers attesting to the brutality of the system. *A Key* reflects Stowe's lawyerly recognition that the most credible and damning evidence of wrongdoing comes from the mouth of the wrongdoer. In *Lady Byron Vindicated*, Stowe merges her literary role with that of a defense attorney. In her "opening statement," Stowe asserts, "I claim, and shall prove that Lady Byron's reputation has been the victim of a concerted attack, begun by her husband during her lifetime, and coming to its climax over her grave." Defending a "revered friend," Stowe aims to demonstrate that Lord Byron was responsible for the failure of his marriage. She skillfully uses the poet's contradictory characterizations of his wife and his penchant for exaggerating and fictionalizing his life story to impeach his credibility. Given the fact that he trifles with the truth on such an important subject as the nature of his father's sanity and death, Stowe contends it is highly likely that he will "give false testimony with equal indifference" on the issue of his wife's character and the cause of their separation. Marrying the conventions of sentimental fiction to the practices of the trial lawyer, *Lady Byron Vindicated* offers a melodramatic polemic in which the incest, adultery, and psychological cruelty of Lord Byron are juxtaposed with the stoic endurance of his wife.[4]

Whether the law actually works toward the goal of creating a just society crucially depends, for Stowe, on its correspondence with the citizenry's moral faith. To achieve this goal, the Declaration of Independence and the Constitution must represent something nobler than a political majority's will. In expressing such principles as "the absolute equal brotherhood of man" and universal human rights, these foundational documents "crystallized religious teaching within a political act" (*Men of Our Times*, vi). When the law clearly and substantially deviates from such fundamental values, citizens have a right and a duty to point out the conflict and argue for the better, truer conception. Thus, Stowe praises Massachusetts Senator Charles Sumner and other leading anti-slavery advocates "for the clearness, the fullness, the triumphant power with which [they] brought out the true intention of the constitution, and the spirit of its makers." The passage of the Civil War Amendments validated the arguments of Sumner and his amateur and professional allies (including Stowe herself) for the compassionate and moral nature of the Constitution despite its flaws, its concessions to slavery (*Men of Our Times*, 232).

For Stowe and her allies, nothing more strikingly illustrated the need to reconnect the nation's law to its ethical principles than the Fugitive Slave Act of 1850, which forbade good-hearted people from offering aid and comfort to those fleeing bondage. Flatly denying "that the Constitution recognizes property in man," Senator William Seward argued that the measure should not be adopted because American law had to conform to "a higher law."[5] The notion of higher law controversially invoked by Seward to read slavery out of the Constitution is complex and includes a wide range of formulations, but the core idea is constant and may be expressed (if not implemented) simply: to be legitimate the law must be just. Of course, slavery was defended as well as attacked on the grounds that a higher law sanctioned it. George Fitzhugh, for instance, argued that benevolently authoritarian institutions, such as slavery and marriage, represented the only benign and productive way of addressing pervasive and apparently natural human inequalities.[6] In contrast to his opponents' attempts to fix higher law in divinely created hierarchies or the timeless constitutional bargains made between the sections at the nation's inception, Seward recognized both that the moral consensus of society delimits the scope and effect of law and that this consensus is mutable. Like other opponents of slavery, Seward was confident that his age's moral consensus was moving in an anti-slavery direction. As numerous critics recognized, Seward's conception of higher law suggested that amateurs, such as literary and religious figures, could play an important role in shaping the nation's jurisprudence by revising its public morality.[7]

Stowe's sense of the power of literature to reshape public policy and law is expressed in an 1853 letter she wrote to Lord Denman (formerly the Lord Chief Justice of England), urging the English to take up literary cudgels against American slavery: "In your reviews[,] in your literature, you can notice & hold up before the world, those awful facts, which but for you, they would scornfully go on denying as they have done." Demurely admitting that law was "not her work" or her "field," Stowe, nonetheless, was sure that amateur or literary jurisprudential efforts could lead to institutional revision: "It seems to me, that this tremendous story cannot be told in the civilised world, without forcing attention."[8] Fans and foes, alike, understood the jurisprudential and political aims of Stowe's anti-slavery writing. A review of *Dred* praised Stowe for showing the novel to be "so potent an instrument for doing good . . . we cannot afford to give it up." A Richmond *Enquirer* review of George Fitzhugh's *Cannibals All!* lamented the fact that, though "In every mode of argument the champions of the South excel," "they have produced no romance quite equal to 'Uncle Tom's Cabin.'" Denouncing the attempt to put the south on trial by "'higher law' men . . . in their Uncle Tom's Cabins, pulpits, schools and rostrums," southern critic George Frederick Holmes feared that the images of Stowe's fiction would effectively frame the national debate, providing the symbols and vocabulary of the constitutional struggle over slavery.[9]

Describing literature as the slave's ally and a powerful tutor of the nation's conscience, Charles Sumner's first great address as a senator, "Freedom National, Slavery Sectional" (1852), praises *Uncle Tom's Cabin* as inspiring a popular nullification of the Fugitive Slave Act:

> The literature of the age is all on [the slave's] side. Songs, more potent than laws, are for him. . . . And now, Sir, behold a new and heavenly ally. A woman, inspired by Christian genius, enters the lists, like another Joan of Arc, and with marvelous power sweeps the popular heart. . . . In a brief period, nearly one hundred thousand copies of "Uncle Tom's Cabin" have been already circulated. But this extraordinary and sudden success, surpassing all other instances in the records of literature, cannot be regarded as but the triumph of genius. Better far, it is the testimony of the people, by an unprecedented act, against the Fugitive Slave Bill.

Sumner shared with Stowe a belief that the escape-from-slavery story could effectively fuse higher-law intuition and literary affect. As Sumner put it in "Freedom National,"

> [I]n their very efforts for Freedom[,][fugitive slaves] claim kindred with all that is noble in the Past. Romance has no stories of more thrilling interest. Classical antiquity has preserved no examples of adventure and trial more worthy of renown. They are among the heroes of our age. Among them are those whose names will be treasured in the annals of their race. By eloquent voice they have done much to make their wrongs known, and to secure the respect of the world. History will soon lend her avenging pen. Proscribed by you during life, they will proscribe you through all time. Sir, already judgment is beginning. A righteous public sentiment palsies your enactment.[10]

The justice of the fugitives' claims to freedom is linked in these passages (as it is in *Uncle Tom's Cabin*) to the affective power of their exciting, adventurous, compelling romantic narratives of personal heroism. The force of the reader's recognition of the fugitive slaves' humanity and moral strength is proportional to the affective success of their narratives. Behind Sumner's appreciation of Stowe's fiction as opening the public's mind by stirring its heart lies an implicit appreciation of literary innovation. Literature can offer persuasive new conceptions of old truths ("all that is noble in the Past"). Reflecting an intuition that tastes in narrative and the stories we tell of fundamental justice are inseparable, Sumner's comments suggest that shifts in culturally authoritative narratives of justice move in tandem with shifts in political theory and jurisprudence.

While Sumner's appreciation of the political and legal authority of Stowe's novel may seem hyperbolic, the fact that Sumner, a politician centrally involved in revising the nation's highest law, believed the literary efforts of Stowe and others had this kind of jurisprudential authority is evidence that they in fact did. Indeed, legislative debates on the issues of slavery, race, and citizenship bear many signs of Stowe's influence. Ohio Representative John Bingham (the prosecutor in Andrew Jackson's impeachment trial and primary drafter of the 14th Amendment) clearly alluded to one of the most dramatic moments in *Uncle Tom's Cabin* in objecting to an amendment of the Fugitive Slave Law proposed in 1860 as part of an eleventh hour union-saving compromise. Noting that his comments would provoke sneers of "higher law," Bingham argued

> that the amendment proposed . . . does not relieve the American people from the unjust obligations imposed upon them by the act of 1850, by which, at the beck of the marshal, they are compelled to join in the hunt – to make hue and cry on the track of a fugitive slave woman who is fleeing, with her babe lashed upon her breast, from the house of bondage. I will not perform that service, and I ask any man on that side whether he will?[11]

Given the fact that, in 1860, the Fugitive Slave Law was still the law of the land, Bingham's comments derive jurisprudential authority solely from the higher-law tradition that unjust laws do not merit obedience. The compelling emotional force of his higher-law position is furnished by the image of the fugitive mother and her babe made famous by Stowe's vivid rendering of Eliza Harris's escape in *Uncle Tom's Cabin*. Asserting that equality before the law means "that the poor man's cabin, though it may be the cabin of a poor freedman in the depths of the Carolinas, is entitled to the protection of the same law that protects the palace of a Stewart or an Astor," Senator Henry Wilson's comments on the Freedmen's Bureau Bill indicate the degree to which Uncle Tom's humble cabin had permeated the era's lexicon of fundamental justice.[12] The success of Stowe's aim of infusing the language of law with sympathy and fellow feeling can be felt in Representative Jehu Baker's description of the 14th Amendment's equal protection clause. Equal protection of the laws, says Baker, "is so obviously right, that one would imagine nobody could be found so hard-hearted and cruel as not to recognize its simple justice."[13] One can modestly observe, I think, that, when in 1868 the dominant political party tests the appropriateness of their Constitutional amendment by reference to kind-hearted justice, we have come a considerable distance from the scorn heaped upon William Seward's invocation of higher law in arguing against the Fugitive Slave Act of 1850 – a shift in jurisprudential consensus that Stowe's anti-slavery writing helped to create.

The narrative focus for her anti-slavery writing came to Stowe in an argument with a friend, Professor Thomas Upham, who lukewarmly recommended obedience of the Fugitive Slave Act as part of the law of the land. When a fugitive appeared at Upham's backdoor the next day, he defied the law, giving the fugitive money and provisions. This incident revealed that the moral invalidity of the Fugitive Slave Act could be driven home by means of vivid images figuratively placing a fugitive at the door of every reader. As she put it in describing her narrative method, "There is no arguing with pictures, and every body is impressed by them, whether they mean to be or not." Transformed by the appearance of the fugitive, Upham, like his literary analogue, Senator Bird in *Uncle Tom's Cabin*, experiences the emerging anti-slavery consensus of the early 1850s as a transcendent moral truth. "Lifelike and graphic" depictions of the fugitives' plight had the power, it seemed, to create a moral consensus at the very instant its authority was needed to defy the enactment.[14] A few months after Seward's controversial higher-law argument against the Fugitive Slave Act, Stowe published "The Freeman's Dream: A Parable" in the anti-slavery newspaper the *National Era* – the venue for the initial publication of *Uncle Tom's Cabin*. In this brief sketch, Stowe imagines the northern farmer who obeys the Fugitive Slave Act refusing to aid "a poor black man, worn and wasted, his clothes rent and travel-soiled, and his step crouching and fearful" and his wife, "a thin and trembling woman, with a wailing babe at her bosom, and a frightened child clinging to her skirts." The fugitives are retaken, and subsequently, in a dream, the farmer foresees his fate for obeying the iniquitous Fugitive Slave Act: "Depart from me ye accursed! For I was an hungered, and ye gave me no meat; I was thirsty, and ye gave me no drink; I was a stranger, and ye took me not in." Explicitly siding with Seward, Stowe censures those "who seem to think that there is no standard of right and wrong higher than an act of Congress or an interpretation of the United States Constitution."[15]

The success of Stowe's anti-slavery writing derives largely from the iconic power of her higher law images. Her characters, their appearances, actions, and words, are types of justice and injustice, whose higher law significance is quickly and unmistakably interpreted. The moral pattern of compassion and Christian forbearance embodied in Uncle Tom is set against the tyrannical type of unregulated power represented by Simon Legree. The dramatic interactions Stowe stages between such characters are designed to trigger in the reader an immediate intuition of slavery's moral impracticability. This intuition seems conclusive and unimpeachable because it springs unbidden from the well of sympathy innate to human nature. Stowe derives her notion of sympathy in part from the moral sense philosophy central to the Founding Fathers' republicanism. Sympathy was an important aspect of the faculty of moral insight, shared by the ploughman and the professor, as Thomas Jefferson put it, which authoritatively discerned the ethical norms upon which law must be based to be legitimate, but which, in any event, must be obeyed if one is to live morally. Stowe famously posits the authority of this form of intuition in the "Concluding Remarks" to *Uncle Tom's Cabin*: "[W]hat can any individual do? . . . They can see to it that they feel right. An atmosphere of sympathetic influence encircles every human being; and the man or woman who feels strongly, healthily, and justly on the great interest of humanity, is a constant benefactor to the human race."[16] The spontaneous eruption of sympathy in a reader confronting a telling image of the clash between the Fugitive Slave Law and the higher law of Christian charity, for Stowe, was a sure signal of the statute's invalidity and the entitlement of the enslaved to certain fundamental human rights.

In describing the moral responses of an individual, Stowe portrays sympathy as capable of creating a new jurisprudential consensus, as, for instance, when, in *Uncle Tom's Cabin*, Senator Bird is moved by the appearance of Eliza Harris and her son to accept his wife's position condemning the Fugitive Slave Act (77). However, certain complications in the jurisprudence of sympathy emerge in Stowe's visualization of the ideal moral community in *Uncle Tom's Cabin*. The Quaker society of Rachel and Simeon Halliday is united in and governed by its collective moral sense. Rachel Halliday leads this benevolent and peaceful polis not by virtue of some power that she possesses but by reason of the moral authority manifest in her "loving words, gentle moralities, and motherly loving kindness," which solve "spiritual and temporal" problems. Her gentle commands, "Thee had better" and "Had n't thee better?" do not refer to the threat of punishment or the promise of reward but to the auditor's sense of morality (121). In this busy but harmonious society, the dictates of conscience and the rule of law are identical. Revealingly, two outsiders, George Harris, and Phineas Fletcher, a convert to Quakerism, interrupt the Quakers' consensus of pacifism, sympathy, and self-sacrifice with expressions of rebellious indignation and revolutionary intent. When cautioned by Simeon Halliday against acting violently out of the heat of his "young blood," George responds that he would "attack no man" but would fight to the death to prevent the recapture of his wife and son. And, while Phineas agrees with Simeon that the "temptation" of armed resistance is best avoided, he adds, "if we are tempted too much, – why, let them look out, that's all" (163–164). The combination of George and Phineas's unapologetic willingness to use force and their status as outsiders suggests that the good-hearted rule of a sympathetic consensus may be impracticable in the face of social diversity and the resulting competition for power.

Indeed, at times, one can sense Stowe's attraction to force as an alternative to or outcome of the sympathetic response. In Eliza Harris's harrowing escape, for instance, one is carried from sympathy to an intense desire for the power to challenge the legal tyranny of slavery with violent means. Despite the Quakers' reservations, the resolve of George Harris and Phineas Fletcher to repel the slave catchers by violent means is plainly heroic, and their battle with Tom Loker on a rocky promontory recalls similar scenes of romantic heroics in James Fenimore Cooper's *The Last of the Mohicans*. As a kind of authorial expiation for her indulgence in the satisfying violence of the action–adventure tale, Stowe does not kill Loker but merely wounds him so that he can be converted while convalescing in a Christian home (168–176). Even in the climax of her novel, Uncle Tom's martyrdom, an apotheosis of Christian compassion and self-sacrifice, Stowe cannot wholly resist the temptation of force, and she has George Shelby strike Tom's murderer Legree to the ground. It is simply not enough to know that Legree will suffer an adverse divine judgment. We must see his malign force answered here and now (364).

Stowe's second anti-slavery novel, *Dred*, explores in greater detail the relation of power to the formation and enforcement of law. In *Dred*, the comments of three slaveholders about the peculiar institution reveal the ubiquity of power in what seem to be different theories of law. Each of these men is a lawgiver, adjudicating disputes and legislating rules for his slave population. Edward Clayton, a sympathetic southerner and a lawyer, conceives of the law as grounded in the sympathetic feelings of the moral sense. His vision of legal authority takes the form of a paternalistic benevolence not unlike that espoused by George Fitzhugh:

> "It is a debt which we owe," he said, "to the character of our state, and to the purity of our institutions, to prove the efficiency of the law in behalf of that class of our population whose helplessness places them more particularly under our protection. They are to us in the condition of children under age; and any violation of their rights should be more particularly attended to."[17]

Mr. Jekyl, another slaveholder and lawyer, argues that law is properly based on majority tradition. The law of slavery is justified not by power but on the theory that "the white race had the largest amount of being" and therefore "had a right to take precedence." Jekyl's incorporeal notion of "being" in its metaphoric emphasis of size simultaneously registers and evades the importance of actual physical might to the legitimating principles of majority

tradition (169). Like Simon Legree, Tom Gordon bluntly accepts the posi-
tivistic reality of slavery: "The best way of educating is, to show folks that
they can't help themselves. . . . Just let them know that there are no two ways
about it, and you'll have all still enough" (163). For Gordon, all human interaction boils down to the question of power, and the undeniable reality of
the unequal distribution of power is the sole justification necessary for its
exercise.

The presence of power in all three versions of temporal authority (the
higher-law argument of Clayton that his "helpless" slaves should obey him
because "what I command is right in the sight of God," the pragmatic view
of Mr. Jekyl that the metaphysical largeness of the white race's being autho-
rizes the white domination, and the frank and brutal positivism of Gordon
that the white race has "the power" and need only teach slaves the "weight"
of its "fist") and the marked absence of moral consensus conveys Stowe's
own concern that the law may prove to be chiefly if not solely an expression
of power (297, 163, 169, 161). This concern is particularly manifest in the
failure of Edward Clayton, the most sympathetic of the novel's white characters, to enter into partnership with the black Americans he defends. Unlike
Mr. Wilson, who, in *Uncle Tom's Cabin*, is converted to civil disobedience
by George Harris's eloquent declaration of independence, Clayton is not
transformed by the revolutionary jeremiad of Dred, the novel's black hero.
Instead, Clayton trivializes Dred as a "curious psychological study" and a
subject of "quaint and poetic interest" and reduces his revolutionary declaration to a "wild jargon of hebraistic phrases, names, and allusions" (509).
Clayton's alternative to Dred's visionary revolution is a project of black education and uplift, which, due to the intransigence of racism among whites,
necessitates emigration. Accepting both the practical necessity of emigration and majority power as the only means of securing one's rights, Stowe's
second novel clearly foreshadows the black nationalism of Martin Delany's
Blake; or The Huts of America (1861–62).[18]

In Stowe's figurations of justice, the tension between moral consensus and
power is accompanied by a kindred oscillation between contract and status.
When depicting contract as a sign and means of just human relations, Stowe
imagines characters who, in agreeing to the terms of their association, overcome differences of birth and background. Such moments differ significantly
from those where Stowe figures decent human interaction as an adherence
to roles prescribed by God or nature. The vacillation between contract and
status in Stowe's writing can be seen by comparing a pair of scenes from
Uncle Tom's Cabin: the debate between Mr. and Mrs. Bird and the colloquy
between George Harris and Mr. Wilson. While Stowe is uncompromisingly

critical of the displacement of moral feeling by profit motive whether it occurs in slavery or capitalism, she clearly does not condemn contract as inherently coercive (whether deluded or not, Stowe's views differ significantly from those of more recent commentators, such as Michele Foucault, Louis Althusser, and Carole Pateman, who are variously skeptical of the distinction between coercion and consent).[19]

The Birds' cozy home provides the setting for the first of these scenes. Worn out by the "tiresome business" of legislating, the Senator has returned for some "good, home living" (67). Senator Bird's relaxation is broken by Mary Bird's inquiry about the Fugitive Slave Act. While she does not normally "trouble her head" about the affairs of state, the moral issues involved compel Mary Bird to interrogate her husband. Senator Bird replies, "Your feelings are all quite right, dear . . . I love you for them; but . . . we mustn't suffer our feelings to run away with our judgment; you must consider it's not a matter of private feeling, – there are great public interests involved." Mrs. Bird's answer to her husband's separate spheres argument – "I don't know anything about politics, but I can read my Bible; and there I see that I must feed the hungry, clothe the naked and comfort the desolate" – is disingenuous to the extent that it seems to separate the moral and legal areas of expertise (69). Her objection to the Fugitive Slave Act accords with the Founding Fathers' belief in a legal system grounded in virtue and sanctioned by the citizenry's moral sense.

Mrs. Bird's higher-law argument is decisively advanced when Eliza Harris appears at their door, a veritable picture of "the real presence of distress" – "a young and slender woman with garments torn and frozen, with one shoe gone, and the stocking torn away from the cut and bleeding foot" (77, 70). Punctuated by the emotionally compelling appearance of Eliza and her son, the Birds' debate closes with a new consensus between husband and wife, and Senator Bird's ideas of law are re-grounded in the moral sense expressed by Mrs. Bird. Far from representing an opposition of law and morality, the Birds' dialogue embodies the process of inspiration and conversation through which the public conscience is animated and the law is revised.

However, by rooting this consensual process within the family and the domestic setting, the original site of status-based relations, Stowe mutes the open-ended potential of consent as a mechanism of civic and social relation. Instead of acknowledging the fact, as George Fitzhugh would insist, that human beings can agree to anything, even monstrous forms of social innovation (Fitzhugh cites the practice of polygamy), Stowe's vision of consent is comfortingly predetermined and limited by status.[20] Moral sentiment and spousal negotiation flow in the channels provided by their respective roles as husband and wife. Senator Bird brings his worldly experience and rationalist argument to bear on the topic of the Fugitive Slave Law, Mrs. Bird responds with the moral intuition and sympathy native to women, and as parents they are both particularly susceptible to Eliza's appeal on behalf of her son. The happy outcome of their discussion depends in part on each performing his or her role. Mrs. Bird's moral intuition, her birthright as a woman and a mother, must trump Mr. Bird's worldly experience and professional expertise for the latter to be legitimate.

Like the seal of the anti-slavery society – slave in manacles, kneeling on one knee, hands uplifted in a prayerful pose of supplication, asking "am I not a man and a brother" – the appeal to conscience made by Eliza's appearance does not disrupt status or verge on contract. Eliza asks for charity not partnership, and charity does not necessitate any renegotiation of civic values. In planning the next leg of Eliza's escape, the Birds do not need to seek her consent, despite the substantial evidence of Eliza's agency as the author of her own bold escape. As a woman and a supplicant, she must take what they give. The passage thus advances and withdraws consent as a guide for human relations, pushing simultaneously toward the higher-law mix of conscience and consent (within the white National Family) *and* the paternalistic ethics requiring the strong (white Americans) to care for the weak (black Americans), which is as Fitzhugh points out the ethical basis of slavery. Focusing solely on this scene, one might suspect, that for Stowe, moral feelings and the legal and political consensus they inspire are innately connected to and derive legitimacy from the participants' adherence to role or type.

But this impression is qualified when we turn to the second scene – the conversation between Mr. Wilson and George Harris. Harris and Wilson meet in a tavern, a place of business and politics (just pages earlier we witness the tavern negotiations between Haley, the slave trader, and Tom Loker, the slave hunter). In their discussion, Harris and Wilson seek to persuade each other of the propriety or impropriety of Harris's plan of escape. Harris begins with the tools of logical argument. He offers Mr. Wilson an analogy:

> "I wonder, Mr. Wilson, if the Indians should come and take you a prisoner away from your wife and children, . . . if you'd think it your duty to abide in the condition in which you were called." (95)

Harris suggests an imagined reversal of positions, but analogy – the forte of lawyers and judges – is not Wilson's strong suit (in a neat, though incomplete, reversal of racial types). When Wilson responds that Harris's desperate state of mind drives him to break "the laws of your country," Harris sounds a theme taken up by Douglass's "What to the Slave is the Fourth of July?" address:

"My country again! Mr. Wilson, you have a country; but what country have
I, or any one like me, born of slave mothers? What laws are there for us? We
don't make them, – we don't consent to them, – we have nothing to do with
them; all they do for us is to crush us, and keep us down. Haven't I heard your
Fourth-of-July speeches? Don't you tell us all, once a year, that governments
derive their just power from the consent of the governed?"   (95–96)

Harris's conclusion is inescapable, by the founders' own principles, the duty
to obey is predicated on the right to participate. The nullity of the latter
voids the former. To drive home the point of his rational argument, Harris
speaks to Wilson's heart, reducing the latter to tears with a vivid portrait of
the cruelties inflicted on his family by the system of slavery.

As with the Birds' debate, this scene ends in consensus, but it is a different
kind of consensus. Separated by racial and legal status as well as differing
views of religion and civic duty, Harris and Wilson manage to come to terms,
and the two men become, in effect, co-conspirators defying the Fugitive Slave
Act. Even though Harris's independence and intelligence – his competence
to enter into contract – is figured as an inheritance from his white father, this
scene comes close to suggesting that the processes of consent may enable
people to decide what is right rather than simply referring moral questions
to intuitions and feelings which Stowe overtly connects to status. One result
of George's successful participation in this debate is his transformation. As
Mr. Wilson notes at the conclusion of their discussion, "George, something
has brought you out wonderfully. You hold up your head, and speak and
move like another man" (98). The figure of George's transformation connects contract with change and change with value; George's mutability is a
sign of the mutability of ethical consensus, which gives the higher-law tradition its continuing power. In connecting the new ethical–legal consensus
between Harris and Wilson to George Harris's new manner of being, Stowe's
novel suggests not only that values may shift or receive new impressions
but also that transformation may itself be a gauge of ethical and aesthetic
value.

Early in her career, Stowe conceived of America's willingness to transform
itself by social and legal experiment as a sign of moral health. In "Uncle
Enoch," an 1839 temperance tale recommending prohibition as a remedy
for alcoholism, Stowe's eponymous hero applauds his country as a place
"where they are continually finding out new things, and when a man has
invented a new machine, if it's useful, we praise him and pay him too."[21] In
celebrating the end of slavery after the war, Stowe overtly connects personal
development to legal and societal transformation – in both cases, mutability
is a sign of moral vitality. The very possibility of personal transformation
functions as a measure of the virtue of the American legal system:

> It is the pride and the boast of truly republican institutions that they give to
> every human being an opportunity of thus demonstrating what is in him. If a
> man *is* a man, no matter in what rank of society he is born, no matter how
> tied down and weighted by poverty and all its attendant disadvantages, there
> is nothing in our American institutions to prevent his rising to the very highest
> offices in the gift of the country.   (*Men of Our Times*, 380–381)

Citizens, such as Frederick Douglass, who fully embody this process of personal transformation, best represent the nation's values:

> Now if we think it a great thing that [Henry] Wilson and Lincoln raised them-
> selves from a state of comparatively early disadvantage to high places in the
> land, what shall we think of one who started from this immeasurable gulf
> below them? Frederick Douglass had as far to climb to get to the spot where
> the poorest free white boy is born, as that white boy has to climb to be president
> of this nation, and take rank with kings and judges of the earth.
>   (*Men of Our Times*, 381–382)

Stowe similarly locates the Constitution's ethical value in its "progressive
character," commending Charles Sumner for demonstrating that the Constitution is not graven in stone but is and was intended by the framers to be
revisable so as "to suit new exigencies and new conditions of feeling" (*Men
of Our Times*, 223).

Lady Byron Vindicated underscores the trend in Stowe's thought from status to contract and her willingness to revise fundamental aspects of American
society including the legal status of women and the nature of marriage. More
than an anecdotal defense of Lady Byron from charges that she had failed
her wifely obligations, Stowe's text is a defense of women's rights and an
argument for gender equality in marriage. Clearly perceiving the broader
import of *Lady Byron Vindicated* and being eager to defend Stowe from
charges of sensationalism, Elizabeth Cady Stanton commented that

> Mrs. Stowe's fearful picture of the abominations of our social life, coming
> out simultaneously with John Stuart Mill's philosophy of the degradation of
> woman, will do much to rouse wise men to new thought on the social wrongs
> of the race, for whatever enslaves woman debases man; together we must rise
> or fall."[22]

In *Lady Byron Vindicated*, Stowe rejects as "slavery for woman" the anti-
contractual conception of marriage in which

> a man may sink himself below the brute, may wallow in filth like the swine, may
> turn his home into a hell, beat and torture his children, forsake the marriage-
> bed for foul rivals; yet all this does *not* dissolve the marriage-vow on her part,
> nor free his bounden serf from her obligation to honor his memory.

Stowe adds, if Lady Byron *"as a wife* has no rights, what is the state of the cotter's wife?" (*Lady Byron*, 114, 119–120). Stowe's defense of Lady Byron's right to separate from her husband for *his* breach of their marital relation reduces the significance of Lady Byron's status as a woman and wife and advances a more frankly contractual conception of the marriage relation in which both spouses, as equal partners, are governed not by respective, naturally or divinely inscribed roles, but by the contract setting forth the terms of their mutual obligation. Moving away from status toward a consensual notion of human development and association, Stowe's depictions of the law illustrate how a jurisprudence of moral and religious absolutes can become a jurisprudence of human consent. And the increasing emphasis on the value of transformation in her writing suggests that we reconsider both her notions of sentiment and law in relation to the long line of American intellectuals and authors weighing the costs and benefits of more fluid conceptions of existence and meaning.

NOTES

1. Brook Thomas, *Cross-Examinations of Law and Literature: Cooper, Hawthorne, Stowe, and Melville* (Cambridge: Cambridge University Press, 1987). James M. Cox, "Harriet Beecher Stowe: from sectionalism to regionalism," *Nineteenth Century Fiction* 38 (1984), 455. Lisa Whitney finds that the discourses of sentiment and law are so different as to foreclose any attempt on Stowe's part to marry them in *Dred*. Whitney, "In the shadow of *Uncle Tom's Cabin*: Stowe's vision of slavery from the Great Dismal Swamp," *New England Quarterly* 66 (1993), 555.
2. Harriet Beecher Stowe, "Love versus Law," in *Stories, Sketches and Studies* (Boston: Houghton, Mifflin and Company, 1896), 32–73; subsequent references to this text are made parenthetically in the essay.
3. Harriet Beecher Stowe, *Men of Our Times; or, Leading Patriots of the Day* (Hartford, CN: Hartford Publishing Co., 1868), 24; subsequent references to this text are made parenthetically in the essay.
4. Stowe's use of documentary evidence in *A Key to Uncle Tom's Cabin* (Boston: John P. Jewett, 1853) drew on the precedent established by Theodore D. Weld's *American Slavery As It Is: Testimony of a Thousand Witnesses* (New York: American Anti-Slavery Society, 1839). Harriet Beecher Stowe, *Lady Byron Vindicated: A History of the Byron Controversy, from its Beginnings in 1816 to the Present Time* (Boston: Fields, Osgood, & Co., 1870), 2, 19–29, 303; subsequent references to this text are made parenthetically in the essay. The merger of the romantic and sentimental literary conventions and trial practice has been thoughtfully discussed in the following essays: Robert A. Ferguson, "Story and transcription in the trial of John Brown," *Yale Journal of Law and the Humanities* 6 (1994), 37–73, and Laura Hanft Korobkin, "The maintenance of mutual confidence: sentimental strategies at the adultery trial of Henry Ward Beecher," *Yale Journal of Law and the Humanities* 7 (1995), 1–48.

5. For a discussion of Seward's speech and the higher-law tradition, see Gregg Crane, *Race, Citizenship, and Law in American Literature* (Cambridge: Cambridge University Press, 2002), 12–55.
6. George Fitzhugh argues that the authority of the slaveholder is as natural and inevitable as that of the parent. Fitzhugh, *Sociology for the South; or the Failure of Free Society* (Richmond, VA: A. Morris, 1854), 25–26, 89.
7. Critics blasted Seward for opening constitutional jurisprudence to "the casuistry of theologians, the dicta of modern philosophers, and the suggestions of metaphysical theorizers. Higher law, *The Republic* charged, "gives [Seward] a scope as wide as the winds." *The Republic*, March 15, 1850, quoted in the *New York Tribune*, March 19, 1850.
8. Letter, dated January 20, 1853, from Harriet Elizabeth [Beecher] Stowe to Thomas Denman, 1st Baron Denman, Huntington Library, San Marino, California.
9. "Review of *Dred*," *New Englander* 13 (November 1856), 515; Richmond *Enquirer*, January 23, 1857; George Frederick Holmes, "Editorial and literary department," *De Bow's Review* 13 (September 1852), 319.
10. Charles Sumner, "Freedom National, Slavery Sectional," *The Works of Charles Sumner*, 15 vols. (Boston: Lee and Shepard, 1872), III, 181–182, 184.
11. Representative Bingham, *Congressional Globe*, 36th Congress, 2nd Session, Jan. 23, 1861, appendix, 83.
12. Senator Henry Wilson, *Congressional Globe*, 39th Congress, 1st Session, Jan. 22, 1866, 343.
13. Rep. Jehu Baker, *Congressional Globe*, 39th Congress, 1st Session, July 9, 1866, appendix, 256.
14. Joan D. Hedrick, *Harriet Beecher Stowe: A Life* (New York: Oxford University Press, 1994), 205–206, 208.
15. Stowe, "The Freeman's Dream: A Parable," in *The Oxford Harriet Beecher Stowe Reader*, ed. Joan D. Hedrick (New York: Oxford University Press, 1999), 57–58.
16. Harriet Beecher Stowe, *Uncle Tom's Cabin* (New York: Norton, 1994), 472; subsequent references to this text are made parenthetically in the essay. Thomas Jefferson, *The Portable Thomas Jefferson*, ed. Merrill Peterson (New York: Penguin, 1975), 385; Hedrick, *Stowe*, 5, 86; Charles H. Foster, *The Rungless Ladder: Harriet Beecher Stowe and New England Puritanism* (Durham: Duke University Press, 1954), 14; Robert Forrest Wilson, *Crusader in Crinoline: The Life of Harriet Beecher Stowe* (Philadelphia: J. B. Lippincott, 1941), 71; Charles Edward Stowe and Lyman Beecher Stowe, *Harriet Beecher Stowe: The Story of Her Life* (Boston: Houghton-Mifflin, 1911), 41.
17. Harriet Beecher Stowe, *Dred: A Tale of the Great Dismal Swamp* (New York: Penguin, 2000), 297; subsequent references to this text are made parenthetically in the essay.
18. Crane, *Race, Citizenship, and Law in American Literature*, 138–157.
19. Under the influence of Michel Foucault's view of all law as coercive, for instance, one may feel that the notion of a consensual legal mechanism is a contradiction in terms. See, for example, image of law presented in the famous opening pages of Foucault's *Discipline and Punish: The Birth of the Prison* (New York: Pantheon, 1977). See, also, Louis Althusser, "Ideology and ideological state apparatuses

(notes towards an investigation)," in *Lenin and Philosophy and Other Essays* (New York: Monthly Review Press, 1971), 156–157, 167–168; Carole Pateman, *The Sexual Contract* (Stanford: Stanford University Press, 1988), 8.

20. George Fitzhugh, "The Conservative Principle; or, Social Evils and their Remedies," *De Bow's Review* 22 (1857), 427.
21. Stowe, "Uncle Enoch," in *The Oxford Harriet Beecher Stowe Reader*, 32.
22. As quoted in Hedrick, *Stowe: A Life*, 364.

9

RONALD G. WALTERS

Harriet Beecher Stowe and the American reform tradition

One of the more curious passages by Harriet Beecher Stowe appears in a novel by someone else. In August 1857 she contributed a "Preface" for the second novel by an African-American author, Frank J. Webb's *The Garies and Their Friends*. After acknowledging violence against free black people and abolitionists in the north, especially virulent in the 1830s and a matter central to the novel, Stowe claimed that "this spirit was subdued, and the right of free inquiry established . . ." Had she concluded there, this might simply be an example of a northerner congratulating her section on its moral superiority to the south. She added, however, that "the question [of freedom for African Americans], so far from being dangerous in the Free States, is now begun to be allowed in the slave States . . ." Stowe must have known how wrong this was. Her second anti-slavery novel, *Dred: A Tale of the Great Dismal Swamp* (1856), appeared a year before *The Garies* and a large part of its plot revolved around southern suppression, often violent, of anti-slavery speeches and publications.

The key to understanding how someone who went to great lengths to defend her accuracy could be so misguided is in the final words of the paragraph. "[T]here are," she wrote, "some subjects the mere discussion of which is a half-victory."[1] Stowe was less interested in southern openness to anti-slavery views – which hostile southern responses to her novels should have led her to doubt – than in defending the power of words to change individuals and, through them, society. As she put it in her 1854 "Appeal to the Women of the Free States," "there is not a woman in the United States, when the question [of slavery] is fairly put before her, who thinks these things are right."[2] In staking this position, she both asserted the value of her work as an author and placed herself within one part of a spectrum of contemporary reform thought. This was, nonetheless, a position her fiction sometimes betrayed. In each of her anti-slavery novels – *Uncle Tom's Cabin*, *Dred*, and *The Minister's Wooing* (1859) – words, her chosen instrument of social change, failed, often with catastrophic results.

Stowe's faith in the power of language in the face of contrary evidence reveals some of the costs as well as benefits in her marriage of reform and popular fiction. At issue here are not the fine points of her racial thought, the influence of her novels on public opinion, or whether or not her work subverts or reinforces male dominance, matters often treated by scholars. The question instead is what does Stowe tell us about the possibilities and problems in the fusion of her kind of fiction with larger reform impulses in American culture? The enormous popularity of *Uncle Tom's Cabin*, and the substantial readership for her other anti-slavery novels, testify to the ability of fiction to bring a controversial message to a large audience in a powerful and compelling fashion. Less obvious are some of the limitations in Stowe's use of popular fiction as an instrument of reform. In order to understand these limitations and their consequences for her novels, however, it is first necessary to locate her within the two great and rising currents in antebellum America that she brought together, often passionately and sometimes courageously: commercial popular culture and social reform.

The power and profit of words

By the time of Harriet Beecher's birth in 1811 a profound shift was underway in how Americans spent leisure time. Before 1800 there was little commercial popular culture and much of what existed was imported from Europe. Theatres were small, few in number, and expensive. Traveling performers had to deal with slow and unreliable transportation. Books and sheet music of popular songs were costly to print. In the New England of Stowe's parents' generation commercial popular amusements also faced deep skepticism about their morality.

Much had changed by the 1830s and 1840s, when Stowe began her literary career. Better transportation in the form of improved roads, canals, steam boats, and, eventually, the railroad made possible far greater circulation of performers, magazines, and books. New printing technologies lowered the cost of all kinds of publications. Americans also had become creators and exporters of popular culture, most notably in the 1840s with the rise of the deeply racist minstrel show, a form that traveled around the world (and produced numerous parodies of *Uncle Tom's Cabin*).

Within this proliferation of popular culture there were many strands, one heavily masculine, irreverent, and occasionally bawdy, best represented by minstrel shows and "dime novels" aimed largely at boys and young men. Its stock-in-trade were racial and ethnic stereotypes and raucous characters like Davy Crockett, who swaggered, had fantastic adventures, told tall tales, and mocked the virtues of Stowe's pious heroes and heroines. At the other extreme was popular culture primarily aimed at the parlor and at women, represented by sheet music of sentimental songs, uplifting novels, and short fiction and poetry in nationally circulated magazines like the pioneering *Godey's Ladies' Book*, in which Stowe first published in 1839. She was well aware of the masculine strand – early in both *Uncle Tom's Cabin* and *Dred* a slave child amuses whites by performing a popular minstrel number, "Jump Jim Crow" in one case and "I'll Bet my Money on a Bob-tail Nag" in the other.[3] Her writings, however, were within its antithesis, the highly religious, respectable, and heavily feminine second variety of popular culture. Its moralism had a special affinity for another deep current in antebellum culture: a reformist spirit.

If there were few forms of commercial popular culture available in the United States before 1800, there were also few reformers. With important exceptions, the most notable eighteenth-century Americans who sought to improve society were people like Ben Franklin or the Puritan minister Cotton Mather. For them, reform was a part-time or retirement activity, not their primary work.

By 1830, there were substantial numbers of men and women engaged in a wide range of crusades to uplift America, others, themselves, and the world. The same improvements in transportation and communications that fostered commercial popular culture also made large-scale reform movements possible by easing the difficulty and lowering the cost of a national, even international, flow of speakers, pamphlets, books, and ideas. In contrast to Franklin and Mather, some of these new reformers, like the fiery Boston abolitionist William Lloyd Garrison, would have no other career. They advocated so many causes that one participant, Stowe's fellow New Englander, Thomas Wentworth Higginson, recalled about the 1840s, "there prevailed then a phrase, 'the Sisterhood of reforms'" referring to "a variety of social and physiological theories of which one was expected to accept all, if any."[4] Also telling was his use of "Sisterhood," tacit acknowledgment of the importance of women as organizers, speakers, and writers. The last role was most congenial for Stowe.

Within antebellum reform there were three answers to the question of "where does change begin?" The first was collective and potentially coercive. It sought reform through organized efforts to pass laws or create institutions such as schools, or more humane asylums and prisons, designed to educate and improve individuals, even while incarcerating them. Stowe moved from Cincinnati to Maine in time for a major victory for this approach. In 1851 that state put into effect the so-called Maine Law, the first successful statewide attempt to limit consumption of alcoholic beverages. Although hardly a supporter of rum-sellers, Stowe's sympathies were not with this method of reforming society. In her anti-slavery novels the law most commonly upholds evil rather than prevents it and the only truly sound reform institutions are Christian families and New England-style schools.

A second approach to reform also involved institutions, but creating utopian ones separate from conventional society, not coercive ones within it. During the antebellum years there was a remarkable flowering of communitarian groups, some religious like the Shakers, and some with scandalous sexual practices like the Oneida community, in which all men and women were considered married to each other. One, Brook Farm, is best remembered for its association with famous New England Transcendentalists and as the inspiration for a novel, Nathaniel Hawthorne's dark meditation on reformers, *Blithedale Romance*. Some of these little utopias were anti-reform in the sense that members joined to withdraw from a corrupt world, not to purify it. Others like Oneida, however, were meant to demonstrate the perfectability of human beings or to build models of an ideal society, often drawing upon the theories of European utopians like Charles Fourier and Robert Owen, who founded his own American community in New Harmony, Indiana. This was reforming by example and by creating an ideal against which to measure the imperfection of one's own society.

Scant traces of utopianism appear in Stowe and we shall see that a problem in her anti-slavery fiction was her inability to imagine a perfect new America after the end of slavery. Although drawn to the New England of her parents' childhood, the setting of *The Minister's Wooing*, Stowe nonetheless refused to see it as an ideal society, or even one in which she might have lived happily. "[T]he keen New England air," she declared, "crystalizes emotions into ideas, and restricts many a poetic soul to the necessity of expressing itself only in practical living."[5] (The latter was not the realm in which Stowe was most comfortable.) The closest she came to conjuring a utopian alternative is in lyrical passages about a timeless model of domesticity. In *The Minister's Wooing* it appears as "that appointed shrine for woman, more holy than cloister, more saintly and pure than church or altar, – *a Christian home*" that "by faith and prayer and love redeems from grossness and earthliness the common toils and wants of life" (326). How such a little utopia might end slavery or other sins is not apparent. Within her own family there were painful reminders that Christian mothers did not always succeed, and her anti-slavery novels have bad characters who were raised in pious families, notably Simon Legree in *Uncle Tom's Cabin* and Aaron Burr in *The Minister's Wooing*.

Stowe's heart was with a third answer to the question of where change begins – with the individual. By this line of reasoning, reform was the sum of personal conversions to the cause, brought about by, in the nineteenth-century term, *moral suasion*, not coercion. In real life, any number of means could produce such a conversion, including first-hand experience with the evils of slavery, as happens in *Uncle Tom's Cabin* and *Dred*. Or it could occur through words in reform propaganda, in sermons, or even in everyday conversation. It might also come from reading sentimental novels that reproduce all these other forms of writing and speaking. Although compatible with other approaches to reform, moral suasion was Harriet Beecher Stowe's weapon of choice. It was an anti-slavery tactic that fit hand-in-glove with her deep conviction that sympathy for the slave, once evoked in a person, produced an instant abolitionist. As she imagined it in action in *The Minister's Wooing*, slavery in New England "fell before the force of conscience and moral appeal" (326). Stowe's wholehearted acceptance of moral suasion influenced her fiction in positive ways – it helped her create memorable exchanges between her characters – but its emphasis on individual experience also made it easier for her to envision a person becoming free than a free society.

The first variety of freedom that attracted Stowe's attention was freedom from alcohol. Of all the causes in her day, temperance was the longest-lived and largest in terms of membership. Less a movement than a collection of groups and agendas, it was a broad assault on selling and drinking alcoholic beverages. Stowe might reasonably have made it her special crusade: her father, Lyman Beecher, was one of its early powerful voices, thanks to his thundering *Six Sermons on Intemperance* (1826), and her son Fred's alcoholism was among the sorrows of her life. Stowe's first publications included one entitled "The Drunkard Reclaimed."[6] If the temperance cause was familiar to her, the intricacies of the American anti-slavery movement apparently were not. The *Liberator* claimed that she did not learn about a major schism within the movement until over a decade after it happened, and then only when she visited Glasgow, Scotland, following publication of *Uncle Tom's Cabin*.[7] It was, however, the Fugitive Slave Law of 1850, not temperance, that most fired her moral indignation and made her a central figure in the history of American abolitionism.

Opposition to slavery went back well before Stowe's birth. A major character in *The Minister's Wooing*, Samuel Hopkins, wrote an important pamphlet against the institution in 1776, somewhat overshadowed by other events that year. By 1831, abolitionist views and strategies had changed considerably from the dominant ones in Hopkins's day. Earlier anti-slavery advocates tended to be moderate and conciliatory in language, and to foresee slavery ending over an unspecified period of time through the benevolence of slaveholders. Prior to the 1830s, abolitionists also often imagined an America without slavery as one without black people, a view promoted by the American Colonization Society, founded in 1816. A major part of its mission was to send all freed slaves to its African outpost, Liberia, to make that continent Christian and America white.

Quite different was the position that emerged in the 1830s, articulated with extraordinary vehemence in William Lloyd Garrison's the *Liberator*, first published on January 1, 1831. It saw slavery as inconsistent with Christianity and a sin to be denounced passionately, not an unfortunate institution inflicted on white Americans by the British, as The Declaration of Independence would have it, or a benevolent one as defenders argued. And if slavery was a sin, it must be repudiated immediately: Christians, after all, are not supposed to cease fornication gradually. Why should slaveholding be different? A radical corollary to this new kind of abolitionism, called "immediatism," was "come-outerism," a conviction that abolitionists must separate themselves from institutions, including churches and political parties, that supported slavery, even tacitly.

If immediatists were willing to leave sinful institutions, they were not willing to separate themselves or the north from moral complicity in slavery. The national union – the Constitution and federal laws that upheld slavery – made the guilt America's, not simply the south's. This was a crucial point: there could be no anti-slavery movement if men and women in the free states regarded slavery as none of their business. *Uncle Tom's Cabin* would have had far less impact if members of Stowe's northern audience believed themselves to be reading about something morally remote from their own lives.

Not content simply to assert the sinfulness of slavery, immediatists pursued a two-fold strategy in attacking southern portraits of slavery as benign and paternalistic. The first part was to present, often from southern sources, examples of extreme cruelty to slaves, one major compendium of which was *American Slavery as It Is*, assembled in 1839 by Theodore Dwight Weld, his wife, Angelina Grimké Weld, and her sister, Sarah Grimké. The second response was to deny that brutality was the primary objection to slavery. As *American Slavery as It Is* put it, "cruelty is the spontaneous and uniform product of arbitrary power."[8] The real evil of slavery was not in how masters used their power over slaves, but rather in the fact that they had it. A corollary of this was that even the best-treated, most loyal slaves yearned for freedom, as they do in each of Stowe's abolitionist novels.

A final plank in the post-1830 abolitionist platform was its rejection of colonization. Immediatists denied that an end to slavery required expulsion of African Americans from the United States. On every point with the debatable exception of this one, Stowe's anti-slavery novels stood with the new, more radical abolitionism. Even on colonization, her position is not entirely clear, a matter to which we will return after examining her three anti-slavery novels.

Stowe as abolitionist

When Stowe wrote *Uncle Tom's Cabin*, the prospects for producing an abolitionist best-seller must have seemed dim. In 1836 Massachusetts native Richard Hildreth published an anti-slavery novel, *The Slave: or Memoirs of Archy Moore*, that went through multiple editions, but was not a popular success. Even the *Liberator*, trumpeting the importance of Hildreth's text in the wake of *Uncle Tom's Cabin*, could only say that "there is scarcely an anti-slavery man of more than ten years' standing, who does not look back to the perusal of the book as adding fresh fuel to his zeal, and giving additional force and clearness to his convictions."[9] In other words, it appealed to the small number of Americans already converted to the cause, and so did much other anti-slavery fiction, like works aimed at children bearing such titles as *The Slave's Friend* or the *Anti-Slavery Alphabet*.[10]

Abolitionists were despised in the south and widely regarded as extremists in the north – not promising credentials for a popular author, as Stowe well knew. While she was living in Cincinnati in 1835 a mob destroyed the press of an anti-slavery editor, James G. Birney, along with the homes of black families. Although it was much safer to be an abolitionist in the 1850s, to attack slavery was to enter into controversial territory, not a formula for reaching a mass audience. Stowe may have had the popularity of *Uncle Tom's Cabin* in mind, and tongue in cheek, when in *The Minister's Wooing* the unworldly Dr. Hopkins finally publishes his dense "theological system." "Quite unexpectedly to himself," she wrote, "the work proved a success . . ." (327).

Part of *Uncle Tom*'s popularity came from the fact that audiences could separate its vivid characters, comic interludes, and melodramatic storytelling from the anti-slavery message. There is good evidence of that in the durability of stage versions of *Uncle Tom's Cabin* long after the end of slavery. It continued to inspire music well into the 1880s, when a "New American Opera" (1887) version appeared, as well as a ditty, "Uncle Tom's Gwine to Stay" (1881), written for the great African-American performer, Sam Lucas. The story, often loosely adapted, appeared in at least fourteen movies, beginning in 1903 and including a 1965 German one with a Hungarian director. As late as 1987 a "contemporary version" surfaced as a made-for-television movie. Whatever else these homages to Stowe's novel accomplished, they were not using moral suasion to create new abolitionists.

Yet the author herself – although never averse to selling books – denied any interpretation of *Uncle Tom's Cabin* or *Dred* other than an anti-slavery one. "The object of these sketches," she tells readers in her "Preface" to *Uncle Tom's Cabin*, "is to awaken sympathy and feeling for the African race, as they exist among us; to show their wrongs and sorrows under a system so necessarily cruel and unjust as to defeat and do away with the good effects of all that can be attempted for them, by their best friends, under it" (xiii).

Appealing to "sympathy and feeling," however, put Stowe in a difficult position because these were the standard fare of sentimental novels having nothing to do with reform or social realities. She countered claims that her works were similarly "mere fiction" by asserting the reality of their portrait of slavery. In the final chapter of the book *Uncle Tom's Cabin*, she responded to critics of the earlier serial version run in the *National Era* by declaring that "The separate incidents that compose the narrative are, to a very great extent, authentic, occurring, many of them, either under her [Stowe's] own observation, or that of her personal friends" (381).

Stung by assaults on her veracity and threatened with a libel suit by a clergyman, Joel Parker, she produced *A Key to Uncle Tom's Cabin* in 1853, a collection of documents linked to chapters in the novel. Her "Preface" to *A Key* thanked "those legal gentlemen who have given her their assistance and support in the legal part of the discussion" of slavery, and others "at the North and at the South, who have kindly furnished materials for her use."[11] This marked an expansion of her claim to have drawn upon first-hand observations or those of friends. Now she had the legal profession and southerners as well as northerners behind her.

An intriguing thing about *A Key* is that it was unnecessary. The material in it was irrelevant for any legal action against her by Parker. She could simply have referred readers to *American Slavery as It Is* for further documentation. The strategic significance of *A Key* is that it allowed her to insist upon the truth of her novel, page by page, rather than in a looser, more metaphorical manner. The result was a devastating counter-attack on her southern critics and, once again, on slavery itself.

After *Uncle Tom's Cabin* she pursued progressively less ambitious strategies for convincing readers of the reality of her fiction. To *Dred* she added three appendices. One was a white lawyer's transcription of the *Confessions* of the slave rebel, Nat Turner, slightly expurgated. The second consisted of documents supporting the "terrible stories" of slave abuse told in one chapter. The final appendix perhaps indicated that Stowe was weary of defending herself from charges of presenting falsehoods in the service of abolition. It consisted of extracts from *A Key*. In her final anti-slavery novel, *The Minister's Wooing*, her claim to be presenting a true picture of slavery is largely implicit and made through incorporation of real figures and incidents into a romantic narrative. By then, nonetheless, she played fast and loose with history in ways that say more about her commitment to her plot than about her commitment to accuracy.

Stowe's problem was one inherent in using sentimental novels as a form of moral suasion. She had to convince readers that they were both fiction and not fiction, a difficulty she exacerbated by asides to readers and other devices that marked her works as novels, while contradictorily asserting in *A Key* that *Uncle Tom's Cabin* "has a purpose transcending the artistic one" and that "therefore as a reality it may be proper that it should be defended" (5). This was the mirror image of the problem abolitionist editors like Garrison confronted in persuading readers that their factual accounts of slavery were not fiction.

Whether or not Stowe convinced readers of the truth of her anti-slavery novels, they set forth an abolitionist agenda scarcely less radical than Garrison's. In doing that, she reached a mass audience that eluded immediatists like him in part because of differences in how they understood moral suasion and words as instruments of reform. Although Garrison was extreme in his harsh language, for him and his colleagues moral suasion meant denouncing sin and sinners without compromise. Where much immediatist rhetoric was abstract and confrontational, Stowe's mode of persuasion was to embed the argument in memorable characters and to use them to juxtapose conflicting positions, at times violently and at other times in a conversational manner. Where the polemics of Garrison bore witness against the sin of slavery and called upon others to do the same, Stowe's fiction encouraged readers to imagine it in practice and sympathize with the slave.

The Fugitive Slave Law of 1850 that provoked Stowe to write *Uncle Tom's Cabin* merely confirmed what abolitionists had been saying for two decades: that northerners were morally implicated in the sin of slavery. The law emerged out of an unsavory congressional compromise – further evidence to abolitionists of the corruption of the political system – and mandated northern assistance to southerners attempting to recapture escaped slaves. After this, for northerners to maintain that slavery was the south's "peculiar institution" was to ignore the law of the land. In an aside to northern readers of *Uncle Tom's Cabin*, Stowe warned "the [slave] trader and catcher may yet be among our aristocracy" (62). In a later passage she both reinforces the point about northern complicity in slavery and offers a more optimistic scenario, one asserting her faith in moral suasion, in sympathy, and in fiction to portray the human realities that lay beyond moral abstractions. She presents the reader with her fictitious Ohio Senator Bird, who supported the Fugitive Slave Law, confronted with the escaped slave mother Eliza and the child from whom she could not bear to be separated. Faced with "The magic of the real presence of distress," he breaks the law he helped pass by aiding her flight for freedom. "He had never thought," Stowe explains, "that a fugitive might be a hapless mother, a defenceless [sic] child . . . ." Reluctant to leave the moral of a story implicit, she concludes that "in Kentucky, as in Mississippi, are noble and generous hearts to whom never was a tale of suffering told in vain" (77). The problem was getting such stories to them. Or, perhaps – a more disturbing possibility – telling tales might not always be sufficient to produce change.

The theme of northern moral complicity in slavery follows Uncle Tom southward from the relatively mild version of the institution in Kentucky to its most vicious incarnation in Louisiana. Rather than let readers in the free states revel in moral superiority, Stowe repeatedly insists that the institution knows no sectional bias in its ability to corrupt. The indecisive planter, Augustine St. Clare, reminds Miss Ophelia (who must confront her own prejudice) that his father was a New Englander like herself, yet pro-slavery and deeply racist (194–195). His father's wicked overseer, Stubbs, was "a great, tall, slab-sided, two-fisted renegade son of Vermont . . ." (196). St. Clare later declares that "the unchristian prejudice of the north is an oppressor almost equally severe" as slavery (283). The novel's arch-villain, Simon Legree, was the New England born son of "a fair-haired woman" who "had led him, at the sound of Sabbath bell, to worship and pray" (322). (Unfortunately, he took after his father.) The true location of slavery, Stowe insisted, was not in the south, but in the human heart, especially the male one, and its lust for power over others, precisely the message radical abolitionists preached.

If the novel's trajectory of slavery and moral responsibility follows Uncle Tom southward, a second trajectory, one of freedom, follows Eliza, her husband George, and other escapees from slavery. It first runs northward, then eastward to France, where George receives the education he long sought, and finally to Africa, where he, Eliza, their children, and his mother and sister settle, as does another character, Topsy. Here Stowe opens herself to the charge that Uncle Tom's Cabin is a colonizationist tract masquerading as an anti-slavery novel. Although plausible, this accusation obscures the degree to which the novel embodies radical abolitionist principles and makes the ending appear more consistent than it is.

At points in the concluding section, George does indeed proclaim a message near and dear to colonizationists – and many other Americans – that he has a duty to bring civilization and Christianity to Africa. Yet in a lengthy letter to a friend, he notes "the struggle between abolitionist and colonizationist" and accepts the abolitionist critique that his destination, Liberia, "may have been used, in unjustifiable ways, as a means of retarding our emancipation . . ." He regards it, nonetheless, as his nation and the mother of future Christian republics in Africa. Stowe then puts words in George's voice that break with colonizationist logic and could have been written by a radical black abolitionist like Frederick Douglass, the novel's most prominent African-American defender. "But," George continues, "you will tell me, our race have equal rights to mingle in the American republic as the Irishman, the German, the Swede. Granted, they have. We *ought* to be free . . . We ought, in particular, to be allowed *here*" (374–375). With this passage, Stowe casts George's decision to go to Africa as a personal one, not a racial imperative. Stowe's biographer believes *Uncle Tom's Cabin* sent a colonizationist message because of "a certain lack of attention" to anti-slavery politics on the author's part.[12] Given the mixed signals in George's letter, it is more likely that the problem was Stowe's inability to envision what America might look like after emancipation, a reading her other anti-slavery fiction supports. This was, moreover, an inability she shared with many radical abolitionists and one directly related to her commitment to moral suasion.

Like *Uncle Tom's Cabin*, Stowe's second abolitionist novel, *Dred*, responded to current events – violence between pro- and anti-slavery forces in Kansas, and a South Carolina congressman's vicious attack on Massachusetts's anti-slavery senator, Charles Sumner, on the floor of the Senate. Stowe also sought to meet criticisms of the earlier novel, including from African Americans offended by her portraits of black men as either the Christ-like, simple Uncle Tom, or good-natured comic characters, or the rebellious, half-white George, who has no future in the United States. She reacted by creating a greater range of black male characters. Among them is the thoughtful, heroic slave, Harry, devoted to the white heroine, Nina Gordon, his half sister. (She dies unaware of the relationship.) Even more striking is the title character, Dred, who embodies an element missing in *Uncle Tom's Cabin*: black rage. He is an insurrectionary with an impeccable lineage. Stowe presents him as the son of Denmark Vesey, hanged in South Carolina in 1821 as the ringleader of a slave conspiracy, a man whom one anti-slavery character compares to the "best men" of Italy, Austria, and Hungary, a reference to much-admired leaders of nationalist insurrections in those countries (316). Stowe also has him in possession of Nat Turner's Bible (446). Dred himself notes that Turner's 1831 uprising "almost drove them [Virginians] to set free their slaves!" and models his own unrealized insurrection after it (341).

Although *Dred* contains many of the stereotypical black characters found in *Uncle Tom's Cabin*, Harry's nobility and Dred's rage are significant additions to her repertoire. Dred does not live to carry out his slave uprising, but his fury and passion produce one of the novel's more powerful moments.

It occurs during a religious camp meeting, after nightfall, when his eerily disembodied voice thunders down from treetops, across which he is moving to avoid capture, preaching hellfire and damnation to hypocrites below who claim slavery is a Christian institution (vol. 1, ch. XXIII).

In spite of such remarkable scenes, this hastily-written novel is a muddle, even by Stowe's relaxed standards for plots. Part of the difficulty is that her heroine, Nina, dies her obligatory, exquisitely Christian death early, leaving the remainder of the story to be carried primarily by male characters, Harry and Edward Clayton, her former suitor. This is an unfamiliar role for men in Stowe's fiction and they do not play it comfortably. Along the way, however, she makes the same criticisms of slavery that she does in *Uncle Tom's Cabin*, with slightly different inflections. Her attacks on pro-slavery Christians, especially clergy, and on the law for upholding slavery, are particularly impassioned. Dred's rage also enables her to stress an abolitionist point muted in *Uncle Tom's Cabin* – that if slavery does not end peacefully and voluntarily (in other words by moral suasion) it may end violently at the hands of future Nat Turners. She underscores that through the novel's most clever plot device. The reader does not know of the existence of Dred, or of his community of escaped slaves in the Great Dismal Swamp, until roughly a third of the way into this very long novel. After the secret is out, it becomes clear that the white characters have, at best, a dim awareness of Dred, while all of the African-American ones have known about his community from the beginning. There is a hidden, dangerous world of black anger, she tells white readers, of which even those who claim to know their own slaves have no comprehension.

As in *Uncle Tom's Cabin*, freedom lies outside the south. Stowe is caustic about southern suppression of antislavery sentiment, as in a harrowing scene of mob violence against an abolitionist minister and his family (vol. II, ch. XXV). One character accurately advises Clayton that "you shouldn't set up for a refomer in the Southern states" (467). Several pages later, he is beaten, a clear reference to Sumner (493), and white hostility ends an attempt by him and his sister, Anne, to educate their slaves (vol. II, ch. XXXII). In this case, however, freedom for blacks does not lie in Africa, although whether or not it lies in the United States is ambiguous. Clayton and Anne take their former slaves to a part of Canada "where the climate is least severe," to found an agricultural community (543). Under Harry's leadership it thrives. Two other contingents of African Americans settle in New York and in Massachusetts, where we are assured that their stories end happily. Her vague account of them runs a scant four pages (vol. II, ch. XXXIV). Once again, Stowe had difficulty writing about black freedom.

With her final anti-slavery novel, *The Minister's Wooing* (1859), Stowe shifted to a more congenial plot – one in which men are clueless about their dependence on women, peripheral, evil, dead, flawed, or absent. (For much of the story, the romantic hero, James Marvyn, is presumed lost at sea.) She also set the novel in what would prove to be a very comfortable time and place for her fiction: New England after the American Revolution, perhaps a sign that her abolitionist muse was deserting her on the eve of the Civil War. The title of the first chapter establishes the distance from Stowe's day: "Pre-Railroad Times."

The story in *The Minister's Wooing* is simple and light compared to its two predecessors, and slavery is on its margin rather than central, as it had been in them. The devout heroine, Mary Scudder, lives in Rhode Island with her widowed mother and an aging boarder, the Reverend Samuel Hopkins, in real life (but not in the novel) the author of a remarkable anti-slavery pamphlet, *A Dialogue, Concerning the Slavery of the Africans* . . .[13] Early in the story, Mary recognizes her love for her childhood friend, James Marvyn, just as he is about to embark on a long voyage. After hearing that he has perished at sea, she and James's mother agonize over their fear that when he died he was not a true Christian, thus doomed by Puritan theology to damnation. Their inability to accept that possibility gives the novel an intellectual complexity very different from its more polemical abolitionist predecessors. This theme also reflects Stowe's anguish over the drowning death of her son, Henry, two years earlier and allows her to meditate upon the emotional demands of her family's New England religious tradition.

With James dead and damned, Mary agrees to marry Hopkins, whose intellect and piety she respects, but whom she does not love as she did the younger man. Shortly before the wedding is to take place, James reappears, a true Christian (converted by Mary's influence, of course), and prosperous. Hopkins realizes the truth – once a woman explains it to him – blesses the couple, and all ends well.

Slavery figures into this romance by virtue of New England's complicity in it, largely figurative in *Uncle Tom's Cabin* and *Dred* and quite literal in *The Minister's Wooing*. Among Hopkins's parishioners are prominent slaveholders and others involved in the slave trade. His decision to denounce slavery, and the consequences he suffers as a result, highlight what was admirable about him and attractive to Mary. In order to make this point, however, Stowe had to rewrite history and rearrange chronology, as she did elsewhere in *The Minister's Wooing*. It takes place in the 1790s. The historical Samuel Hopkins published his great anti-slavery manifesto two decades earlier, in 1776. Moving Hopkins's conversion to abolitionism after the Revolution enabled Stowe to make, once again, the point that slavery was a national, as well as an individual, sin.

Another bit of tampering with history, replacing Hopkins's pamphlet with a sermon, was an effective way for Stowe to reinforce the argument that any implication in slavery – even failure to speak against it – was a personal sin. As she has Hopkins proclaim to his congregation, "all the individuals in private stations who have in any way aided in this business [the slave trade], or have not opposed it to the utmost of their ability, have a share in this guilt" (143). Her Hopkins, however, was remarkably concise. The sermon sequence lasts just under two pages from his first words to the audience's departure. The chapter's final image is not an anti-slavery one, but rather one of virtue imperiled. Mary marches out of the church on Hopkins' arm, receiving a smile and a bow from the rakish Aaron Burr, hoping to add her to his list of conquests (ch. xv). In Stowe's third novel, abolitionism moved from the passion driving the story to a plot device.

In one significant respect, nonetheless, *The Minister's Wooing* does what *Uncle Tom's Cabin* fails to do and at which *Dred* only hints. It briefly addresses the question of what society might be like after freedom. The answer in this case is "very much the same." The novel shows slavery falling away easily in New England when masters see the light or hear the right words. Hopkins encourages kindly Mr. Marvyn, James's father, to ask his slave, Candace, if she and her husband, Cato, want to be free. Assuring him that she feels well treated and that "I couldn't hab no better friends 'n you an' Missis" (104), she declares that she would indeed like her freedom, harking back to Uncle Tom telling St. Clare that he would rather be free than have a good master (265). Marvyn immediately emancipates her and she tells him "dat it's my will an' pleasure to go right on doin' my work jes' de same . . ." (104). Freedom comes down to Candace and Cato remaining with the Marvyns, working for wages.

Stowe herself casts doubt on whether or not Candace's emancipation is a contemporary model for freedom. "In those days," she wrote, "when domestic slavery prevailed in New England, it was quite a different thing in its aspects from the same institution in more southern latitudes." In Yankee land, the institution "was something foreign, grotesque, and picturesque . . ." (65–66). Moral suasion, she implies, might not work so easily to end slavery outside of New England, nor, for that matter, would relations between ex-slaves and their former masters necessarily remain so cordial after emancipation.

Taken as a whole, however, Stowe's anti-slavery novels hit the main notes of the abolitionist argument since 1831: that slavery is contrary to the principles of the American Revolution and Christianity, that slavery is a sin to be renounced immediately, that all righteous people must come out of corrupt churches and other institutions that uphold slavery, that northerners bear moral responsibility for slavery, that the self-interest of masters provides no protection for slaves, that the essence of slavery is arbitrary power, and that the institution is evil even when the treatment of slaves is humane.

In a quiet way, Stowe went on to make a further radical suggestion at which some abolitionists balked: that interracial sexual relationships might be consensual, based on love, and not especially remarkable. When George, Eliza, and their party sail for France at the end of *Uncle Tom's Cabin*, their numbers include Cassy's daughter, Emmeline, rescued from Simon Legree. On the voyage, she "won the affection of the first mate of the vessel and, shortly after entering the port, she became his wife" (373). Although the husband's race is unspecified, the most plausible reading is that he is white, a possibility Stowe – seldom given to frivolous ambiguity – refuses to foreclose. More daring is a subplot in *Dred* involving the mulatto children of the father of the heroine, Nina Gordon, one of whom becomes the loving wife of a white man. After his death, and in spite of his best intentions, the law does not protect her from her white half-brother, Tom Gordon, and his plan to reenslave her and take her property (339–340). This melodramatic story of interracial love and betrayal, like Dred's murderous rage, put Stowe in risky territory for a popular novelist.

Her abolitionism's greatest lapse was in failing to comprehend what it would take to achieve a truly free, multi-racial America, but in this failure she had an enormous amount of company. Even many of the most radical abolitionists believed that the job was finished at the end of the Civil War. Among them was William Lloyd Garrison, who in 1865 moved to dissolve the American Anti-Slavery Society and cease publication of the *Liberator*, actions Stowe applauded, noting "He acknowledges the great deed done . . ."[14]

Words and deeds

The immediate problem for Stowe in the 1850s was not the future, but rather putting her anti-slavery agenda into action. Since 1831, the answer for abolitionists was to use a mixture of anti-slavery organizations, public agitation, and various other forms of moral suasion. For some, by 1840 the list of acceptable means included political action and in 1859, three years after *Dred*, John Brown added violence to it. For Stowe, the answer was always moral suasion through the power of words. Yet this was a power her own fiction sometimes called into question, a sign of instability in her union of reform and popular culture.

For words to serve as means to reformist ends, they must do several things. They must connect people across time and space, otherwise there can be no movement like the anti-slavery one. That they do in Stowe's three abolitionist novels, primarily through letters and through books her characters read and discuss, especially the Bible. Words also allow reformers to bear personal witness to their own moral commitment, as Reverend Hopkins declares when deciding to give his anti-slavery sermon: "I must utter my voice . . . I must testify" (85). Above all, if words are to be instruments of moral suasion, they must evoke sympathy by revealing the truth and persuading men and women to accept it. That occurs in each of the three novels, and faith in the power of words helped drive Stowe to write *Uncle Tom's Cabin* in the first place. As a writer of fiction, however, Stowe also had to have words advance the plot. And here is where we begin to see a dark side – a place where reform and the imperatives of popular culture came into conflict. The drama of Stowe's stories often depended on words that failed, something that must not happen if moral suasion is to work.

These failures come in multiple varieties. There are words that do not reach the right person in timely fashion. In all three novels, tardy letters play major roles in the plot. The slow course of one from Miss Ophelia to Mr. Shelby results in Uncle Tom's death (360); the leisurely path of one from Nina to Clayton costs the couple precious moments together as she lies dying (375); and yet another delayed letter, one from James, almost leads to Mary's marriage to Dr. Hopkins (293). In using such a device to advance the story Stowe calls into question her own faith in words as means of reform: what if people simply do not get the message?

Also problematic for her commitment to moral suasion are cases in which godly words fail to convert willful sinners. Hopkins is sanguine that Simeon Brown will give up the slave trade once the doctor shows "him that it follows logically from his principles; I am confident of that" (870). He is wrong. In *Uncle Tom's Cabin*, Simon Legree seals his perdition by burning a letter telling him that his dying mother forgave him for his sins (323). Dred's righteous preaching from the treetops fails to convert pro-slavery whites below (vol. I, ch. XXIII). Later in the same novel a mob deals with an abolitionist minister by silencing, not heeding, him (vol. II, ch. XXV). Further compromising Stowe's faith in moral suasion are words that deceive, a common enough plot device in sentimental fiction. All three novels contain examples of authority figures – clergymen, political leaders, lawyers, and judges – who spout false doctrines that convince their followers. If their words should not be believed, whose can be?

At this point Stowe confronted a fundamental problem for moral suasion as an approach to reform in a democracy: how to tell true words from false, or even to be sure that the right words reach the right people? Unless that can be done, how can reformers make the sum of individual consciences add up to a majority, especially with powerful interests and strong arguments arrayed against change? She offers no persuasive answer. Womanly feeling, common sense, Christian upbringing, and education are among her prime candidates for sorting true words from false, but each fails at important moments in her anti-slavery novels. In her popular fiction, there are times when the complexity of plot triumphs over the clarity and simplicity of reform.

Tensions between Stowe's dual commitments to moral suasion and sentimental fiction help explain another problem we have seen in the anti-slavery novels: the mostly unanswered question, "what happens when freedom comes?" After *The Minister's Wooing* her writings largely took place in a world of whiteness, and there are signs that she continued to have trouble conceiving of a new, racially egalitarian society. After the Civil War she supported education for blacks as a panacea for both races, as she had in her anti-slavery novels, writing two long pieces on the subject for the *North American Review* in 1879. In them she confidently asserted – using the future tense – that "Education will bring quiet, refinement, respect for law, respect for the mutual rights of races; and America, where so many races meet and mingle, will be the true millennial ground, where the fatherhood of God is shown in the brotherhood of man."[15] Those words appeared two years after the collapse of Reconstruction in the south and during a long period of extreme violence against African Americans.

In the same year, she published a story in the *Atlantic Monthly* that may inadvertently tell more of the truth of the matter. Drawing on experiences with winter homes the Stowes purchased in Florida after the War, she described life upon "Our Florida Plantation" – the story's revealing title – in terms that could have come from the antebellum south, except for the presence of wages and education and the absence of whipping.[16] The tale even repeats pre-War racial stereotypes. In addition to commenting on dancing as "the one thing which every negro man or woman can do *well* by nature," she evoked her own most famous character by describing one man as "our 'Tom,' a great Hercules of a fellow . . ." (648). The piece ends with the plantation an economic disaster (perhaps slavery had been more efficient, after all?) and the white characters congratulating themselves on at least having paid their black workers. Neither they nor the author contemplate how much the new order of freedom resembled the old one of slavery, with whites in charge and blacks in the fields.

On this score it would be convenient to fault Stowe for being "racist," or to excuse her because none of the New World former slave societies – notably

Haiti and Jamaica – provided a model she wished America to emulate. Her inability to conjure a vision of an America purged of slavery, however, stemmed from the same commitment to moral suasion that made her an anti-slavery novelist in the first place and that enabled her to create a memorable assortment of characters. At times Stowe might think of guilt in collective terms, but even then moral responsibility rested with individuals: it was their duty to leave corrupt churches or denounce the national sin of slavery. She could only conceive of change one person at a time, not in terms of social relations, whether the change was conversion to abolitionism or emancipation. "What is freedom to a nation," she asked in *Uncle Tom's Cabin*, "but freedom to individuals in it?" (332).

However much Harriet Beecher Stowe's three anti-slavery novels may unravel upon close inspection, they represent a remarkable achievement. Over a seven-year span in which passions about slavery dominated American politics and produced atrocious acts of violence, she grafted an unpopular message onto a popular literary form and gained a sympathetic hearing from a large audience previously hostile or indifferent to abolitionism. She helped move the controversy over slavery from polemics, legislative debates, and mobs to parlors and to the popular stage, where *Uncle Tom's Cabin*, and answers to it, quickly became a staple. Through the power of her prose, she – in common with authors of ex-slaves' narratives like Frederick Douglass – took abolitionists' abstractions and embodied them in striking characters, dramatic dialogue, and emotionally compelling human predicaments.

And yet, behind Stowe's seemingly rock-solid moral certainty lie two related and unsettling questions that her own prose, plot devices, inconsistencies, silences and assumptions about reform raise: What will be the place of black people in an America without slavery? Can moral suasion transform the world? The long quest for racial justice from Stowe's day to our own is a reminder that the first question is still an open one. The carnage of the Civil War is a reminder that, in the end, words failed.

NOTES

1. Frank J. Webb, *The Garies and Their Friends*, ed. Robert Reid-Pharr (Baltimore and London: The Johns Hopkins University Press, 1997 [1857]), xix, xx.
2. Harriet Beecher Stowe, "Appeal to the women of the free states," in *Uncle Tom's Cabin; or, Life Among the Lowly*, ed. Elizabeth Ammons, Norton Critical Editions (New York and London: W. W. Norton & Company, 1994 [1852]), 427.
3. Harriet Beecher Stowe, *Uncle Tom's Cabin; or, Life Among the Lowly*, ed. Elizabeth Ammons, Norton Critical Editions (New York and London: W. W. Norton & Company, 1994 [1852]), 3; Harriet Beecher Stowe, *Dred: A Tale of the Great Dismal Swamp*, ed. Robert S. Levine (New York and London: Penguin Books, 2000 [1856]), 47.

4. Higginson quoted in Ronald G. Walters, *American Reformers: 1815–1860*, rev. ed. (New York: Hill and Wang, 1997 [1978]), xiii. Another general work on antebellum reform is Steven Mintz, *Moralizers and Modernizers: America's Pre-Civil War Reformers* (Baltimore and London: The Johns Hopkins University Press, 1995).

5. Harriet Beecher Stowe, *The Minister's Wooing*, ed. Susan K. Harris (New York and London: Penguin Books, 1999 [1859]), 16.

6. Joan D. Hedrick, *Harriet Beecher Stowe: A Life* (New York: Oxford University Press, 1994), 135.

7. Anon., "Mrs. Stowe in Edinburgh," *Liberator*, November 14, 1856 (Boston).

8. Quoted in Ronald G. Walters, *The Anti-slavery Appeal: American Abolitionism After 1830* (Baltimore and London: The Johns Hopkins University Press, 1976), 70, which also deals more extensively with this theme.

9. William Lloyd Garrison, "The Anti-slavery Novels," *Liberator*, January 5, 1855 (Boston).

10. Walters, *Anti-slavery Appeal*, 97, 107.

11. Harriet Beecher Stowe, *A Key to Uncle Tom's Cabin; Presenting the Original Facts and Documents . . . .* (Bedford, MA: Applewood Books, n.d. [1853]), iii.

12. Hedrick, *Harriet Beecher Stowe*, 235.

13. Samuel J. Hopkins, *A Dialogue Concerning the Slavery of the Africans; Shewing It to Be the Duty and Interest of the American Colonies to Emancipate All Their African Slaves: With an Address to the Owners of Such Slaves* (Norwich, CT: Judah P. Spooner, 1776).

14. Hedrick, *Harriet Beecher Stowe*, 325.

15. Harriet Beecher Stowe, "The Education of Freedmen," *The North American Review* 128:271 (June 1879), 94.

16. Harriet Beecher Stowe, "Our Florida Plantation," *Atlantic Monthly* 43:259 (May 1879)

IO

LAWRENCE BUELL

Harriet Beecher Stowe and the dream of the great American novel

The first critical call on record for "the great American novel" (by novelist John W. DeForest in 1868) names *Uncle Tom's Cabin* as the closest approximation yet. Small wonder. One can imagine at least four reasons why, especially in the aftermath of the Civil War. First, the novel's foregrounding of slavery as *the* defining national issue. Second, the book's sensational impact, provoking a vast array of imitations and refutations, perhaps even the Civil War itself (if we take seriously Abraham Lincoln's *bon mot*).[1] Third, its record-breaking sales, which demonstrated the reality of national literary emergence as a hard economic fact: the United States was now the largest book market in the English-speaking world. And fourth, the novel's panoramic reach, combining the geographical scope of a Whitman with the sociological profusion of a Dickens.

This last was the point that especially interested DeForest. Though he scoffed at the book's idealizing exoticization of Tom and Eva, he praised "the national breadth to the picture, truthful outlining of character, natural speaking, and plenty of strong feeling." By contrast, all the other authors on his radar screen seemed provincial, even the incomparable Nathaniel Hawthorne; and he was harshly dismissive of Stowe's own regionalist turn as well. ("Stricken with timidity, the author shrank into her native New England.")[2]

DeForest's assessment of *Uncle Tom's Cabin*'s landmark significance can be disputed both on its own terms and on its premises. His comparison list has some glaring lacunae, starting with Herman Melville's *Moby-Dick*, which certainly meets the spatial mobility and the demographic heterogeneity tests. (Of course it would take another half-century before that book lodged itself in Americanist critical consciousness even to the extent of James Fenimore Cooper and Washington Irving, let alone Hawthorne.)

Against the governing critical premise, at least two charges might be laid. First, the anachronism of imputing *novelistic* intent to several of the writers mentioned, including Stowe. Although Stowe *did* write a number of books we now call novels, it ran counter to her evangelical conditioning, as well as the not-yet-fully-differentiated-and-established standing of "the novel" in antebellum US critical discourse, for Stowe to think of herself as a novelist by *vocation*.[3] That's doubtless part of the explanation why the "great American novel" mantra didn't start until later, and why the preferred promotional rubric used by Stowe's publisher for *Uncle Tom* was simply "the greatest book of its kind" – or, occasionally, the "greatest of all American tales."[4]

Second, and related, DeForest's critical horizon is limited also by the proto-realist assumption that "truthful outlining of character" and "natural speaking" are decisive and definable measures of fictive achievement. Indeed, arguably the whole idea of a Great American novel has always been more or less tethered to an aesthetic of representational realism, not only in this instance but in all its future avatars of articulation, which amazingly persist down to this very day notwithstanding a century of debunking as a vacuous media hype.[5] In this sense there's a direct line between *Uncle Tom's Cabin* and the most mammoth of all the major national narrative projects ever to be conceptualized as a single project, Dos Passos's *USA* trilogy (1930–36), which undertakes, on an even vaster canvas, for the subject of class in the United States what Stowe did with race and region.[6] In fact Stowe herself gives reinforcement to such linkage. Though *Uncle Tom's Cabin* is notoriously replete with gothic heightening, strange coincidence, and supernatural occurrence, Stowe accepted a realist litmus test in defending its facticity in *A Key to Uncle Tom's Cabin* (1853).

> [My] book had a purpose entirely transcending the artistic one, and accordingly encounters at the hands of the public demands not usually made on fictitious works. It is *treated as a reality* – sifted, tried, and tested, as a reality; and therefore as a reality it may be proper that it should be defended.[7]

It's an intriguing paradox of Anglo-American fiction history that we associate the maturation of the novel with the emergence of fictional realism, whereas "reading for realism" in the first instance meant reading *against* novelism, against the fictive, or rather through and against that in order to grasp the supposed factual bedrock at the heart of the fable.[8] Indeed, this paradox has a history almost as old as the novel itself. In the early English novel, a favorite genre is the autobiographical fiction that sets forth the case for its existence in the ground that it is a narrative of actual fact, like Daniel Defoe's *Moll Flanders* and *Robinson Crusoe*, whether or not the narrator did in fact have an historical antecedent. Several of Herman Melville's early novels belong to this tradition, including the book for which he was most famous in his lifetime, *Typee: A Peep at Polynesian Life*, a fictionalized account of the author's adventures in Polynesia. *Typee*'s publishers, both in England and the United States, worried greatly about its possible fabrications or distortions; and Melville himself, whether earnestly or tongue-in-cheek, insisted in his "Preface" that the book was "the unvarnished truth."[9] In other contexts, Melville defended fiction's "truth" in a very different and much more visionary sense (as in his praise of Shakespeare and Hawthorne as masters of "the great Art of Telling the Truth"),[10] as did Stowe herself in effect at those times when she claimed that *Uncle Tom's Cabin* had been written from a kind of divine dictation and when she characterized its primary aim in her "Preface": "to awaken sympathy and feeling for the African race" (Norton Critical Edition, xiii).

To give DeForest his due before leaving him behind, when he praised *Uncle Tom's Cabin* for its "strong feeling" as well as "truthful outlining," he did implicitly recognize the inadequacy of the documentary yardstick Stowe imposed on herself in *A Key*. And in acknowledging "the national breadth to the picture," he named one of the novel's great and still underappreciated coups: the effort, if not the full success, to deprovincialize national fiction so as to take on more of the full geo-cultural range of the fast-expanding United States than had any previous novelist, and in such a way as both to recognize and to cut across the salient fault lines: region, race, gender, and class. One is reminded, by contrast, of Cooper contemplating a mammoth series of thirteen novels about the thirteen British-American colonies and abandoning it after the first book. The sheer territorial sweep of Stowe's fictive panorama DeForest himself was well prepared to appreciate, since he himself had tried a similar thing the year before on a more modest scale, in *Miss Ravenel's Conversion from Secession to Loyalty* – one of those perennial nominees for best underrated US novel that keeps falling out of print.

Uncle Tom's Cabin and *Miss Ravenel* actually belong to a longer sequence of US narratives, from certain novels of the 1820s (for example, Catharine Maria Sedgwick's *Redwood* and Sarah Josepha Hale's *Northwood*) to William Faulkner's *Light in August* and beyond, that negotiate lines of sectional division – especially but not merely between north and south – often enlisting the trope of family to image nationness – or fracture of nationness. As one might expect, such projects are especially rife in the successive epochs of antebellum anxiety about national fission and postbellum "romance of reunion," as Nina Silber has called it.[11] Stowe's deployment of the Shelbys, the Harrises, and especially the St. Clares are all variants on the basic nation–family template, the quintessential form of which foregrounds the vicissitudes of a white heterosexual couple who exemplify each of the regional sides – Hale's *Northwood*, Caroline Lee Hentz's *The Planter's Northern Bride*, to some extent DeForest's *Miss Ravenel* too. Much more might be said about the permutations and history of this plot form, which has certainly been one of the main templates or *gestalts* in terms of which US national novel projects have been conceived. For example, one of the arresting – and disturbing – facets of its early history, which the transit from Stowe to DeForest also illustrates, is that it starts as a comparatively gyno-centric mode of imagination but after the Civil War tends to get hijacked by a masculinist ideology. Henry James's *The Bostonians* is another striking case in point, unless one can bring oneself to believe that the satire directed toward Basil Ransom somehow implies a positive verdict on feminized New England reform culture as represented by Miss Birdseye, Olive Chancellor and Verena Tarrant. In modern times, William Faulkner's treatment, in *Light in August* (1932), of the pathological amour instigated by a do-gooding white woman of carpetbagger background with a southern man, thought to have black blood, gives a still more grotesque twist to the postbellum misogynistic undoing of the classic intersectional conversation plot as first developed through *Uncle Tom's Cabin*. But I forbear further elaboration in order to focus more squarely on Stowe's fictional practice.

In what follows I shall mainly focus on *Uncle Tom's Cabin*, but I also want at least briefly to discuss its successor *Dred: A Tale of the Great Dismal Swamp*. For not only does *Dred* shed valuable retrospective light on Stowe's most famous and influential work; it is also a much more significant achievement in its own right than has been recognized until very recently.[12]

My preferred way of characterizing the project of *Uncle Tom's Cabin* in summary terms without falling into the usual extremes of gush or blame is as an admirable but uneven attempt to think beyond one's sociohistorical position according to two opposing logics I shall unpack momentarily. *Uncle Tom's Cabin* is a northerner's attempt to imagine also the south. It is a white person's attempt to imagine also non-whites. It is a woman writer's attempt in an age of separate spheres to imagine also the male world of affairs. It is a middle-class author's attempt to imagine also both grandees and down-and-outers. It is an evangelical Protestant believer's attempt to imagine also people of other faiths including even agnostics and atheists. In all these outreach attempts the novel achieves some impressive results, however constrained by various forms of tribalism. For degree of difficulty attempted, *Uncle Tom's Cabin* deserves at least a 9.5 out of 10, although for execution rather less.

How much less I shall not try to adjudicate precisely. Rather I shall focus on the opposition of logics by which the polarities I have just mentioned are negotiated. Stowe is by turns a *reifier* of binaries (men are like this, women are like that; whites are like this, Africans are like that, and so forth) and by turns a *universalizer* who dissolves the binaries that elsewhere bind her.

The book's most luminous and telling moments come when the two logics get deployed concurrently. A symptomatic case in point is nomology.

All readers of *Uncle Tom's Cabin* notice Stowe's curious economy of names, especially the duplicates across the color line. Senator and Mrs. Bird give their dead son Henry's clothes to Eliza's son Harry. The leading African-American protagonist, whom the novel compares at one point to a Hungarian freedom fighter, has the same name as young George Shelby, who strikes down Simon Legree over Tom's dead body and returns home to become "liberator" to his plantation. "Emily" is another name that migrates across the color line, both Mrs. Shelby and George Harris' sister sharing a version of it. Such duplications give low-key reinforcement to more explicit universalizing moves in other contexts, like direct narrative appeal to readers, as in "If it were *your* Harry, mother, or your Willie, that were going to be torn from you by a brutal trader . . . how fast could *you* walk?" (Norton, 43–44). One recent critic thoughtfully argues that this strategy of "reflective naming" amounts to "a rhetoric of equality," designed to make us "see whites and blacks as equals";[13] and up to a point I agree. Yet naming is sometimes used to drive wedges between the races as well. Consider the following lists. (1) Cassy, Chloe, Cudjoe, Quimbo, Sambo, Topsy. (2) Arthur, Augustine, Evangeline, Marie (or Mary), Ophelia. Can one imagine such monikers transposed to the other side?

Well, perhaps one can. So the novel suggests at an especially provocative moment in Chapter XVI. Tom has recently arrived at the St. Clare estate. St. Clare has just reproached Ophelia for the hypocrisy of principled abolitionism *versus* physical revulsion from real-live black people. The scene now switches to Tom and Eva, with emphasis on the innocent pleasure Tom is taking in the gorgeousness of this "Aladdin's palace" of an establishment. Here ensues one of the novel's most fulsomely "orientalizing" moments, in its essentialization of both southernness and of Africanness. The narrator gets swept up by the romantic religio-utopic racialism Stowe imbibed from Alexander Kinmont's *Twelve Lectures on Man*: the thesis that blacks make inherently better Christians than whites because they are more submissive, that the essentially childlike nature of Africans is destined to make them the first truly Christian race.[14] But just before this happens, the narrator pauses to sketch a thumbnail portrait of Tom decked out in his new livery: in "his well-brushed broadcloth suit, smooth beaver, glossy boots, faultless wristbands and collar," the text says, Tom "looked respectable enough to be a Bishop of Carthage, as men of his color were, in other ages" (Norton, 155).

This sounds jocose, but it's really a bombshell. To whom does the text refer here? To more than one individual, it would seem, judging from what the

The dream of the great American novel

language of the text implies; but among them almost surely St. Augustine, often traditionally (and still today) thought to be non-white.[15] If you're looking for the *true* patriarch, the text insinuates, here's your man. Here's the *true* Augustine, not the *papier-maché* Augustine St. Clare who happens to be Tom's legal master. Stowe could hardly have conjured up a more formidable image of spiritual authority among the church fathers from the standpoint of the Protestant Christian imagination. Catch the allusion, and it shrewdly disrupts the ostensively dominant symbolism the novel builds up when it names the two brothers St. Clare after opposite types of heroes of the "Dark Ages": Augustine (the great spiritual hero) and Alfred (the greatest of the Anglo-Saxon kings). Catch the allusion, and it snaps into place a skein of other references to Tom, as far back as our first glimpse of him in his cabin at the Shelby place, as "a sort of patriarch in religious matters" (26). Catch the allusion, and it also forces you to take more seriously the droll-seeming reference in that same earlier chapter to the portrait on the cabin wall of "General Washington, drawn and colored in a manner which would cartainly have astonished that hero, if ever he had happened to meet with its like" (18). Yes, maybe the world of canonical heroes is not so remote from the world of humble folksy African Americans after all.

IF you catch the allusion. That moment in Chapter XVI is indeed one of those incipiently epiphanic passages in the novel that have the potential to override most grandly, most extravagantly, any and all romantic racialist counter-suggestions about black inferiority implied by Tom's phenomenal forbearance and the fantasy of "poor Africa" humbly and belatedly emerging from "the furnace of affliction" to take its place as "the highest and noblest in that kingdom which [God] will set up" (156). *Uncle Tom's Cabin* here comes very close indeed to asserting a vision of inseparable consanguinity between the races not only at the level of human affection but even at the profoundest level of spiritual intellection. Perhaps too dangerously close for antebellum white comfort. In any case, the assertion is not allowed to complete itself. The narrator makes a vague, hasty gesture and then moves on. No less provocative and fascinating than the decision to drop the hint about the two Augustines is the decision to muffle it. Should this be understood in light of the self-consciousness about the duplicity of northern abolitionist racism that the just-completed encounter between Ophelia and St. Clare has laid bare? Did the novel pull its punches for fear that flatly stating the historical St. Augustine (or St. Cyprian, or any other early Christian hero) was black would have given too much offense to white readers? Or did the novel lack the courage of its best convictions, shrinking from the claim of truly equivalent authority across the color line, hesitating to insist that Tom's humble folk-spirituality *was* up to the Augustinian mark, even though

195

for a moment he might have "looked" that way, and/or the author might have wished to feel that way? Might part of the reason why the text holds back from a more grandiose insistence be the sense of documentary "realist" accountability of which Stowe made so much *ex post facto* – a sense that under slavery "realistically" the analogy between a barely literate slave and the greatest thinker of the patristic age is too absurd to press seriously? Or was the equation of true spirituality with Christian submission so compelling for Stowe as to deflect her away from an image that smacked of patristic authoritarianism?

We simply do not know. At the least, though, the very existence of the passage shows how audaciously spirituality could prod Stowe to think across the color line, at least in flashes. Of course the one-two martyrdom of Eva and Tom also exposes her inability to avoid falling into divisive stereotypes that compromise the universalizing claims elsewhere ascribed to Christian spirituality. But there's also another sense in which this double disaster overrides such division for the sake of a common vision of how in an unjust world the saints are always crucified. Altogether, *Uncle Tom's Cabin* stands as one of the most high-stakes attempts in US fiction to imagine unifying vocabularies against background assumptions of essentialized difference. And the greatest and also the riskiest of these vocabularies is the religious, because of its almost equal susceptibility – in Stowe's hands, anyhow – to become an instrument either of democratic leveling or of rehierarchicalization.

One suspects that Stowe herself sensed all this, at least dimly. One suspects that she sensed that to make a willing martyr out of Tom, and of Eva too, was not an adequate solution even to the problem of right conduct, white *or* black, much less to the challenge of charting a path to national salvation from the curse of slavery. Hence the George Harris subplot. Hence too the author's decision to go on and invent a far more radical figure like Dred – half Biblical prophet, half Denmark Vesey or Nat Turner – a figure of more formidable intelligence as well, a fully literate figure, and a figure of commanding eloquence who can bring an entire community (white as well as black) to its knees when he speaks to it as an unseen mysterious voice of divine judgment from the treetops at the height of a local revival meeting.

Even in the early 1850s, but far more as sectional conflict intensified, Stowe seems to have sensed a problem with Christian submission that didn't just have to do with the envisagement of blacks. "How the blood & insults of [Senator Charles] Sumner and the sack of Lawrence, [Kansas,] burn within us I hope to make a voice to say."[16] Far more than *Uncle Tom's Cabin*, *Dred* is imbued with this spirit of righteous wrath. In fact it explicitly mentions the battle for "bleeding Kansas" between northern free-soilers and southern slavery expansionists and stages near its climax an attack on the white hero Edward Clayton by Tom Gordon, the novel's arch-villain, that replays the notorious incident on the floor of the US Senate when South Carolina Congressman Preston Brooks caned the abolitionist firebrand Charles Sumner into insensibility. (The battered Clayton is rescued from a worse fate by the nick-of-time appearance of Dred, who breaks Gordon's arm and bears the wounded man away.)[17] Although Stowe carefully keeps Dred from killing Gordon (or anybody else during the novel, for that matter), *Dred* displays an even more uneasy conscience about the virtues of Christian submission than does *Uncle Tom's Cabin*, which itself acknowledges that the only way out of slavery in this world is the path of defiance taken by George and Cassy. Stowe is well on her way to achieving the affectionate but decisive disengagement from the submission ethic that we later find in her treatment of the title figure of her third novel, *The Minister's Wooing*. There the Reverend Samuel Hopkins's renunciation of his reluctant fiancée is seen both as a heroic act of generosity and as a confirmation of his unworldliness – both a reenactment and a parody of the historical Hopkins's central doctrine of "disinterested benevolence."[18]

Dred seemed to DeForest a distinctly inferior work – clear evidence that the author "was losing [her] hold on the vast subject which had so stirred us."[19] He was right in a pragmatic, box-office sense: *Dred*'s sales and staying power did not begin to match *Uncle Tom's Cabin*. None of *Dred*'s characters took hold of readerly imagination as Eliza, Tom, Eva, and Topsy did. Nor was *Dred* so comprehensively a "national" achievement with respect to geographical range, to regional diversity. (The novel confines itself largely to a particular district of North Carolina.) All the same, in at least three ways *Dred* stands as a more ambitious and impressive fictionalization of the greatest "crisis in the history of the nation" (3).

First, to turn DeForest's pronouncement on its head, the novel's project seems quite deliberately to depict a situation that has spun out of control, that admits of no solution. The stakes are (even) higher than in *Uncle Tom's Cabin*; the state of emergency has intensified. The author writes in horrified awareness that the country may be in the process of allowing pro-slavery interests dominance "over broad regions, where, till now," the American people "have solemnly forbidden it to enter" (3–4). Second, in consequence, the novel itself pushes into "forbidden" territory that *Uncle Tom's Cabin* either evades or relegates to shuddering sideglimpses. The titular African-American character is a southern white man's nightmare embodiment of black insurgency – despite his partial taming by the ministrations of a female quasi-Uncle Tom figure near the end. The scandal of forced miscegenation under planter patriarchy is foregrounded by the *dramatis personae* of the book's leading family, the Gordons, whose white scion is even more malevolent than Simon Legree and whose more virtuous and intelligent bira-cial elder brother is even more waspish about white do-gooderism than his *Uncle Tom*-counterpart, George Harris. If this is the family as synecdoche of nation, it is a toxic image indeed; and it comes as no surprise to find the Gordon family devastated and torn apart during the course of the novel. On top of that, the book's premier experiment in benign top-down reform of the system from within is utterly defeated when evil Tom Gordon incites the locals to mob violence against the genteel reformers, Clayton and his sister Anna, for illegally teaching their slaves to read. Their ensuing exodus to Canada with their African-American dependants spells the end of liberal-ism in the south and by implication the prospect of a viable biracial society anywhere in the US that the long arm of slavery can reach. Superficially, this denouement may look like the much-criticized back-to-Africa closure of *Uncle Tom's Cabin*; but it is actually quite different, since nobody in *Dred* leaves North America, some of the escapees even relocate in New York City, and exodus in either case is clearly meant to betoken authorial despair at fixing the system rather than discomfort at the prospect of black–white coex-istence.

Third, *Dred* undertakes a more explicit, intricate, clear-eyed, and search-ing anatomy of the sociopolitical institutions than does *Uncle Tom's Cabin* – acknowledging to a greater extent the dominance of the status quo over indi-vidual reform efforts and the worldly triumph of economic self-interest over the power of benevolent emotion and spiritual purity. The reactionary force of the judicial system and organized religion are more fully dramatized here, as is the weight of group affiliation: of kin, of class (planters and poor whites especially), of mobs, of resistance networks and secret communication chan-nels among slaves. Although it oversimplifies the novel's complex balancing of values, characters, and incidents to think of *Dred* as positively disowning "sentimentalism disconnected from specific political activism," the novel's numerous episodes of heat-of-the-moment conversions giving way to apathy or recidivism are indeed a far cry from such moments in *Uncle Tom's Cabin* as Senator Bird's seeming conversion to abolitionism by the emotional force of personal encounter with Eliza. "In *Dred*," as critic John Carlos Rowe goes on to observe, Stowe repeatedly argues that "emotional identification with African-American slaves will do nothing positive and very often has tragic consequences, unless it is part of a specific program of political, legal, social, educational, and economic reforms."[20] This requires a bit of qualification, but not too much. Throughout the novel, the reader is left in no doubt as to whether the leading white male protagonist Clayton, whose conscience prompts him to abandon the legal profession and to press his program of uplifting the lot of his slaves in the teeth of local opposition, is inherently nobler than his old chum Frank Russel, a genial, worldly-wise racist headed for a political career. Yet the reader is also made to feel, at the end, completely convinced by the prudential logic of Russel's (successful) attempt to persuade Clayton away from self-destruction: "Your plans for gradual emancipation . . . are utterly hopeless" because the south is obdurate and "the mouth of the north is stuffed with cotton" (537).

No less significant, however, is the fact that the embracement of "realism" in this climactic, pivotal exchange is obviously calculated to enrage the reader against the restraints of "realism" as such. Here we can see a fourth major shift, not a complete shift but a decisive one, from *Uncle Tom's Cabin* to *Dred*. Both novels alternate, sometimes disconcertingly, between a mode of attempted sociological realism and a mode of visionary melodrama. But *Dred* seems more willfully divided against itself in this respect than *Uncle Tom's Cabin*. *Dred* is both more cognizant of the actual limits governing human behavior and social change and more insistent on presenting characters and experiments that offer counter-models to the status quo, which the novel's sociological analysis has shown to be wildly aberrant if not impossible: for example, a local Protestant minister who is an outspoken abolitionist, the by-and-large dutiful son of a pillar of the local judiciary, who deliberately breaks the law against teaching slaves to read, a community of swamp-based maroons who can make sorties onto plantations at will and almost never get caught, and the delegation of effective attack against these (by 1850s North Carolina standards) acts of blatant defiance of the slaveocracy to one or two very bad apples, who galvanize an otherwise rather amazingly tolerant populace. The figure of Dred himself is the most striking example of the shift (farther) away from realism. Although Uncle Tom is presented within the novel as unique (a "moral miracle," St. Clare calls him) whereas Dred is explicitly compared to famous leaders of slave revolts, Dred is from start to finish much more the mythic figure at the level of narrative representation. By contrast, Tom's language and manners remain pretty closely bound to Stowe's (stereotype-ridden) conception of how an earnest untutored slave would behave and talk. With Dred she barely makes any such pretense. He talks like Moses and behaves like a demigod, popping up at crucial moments in the plot like a *deus ex machina*. Even if not all of the elements of *Dred* were under control, as seems certain given how hastily it was composed, those who would complain about the novel's "inconsistency" or "improbability" miss the point that a figure like Dred is "improbable" not by chance or incompetence but by design. The design of the novel is to pit "realistic" against "utopian" elements much more starkly than is the case with *Uncle Tom's Cabin*.

None of these departures from its predecessor, in and of themselves, make *Dred* a superior *novel*. But they do underscore *Dred*'s claim to be taken as a more far-sighted act of national imagination in certain crucial ways. Most crucially: the momentum of Stowe's work from *Uncle Tom's Cabin* to *Dred* suggests that she came increasingly to sense that the only legitimate path for a grand national fiction in the age of slavery had to be tragic rather than comic. That in the long run might well have been the most decisive reason why the only "happy" ending for *Uncle Tom* the author seems to have been able to imagine entailed hustling out of the country the surviving black characters she most cared about – and in *Dred* the surviving white characters as well. If Stowe had had to choose on the eve of the Civil War which of her two novels about slavery was the truer national representation, she might well have chosen *Dred*. Of course posterity has since chosen for her by remembering *Uncle Tom's Cabin* and largely forgetting *Dred*. But a more careful analysis suggests that the choice should not be so easy. The two books should rather be seen as part of a larger, continuous, evolving attempt at bringing off the impossible dream of narrating the nation, as it looked to the author in the aftermath of the Compromise of 1850. It was a dream of unification across social divides, a dream of personal and spiritual equality frustrated not so much by the author's limited horizon of apprehension as by increasing awareness of the intractability of the divides in need of bridging, as well as by the bald fact that national situations are too messy and unstable to be novelized definitively. In *Uncle Tom's Cabin* the author sensed this; in *Dred* she built more self-consciously upon this realization. Altogether, notwithstanding whatever might be said against it, Stowe's anti-slavery fiction was a remarkable achievement. She herself was never able to equal it, even as she increased in seasoning and polish as a literary professional. Indeed, few other writers in US history have addressed themselves more eloquently to what still remains, even after a century and a half, this nation's most defining crisis.[21]

NOTES

1. According to Stowe family report (published by Annie Adams Fields in 1897), during her 1862 meeting with Lincoln at the White House, the president greeted her in some such fashion: "Is this the little woman who made this great war?" But in Stowe's report at the time no such remark is mentioned (Joan D. Hedrick, *Harriet Beecher Stowe: A Life* [New York: Oxford University Press, 1994], 306; Elizabeth Young, *Disarming the Nation: Women's Writing and the American Civil War* [Chicago: University of Chicago Press, 1999], 25).
2. John W. DeForest, "The great American novel," *The Nation*, 6 (January 9, 1868), 28. Among modern critics, Stowe's "lapse" from national to regional writer is

most perceptively discussed by James M. Cox, "Harriet Beecher Stowe: from sectionalism to regionalism," *Nineteenth-Century Fiction*, 38 (March 1984), 444–466.

3. The history of "novel" as a rubric for designating American fiction in English is much contested, especially with regard to the issue of genre and genderization. Nina Baym, *Novels, Readers, and Reviewers: Responses to Fiction in Antebellum America* (Ithaca: Cornell University Press, 1984), argues strongly and resourcefully that traditional critical identification of the "romance" mode as the defining mark of US fictional practice relative to British is an androcentric critical artifact based on the male canon, and that antebellum domestic fiction ("woman's" fiction as Baym characterizes it elsewhere) represents the first wave of a vigorous novelistic tradition. On the other hand, Emily Budick's *Engendering Romance: Women Writers and the Hawthorne Tradition, 1850–1990* (New Haven: Yale University Press, 1994), argues for the strength of romance modality in fiction by US women writers. These two points seem incontestible, however: that "novel" gained legitimacy as a term of reference as the nineteenth century progressed, and that Stowe was retrospectively classified as a forerunner of "the genuine novel" in a critical conflation of "novel" as the preferred imaginative vehicle of the "real" that she herself eschewed. For the 1883 review crediting Stowe as pioneer in the art of "the genuine novel," see G. R. Thompson and Eric Carl Link, *Neutral Ground: New Traditionalism and the American Romance Controversy* (Baton Rouge: Louisiana State University Press, 1999), 141.

4. Michael Winship, "'The Greatest Book of Its Kind': a publishing history of *Uncle Tom's Cabin*," *Proceedings of the American Antiquarian Society*, 109 (1999), 309–332. "This greatest of American tales" was a much-recycled phrase lifted from a notice in the *Barre Patriot* for the end-of-book advertisement section during the first (1852) edition print run (see for example p. 166 of the paperback edition, Stowe-Day Foundation, Hartford, #G526.S892.U852e).

5. On the durability of the dream (or chimera) of the great American novel, see my "The rise and 'fall' of the great American novel," *Proceedings of the American Antiquarian Society*, 104 (1994), 261–284.

6. I have especially in mind of course the narrative method of *USA*'s principal chapters, rather than the more experimental "Camera's Eye" and "Newsreel" sequences.

7. Harriet Beecher Stowe, *A Key to Uncle Tom's Cabin* (Boston: John P. Jewett, 1853), 5.

8. See Nancy Glazener, *Reading for Realism: The History of a US Literary Institution* (Durham: Duke University Press, 1997), for an account of the importance of (a certain selective kind of) fiction-reading response to the construction of what was thought to count as realism.

9. Herman Melville, *Typee* (1846), ed. Harrison Hayford, Hershel Parker, G. Thomas Tanselle (Evanston: Northwestern University Press, 1968), xiv. Leon Howard's "Historical Note" explains the publishers' and author's attempt to revise the text so as to compensate for the suspected "taint" of fiction (279–294) – less of a problem for American audiences, or so Howard surmises, partly because Americans were more prepared to accept that common sailors might be capable of articulate writing.

10. Herman Melville, "Hawthorne and His Mosses," *The Norton Anthology of American Literature: American Literature 1820–1865*, 6th ed., vol. B., ed. Nina Baym *et al.* (New York: Norton, 2003), 2297.

11. Nina Silber, *The Romance of Reunion: Northerners and the South, 1865–1900* (Chapel Hill: University of North Carolina Press, 1993).

12. Deprecations of *Dred* as a hasty botch began as early as Calvin Stowe's pre-publication warnings to his wife to slow down and write more deliberately (Hedrick, *Harriet Beecher Stowe*, 160, in the course of seconding the traditional verdict of *Dred*'s mediocrity). The contemporary upward assessment of *Dred*'s accomplishment and significance effectively starts with Eric Sundquist's discussion of it in *Faulkner: The House Divided* (Baltimore: Johns Hopkins University Press, 1983), 96–100.

13. Michael J. Meyer, "Toward a rhetoric of equality: reflective and refractive images in Stowe's language," *The Stowe Debate: Rhetorical Strategies in "Uncle Tom's Cabin"*, ed. Mason I. Lowance, Jr., Ellen E. Westbrook, and R. C. De Prospo (Amherst: University of Massachusetts Press, 1994), 241.

14. George Frederickson, *The Black Image in the White Mind: The Debate on Afro-American Character and Destiny, 1817–1914* (New York: Harper, 1971), 104–106; Thomas Y. Gossett, *Uncle Tom's Cabin and American Culture* (Dallas: Southern Methodist University Press, 1985), 83–85.

15. I say "almost surely," because Augustine (354–430) was literally Bishop of Hippo (farther west on the North African coast), although his formative educational years were famously spent in Carthage. Stowe would have been aware both of this fact and also that the most noted early Christian era Bishop of Carthage itself was Cyprian (200–258), whom in fact she quotes for support in *A Key to Uncle Tom's Cabin* (432). It seems almost certain that the passage would have been alluding to both saints. Both Cyprian and Augustine are today regularly claimed to have been black (see Michael Scott, "Black Catholic History Month" (1999), www.adw.org/cultures/officeblack_month.html).

16. Stowe to the Duchess of Argyle, quoted in Hedrick, *Harriet Beecher Stowe*, 258.

17. Here and elsewhere, Stowe makes sure that readers catch the topical allusions: "Tom Gordon . . . proved his eligibility for Congress by beating his defenseless acquaintance on the head, after the fashion of the chivalry of South Carolina" (*Dred: A Tale of the Great Dismal Swamp* ed. Robert S. Levine [New York: Penguin, 2000], 493). Quotations below are from this edition.

18. For more on Stowe's fictionalization of Hopkins, see my *New England Literary Culture* (Cambridge: Cambridge University Press, 1986), 263–280.

19. DeForest, "The great American novel," 28.

20. John Carlos Rowe, "Stowe's rainbow sign: violence and community in *Dred: A Tale of the Great Dismal Swamp (1856)*," *Arizona Quarterly*, 58 (Spring 2002), 40.

21. My sincere thanks to Jared Hickman for research assistance.

II

CAROLYN L. KARCHER

Stowe and the literature of social change

No other American author has ever attained the international celebrity status
to which the publication of *Uncle Tom's Cabin* catapulted Harriet Beecher
Stowe. A leading German literary journal of the day ranked the novel above
"the whole modern romance literature of Germany, England, and France,"
asserting that Stowe eclipsed such luminaries as George Sand, Charles
Dickens, and Edward Bulwer-Lytton in "eloquence," "truth to nature," intellectual scope, and "artistic faultlessness." "[O]ur English fiction writers had
better shut up altogether and have done with it," agreed the prominent British
reformer Harriet Martineau, who claimed Stowe had whetted a public taste
for "didactic" novels that no one else could satisfy. Sales of *Uncle Tom's
Cabin* abroad the first year – a million and a half copies in England alone –
dwarfed the already astounding record of 300,000 set in the United States.
Translations in twenty European languages – among them not only French,
German, Spanish, and Russian, but Armenian, Finnish, Hungarian, Illyrian,
and Serbian – appeared almost overnight, and more proliferated across the
globe as far away as China and Japan. Stowe's international audiences also
"translated" her message, reapplying her indictment of American slavery to
the wrongs their own peoples endured. For example, Chinese theater-goers
in 1917, seething with resentment against discrimination in the United States
and imperialist domination at home, wildly applauded the play version of
Uncle Tom's Cabin "because they 'knew by bitter experiences the sufferings and humiliations of an oppressed race.'" Similarly capitalizing on the
versatility of Stowe's masterpiece, a Soviet stage adaptation of the 1930s
eliminated the Christian preaching and recast little Eva as "something of an
American forerunner to a vigorous present-day Komsomol (Young Communist) championing the cause of the downtrodden proletarian Negro."[1]

The worldwide appeal *Uncle Tom's Cabin* has exerted indicates that Stowe
deserves recognition as the chief architect of a school I am calling the
"literature of social change" – a school one of her disciples, Elizabeth Stuart
Phelps, called "Art for Truth's Sake."[2] Stowe perfected and blended two

varieties of this art – protest literature, aimed at promoting social change by exposing current injustices; and regional, or as I prefer to term it, sociological fiction, aimed at capturing a changed or changing way of life by portraying the customs, manners, and personalities that typify it. Besides *Uncle Tom's Cabin* (1852), Stowe's overt protest works include its factual companion-piece *A Key to Uncle Tom's Cabin* (1853), her second anti-slavery novel, *Dred* (1856), and her outcry against the sexual double standard, *Lady Byron Vindicated* (1870). Stowe's sociological fiction – into which she wove testimony against New Englanders' role in the slave trade, critiques of Calvinist theology, pleas for a liberalized Christianity, and interventions in debates on the "woman question" – encompasses both her New England novels *The Minister's Wooing* (1859), *The Pearl of Orr's Island* (1862), *Oldtown Folks* (1869), and *Poganuc People* (1878) and her New York trilogy *My Wife and I* (1871), *Pink and White Tyranny* (1871), and *We and Our Neighbors* (1875).

In assessing Stowe's contributions to the literature of social change, I will concentrate on her most influential protest work, *Uncle Tom's Cabin*; her most accomplished New England idyll, *The Minister's Wooing*; and her neglected sketch of modern urban society, *My Wife and I*. My essay falls into two main sections, corresponding to the division of Stowe's corpus into "protest" and "sociological" categories. Each section will examine in turn the hints Stowe took from her predecessors, the ways she reshaped the forms and conventions she inherited, and the models she bequeathed to her successors. Section One will additionally examine the multiple revisions *Uncle Tom's Cabin* inspired as Stowe's successors appropriated her model for new ends.

I

When Stowe set out to write a novel that would impel Americans to repent of their national sin, the controversy over slavery had been raging for two decades, during which the propriety of a woman's taking a public position on a political issue outside her "sphere" had been hotly contested. Hence, she could hardly have overlooked the best-known woman who had entered this fraught arena before her: Lydia Maria Child. A popular author of historical novels, short stories, domestic advice books, and children's literature, Child had produced a comprehensive indictment of slavery and racial prejudice, *An Appeal in Favor of That Class of Americans Called Africans* (1833), which had alienated her fans but propelled her to the forefront of the abolitionist movement. Child had also invented the genre of anti-slavery fiction, orienting the stories she wrote for periodicals and gift books in the 1830s and '40s especially toward mothers and children – the readers Stowe would target in *Uncle Tom's Cabin* – and focusing on themes Stowe would likewise tackle: the separation of families, the sexual exploitation of slave women, and the cycle of violence slavery generated.

Two of Child's stories for young folk, "Jumbo and Zairee" (1831) and "Mary French and Susan Easton" (1834), both published in her magazine the *Juvenile Miscellany*, featured children kidnapped into slavery and subjected to savage beatings, leaving their bereft parents helpless to rescue them. These stories invited white children and their mothers to put themselves in the place of their black counterparts, much as Stowe would ask readers of *Uncle Tom's Cabin* to imagine what they would do "[i]f it were *your* Harry, mother, or your Willie, that were going to be torn from you by a brutal trader."[3] Intended instead for a mature female audience, "The Quadroons" (1842) and "Slavery's Pleasant Homes" (1843), published in the abolitionist gift book *The Liberty Bell*, dramatized the plight of slave women who could not defend their bodies against violation without risking their lives. To bridge the gap between them and the genteel white women she was addressing, Child created the figure of the tragic mulatta – a light-skinned, ladylike heroine who shared the white reader's feminine delicacy and idealization of sexual purity, but faced the sordid prospects of concubinage or rape. Both in "Slavery's Pleasant Homes" and in an earlier *Liberty Bell* story, "The Black Saxons" (1841), Child turned her lens as well on what she saw as the chief dilemma male slaves confronted – whether or not to strike back against the masters who whipped and tortured them, defiled their wives, and sold their children. To arouse the sympathies of her male readers, she allowed them to eavesdrop on a conclave in the woods during which slaves debated this question – a strategy Stowe would emulate in *Dred* – and she portrayed as a heroic martyr a slave who avenged the rape and murder of his wife.[4]

Child furnished Stowe with nuclei of many plot devices and character types she would incorporate into *Uncle Tom's Cabin*, among them the stories of Cassy, Emmeline, Eliza, and George Harris – variations of the tragic mulatta and slave rebel. A writer closer in temperament to Stowe, however, Catharine Maria Sedgwick, suggested elements crucial to making *Uncle Tom's Cabin* a popular success. In *Redwood* (1824), the earliest novel to consider the issue of slavery, Sedgwick introduced a precursor of Uncle Tom – a bondsman whose martyrdom and dying exhortation inspire a young master to emancipate his slaves. She also conjured up a vision of regenerating the south through the north's Christian example, thereby ending slavery peacefully while maintaining national unity – an outcome Stowe sought to achieve in *Uncle Tom's Cabin*.[5]

Sedgwick and Child hardly exhaust the list of authors from whom Stowe borrowed, of course. As critics have noted, *Uncle Tom's Cabin* reveals traces of widely disparate sources: the comic caricatures and pathetic waifs of Dickens, transplanted in American soil and painted in blackface; the anti-slavery novel that had launched the genre, *The Slave: or Memoirs of Archy Moore* (1835); the slave narratives of Frederick Douglass, Henry Bibb, Josiah Henson, and William and Ellen Craft; the abolitionist tracts of Child, Angelina Grimké, and above all Theodore Dwight Weld, whose *American Slavery As It Is* supplied Stowe with so many facts and arguments; and abolitionist newspapers like Gamaliel Bailey's *National Era*, which serialized *Uncle Tom's Cabin*, and William Lloyd Garrison's *Liberator*, which gave Stowe the title of her penultimate chapter.[6]

Whatever Stowe owed to her sources and predecessors, she revolutionized the genre of anti-slavery fiction. The broader canvas of the novel enabled her to combine and develop the plots of children torn away from their parents, young women hounded by lecherous slaveholders, husbands and wives severed from each other, and slaves lashing out against their masters that Child had relegated to separate stories and compressed into brief vignettes. Readers come to know Uncle Tom and Aunt Chloe, Eliza and George, Cassy and Emmeline with an intimacy unprecedented for African-American characters. And readers arrive at a visceral understanding of how slavery perverts family life as Stowe takes them from the flawed patriarchal household of the Shelbys, in which a well-meaning wife is powerless to prevent her husband from selling his most faithful slave, to the overtly dysfunctional household of the St. Clares, dominated by a monstrously selfish wife and mother who keeps her slaves apart and puts them up for auction in defiance of her husband's wishes, to the pandemonium of Simon Legree's plantation, where a bachelor master imposes a sadistic regime of rape and concubinage.

Brilliantly structured, *Uncle Tom's Cabin* advances formally the ethical principles Stowe preaches in direct addresses to the reader and speeches put in the mouths of characters. Through paired scenes, doubled characters, and identical names Stowe shows that all human beings are interconnected, that they form one family despite their superficial differences in skin color, status, and political affiliation. Thus, Stowe's opening chapter, "In which the Reader is Introduced to a Man of Humanity," juxtaposes the crude slave trader Haley with the gentlemanly slaveholder Mr. Shelby and prompts readers to ask whether either can claim to be humane while buying or selling a father or child away from his family. Similarly, chapters VIII and IX align Senator Bird, who has just voted for a state law prohibiting citizens of Ohio from "aiding and abetting" fugitive slaves (68), with the minstrel-like slave Sam, whose "strict look-out to his own personal well-being . . . would have done credit to any white patriot in Washington" (37). Invoking "principles" and "gen'l interests of s'ciety," Sam's patently self-aggrandizing "oratory" parodies the rhetoric the senator uses to justify the Fugitive Slave Law – "we must put aside our public feelings" for the sake of "great public interests" – unmasking its moral bankruptcy (64, 66, 69).

Heading the roster of the novel's countless doubled characters are the Christlike Uncle Tom and little Eva. Both sacrifice themselves to save others, Uncle Tom by choosing to be whipped to death rather than betray the whereabouts of the fugitives Cassy and Emmeline, Eva by wasting away in the hope that "my dying could stop all this misery" (240). Both stage their death scenes in accordance with the iconography of the Crucifixion, Tom by echoing Christ's forgiveness of his torturers and praying for the souls of the slave drivers Sambo and Quimbo, the counterparts of the two thieves between whom Christ hangs on the cross (358–360), Eva by giving away locks of her hair with the words "shear the sheep" (249). Both convert three people, one of whom vows to work for abolition: Tom not only wins over Sambo and Quimbo, but induces George Shelby, the son of his former master, to emancipate his slaves and undertake "*what one man can* to drive out this curse of slavery from my land" (365); correspondingly, Eva regenerates the "goblin-like" slave child Topsy, empowers the upright but loveless New Englander Miss Ophelia to overcome her racial prejudices, and obtains her father Augustine St. Clare's promise to speak out publicly against slavery (209, 241, 244–246).[7]

Stowe's most original device for linking her black and white characters is assigning them the same given names: George Harris and George Shelby; Uncle Tom and the slave catcher Tom Loker; Eliza's son Harry, the Birds' dead son Henry, Eva's cousin Henrique, and Cassy's son Henry; Emily Shelby, Emily de Thoux, and Emmeline; Senator John Bird, John Van Trompe, the "article enumerated as 'John, aged 30'" (106), John the drover, and John Stedman the Quaker. The proliferation of homonyms undermines the distinctions between slave and master, black and white. In the case of Uncle Tom and Tom Loker, the shared names underscore the common humanity of saint and sinner and with it, the possibility of almost every sinner's redemption. This message, indeed, is reinforced by Tom Loker's eventual conversion, as well as by scenes in which the narrative flashes back and forth between "[Uncle] Tom in the hands of his persecutors" and "Tom Loker . . . groaning and touzling in a most immaculately clean Quaker bed" (331).

In addition to these structural innovations, Stowe enlivened anti-slavery fiction (and the larger genre of the protest novel) with a pantheon of vividly portrayed characters representing every conceivable shade of opinion. She created unforgettable types whose very names became bywords. She also endowed her characters with a psychological depth till then unseen in protest literature. Miss Ophelia, "the absolute bond-slave of the '*ought*,'" whose unattainable standards of moral perfection leave her "burdened with a constant and often harassing sense of deficiency" (138), Augustine St. Clare, who despite warm sympathies and high intellectual gifts, "has floated on, a dreamy, neutral spectator of the struggles, agonies, and wrongs of man, when he should have been a worker" (272), and even Legree for whom, having "set all the force of his rough nature against the conviction of his conscience," "perfect love" has become "the most fearful torture, the seal and sentence of the direst despair" (323), come alive as complex human beings and linger in the reader's memory long after the details of the plot have faded.

Stowe's crowning achievement lay in infusing *Uncle Tom's Cabin* with the religious fervor that gave the novel its irresistible power. By wrapping her anti-slavery message in evangelical garb, Stowe succeeded in reaching "a much larger class of readers, who are not in the habit of taking in much humanity, unless stirred up with a portion of theology; like brimstone and molasses," as Lydia Maria Child remarked wryly.[8] Yet readers of other religious persuasions – Unitarians, Quakers, Catholics, and even freethinkers and devotees of non-western faiths – found themselves no less moved by Uncle Tom's and Eva's sacrificial deaths and the core belief they symbolized: that men and women willing to lay down their lives for a cause could transform their fellows and ultimately the world.

Stowe's contemporaries immediately recognized in *Uncle Tom's Cabin* a model they could adapt to their own purposes, and later generations followed suit. African-American writers offer some of the earliest and most striking instances. In such revisions of *Uncle Tom's Cabin* as William Wells Brown's *Clotel; or, The President's Daughter* (1853), Frederick Douglass's "The Heroic Slave" (1853), Martin R. Delany's *Blake; or The Huts of America* (1859), Frances Ellen Watkins Harper's *Iola Leroy; or, Shadows Uplifted* (1892), and Richard Wright's *Uncle Tom's Children* (1936, 1940), they extended Stowe's target to encompass a thoroughgoing indictment of white supremacy; inverted the roles of black and white characters to emphasize black agency and relations within the black community and to undercut the authority of whites, whether as benevolent intercessors or as oppressors; and challenged racial stereotyping by portraying a broad range of African Americans, rendered with subtlety and complexity.

Brown's *Clotel*, for example, delineates slavery with a brutal realism that includes graphic scenes of lynching, slave hunting, casual violence, and squalor. At the same time, *Clotel* shows slaves fighting back and forming maroon strongholds in the swamps, rather than welcoming Christian martyrdom. This "larger context of suffering and rebellion," as Robert Levine points out, decenters the tragic mulatta plot Brown borrows from Child and Stowe. Moreover, by identifying his light-skinned heroines as daughters of Thomas Jefferson, sold at auction by "the writer of the Declaration of American Independence," Brown highlights the blatant hypocrisy that corrodes the nation's founding creed.[9]

While Brown omits Uncle Tom entirely, Harper's *Iola Leroy*, which carries the history of African Americans' struggle for freedom into the 1890s, relegates the Tom-like Uncle Daniel to a minor role in a varied cast of slave characters. For Harper's protagonists, who hold secret prayer meetings in the woods to plan a mass flight to Union army lines, religion and resistance are inextricable. Indeed, martyrdom occurs in combat as Tom Anderson, another analogue of Uncle Tom, exposes himself to Confederate bullets to rescue his comrades – an episode serving to remind readers that African-American soldiers had proved instrumental in rescuing the country from slavery during the Civil War. By representing African Americans as battling side by side with white soldiers, Harper substitutes relations of solidarity for the relations of dependency Stowe had limned in her scenes of benevolent whites helping slaves to escape. Harper redefines the significance of the tragic mulatto as well, using her light-skinned characters both to discredit racial categories as arbitrary and illusory constructs and to establish racial identity as a political choice rather than a biological given. In contrast to Stowe's Cassy, Harper's Iola is "[t]ried, but not tempted" by white men;[10] not only does she fiercely resist the concubinage to which Cassy succumbs, but she also rejects the option of marrying her white suitor and passing for white. Instead, she proudly embraces her African-American heritage and dedicates herself to completing the liberation of her people.

As Brown and Harper illustrate, most African-American writers have revealed discomfort with the figure of Uncle Tom. Hence, Frederick Douglass in "The Heroic Slave" and Martin Delany in *Blake* substitute a revolutionary hero for Stowe's Christlike martyr. Douglass makes his hero Madison Washington palatable to white readers by imbuing him with Tom's fatherly "kindliness and benevolence," as Robert Stepto has noted,[11] but he lets the "Herculean" Madison kill rather than die to free his fellow slaves. Delany rejects Tom altogether, patterning his messianic hero not on Christ, but on Moses.

Thus, it is all the more remarkable to find a full-fledged Uncle Tom in Richard Wright's "Bright and Morning Star," published in the Communist journal *New Masses* (1938) and reprinted in the second edition of the short story collection pointedly titled *Uncle Tom's Children*. Perhaps acknowledging the feminine qualities so many critics have recognized in Tom,[12] Wright turns him into a woman, Aunt Sue. Member of a Communist cell, along with her sons, Sue fuses the militancy of the political creed she has espoused with the need for self-sacrifice she derives from her Christian upbringing. Wright explicitly links the two: "The wrongs and sufferings of black men had taken the place of Him nailed to the Cross; the meager beginnings of the party had become another Resurrection; and the hate of those who would destroy her new faith had quickened in her a hunger to feel how deeply her new strength went."[13] In the climactic scene, Sue carries a pistol wrapped in a sheet to the site where the sheriff and his henchmen are torturing her son to make him divulge the names of his comrades. Her aim is to protect these comrades by shooting the "Judas" who has betrayed her son and is about to identify the other members of the cell. But to do so, she must witness her son's agony without being able to save him, and she must ultimately trigger her own murder. In casting this Communist mother as Virgin Mary and Christ rolled into one, Wright taps into the source of Stowe's greatest power while translating Uncle Tom from a Christian saint into a revolutionary martyr. No revision better testifies to the enduring appeal of *Uncle Tom's Cabin* as a model protest novel.

The versatility of Stowe's model becomes especially apparent in the adaptations that strive to do for (white) industrial workers what *Uncle Tom's Cabin* had done for slaves. Rebecca Harding Davis's "Life in the Iron-Mills" (1861), Elizabeth Stuart Phelps's *The Silent Partner* (1871), and above all Upton Sinclair's *The Jungle* (1906), hailed by fellow socialist Jack London as "the 'Uncle Tom's Cabin' of wage slavery,"[14] all seek to awaken middle- and upper-class readers to the hellish conditions in which factory operatives work and live. All seek as well to arouse their readers' sympathies for a class perceived as utterly repugnant – squalid, animalistic, depraved, and so degraded as to be virtually irredeemable – traits interchangeable with those ascribed to slaves. The three writers accomplish these aims by imitating Stowe's techniques.

Just as Stowe had led readers up to the auction block, into slave huts, through cotton fields, so Davis, Phelps, and Sinclair lead their readers into workers' hovels, iron mills, cotton mills, slaughterhouses, and fertilizer factories. Like Stowe, they engage readers' sympathies by humanizing the victims of the draconian institutions they indict. Davis portrays the iron-puddler Hugh Wolfe as a soul-starved artist, condemned never to sate the hunger he expresses in the gigantic statue he sculpts out of iron-ore refuse. Phelps ennobles the textile worker Sip Garth as a self-sacrificing maternal figure who preaches a "poor folks' religion" to the fellow operatives she devotes her life to redeeming.[15] Sinclair opens *The Jungle* with the wedding of Lithuanian immigrants Jurgis and Ona Rudkus, a setting that introduces them as young lovers and heirs of a vibrant culture.

Sinclair and Davis also trap readers, as Stowe does, in a downward spiral illustrating the oppressive institution's inevitable tendency to crush its victims. Just as Uncle Tom ends up on Simon Legree's plantation after being twice sold away from "kind" masters, Hugh Wolfe lands in prison when he takes too literally the bourgeois philanthropist's exhortation to "remember it was his right to rise," and Jurgis slides from the slaughterhouse to the fertilizer plant, the "place that waits for the lowest man."[16]

Sinclair even emulates Stowe in highlighting the destruction of families and the sexual exploitation of women as the most tragic consequences of the system he explicitly likens to slavery. The capitalist bosses' foremen, writes Sinclair, are "every bit as brutal and unscrupulous as the old-time slave drivers; under such circumstances immorality [is] exactly as inevitable, and as prevalent, as it was under the system of chattel slavery" (104). Threatening to "hound" Ona and her family "to death" if she does not yield, her foreman coerces her into prostitution, with the result that Jurgis eventually deserts her (146).[17]

The champions of industrial laborers pattern their protest novels after Stowe's in their solutions as well as their indictments. Davis offers redemption through a Quaker reformer recalling Stowe's Rachel Halliday, the Quaker matriarch whose home serves as an underground railway station for fugitive slaves. Phelps forges a partnership akin to that of slaves and white abolitionists, between the working-class preacher Sip Garth and the benevolent mill owner Perley Kelso. And Sinclair brings Jurgis into contact with the socialist Comrade Ostrinski, who converts him to "the new religion of humanity – or you might say it was the fulfillment of the old religion, since it implied but the literal application of all the teachings of Christ" (304).

The influence of *Uncle Tom's Cabin* extends even further than these adaptations by labor sympathizers and advocates of racial equality indicate. In the century and a half since its publication, Stowe's masterpiece has won near-universal recognition as the prototype of the work that succeeds in inflaming mass enthusiasm for a cause. Indeed, as Jack London's tribute to *The Jungle* testifies, virtually every writer who has approached Stowe's achievement has been credited with producing "The *Uncle Tom's Cabin* of" her or his cause, be it Native American rights (Helen Hunt Jackson's *Ramona* [1886]), the prevention of cruelty to animals (Anna Sewell's *Black Beauty* [1877]), world peace (Bertha Von Suttner's *Lay Down Your Arms!* [1896]), Alaska statehood (Edna Ferber's *Ice Palace* [1957]), or modern environmentalism (Rachel Carson's *Silent Spring* [1962]), to name only a few.[18] Yet none of the writers who have inherited Stowe's mantle have ever matched her worldwide fame. *Uncle Tom's Cabin* still stands unrivaled as the quintessential protest novel.

II

The protest novel nevertheless represents only the best known of Stowe's contributions to the literature of social change. As I suggested at the outset, Stowe's portrayals of manners and mores in the rural New England of a bygone era and the urban New York of the 1870s likewise focus on social change. Her greatest New Engand novel *The Minister's Wooing* (1859), for example, centers around the struggle over the slave trade in post-Revolutionary Newport and the concurrent rebellion against Calvinist theology that heralds Stowe's liberalized evangelicalism. Similarly, *My Wife and I; or, Harry Henderson's History* (1871), which inaugurates Stowe's New York trilogy, highlights the ongoing controversy over women's rights and the increasing secularization wrought by scientific discoveries that clash with Biblical truth.

As a social critic and observer of regional manners, Stowe owed a large debt to Catharine Maria Sedgwick. In *A New-England Tale; or, Sketches of New-England Character and Manners* (1822), whose title Stowe echoed in her first published story, "A New England Sketch" (1834), Sedgwick created the genre Stowe brought to fruition in *The Minister's Wooing* – a genre peopled with distinctive regional types. Indeed, *A New-England Tale*, like *The Minister's Wooing*, condemned the harshness of Calvinist theology, though Sedgwick sought to convert her readers to Unitarianism rather than liberal evangelicalism. Setting yet another precedent for *The Minister's Wooing*, Sedgwick's *Redwood* (1824) and *The Linwoods* (1835) intertwined the depiction of regional types with the exploration of a key national problem – slavery. Besides regional fiction, Sedgwick pioneered the urban novel as Patricia Kalayjian has pointed out in her analysis of *Clarence* (1830).[19] Both Sedgwick's critique of urban fashionables in *Clarence* and her treatment in *Married or Single?* (1857) of marriage and women's rights activism anticipated Stowe's *My Wife and I*. Last but not least, Sedgwick laid the groundwork for Stowe in her sophisticated narrative strategies. By allowing her characters to narrate parts of the story through interpolated letters, she opened her novels to multiple voices and points of view – a democratizing technique Stowe would raise to new heights in *The Minister's Wooing*.

Stowe revised Sedgwick's models of regional and urban fiction almost as radically as she had Child's versions of anti-slavery fiction, however. Eliminating the melodramatic subplots Sedgwick derived from the seduction novel, developing dialogue into a prime means of revealing character, and skillfully capturing the accents of different regions and social classes, Stowe carried literary realism much farther than her predecessor had.

Unlike Sedgwick's novels, moreover, *The Minister's Wooing* accords an African-American character a pivotal role in the plot. The "majestic" Candace not only inspires her pastor Dr. Hopkins to begin preaching against slavery, but usurps his ministerial function when she "talk[s] *gospel*" to save her mistress Mrs. Marvyn from the despair that Hopkins's Calvinist theology has induced in her. Explicitly rejecting Hopkins's doctrine of eternal damnation for all but a chosen few as unfit for "sick" souls, Candace articulates the religion of love that Stowe proffers in the place of Calvinism:

> Jesus didn't die for nothin', – all dat love a'n't gwine to be wasted. . . . Dar's de *Spirit.* . . . [A]s we's got to live in dis yer world, it's quite clar de Lord must ha' fixed it so we *can*; and ef tings was as some folks suppose, why, we *couldn't* live, and dar wouldn't be no sense in anyting dat goes on.[20]

Candace speaks for earthly as well as heavenly love. Arguing that "[d]ar's a good deal more reason in two young, handsome folks comin' togeder dan dar is in" a sexless marriage between a girl in her twenties and a minister twice her age, Candace helps effect the consummation she favors (313). She thus links the political, religious, and romantic themes of *The Minister's Wooing*.

The most experimental of Stowe's novels, *The Minister's Wooing* eschews a linear plot and dominant character. Instead it tells the story of a New England community. Stowe's narrator speaks as a member of this community, setting herself on a par with the other characters comprising it, and aligning her own art of narration with the domestic arts its female members practice: baking, sewing, spinning, ironing, and above all quilting, on which she patterns her storytelling.[21] As she explains in her second paragraph: "When one has a story to tell, one is always puzzled which end of it to begin at. You have a whole corps of people to introduce that *you* know and your reader doesn't; and one thing so presupposes another, that, whichever way you turn your patchwork, the figures still seem ill-arranged" (3). Her narrative, she hints, will take the shape of a patchwork quilt rather than a yarn with an obvious beginning and "end."

The intimate "you" the narrator addresses likewise draws readers into the community and involves them in the process of narration by prompting them to ask the questions that will "start me systematically on my story" (3). At critical moments, the narrator lets readers not simply propel but interfere with her storytelling by objecting to the direction the plot is taking: "Will our little Mary really fall in love with the Doctor? – The question reaches us in anxious tones from all the circle of our readers" (107). While playfully chiding readers for demanding fictional outcomes contrary to those they have chosen in real life, the narrator ultimately allows her surrogates, Candace and the seamstress Miss Prissy, to rearrange the "patchwork" of her plot.

Miss Prissy, who sews wedding gowns, designs wedding quilts, presides over quilting bees, and slips precipitously from a vision of the Millennium into a "discourse on her own particular way of covering piping-cord" (120), rejects the literary conventions requiring a linear plot. "I always told folks that I should spoil a novel before it got half-way through the first volume, by blurting out some of those things that they let go trailing on so," she confesses (313). At the same time, she personifies the aesthetic governing Stowe's novel, as the narrator articulates it: "Two worlds must mingle, – the great and the little, the solemn and the trivial, wreathing in and out, like the grotesque carvings on a Gothic shrine; – only, did we know it rightly, nothing is trivial; since the human soul, with its awful shadow, makes all things sacred" (120). Because Miss Prissy, like Candace, recognizes that "we have [both] a body and a soul," she thwarts the marriage with the minister that would have forced Mary to repress her sexual desires. Having rewritten the plot of "The Minister's Wooing," which ends two chapters before the novel's actual conclusion, Miss Prissy fittingly takes over from the narrator the task of describing "The Wedding" she has engineered between Mary and her young lover James Marvyn.[22]

With its non-linear plot, its hybrid aesthetic, its ensemble cast, and its focus on a regional community rather than a dominant character, *The Minister's Wooing* fundamentally altered the genre Stowe had inherited from Sedgwick and set new directions for her successors. As many critics have noted, Sarah Orne Jewett and Willa Cather developed these aspects of Stowe's legacy in such works as *The Country of the Pointed Firs* (1896) and *O Pioneers!* (1913).[23]

Stowe's well-recognized contributions to the tradition of women's regional fiction, however, have tended to eclipse her role as a trendsetting observer of modern urban society in transition – hence my preference for the term "sociological," which illuminates the complementary relationship between her New England and New York novels as literary explorations of social change. Stowe herself highlights this complementarity in *My Wife and I*, whose narrator Harry Henderson grows up in a New England village but moves to New York City.

Harry's career recapitulates the seismic shift American culture has undergone between the post-Revolutionary past of *The Minister's Wooing* and the post-Civil War present of *My Wife and I*: though himself the son of a minister, he has lost his faith and renounced the religious calling of his father for the secular profession of journalism. "[T]he literature of newspapers and magazines," explains Stowe through her characters, is "getting to be in our day . . . a power far out-going that of the pulpit, and that of books."[24] She playfully reminds readers that like her narrator, she is exploiting the latest medium of moral influence, the newspaper serial. "It is understood now that no paper is complete without its serial story" and that "whoever wishes to gain the public ear . . . must do it in a serial story," she has Harry announce in the novel's "Introductory Note," which identifies the text readers are perusing as a serial for the *Christian Union* (ix, x). The editor of the *Christian Union*, Stowe's brother Henry Ward Beecher, is sponsoring her serial, she hints, because he, like she, is anticipating the day when "every leading clergyman" will have to couch his theology in the form of a "serial story, to be delivered from the pulpit Sunday after Sunday" (ix).

While capitalizing on the expanded audience the periodical press affords, Stowe exposes the profession of journalism as a minefield for the writer aspiring to raise moral standards (at least in the pre-muckraker era). Although Harry hopes to use the power of the press to further the ideals he espouses, he quickly discovers that his advancement as a journalist depends on pleasing his employer and the public. When he upholds "abstract moral principles," he is praised for his "firm, moral tone, and steady religious convictions"; when he "attack[s] a specific abuse in New York administration," on the other hand, he is sharply reprimanded (149–151). Both his own newspaper, *The Great Democracy*, and its rival, *The Moral Spouting Horn*, prove equally "humbug."

Stowe's focus on social change in *My Wife and I* encompasses not only the decline of religion and the rise of the journalistic profession but "the subject which is in everybody's mind and mouth, discussed on every platform, ringing from everybody's tongue, and coming home to every man's business and bosom": women's rights (x). Her female characters represent a range of positions in the debates over what reforms are needed in women's status. Caroline Simmons and Ida Van Arsdel yearn for "a life-work worth doing," education that will prepare them for their chosen profession of medicine, an income of their own, the opportunity to live single and independent, and suffrage when women as a group are ready for it (111, 248). Eva Van Arsdel wants to escape both the triviality and emptiness of fashionable life and the commodification of women on the marriage market. Mrs. Stella Cerulean, a caricature of Stowe's younger sister, Isabella Beecher Hooker,[25] feels "called to the modern work of society regeneration" and has "one simple remedy for the reconstruction of society" – to put "the affairs of the world into the hands of women, forthwith" (245). And Audacia Dangereyes, a lampoon of Victoria Woodhull, demands the right "to do anything that men do," including smoke, drink, and enjoy free love (251). Stowe's sympathies clearly lie with Caroline and Ida, who speak for the more conservative and practical faction of the women's rights movement, then titularly led by Henry Ward Beecher himself. Hence, she uses the columns of Henry's newspaper to differentiate women's legitimate claims from the travesty of their cause that threatens, she fears, to discredit the movement. Appropriately, Stowe concentrates her attack on Woodhull's newspaper, using her journalist narrator as her mouthpiece: "It was particularly annoying to me that this paper, with all its coarseness and grossness, set itself up to be the head leader of Woman's Rights; and to give its harsh clamors as the voice of woman" (269).

Stowe's intervention into the "woman question" boomeranged by goading Woodhull into accusing Henry Ward Beecher of committing adultery with the wife of his erstwhile colleague Theodore Tilton. Overshadowed by the scandal it precipitated, *My Wife and I* has never received the attention it deserves in literary history. Yet it heralded and may well have prompted a long series of novels delving into the same modern social problems that Stowe had been the first to investigate. As a snapshot of the new profession of journalism, for example, *My Wife and I* predates William Dean Howells's *A Modern Instance* (1882). As an adumbration of women's search for meaningful careers, especially in the field of medicine, it paves the way for Elizabeth Stuart Phelps's *Doctor Zay* (1882) and Sarah Orne Jewett's *A Country Doctor* (1884). As a view of the women's rights movement and a critique of its most flamboyant leaders, *My Wife and I* precedes Henry James's *The Bostonians* (1886). And as a satiric depiction of urban fashionables and the marriage market, it foreshadows Edith Wharton's *The House of Mirth* (1905).

Rarely, if ever, has one author bequeathed to posterity three literary models that span as wide a range as *My Wife and I*, *The Minister's Wooing*, and *Uncle Tom's Cabin* – prototypes, respectively, of the urban, regional, and protest novel. Even more rarely has any author produced such an extraordinary number and diversity of literary heirs. And never has an American novel reached a larger audience worldwide than *Uncle Tom's Cabin*. Judged by all these criteria, Stowe surely ranks at the head of the school I have called the literature of social change.

NOTES

1. Quotations are from Charles Edward Stowe, *Life of Harriet Beecher Stowe, Compiled from Her Letters and Journals* (Boston: Houghton-Mifflin, 1889), 195, 309; and Thomas F. Gossett, *Uncle Tom's Cabin and American Culture* (Dallas: Southern Methodist University Press, 1985), 387.
2. Elizabeth Stuart Phelps, *Chapters from a Life* (Boston: Houghton-Mifflin, 1897), 259–266. I am indebted to Cindy Weinstein for suggesting the term "literature of social change."

3. Harriet Beecher Stowe, *Uncle Tom's Cabin; or, Life among the Lowly*, ed. Elizabeth Ammons (New York: Norton, 1994), 43. Subsequent page references will be given parenthetically in the text.
4. For detailed discussions of these stories, see Carolyn L. Karcher, *The First Woman in the Republic: A Cultural Biography of Lydia Maria Child* (Durham: Duke University Press, 1994), 161–168, 333–343.
5. For a more extensive discussion of Sedgwick's legacy to Stowe, see Carolyn L. Karcher, "Catharine Maria Sedgwick in literary history," in *Catharine Maria Sedgwick: Critical Perspectives*, ed. Lucinda Damon-Bach and Victoria Clements (Boston: Northeastern University Press, 2003), 5–15.
6. For discussions of Stowe's sources and antecedents, see Jean Fagan Yellin, *The Intricate Knot: Black Figures in American Literature, 1776–1863* (New York: New York University Press, 1972), chapters 6–7; Yellin, "Doing it herself: *Uncle Tom's Cabin* and woman's role in the slavery crisis," and Robert B. Stepto, "Sharing the thunder: the literary exchanges of Harriet Beecher Stowe, Henry Bibb, and Frederick Douglass," both in *New Essays on Uncle Tom's Cabin*, ed. Eric J. Sundquist (Cambridge: Cambridge University Press, 1986), 85–105, 135–53; Gossett, *Uncle Tom's Cabin and American Culture*; and Joan D. Hedrick, *Harriet Beecher Stowe: A Life* (New York: Oxford University Press, 1994), chapters 18–19.
7. For earlier discussions of some of these parallels, see Elizabeth Ammons, "Heroines in *Uncle Tom's Cabin*," in *Critical Essays on Harriet Beecher Stowe*, ed. Ammons (Boston: G. K. Hall, 1980), 156–159; and Ammons, "Stowe's dream of the mother-savior: *Uncle Tom's Cabin* and American women writers before the 1920s," in Sundquist, ed., 166–168. For an influential analysis of how "Christian soteriology," the iconography of the Crucifixion, and "the eschatological vision" structure *Uncle Tom's Cabin*, see Jane Tompkins, *Sensational Designs: The Cultural Work of American Fiction, 1790–1860* (New York: Oxford University Press, 1985), chapter 5, especially 128–139.
8. Milton Meltzer, Patricia G. Holland, and Francine Krasno (eds.), *Lydia Maria Child: Selected Letters, 1817–1880* (Amherst: University of Massachusetts Press, 1982), 264.
9. William Wells Brown, *Clotel; or, The President's Daughter: A Narrative of Slave Life in the United States*, ed. Robert S. Levine (Boston: Bedford/St. Martin's, 2000), 21, 88.
10. Frances E. W. Harper, *Iola Leroy; or, Shadows Uplifted*, ed. Hazel V. Carby (Boston: Beacon Press, 1987), 115.
11. Robert B. Stepto, "Sharing the thunder," 150–151; for a fine analysis of both Douglass's and Delany's dialogue with Stowe, see Robert S. Levine, *Martin Delany, Frederick Douglass, and the Politics of Representative Identity* (Chapel Hill: University of North Carolina Press, 1997), 83–85, 175–178.
12. See, for example, James Baldwin's famous attack on Stowe in "Everybody's protest novel" (1948), reprinted in Ammons, ed., *Critical Essays on Harriet Beecher Stowe*, 92–97, especially 94; and Ammons, "Heroines in *Uncle Tom's Cabin*," 152–154, 159–161.
13. Richard Wright, *Early Works: Lawd Today!, Uncle Tom's Children, Native Son* (New York: Viking Press Library of America, 1991), 410. See also Wright's essay, "How 'Bigger' was born," reprinted in the same volume, 851–881, in which he ultimately repudiates the model of sentimental protest fiction he had borrowed

from Stowe because he wants readers to face the harsh truths of black life in America "without the consolation of tears" (874). For a fine analysis of "Bright and Morning Star," and of *Uncle Tom's Children* generally, see Cheryl Higashida, "Aunt Sue's children: re-viewing the gender(ed) politics of Richard Wright's radicalism," *American Literature* 75 (June 2003), 395–425.

14. Quoted in Walter B. Rideout, *The Radical Novel in the United States, 1900–1954*, 2nd ed. (New York: Columbia University Press, 1992), 30.

15. Elizabeth Stuart Phelps, *The Silent Partner* (Old Westbury, NY: Feminist Press, 1983), 296.

16. Rebecca Harding Davis, *Life in the Iron-Mills*, ed. Cecelia Tichi (Boston: Bedford/St. Martin's, 1998), 58; Upton Sinclair, *The Jungle*, ed. James R. Barrett (Urbana: University of Illinois Press, 1988), 123.

17. Despite these similarities, Sinclair's portrayal of family life as a trap men should avoid, at least until the triumph of a socialist revolution, is very different from Stowe's, as is his narrative voice, which eschews the moralizing direct addresses to the reader so characteristic of *Uncle Tom's Cabin*. Sinclair's championship of white workers at the expense of blacks, whom he denigrates viciously in the famous strike scene in chapter 26, further distinguishes *The Jungle* from its model.

18. I am indebted to H. Bruce Franklin for suggesting the Google search that turned up these examples, and many more.

19. Patricia Larson Kalayjian, "Disinterest as moral corrective in *Clarence*'s cultural critique," in Damon-Bach and Clements (eds.), 104–117.

20. Harriet Beecher Stowe, *The Minister's Wooing*, ed. Susan K. Harris (New York: Penguin Books, 1999), 201, 202. Subsequent page references will be given parenthetically in the text.

21. On the structural significance of quilting and needlework in the novel, see Karen E. Beardslee, *Literary Legacies, Folklore Foundations: Selfhood and Cultural Tradition in Nineteenth- and Twentieth-Century American Literature* (Knoxville: University of Tennessee Press, 2001), chapter 1.

22. For a fine analysis of Miss Prissy's role as surrogate author, see Nancy Lusignan Schultz, "The artist's craftiness: Miss Prissy in *The Minister's Wooing*," *Studies in American Fiction* 20.1 (1992), 33–44.

23. See, for example, Josephine Donovan, *New England Local Color Literature: A Women's Tradition* (New York: Frederick Ungar, 1983); Ammons, "Stowe's dream of the mother-savior," 173–176; Sarah Way Sherman, *Sarah Orne Jewett, an American Persephone* (Hanover, NH: University Press of New England, 1989); and Judith Fetterley and Marjorie Pryse (eds.), *American Women Regionalists, 1850–1910* (New York: Norton, 1992).

24. Harriet Beecher Stowe, *My Wife and I; or, Harry Henderson's History*, vol. 12 of *The Writings of Harriet Beecher Stowe* (Boston: Houghton-Mifflin, 1899), 93. Subsequent page references will be given parenthetically in the text.

25. The caricature was recognized and criticized by readers of the *Revolution*, the women's rights newspaper of the Elizabeth Cady Stanton–Susan B. Anthony faction of the movement, to which Isabella Beecher Hooker belonged. See the article, "Mrs. Cerulian" [sic], signed Observer, in the *Revolution* of July 6, 1871, 7; also Jeanne Boydston, Mary Kelley, and Anne Margolis, *The Limits of Sisterhood: The Beecher Sisters on Women's Rights and Woman's Sphere* (Chapel Hill: University of North Carolina Press, 1988), 262–273, 279, 295, 302 n.9.

12

KENNETH W. WARREN

The afterlife of *Uncle Tom's Cabin*

In the introduction to the Vintage edition of *Invisible Man* Ralph Ellison recalls the Vermont summer of 1945 during which he began to write his soon-to-be-classic novel of race and identity. Ellison remembers that while unsuccessfully "plotting a novel based on the war then in progress," he happened upon

> a poster announcing the performance of a "Tom Show," that forgotten term for blackface minstrel versions of Mrs. Stowe's *Uncle Tom's Cabin*. I had thought such entertainment a thing of the past, but there in a quiet northern village it was alive and kicking, with Eliza frantically slipping and sliding on the ice, still trying – and that during World War II! – to escape the slavering hounds.[1]

Finding Uncle Tom apparently alive and well was certainly a shock to Ellison's sensibilities, and for the novel he thought himself to be writing, the jolt administered turned out to have been terminal. Yet, Ellison's unexpected encounter with what he had presumed to be a dead letter was also highly fortuitous: the Vermont Tom Show conjures up "the spokesman for invisibility" who would become the protagonist of Ellison's first novel (xvi). Uncle Tom's refusal to die becomes the invisible man's insistence on living.

In describing himself as affronted and detoured by what he mistakenly presumed to be an artifact of a dead past, Ellison sketches out what was to become a common reaction to rereading Stowe's novel. To take one example, Ellison's shock was echoed, albeit with contrasting political overtones in Edmund Wilson's observation in *Patriotic Gore* (1962), that, "To expose oneself in maturity to *Uncle Tom* may therefore prove a startling experience. It is a much more impressive work than one has ever been allowed to suspect."[2] Wilson recounts his "startling" re-encounter with Stowe's novel in an assessment of the Civil War that was itself calculated to startle his own readers. Wilson argued that like all "wars fought by human beings" "the Civil War was stimulated . . . by the same instincts as the voracity of the sea slug" that makes its way along the sea bottom "gobbling up smaller organisms through the large orifice at one end of its body" (xi). Virtually acquiescing in the southern view of the Civil War as a war of aggression, Wilson lumps Abraham Lincoln with Otto von Bismarck and V. I. Lenin as "uncompromising dictator[s]" (xviii), not because he agrees with the south's view of slavery (although, tellingly he does express dismay at "the premature enfranchisement of the Negroes," xxii), but because he wants his contemporaries to disabuse themselves of the idea that the USA pursues war out of anything other than an "appetite for aggrandizement." The nation, in Wilson's view, has become so beguiled by its high sounding slogans that it is "very difficult for us to recognize that we, too, are devourers and that we, too, are talking cant." Wilson's rereading of Stowe, then, takes place in service of a rewriting of national history for the present moment – "If we would truly understand at the present time the kind of role that our country is playing, we must go back and try to see objectively what our tendencies and our practice have been in the past" (xiii). *Uncle Tom's Cabin*, then, becomes a text as much for the Cold War present as for the Civil War past.

Again and again Stowe's modern readers have found that far from being safely and inertly ensconced in the past, *Uncle Tom's Cabin* demands reassessments of the literary present. In Lauren Berlant's words, "sentimentality signifies redefinition, and in the US the definitions of power, personhood, and consent construe the scene of value in the political public sphere in such a way that any account of sentimentality has to be an account of change and of an ideology of change."[3] Rereading Stowe's novel becomes simultaneously a rereading of current assumptions about political and literary value as well as literary tradition. In fact, Ellison's 1981 recollection occurred at a moment quite propitious for the scholarly reputation of Stowe's best-selling novel. In 1979 Leslie Fiedler had published *The Inadvertent Epic: From Uncle Tom's Cabin to Roots* based on the Massey lectures that he had delivered the previous year. And by the mid-1980s Elizabeth Ammons, Gillian Brown, Philip Fisher, Walter Benn Michaels, Hortense Spillers, Eric Sundquist, Jane Tompkins, and Richard Yarborough, to name a few, had all published significant essays and books on *Uncle Tom's Cabin* without presuming the need to disparage Stowe's best-seller. Although it would be incorrect to cite all of these authors as straightforwardly engaged in an effort to recuperate *Uncle Tom's Cabin*, the effect of their attention was not only to secure the idea that the novel warranted serious consideration as a major text in American literary history but also to buttress a claim that attending properly to *Uncle Tom's Cabin* requires that we transform the way we think about such matters as American literature, race, the self, and the market.

Fiedler, for example, in the *Inadvertent Epic* announces his intention "to save *Uncle Tom's Cabin* – even if this means re-defining literature as it has been traditionally understood, as well as reconstituting the canon of o.k. fiction as defined by *American Renaissance* and *Studies in Classic American Literature*."[4] Rereading *Uncle Tom's Cabin* once again would be to change everything – an outcome which, of course, describes what Stowe's novel was intended to achieve in the first place, namely to transform one thing into another, most specifically a chattel into a human being and a slave society into a free one. And as I hope to illustrate, the sentimental strategies for effecting transformations on the pages of *Uncle Tom's Cabin* have been reproduced consciously and unconsciously in subsequent rereadings of the novel.

The strange formula for Stowe's sentimental alchemy is laid out in the ninth chapter of *Uncle Tom's Cabin*, "In Which It Appears That a Senator Is But a Man." The chapter's title prompts one to ask, just what does a senator appear to be before Stowe corrects our view? And in considering this question, the possibility raised by the word "but" as a synonym for "only" suggests that Stowe's readers may have been previously misled into thinking that senators were perhaps more than men – a misconception perhaps shared by senators themselves, who have been making laws as if they were more superhuman – the narrator tells us later in the chapter that a statesman "of course, could not be expected to cry, like other mortals."[5] The law that Senator Bird has just helped pass is the Fugitive Slave Act, which Mrs. Bird reviles as "a law forbidding people to give meat and drink to poor colored folks that come along" and thus so heinous that she "didn't think any Christian legislature would pass it!" (142). So Stowe's chapter quickly reveals that the "but" in its title is to be read ironically: senators, in overriding their feelings to enact laws out of a belief that public men "mustn't suffer our feelings to run away with our judgment" have been behaving as something less than men (144). They have enacted an inhuman and thus inhumane law.

Bird's particular virtue, then, is that "our poor senator was not stone or steel, – as he was a man, and a downright noble-hearted one, too" (156). Needing to be inanimate to act his part on behalf of the state, the senator proves himself unable to shed enough of his humanity to enable his conformity with the law he has just helped to pass. The change in his behavior, from agreeing to pass the law in the first place to later choosing not to abide by it, is explained by his having in the meantime been presented with the persons and the story of the fugitive Eliza and her son Harry, who together constitute what Stowe calls the "magic of the real presence of distress, – the imploring human eye, the frail trembling human hand, the despairing appeal of helpless agony," which senator Bird "had never tried" (156). Faced with the almost oxymoronic "magic of the real presence of distress" Senator Bird is revealed to be merely John Bird, husband and father, who cannot avoid being moved by the plight of the fugitive slaves who have appeared within his household. In describing this revelation of the senator as but a man it would not be right to say that Bird has been transformed from stone and steel back into a man. The narrative emphatically states that he never was stone or steel. On the contrary, Bird would have needed to be transformed into stone and steel to withstand the magic of the real presence of distress. The magic worked by the real, then, depends on no real magic but merely on what Philip Fisher has called the capacity of objects of compassion to reveal "the reality of their suffering."[6] If their sufferings were indeed real, conjuring them up would require no real magic at all – the presence of such suffering would merely work like magic.

Fisher's reassessment of *Uncle Tom's Cabin* stresses the novel's "experimental, even dangerous, extensions of the self of the reader" (98), by which he means to point out the work sentimental novels do in drawing into the realm of human regard classes of beings – "prisoners, slaves, madmen, children, and animals" – whose condition, however unfortunate has not been understood as suffering in the order of that experienced by those already regarded as human (100). And both he and Tompkins, whose argument at points works parallel to his, are right in noting that something powerful is at work in fictions like that written by Stowe. Yet words like "dangerous" and "experimental" should not be confused with "uncertain," because one mark of the sentimental is that, whatever the risks it might appear to undertake, it knows its methods to be tried and true. In other words the "truths that Stowe's narrative conveys can only be re-embodied, never discovered, because they are already revealed from the beginning" (134). The only fear of the sentimentalist is that those who would naturally respond sympathetically to the reality of suffering might for one reason or another be in the position of never having tried it. Recall that Mrs. Bird does not center her initial complaint about the Fugitive Slave Act on the possibility of her having to assist in the recapture of runaways (although she does subsequently chastise her husband by reminding him that the new law would require him to throw Eliza in jail [145]). Rather she focuses on the way that the law would prevent her and individuals like her from committing the acts of charity – giving "a warm supper and a bed to poor, starving creatures" – that would place them in the real presence of suffering (144). So while there is no magic capable of transforming men and women into stones or steel, there *is* the possibility that the law could exile them from the reality of suffering and thus prevent them from recognizing that they themselves are but men and women whose feelings and passions need be engaged as reminders of their own humanity. Thus exiled, they would then be in danger of behaving like "political folks" who have a way "of coming round and round a plain right thing" even though they "don't believe in it [them]selves, when it comes to practice" (145). It is against this eventuality that *Uncle Tom's Cabin* organizes itself, and it is against this same eventuality that much of the recuperative criticism of *Uncle Tom's Cabin* in the late twentieth century, albeit in different ways, has been organized.

To be sure, one of the most significant mid-twentieth-century criticisms of Stowe's novel takes direct aim at the tears evoked by Uncle Tom and his children. Richard Wright's assessment of his own volume of short stories, *Uncle Tom's Children* famously proclaims his own sense of having "made an awfully naïve mistake" by having "written a book which even bankers' daughters could read and weep over and feel good about." In response Wright swore "that if I ever wrote another book, no one would weep over it; that it would be so hard and deep that they would have to face it without the consolation of tears."[7] In thinking that he was marking out a departure from Stowe's text with *Uncle Tom's Children*, Wright describes himself as unwittingly replaying its dynamics. His *Native Son* then, as we all know, was put forward as an anti-Tom narrative, meant to substitute for the Christ-like slave a black rapist and murderer who kills the wealthy white daughter who would have wept for him (and possibly slept with him) had she not unfortunately turned out to be his first victim. With her head under rather than on the pillow, Mary Dalton is the beautiful white girl who must be sacrificed for the sake of the narrative and serve as Wright's anti-Eva whose death must not evoke the lachrymose emotions of Stowe's narrative. If the key to the sentimental scene is maternal witnessing – the mother "must be present when all that she values most is torn from her" – *Native Son* mercilessly parodies Stowe's archetypal scene in all its crucial elements. The daughter dies on her own bed with her black retainer at her side and with her mother present but unable to witness the scene of suffering because of her blindness (in this Mrs. Dalton perhaps mirrors rather than parodies Marie St. Clare whose self-indulgence prevents her from truly seeing her daughter's holiness). Kneeling at Mary's bedside to pray not because she thinks her daughter is dead but merely "dead drunk," Mrs. Dalton is more the unwitting accomplice to her daughter's accidental murder than its victim.[8] By entering the room just as Bigger has kissed Mary, who in a drunken stupor has responded to the kiss by moving her hips against Bigger "in a hard and veritable grind," Mrs. Dalton in effect prevents the despoiling of her daughter by the black would-be rapist by precipitating the death that avoids the fate worse than death (84). The beatific face of the dead Little Eva in which "there was diffused over every lineament . . . that high celestial expression" (258), is replaced by the bluish tinged skin and the bulging glassy eyes of Mary Dalton. And the gruesome scene of dismemberment and beheading in the basement through which Bigger seeks to hide his crime also functions to make it absolutely impossible that Mary Dalton present any reenactment of the sentimental picture of Little Eva lying in state.

Ironically, however, despite the great lengths that Richard Wright seems to have gone to avoid making the same error with *Native Son* that he had with *Uncle Tom's Children*, he was to be charged with having done precisely that by James Baldwin, who in two essays, "Everybody's Protest Novel" and "Many Thousands Gone" undertook in the mid-1950s a reassessment of Wright's landmark novel. Baldwin's criticism is searing but not unsparing in its reckoning of Wright's achievements and failures. Nonetheless in detailing *Native Son*'s failures Baldwin charges the novel with having extended rather than ended the sway of Uncle Tom. He writes:

> Below the surface of this novel there lies, as it seems to me, a continuation, a complement of that monstrous legend it was written to destroy. Bigger is Uncle Tom's descendant, flesh of his flesh, so exactly opposite a portrait that, when the books are placed together, it seems that the contemporary Negro novelist and the dead New England woman are locked together in a deadly, timeless battle; the one uttering merciless exhortations, the other shouting curses.[9]

Baldwin virtually rewrites Mary Dalton's death scene (itself, as we have seen, a rewriting of Little Eva's death) so that Bigger is replaced by Wright, who wields his novel instead of a pillow and Mary Dalton by Stowe, who, though already dead in Baldwin's depiction, still has enough strength to prevent her assailant from smothering her completely, if not to vanquish him entirely. It is as if Baldwin has infused Mrs. Dalton's ghostly presence into the moldering corpse of a dead New England woman, enabling Stowe to cling to Wright and creating for Baldwin the nightmarish vision of the young black male writer forever unable to wrench himself free of the dead arms of an elderly white woman.

Baldwin's critique is less important for what it tells us about Wright's novel than for what it can tell us about the often paradoxical way in which the threat of sentimentality circulated in the imaginations of writers and critics from the 1950s into the 1980s. Baldwin's condemnation of sentimentalism employs the familiar strategy of reversal. He writes:

> Sentimentality, the ostentatious parading of excessive and spurious emotion, is
> the mark of dishonesty, the inability to feel; the wet eyes of the sentimentalist
> betray his aversion to experience, his fear of life, and his arid heart; and it
> is always, therefore, the signal of secret and violent inhumanity, the mask of
> cruelty. *Uncle Tom's Cabin* – like its multitudinous, hard-boiled descendants –
> is a catalogue of violence. (14)

Excess emotion means no emotion. Excess feeling, no feeling, and so on.
Rather than staging an abhorrence of violence, the sentimental merely
parades its indulgence in violence and its love of cruelty. These are, to be
sure, hard charges to be brought against a long dead Connecticut lady and
the writers following in her wake. Crediting such charges would almost mean
loading upon Stowe and her hapless train not only the outbreak of the Civil
War as Lincoln is reputed to have done, but the entire history of moral and
political evasion of the Jim Crow era. Of course, whether or not Baldwin
actually believes his own indictment is almost beside the point because the
volume of his vituperation identifies Baldwin not as an implacable foe of
sentimentalism but as an aggrieved disciple. By charging the sentimentalist
with an "inability to feel" Baldwin is not declaring his opposition to trying
to reach and mobilize the feelings of one's readers. Rather he is faulting his
predecessors for *not* having done so and for not having recognized that their
efforts have fallen short of the mark. Baldwin remarks on Stowe's "laudable
determination to flinch from nothing in presenting the complete picture" and
seeks to inquire into what caused her "to leave unanswered and unnoticed
the only important question: what it was, after all, that moved her people to
such deeds" (14). Leaving aside for the moment whether or not Stowe could
have pursued such questions and still written a novel of any power, there is
in Baldwin's remarks a sense that it was the means rather than the ends that
needed to be questioned.

Stowe may have believed with Mrs. Bird in the importance of placing the
individual in "the magic of the real presence of distress," but she had not
succeeded in doing so because in writing a protest novel she constructed a
web of "fantasies, connecting nowhere with reality" (19). Baldwin describes
Stowe as if she were Senator Bird before being confronted with Eliza and
Harry, an individual whose "idea of a fugitive was only an idea of the letters
that spell the word, – or, at the most, the image of a little newspaper picture
of a man with a stick and bundle with 'Ran away from the subscriber' under
it" (77). Aligning Stowe's and Wright's novels of protest with contemporary
sociology and a host of contemporary films, Baldwin faults them all by noting
that the "failure of the protest novel lies in its rejection of life, the human
being, the denial of his beauty, dread, power, in its insistence that it is his
categorization alone which is real and which cannot be transcended" (23).

The magic of the real presence, as Baldwin makes abundantly clear lay not in the categorization but in something more palpable even if quite complex. Nor was this complexity best accessed by those whom Mrs. Bird termed "political folks" who insist on "reasoning on such subjects" (70). Rather, in seeming agreement with Mrs. Bird, Baldwin avers that to find the path to the complex, real vision that eludes *Uncle Tom's Cabin* one must declare "a devotion to the human being, his freedom and fulfillment; freedom which cannot be legislated, fulfillment which cannot be charted" (15). The magic of the real presence, then, could not be the province of merely political folks.

This strand of agreement connecting Baldwin with Stowe and thereby with Wright should make it no surprise that rather than exiling Bigger and Uncle Tom from the psychological profiles of black Americans, Baldwin locates both figures prominently among the furniture of the collective black psyche. Writing in "Many Thousands Gone," Baldwin asserts not only that "the American image of the Negro lives also in the Negro's heart" but also that "no American Negro exists who does not have his private Bigger Thomas living in his skull." Thus it would seem that, however unsuccessful Stowe and Wright may have been in depicting accurately who the Negro was, they had somehow managed to inject their creations inside the Negro mind where they threatened to do damage unless dealt with adequately. Consequently, for the Negro, recognizing and containing this "dangerous and unloved stranger" within himself became a necessary part of self-development and self-realization (38, 42).

So although Baldwin had written Uncle Tom's epitaph early in "Many Thousands Gone" by announcing, "Aunt Jemima and Uncle Tom are dead" (27) he undercut his claim by turning to what might be termed pop psychology to give Uncle Tom his due. In making this psychological turn Baldwin in effect kept the old slave alive by putting him in the mind of every Negro, thus foreshadowing the strategy that was to dominate the Tom revival in the literary academy in the 1970s and 1980s. Small wonder, then, that Richard Yarborough treats Baldwin's "Everybody's Protest Novel" and Ishmael Reed's *Flight to Canada* (1976) as evidence that black writers will continue to "strive to distance themselves from all that *Uncle Tom's Cabin* represents" – which in psychological terms means that they will always return in order to determine just how far they've gotten away.[10]

In stressing the pop psychology dimension of the reclamation of the sentimental, and the concomitant rise of *Uncle Tom's Cabin*, I do not mean to slight the way in which this project was political in the extreme. One could not imagine the rehabilitation of Stowe's novel in the absence of both the feminist movement and the greater democratization of American society in the wake of the Civil Rights, anti-war, and decolonization movements of the 1950s, '60s, and '70s. That is, it is far from coincidental that the rise of Uncle Tom followed upon the increasing visibility of women and blacks in the academy. And yet at the same time, as Hortense Spillers points out, it was not immediately clear how both the feminist and Civil Rights movements could be equally abetted by Stowe's text. Claiming herself "wholly sympathetic to Tompkins's project and to that of other corrective feminist readings of *Uncle Tom's Cabin*," Spillers nonetheless insists that there is something missed by revisionist readings "that Afro-American readers, at least – who, by the way, also come with at least *two* kinds of sexual markings, described as 'female' and 'male' – have palpably *felt* for over a century about *Uncle Tom's Cabin*."[11] But in getting at the concerns that generations of black readers have had about Stowe's novel, Spillers invokes a strategy of reading identified less with those readers than with her mostly white academic audience. Her claim in "Changing the letter: the yokes, the jokes of discourse, or Mrs. Stowe, Mr. Reed," that slavery "remains one of the most textualized and discursive fields of practice that we could posit as a structure of attention," makes sense almost only within the context of academic preoccupations of the 1980s. In order to assert the textualizing of slavery as a move towards, rather than away from, political engagement, one must presume the power that texts have as texts and their availability for rereading. Crucially, then, Spillers's reading of the relationship between Stowe's *Uncle Tom's Cabin* and Reed's *Flight to Canada* takes up at one point the way that "Reed's translation of the fugitive icon strikes an analogy with a scene from *Uncle Tom's Cabin*" (51). Spillers first points out the similarity between the figure of the fugitive that appears in Reed's text as an image on the wall paper of the Slave Hole Café and "the image of the little newspaper picture of a man with a stick and bundle" that in Chapter IX of *Uncle Tom's Cabin* indicates Senator Bird's estrangement from "the real." She then delineates a process analogous to what Stowe attempts to do in "In Which It Appears That a Senator Is But a Man," namely, wresting our apprehension of slavery from its conventionalized representations so that we might "construct and reconstruct repertoires of usage out of the most painful human/historical experience" (52). If under the aegis of deconstruction we could not be sure about approaching the real we could certainly expose the conventions masquerading as its essence.

Spillers presents herself as a black reader experiencing discomfort as a result of having to confront Stowe's text. Admitting that "Mrs. Stowe's 'slavery' demarcates an inexorable grimness, which I really did not want to experience again as a reader," Spillers claims her discomfort to have been alleviated by a dose of Ishmael Reed's novel: "After *Uncle Tom's Cabin*, one needs a drink. Reed provides it" (33). Spillers does, however, confess that

Flight to Canada's experimental structure makes the idea of unwinding with it a little bit of a stretch. And despite her reading of the novel as an insurgent text, she also notes that *Flight to Canada* does not create any "necessary chumminess . . . between Reed and a putative community of Afro-American readers" (48). Reed's novel is in reality the province of the literary specialist. And yet Spillers's use of this text to counteract the effects of what is in the final instance a job requirement (she didn't want to read *Uncle Tom's Cabin*, "[b]ut I had to," 33), gestures toward what may be the most significant factor in the reanimation of Uncle Tom for the American academy, namely the anxieties experienced by black, female, and working-class writers about being in the academy itself.

For novelist and academic alike the demands of the profession appeared to require an estrangement from one's own experience and a removal from the realm of the personal within which one could claim really to feel anything at all. Although for Baldwin the terms are somewhat reversed from what they have been for the scholars who have worked out their anxieties through an encounter with Stowe's novel, the structure of the problem he claims to have confronted on his way to being a writer are instructive. He explains in the introduction to *Notes of a Native Son* that

> One writes out of one thing only – one's own experience. Everything depends on how relentlessly one forces from this experience the last drop, sweet or bitter, it can possibly give. This is the only real concern of the artist, to recreate out of the disorder of life that order which is art. The difficulty then, for me, of being a Negro writer was the fact that I was, in effect, prohibited from examining my own experience too closely by the tremendous demands and the very real dangers of my social situation. (6)

With the demand to address and redress the Negro problem constituting the major obstacle preventing his access to his experience, Baldwin's extended engagement with Stowe seems unavoidable. Well aware that he has joined a prolific industry producing poorly written texts on the Negro Problem – an industry whose origin he traces to *Uncle Tom's Cabin* – Baldwin describes for himself an arc of possibility that rises from the point marked by his own desire to be a writer and then descends upon the point where the writer presumably represents the race without being compelled to plead on its behalf. The story that Baldwin wants to tell us then is the one in which it appears that the Negro writer is but a man – in doing so Baldwin recasts the problem facing the novelist so that it appears to be the problem facing the race as a whole.

For that group of scholars who found themselves embarrassingly classed among the ranks of elite critics extolling the classics of American literature and looking down on the tastes of the public as a whole, the encounter with Stowe became a way of expiating a previous sin of pride in failing to sympathize with the majority of her fellow American citizens. Tompkins recounts with self-directed indignation that during the time she herself lived in the home of Stowe's half-sister, Isabella Beecher Hooker, she had "made a reverential visit to the Mark Twain house a few blocks away, took photographs of his study, and completely ignored Stowe's own house – also open to the public – which stood across the lawn." She continues:

> Why should I go? Neither I nor anyone I knew regarded Stowe as a serious writer. At the time, I was giving my first lecture course in the American Renaissance – concentrated exclusively on Hawthorne, Melville, Poe, Emerson, Thoreau, and Whitman – and although *Uncle Tom's Cabin* was written in exactly the same period, and although it is probably the most influential book ever written by an American, I would never have dreamed of including it on my reading list. To begin with, its very popularity would have militated against it; as everybody knew, the classics of American fiction were, with a few exceptions, all succes d'estime.[12]

The rest of Tompkins's chapter goes on to delineate quite carefully a protocol of reading that illuminates an array of compelling elements within Stowe's novel. Even so, it is also true that for Tompkins *Uncle Tom's Cabin* is first and foremost a proxy for the popular, the feminine, and the emotional, all of which had been given short shrift in a male-dominated academy. Even more to the point, as indicated by her autobiographical introduction to the chapter, *Uncle Tom's Cabin* made it possible for Tompkins herself to find a way out of the narrow world of an unfeeling elite into a larger realm where it was okay to be a critic, a woman, and an appreciative and feeling reader of popular literature.

The story that *Uncle Tom's Cabin* has enabled US writers and Americanist literary scholars to tell about themselves was one in which they themselves have represented and been numbered among the excluded and disregarded. To be sure, the ability to tell this story at all depends on the historical truth that many scholars – many of them women – took on considerable professional risks in championing writers and literary genres that had been neglected and disparaged by mainstream scholarship and criticism. Both the profession and the US literary canon were indeed male-dominated in ways that had to be questioned and challenged. And both the scholarship and pedagogy of American literature changed dramatically as a result of this challenge. In fact, as the introduction to the 1982–83 English Institute Papers, *The American Renaissance Reconsidered* makes clear, during this period the field as a whole was writing itself into a story of prior exclusion and disregard by the field's founding fathers. Donald Pease's introduction to the volume reminds us that the program kicked off with an essay on Edgar Allan Poe, "a figure Matthiessen excluded from his canon" but who "returns from the unconscious literary canon with all the power derived from having been repressed"; that by disclosing "what Matthiessen had to repress (if not quite bury) in order to authorize the canon" Jonathan Arac "discovers another American Renaissance . . . representing the values of 'all the people' rather than those of exclusively Renaissance figures"; and that Pease himself "suggests that Matthiessen repressed the other American Renaissance because of the political demands of World War II."[13]

In other words, American literary scholarship was rewriting its story as a populist revolt in which the literature of all the people was demanding its due by those scholars who had the temerity to label themselves Americanists even though the literature they studied and values they extolled represented only a narrow slice of the tastes and experiences of real Americans. The psychological dynamic of repression and return invoked to describe the process by which the field was undergoing this shift gave a particularly powerful ineluctable cast to the task of literary revisionism. The tearful mothers and inebriate fathers whom we had been too embarrassed to acknowledge were now somehow avatars of broader democratization. It was they who would put us back in the magic of the real presence of distress and thereby enable, in Pease's words, "the creation of a real world consistent with American principles" (xi).

The capacity of Stowe's novel to evoke simultaneously suspicion of and allegiance to its aesthetic and political projects surfaces in both Robyn Wiegman's *American Anatomies* (1995) and Lauren Berlant's "Poor Eliza" (1998), both of which define contemporary agendas significantly inflected by *Uncle Tom's Cabin*, which Wiegman describes as "the text that most haunts my own."[14] As a source for Wiegman's effort as a white feminist critic to confront the inadequacies of contemporary feminist practices, Stowe's failures are as important as her successes, because of the way they serve as cautionary tales for contemporary scholar–activists interested in identifying feminist and anti-racist theory and politics. Wiegman cautions that "while *Uncle Tom's Cabin* tries to forge a political alliance between slaves and white women" the attempt "fractures under the inescapable priority accorded to white racial being" (196). By making contemporary feminism complicit with the sentimentalizing strategies used by Stowe, Wiegman suggests that the posture demanded at the present moment is one of "feminist disloyalty" dictated by the apparent way in which the strategies that make possible the identification of a feminist politics also make it impossible to identify that politics with antiracist concerns (200). Wiegman suggests as a response a strategy of alienation from and return to the very politics one hopes to have, hinged on the possibility of one becoming an outlier to one's own practices (201).

Berlant's essay is likewise a reflection "on the unfinished business of sentimentality" – more specifically, "liberal sentimentality" that "has been deployed mainly by the culturally privileged to humanize those very subjects who are also, and at the same time, reduced to cliché within the reigning regimes of entitlement and value" (636). Like Fiedler's discussion of Stowe's novel, Berlant locates *Uncle Tom's Cabin* in an archive including popular and elite writers and texts (in this case such texts as *The King and I, The Bridges of Madison County,* and *Beloved* cohabit with Stowe's novel), and like Wiegman's study, it marks the radical possibility of sentimentalism as well as its limits – "the forces of distortion in the world of feeling politics put into play by the citation of *Uncle Tom* are as likely to justify ongoing forms of domination as to give form and language to impulses toward resistance" (640). Berlant also highlights the magic of the real presence of distress in Stowe's novel – "in order to benefit from the therapeutic promises of sentimental discourse you must imagine yourself with someone else's stress pain or humiliated identity. The possibility that through identification with alterity you will never be the same remains the radical threat and the great promise of this affective aesthetic" (648). But in highlighting this magic Berlant also tracks and laments the way that consumer culture and the commodities surrounding *Uncle Tom's Cabin* subsume this promise into "the pleasures of entertainment, of the star system, of the love of children, and of heterosexual romance where a political language about suffering might have been considered appropriate" (664). Against this process Berlant tracks a "postsentimental modality" that, even as it consents to the "sentimental contract between its texts and readers – that proper reading will lead to better feeling and therefore to a better self," does not consent to the idea that "in a just world a consensus will already exist about what constitutes uplift, amelioration, and emancipation." She thus supplants the repetition of sentimental plots with the need for reinvention (655–656). In what amounts to a kind of eating your cake and having it, too, Berlant describes a process in which one must actively seek to transform the sentimental tradition to which one is necessarily an heir. The responsibility here is not to repudiate but "to demand of the sentimental project that its protests and complaints be taken seriously in themselves" (665–666).

Likewise taking seriously the efficacy of *Uncle Tom's Cabin*'s sentimentalism, Fisher argues that the more masculinist and modernist "Romance of Consciousness" that displaced the sentimentalist values of Stowe was organized against the magic of real presence of distress because its structure was that of both dramatic and historical irony. For the protagonist of this type of fiction, every "moment of his suffering is only partly suffering because the reader is aware of the coming revenge and nothing so eliminates the reality of suffering as the structure of revenge or the anticipation of revenge. Every insult is only partly an insult because the bloody sword hangs over the scene, visible to the reader but not yet to any of the historical actors" (96–97). It is not quite the case that to know more is to feel less, but Fisher's insight does help make evident why Baldwin's desire for more psychological depth in Stowe's portrayal of her characters, particularly her villains, would have run the risk of stopping the tears so necessary for her narrative success.

Fisher also helps us see the way that in this debate, Stowe's "magic of the real presence of distress" has come to mark the presence of the historical by identifying true history as the province of true emotion. "Historical irony of the modern kind," Fisher writes, is in fact the most unhistorical strategy possible. "No point of view so corrodes the actual meaning of the past as lived experience as the one that sees it as the doomed and unconscious prelude to an irrational catastrophe of which the future alone is in possession of the knowledge" (97). The meaning of the past and the feeling of the past become here intertwined, so that in order to know we must feel, and in order to feel we must not presume to know too much. Or rather, we must acknowledge the ongoing significance of those writers whom Leslie Fiedler deems "inept in form and weak in ideas, but like Shakespeare or Sophocles, Dickens or Mark Twain, endowed – by the grace of God, the muse of their own unconscious – with mythopoeic power" (85). So that although professional inquiry into history and literature requires that we apply reason to the enterprises of understanding both literary creation and the past, the problem apparently presented by a writer like Stowe is that by doing the very thing we are trained to do, professional scholars move away from rather than toward the phenomena we are trying to apprehend.

The definition of art with which Fiedler rehabilitates Stowe is, of course, highly unprofessional. He writes, "It is, indeed the function of all art at its most authentic to release us to dionysiac, demonic impulses; and thus to satisfy our shame-faced longing (otherwise repressed or sublimated) to be driven out of control – to permit us, in short, moments of privileged madness, a temporary return to psychic states which we have theoretically abandoned in the name of humanity and sweet reason" (84). Fiedler leaves open here the question of whether these temporary desublimations and returns to the state of madness contain truly destabilizing power or whether they merely constitute that version of the carnivalesque that underwrites even as it challenges the normative realm of the social world. In all likelihood, the true answer contains a little bit of both possibilities. Changing the profession to accommodate both Stowe and the concerns of scholars who have found themselves and their needs less than welcome in the world of the literary academy has certainly altered not only the texts that we read, but also the way we read texts. And yet, however profound these changes have been, they have left the profession recognizably a profession and not a dionysiac revel, which is to say that however much we might wish to identify Stowe, *Uncle Tom's Cabin*, and even ourselves with Mrs. Bird as one of those people "who don't want to reason about a plain thing," we are all inescapably creatures of the same academy that must – if it is to be what it is – remain to some degree the dry-eyed partisan of reason as a guide to the possibility of creating communities of political and intellectual consent.

NOTES

1. Ralph Ellison, "Introduction," in *Invisible Man* (New York: Random House, 1990), xiv, xvi.
2. Edmund Wilson, *Patriotic Gore: Studies in the Literature of the American Civil War* (New York: Farrar, Straus, and Giroux, 1962), 5.
3. Lauren Berlant, "Poor Eliza!" in *American Literature* 70 (September 1998), 647–648.
4. Leslie A. Fiedler, *The Inadvertent Epic: From "Uncle Tom's Cabin" to "Roots"* (New York: Touchstone, 1980), 16.
5. Harriet Beecher Stowe, *Uncle Tom's Cabin*, ed. Elizabeth Ammons (New York: W. W. Norton & Co., 1994), 150. All further citations from *Uncle Tom's Cabin* will be incorporated in the text.
6. Philip Fisher, *Hard Facts: Setting and Form in the American Novel* (New York: Oxford University Press, 1985), 99.
7. Richard Wright, "How Bigger was born," in *Native Son* (New York: Perennial Classics, 1998), 454.
8. Richard Wright, *Native Son* (New York: Perennial Classics, 1998), 86. All further citations from *Native Son* will appear parenthetically in the text.
9. James Baldwin, "Everybody's protest novel," in *Notes of a Native Son* (Boston: Beacon Press, 1957), 22.
10. Richard Yarborough, "Strategies of black characterization in *Uncle Tom's Cabin* and the early Afro-American novel," in Eric J. Sundquist, ed., *New Essays on Uncle Tom's Cabin* (New York: Cambridge University Press, 1986), 68.
11. Hortense Spillers, "Changing the letter: the yokes, the jokes of discourse, or Mrs. Stowe, Mr. Reed," in Deborah E. McDowell and Arnold Rampersad, eds., *Slavery and the Literary Imagination: Selected Papers from the English Institute, 1987*, new series 13 (Baltimore: The Johns Hopkins University Press 1989), 35.
12. Jane P. Tompkins, *Sensational Designs: The Cultural Work of American Fiction 1790–1860* (New York: Oxford University Press, 1985), 122.

13. John Guillory, *Culture Capital: The Problem of Literary Canon Formation* (Chicago: University of Chicago Press, 1993); Walter Benn Michaels and Donald E. Pease, eds., *The American Renaissance Reconsidered: Selected Papers of the English Institute, 1982–83*, new series 9 (Baltimore: The Johns Hopkins University Press, 1985), x–xi.

14. Robyn Wiegman, *American Anatomies: Theorizing Race and Gender* (Durham: Duke University Press, 1995), 193.

SELECT BIBLIOGRAPHY

Stowe's Writings

NOTE: What follows is a selected list of Stowe's book-length writings, those to which the *Companion*'s contributors refer, as well as a few other well known works. Although for many years *Uncle Tom's Cabin* was the only one of Stowe's novels still in print, recently new editions of several of her other works have been published. Where there is a recent edition widely available, that edition is listed, but the remainder of the citations below refer to first editions. Over her lifetime, Stowe also published hundreds of stories, essays, and articles. Some of those can be found in the 16-volume Riverside Edition of her writings, *The Writings of Harriet Beecher Stowe* (Boston: Houghton-Mifflin, 1896). Joan D. Hedrick's biography, *Harriet Beecher Stowe: A Life*, includes a lengthy list of Stowe's shorter writings as well. Finally, see the Chronology included in this volume for other works by Stowe.

Agnes of Sorrento. Boston: Ticknor & Fields, 1862.
Dred: A Tale of the Great Dismal Swamp. 1856. Ed. Robert S. Levine. New York: Penguin, 2000.
A Key to Uncle Tom's Cabin; Presenting the Original Facts and Documents upon which the Story is Founded, together with Corroborative Statements Verifying the Truth of the Work. Boston: J. P. Jewett & Company, 1853.
Lady Byron Vindicated: A History of the Byron Controversy, from its Beginnings in 1816 to the Present Time. Boston: Fields, Osgood, & Company, 1870.
Men of Our Times; or, Leading Patriots of the Day. Hartford: Hartford Publishing Company, 1868.
The Minister's Wooing. 1859. Ed. Susan K. Harris. New York: Penguin, 1999.
My Wife and I; or, Harry Henderson's History. 1871. Boston: Houghton-Mifflin, 1896.
Oldtown Folks. 1869. Ed. Dorothy Berkson. New Brunswick: Rutgers University Press, 1987.
The Oxford Harriet Beecher Stowe Reader. Ed. Joan D. Hedrick. New York: Oxford University Press, 1999.
Palmetto Leaves. 1873. Ed. Mary B. Graff and Edith Cowles. Gainesville: University Press of Florida, 1999.
The Pearl of Orr's Island: A Story of the Coast of Maine. 1862. Ed. Joan D. Hedrick. Boston: Houghton-Mifflin, 2001.

Pink and White Tyranny. 1871. New York: Plume, 1988.

Poganuc People. 1878. Ed. Joseph S. Van Why. Hartford: Stowe–Day Foundation Press, 1987.

Sam Lawson's Oldtown Fireside Stories. 1872. Ridgewood, NJ: Gregg Press, 1967.

Uncle Tom's Cabin; or, Life Among the Lowly. 1852. Ed. Elizabeth Ammons. New York: W. W. Norton & Company, 1994.

Woman in Sacred History. New York: J. B. Ford, 1873.

Bibliographies and Guides

Ammons, Elizabeth and Susan Belasco, eds. *Approaches to Teaching "Uncle Tom's Cabin"*. New York: Modern Language Association of America, 2000.

Ashton, Jean W. *Harriet Beecher Stowe: A Reference Guide*. Boston: G. K. Hall, 1977.

Gardiner, Jane. "Pro-slavery propaganda in fiction written in answer to *Uncle Tom's Cabin*, 1852–1861: an annotated checklist." *Resources for American Literary Study* 7 (1977): 201–209.

Hildreth, Margaret Holbrook. *Harriet Beecher Stowe: A Bibliography*. Hamden, CT: Archon Books, 1976.

Biographical Studies and Resources

Adams, John R. *Harriet Beecher Stowe*. Updated edn. Boston: Twayne, 1989.

Fields, Annie, ed. *Life and Letters of Harriet Beecher Stowe*. Detroit: Gale Research Company, 1970.

Gerson, Noel B. *Harriet Beecher Stowe: A Biography*. New York: Praeger, 1976.

Gilbertson, Catherine. *Harriet Beecher Stowe*. New York: D. Appleton-Century, 1937.

Hedrick, Joan D. *Harriet Beecher Stowe: A Life*. New York: Oxford University Press, 1994.

Johnston, Johanna. *Runaway to Heaven: The Story of Harriet Beecher Stowe*. Garden City, NY: Doubleday, 1963.

McCray, Florine Thayer. *The Life Work of the Author of "Uncle Tom's Cabin"*. New York: Funk & Wagnalls, 1889.

Mair, Margaret Granville and Earl A. French, ed. *The Papers of Harriet Beecher Stowe: A Bibliography of the Manuscripts in the Stowe–Day Memorial Library*. Hartford: Stowe–Day Foundation, 1977.

Rugoff, Milton. *The Beechers: An American Family in the Nineteenth Century*. New York: Harper and Row, 1981.

Scott, John Anthony. *Woman Against Slavery: The Story of Harriet Beecher Stowe*. New York: Crowell, 1978.

Stowe, Charles Edward. *Life of Harriet Beecher Stowe: Compiled from her Letters and Journals*. Boston and New York: Houghton-Mifflin, 1889.

Stowe, Charles and Lyman Beecher Stowe. *Harriet Beecher Stowe: The Story of her Life*. Boston: Houghton-Mifflin, 1911.

Thulesius, Olav. *Harriet Beecher Stowe in Florida, 1867–1884*. Jefferson, NC: McFarland & Company, 2001.

Van Why, Joseph S. and Earl French, ed. *Harriet Beecher Stowe in Europe: The Journal of Charles Beecher*. Hartford: Stowe–Day Foundation, 1986.

Wilson, Robert Forrest. *Crusader in Crinoline: The Life of Harriet Beecher Stowe*. Philadelphia: Lippincott, 1941.

Studies of Production and Reception

Adams, F. C. *Uncle Tom at Home: A Review of the Reviewers and Repudiators of Uncle Tom's Cabin by Mrs. Stowe*. Philadelphia: Hazard, 1853.

Banks, Marva. "*Uncle Tom's Cabin* and antebellum black response." *Readers in History: Nineteenth-Century American Literature and the Contexts of Response*. Ed. James L. Machor. Baltimore: The Johns Hopkins University Press, 1993. 209–227.

Baym, Nina. *Novels, Novelists, and Reviewers: Responses to Fiction in Antebellum America*. Ithaca: Cornell University Press, 1984.

Furnas, J. C. *Goodbye to Uncle Tom*. New York: William Sloane, 1956.

Hirsch, Stephen. "Uncle Tomitudes: the popular reaction to *Uncle Tom's Cabin*." *South Atlantic Review* 43 (1978): 303–330.

Kirkham, E. Bruce. *The Building of Uncle Tom's Cabin*. Knoxville: University of Tennessee Press, 1977.

Levine, Robert S. "*Uncle Tom's Cabin* in Frederick Douglass' Paper: an analysis of reception." *American Literature* 64 (1992): 71–93.

Smith, Susan Belasco. "Serialization and the nature of *Uncle Tom's Cabin*." *Periodical Literature in Nineteenth-Century America*. Ed. Kenneth M. Price and Susan Belasco Smith. Charlottesville: University Press of Virginia, 1995. 69–89.

Winship, Michael. "'The Greatest Book of Its Kind': a publishing history of *Uncle Tom's Cabin*." *Proceedings of the American Antiquarian Society* 109 (2002): 309–332.

Collections of Critical Essays

Ammons, Elizabeth. *Critical Essays on Harriet Beecher Stowe*. Boston: G. K. Hall, 1980.

Lowance, Mason I., Jr., Ellen E. Westbrook, and R. C. De Prospo, ed. *The Stowe Debate: Rhetorical Strategies in "Uncle Tom's Cabin"*. Amherst: University of Massachusetts Press, 1994.

Sundquist, Eric J., ed. *New Essays on "Uncle Tom's Cabin"*. Cambridge and New York: Cambridge University Press, 1986.

Studies of Stowe

Boydston, Jeanne, Mary Kelley, and Anne Margolis. *The Limits of Sisterhood: The Beecher Sisters on Women's Rights and Woman's Sphere*. Chapel Hill: University of North Carolina Press, 1988.

Crozier, Alice C. *The Novels of Harriet Beecher Stowe*. New York: Oxford University Press, 1969.

Donovan, Josephine. *Uncle Tom's Cabin: Evil, Affliction, and Redemptive Love*. Boston: Twayne Publishers, 1991.

Foster, Charles H. *The Rungless Ladder: Harriet Beecher Stowe and New England Puritanism.* Durham: Duke University Press, 1954.

Goodell, John. *The Triumph of Moralism in New England Piety: A Study of Lyman Beecher, Harriet Beecher Stowe, and Henry Ward Beecher.* New York: Arno Press, 1976.

Hovet, Theodore R. *The Master Narrative: Harriet Beecher Stowe's Subversive Story of Master and Slave in "Uncle Tom's Cabin" and "Dred".* Lanham, MD: University Press of America, 1989.

Kimball, Gayle. *The Religious Ideas of Harriet Beecher Stowe: Her Gospel of Womanhood.* New York: Mellen Press, 1982.

Lewis, Gladys Sherman. *Message, Messenger, and Response: Puritan Forms and Cultural Reformation in Harriet Beecher Stowe's "Uncle Tom's Cabin".* Lanham, MD: University Press of America, 1994.

Moers, Ellen. *Harriet Beecher Stowe and American Literature.* Hartford: Stowe–Day Foundation, 1978.

Reynolds, Moira Davison. *"Uncle Tom's Cabin" and Mid-Nineteenth Century United States: Pen and Conscience.* Jefferson, NC: McFarland and Company, 1985.

Stern, Philip Van Doren, ed. *The Annotated "Uncle Tom's Cabin".* New York: Paul S. Eriksson, 1964.

Wagenknecht, Edward. *Harriet Beecher Stowe: The Known and the Unknown.* New York: Oxford University Press, 1965.

Literary and Historical Studies with Sections on Stowe

Barnes, Elizabeth. *States of Sympathy: Seduction and Democracy in the American Novel.* New York: Columbia University Press, 1997. [*Uncle Tom's Cabin*]

Beardslee, Karen E. *Literary Legacies, Folklore Foundations: Selfhood and Cultural Tradition in Nineteenth- and Twentieth-Century American Literature.* Knoxville: University of Tennessee Press, 2001. [*The Minister's Wooing*]

Bell, Michael Davitt. *Culture, Genre, and Literary Vocation: Selected Essays on American Literature.* Chicago: University of Chicago Press, 1997.

Best, Stephen Michael. *The Fugitive's Properties: Law and the Poetics of Possession.* Chicago: University of Chicago Press (forthcoming).

Bromell, Nicholas K. *By the Sweat of the Brow: Literature and Labor in Antebellum America.* Chicago: University of Chicago Press, 1993. [*Uncle Tom's Cabin*]

Brown, Gillian. *Domestic Individualism: Imagining Self in Nineteenth-Century America.* Berkeley: University of California Press, 1990. [*Uncle Tom's Cabin*]

Budick, E. Miller. *Engendering Romance: Women Writers and the Hawthorne Tradition, 1850–1990.* New Haven: Yale University Press, 1994. [*Uncle Tom's Cabin*]

Buell, Lawrence. *New England Literary Culture: From Revolution through Renaissance.* Cambridge: Cambridge University Press, 1986.

Burnham, Michelle. *Captivity and Sentiment: Cultural Exchange in American Literature, 1682–1861.* Hanover, NH: University Press of New England, 1997 [*Uncle Tom's Cabin*]

Bush, Harold K., Jr. *American Declarations: Rebellion and Repentance in American Cultural History.* Urbana: University of Illinois Press, 1999. [*Uncle Tom's Cabin*]

Camfield, Gregg. *Necessary Madness: The Humor of Domesticity in Nineteenth-Century American Literature*. New York: Oxford University Press, 1997.

Cassuto, Leonard. *The Inhuman Race: The Racial Grotesque in American Literature and Culture*. New York: Columbia University Press, 1997.

Cherniavsky, Eva. *That Pale Mother Rising: Sentimental Discourses and the Image of Motherhood in Nineteenth-Century America*. Bloomington: Indiana University Press, 1995. [*Uncle Tom's Cabin*]

Coultrap-McQuin, Susan. *Doing Literary Business: American Women Writers in the Nineteenth Century*. Chapel Hill: University of North Carolina Press, 1990.

Crane, Gregg. *Race, Citizenship, and Law in American Literature*. New York: Cambridge University Press, 2002. [*Uncle Tom's Cabin, Dred*]

Davis, Mary Kemp. *Nat Turner before the Bar of Judgment: Fictional Treatments of the Southampton Slave Insurrection*. Baton Rouge: Louisiana State University Press, 1999. [*Dred*]

Donaldson, Laura E. *Decolonizing Feminisms: Race, Gender and Empire Building*. Chapel Hill: University of North Carolina Press, 1992. [*Uncle Tom's Cabin*]

Douglas, Ann. *The Feminization of American Culture*. New York: Alfred A. Knopf, 1977.

Felker, Christopher. *Reinventing Cotton Mather in the American Renaissance: Magnalia Christi Americana in Hawthorne, Stowe, and Stoddard*. Boston: Northeastern University Press, 1993. [*The Minister's Wooing*]

Fiedler, Leslie. *Love and Death in the American Novel*. New York: Criterion Books, 1960. [*Uncle Tom's Cabin*]

Fisher, Philip. *Hard Facts: Setting and Form in the American Novel*. New York: Oxford University Press, 1985. [*Uncle Tom's Cabin*]

Frederickson, George M. *The Black Image in the White Mind: The Debate on Afro-American Character and Destiny, 1817–1914*. New York: Harper & Row, 1971. [*Uncle Tom's Cabin, Dred*]

Gilmore, Michael. *Surface and Depth: The Quest for Legibility in American Culture*. New York: Oxford University Press, 2003. [*Uncle Tom's Cabin*]

Goddu, Teresa A. *Gothic America: Narrative, History, and Nation*. New York: Columbia University Press, 1997. [*Uncle Tom's Cabin, Dred*]

Hanne, Michael. *The Power of the Story: Fiction and Political Change*. Providence: Berghahn Books, 1994. [*Uncle Tom's Cabin*]

Heilbrun, Carolyn G. *Women's Lives: The View from the Threshold*. Toronto: University of Toronto Press, 1999.

Hendler, Glenn. *Public Sentiments: Structures of Feeling in Nineteenth-Century American Literature*. Chapel Hill: University of North Carolina Press, 2001. [*Uncle Tom's Cabin*]

Henning, Martha L. *Beyond Understanding: Appeals to the Imagination, Passions, and Will in Mid-Nineteenth-Century American Women's Fiction*. New York: Peter Lang, 1996. [*Uncle Tom's Cabin*]

Herzog, Kristin. *Women, Ethnics, and Exotics: Images of Power in Mid-Nineteenth-Century American Fiction*. Knoxville: University of Tennessee Press, 1983.

Jenkins, Thomas E. *The Character of God: Recovering the Lost Literary Power of American Protestantism*. New York: Oxford University Press, 1997.

Kelley, Mary. *Private Woman, Public Stage: Literary Domesticity in Nineteenth-Century America*. New York: Oxford University Press, 1984.

Kent, Kathryn R. *Making Girls into Women: American Women's Writing and the Rise of Lesbian Identity*. Durham: Duke University Press, 2003. [*Oldtown Folks*]

Kete, Mary Louise. *Sentimental Collaborations: Mourning and Middle-Class Identity in Nineteenth-Century America*. Durham: Duke University Press, 2000. [*Uncle Tom's Cabin*]

Lang, Amy Schrager. *Prophetic Woman: Anne Hutchinson and the Problem of Dissent in the Literature of New England*. Berkeley: University of California Press, 1987. [*Uncle Tom's Cabin*]

Levine, Robert S. *Martin Delany, Frederick Douglass, and the Politics of Representative Identity*. Chapel Hill: University of North Carolina Press, 1997. [*Uncle Tom's Cabin, Dred*]

McFadden, Margaret H. *Golden Cables of Sympathy: The Transatlantic Sources of Nineteenth-Century Feminism*. Lexington: University Press of Kentucky, 1999.

Pattee, Fred. *The Feminine Fifties*. New York: D. Appleton-Century Company, 1940.

Powell, Timothy B. *Ruthless Democracy: A Multicultural Interpretation of the American Renaissance*. Princeton, NJ: Princeton University Press, 2000. [*Uncle Tom's Cabin*]

Roberts, Diane. *The Myth of Aunt Jemima: Representations of Race and Region*. New York: Routledge, 1994.

Romero, Lora. *Home Fronts: Domesticity and its Critics in the Antebellum United States*. Durham: Duke University Press, 1997.

Romines, Ann. *The Home Plot: Women, Writing and Domestic Ritual*. Amherst: University of Massachusetts Press, 1992.

Rourke, Constance Mayfield. *Trumpets of Jubilee: Henry Ward Beecher, Harriet Beecher Stowe, Lyman Beecher, Horace Greeley, P. T. Barnum*. New York: Harcourt, Brace & Company, 1927.

Schriber, Mary Suzanne. *Writing Home: American Women Abroad, 1830–1920*. Charlottesville: University Press of Virginia, 1997. [*Sunny Memories from Foreign Lands*]

Shapiro, Ann. *Unlikely Heroines: Nineteenth-Century American Women Writers and the Woman Question*. New York: Greenwood Press, 1987.

Sizer, Lyde Cullen. *The Political Work of Northern Women Writers and the Civil War, 1850–1872*. Chapel Hill: University of North Carolina Press, 2000.

Smith, Stephanie. *Conceived by Liberty: Maternal Figures and Nineteenth-Century American Literature*. Ithaca, NY: Cornell University Press, 1994. [*Uncle Tom's Cabin, A Key to Uncle Tom's Cabin*]

Tompkins, Jane. *Sensational Designs: The Cultural Work of American Fiction, 1790–1860*. New York: Oxford University Press, 1985. [*Uncle Tom's Cabin*]

Weinstein, Arnold. *Nobody's Home: Speech, Self, and Place in American Fiction from Hawthorne to DeLillo*. New York: Oxford University Press, 1993. [*Uncle Tom's Cabin*]

Wilson, Edmund. *Patriotic Gore: Studies in the Literature of the American Civil War*. New York: Oxford University Press, 1962.

Yellin, Jean Fagan. *The Intricate Knot: Black Figures in American Literature, 1776–1863*. New York: New York University Press, 1972.

—. *Women and Sisters: The Anti-slavery Feminists in American Culture*. New Haven: Yale University Press, 1989.

Young, Elizabeth. *Disarming the Nation: Women's Writing and the American Civil War.* Chicago: University of Chicago Press, 1999. [*Uncle Tom's Cabin*]

Zafar, Rafia. *We Wear the Mask: African Americans Write American Literature, 1760–1870.* New York: Columbia University Press, 1997. [*Uncle Tom's Cabin, A Key to Uncle Tom's Cabin*]

Articles from Journals and Book Collections

Arac, Jonathan. "*Uncle Tom's Cabin* vs. *Huckleberry Finn*: the historians and the critics." *Boundary 2 – An International Journal of Literature & Culture.* 24 (1997): 79–100.

Armstrong, Nancy. "Why daughters die: the racial logic of American sentimentalism." *Yale Journal of Criticism* 7 (1994): 1–24. [*Uncle Tom's Cabin*]

Baldwin, James. "Everybody's protest novel." *Partisan Review* 16 (1949): 578–585. [*Uncle Tom's Cabin*]

Bentley, Nancy. "White slaves: the mulatto hero in antebellum fiction." *English Literary History* 65 (1993): 501–522. [*Uncle Tom's Cabin*]

Berlant, Lauren. "The female complaint." *Social Text* 19 (1988): 237–259. [*Uncle Tom's Cabin*]

—. "Poor Eliza." *American Literature* 70 (1998): 635–668. [*Uncle Tom's Cabin*]

Borgstrom, Michael. "Passing over: setting the record straight in *Uncle Tom's Cabin.*" *PMLA* 118 (2003): 1290–1309.

Boyd, Richard. "Models of power in Harriet Beecher Stowe's *Dred.*" *Studies in American Fiction* 19 (1991):15–30.

Brickhouse, Anna. "The writing of Haiti: Pierre Faubert, Harriet Beecher Stowe, and beyond." *American Literary History* 13 (2001): 407–444.

Brodhead, Richard. "Sparing the rod: discipline and fiction in antebellum America." *Representations* 21 (1988): 67–96. [*Uncle Tom's Cabin*]

Camfield, Gregg. "The moral aesthetics of sentimentality: a missing key to *Uncle Tom's Cabin.*" *Nineteenth-Century Literature* 43 (1988): 319–345.

Cox, James. "Harriet Beecher Stowe: from sectionalism to regionalism." *Nineteenth Century Fiction* 38 (1984): 444–446.

Crane, Gregg. "Dangerous sentiments: sympathy, rights, and revolution in Stowe's anti-slavery novels." *Nineteenth-Century Literature* 51 (1996): 176–204.

Fetterley, Judith. "Only a story, not a romance: Harriet Beecher Stowe's *The Pearl of Orr's Island.*" *The (Other) American Traditions: Nineteenth-Century Women Writers.* Ed. Joyce W. Warren. New Brunswick, NJ: Rutgers University Press, 1993. 108–125.

Fluck, Winfried. "The power and failure of representation in Harriet Beecher Stowe's *Uncle Tom's Cabin.*" *New Literary History* 23 (1992): 319–338.

Foreman, P. Gabrielle. "'This promiscuous housekeeping': death, transgression, and homoeroticism in *Uncle Tom's Cabin.*" *Representations* 43 (1993): 51–72.

Furth, Isabel. "Manifest destiny, manifest domesticity, and the leaven of whiteness in *Uncle Tom's Cabin.*" *Arizona Quarterly* 55 (1999): 31–55.

Grant, David. "*Uncle Tom's Cabin* and the triumph of republican rhetoric." *New England Quarterly* 71 (1998): 429–448.

Hamilton, Cynthia S. "*Dred*: intemperate slavery." *Journal of American Studies* 34 (2000): 257–277.

Harris, Susan K. "The female imaginary in Harriet Beecher Stowe's *The Minister's Wooing*." *New England Quarterly* 66 (1993): 179–198.

Hedrick, Joan D. "'Peaceable fruits': the ministry of Harriet Beecher Stowe." *American Quarterly* 40 (1998): 307–332.

Hoyer, Mark T. "Cultivating desire, tending piety: botanical discourse in Harriet Beecher Stowe's *The Minister's Wooing*." *Beyond Nature Writing: Expanding the Boundaries of Ecocriticism*. Ed. Karla Armbruster and Kathleen R. Wallace. Charlottesville: University Press of Virginia, 2001. 111–125.

Jehlen, Myra. "The family militant: domesticity versus slavery in *Uncle Tom's Cabin*." *Criticism* 31 (1989): 383–400.

Kaplan, Amy. "Manifest domesticity." *American Literature* 70 (1998): 581–606. [*Uncle Tom's Cabin*]

Lang, Amy Schrager. "Class and the strategies of sympathy." *The Culture of Sentiment: Race, Gender, and Sentimentality in Nineteenth-Century America*. Ed. Shirley Samuels. New York: Oxford University Press, 1992. 128–142.

Merish, Lori. "Sentimental consumption: Harriet Beecher Stowe and the aesthetics of middle-class ownership." *American Literary History* 8 (1996): 1–33.

Michaels, Walter Benn. "Romance and real estate." *The American Renaissance Reconsidered*. Ed. Walter Benn Michaels and Donald E. Pease. Baltimore: Johns Hopkins University Press, 1985. 156–182. [*Uncle Tom's Cabin*]

Newbury, Michael. "Eaten alive: slavery and celebrity in antebellum America." *English Literary History* 61 (1994): 159–187. [*Uncle Tom's Cabin*]

Newman, Judie. "Was Tom white? Stowe's *Dred* and Twain's *Pudd'nhead Wilson*." *Soft Canons: American Women Writers and the Masculine Tradition*. Ed. Karen L. Kilcup. Iowa City: University of Iowa Press, 1999. 67–81.

Noble, Marianne. "The ecstasies of sentimental wounding in *Uncle Tom's Cabin*." *Yale Journal of Criticism* 10 (1997): 295–320, and Barnes, Elizabeth. "The epistemology of the 'real': a response to Marianne Noble." *Yale Journal of Criticism* 10 (1997): 321–326.

O'Loughlin, Jim. "Articulating *Uncle Tom's Cabin*." *New Literary History* 31 (2000): 573–597.

Prior, Moody E. "Mrs. Stowe's Uncle Tom." *Critical Inquiry* 5 (1979): 635–650.

Pryse, Marjorie. "Origins of literary regionalism: gender in Irving, Stowe, and Longstreet." *Breaking Boundaries: New Perspectives on Regional Writings*. Ed. Sherrie Inness and Diana Royer. Iowa City: University of Iowa Press, 1997. 17–37.

Railton, Stephen. "Mothers, husbands, and Uncle Tom." *Georgia Review* 38 (1984): 129–144.

Riss, Arthur. "Racial essentialism and family values in *Uncle Tom's Cabin*." *American Quarterly* 46 (1994): 513–544.

Rowe, John Carlos. "Stowe's rainbow sign: violence and community in *Dred: A Tale of the Great Dismal Swamp*." *Arizona Quarterly* 58 (2002): 37–55.

Ryan, Susan M. "Charity begins at home: Stowe's anti-slavery novels and the forms of benevolent citzenship." *American Literature* 72 (2000): 751–782.

Sanchez-Eppler, Karen. "Bodily bonds: the intersecting rhetorics of feminism and abolitionism." *Representations* 24 (1988): 28–59.

Schultz, Nancy Lusignan. "The artist's craftiness: Miss Prissy in *The Minister's Wooing*." *Studies in American Fiction* 20 (1992): 33–44.

Smith, Gail K. "Reading with the other: hermeneutics and the politics of difference in Stowe's *Dred*." *American Literature* 69 (1997): 289–313.

—. "The sentimental novel: the example of Harriet Beecher Stowe." *The Cambridge Companion to Nineteenth-Century American Women's Writing*. Ed. Dale M. Bauer and Philip Gould. New York: Cambridge University Press, 2001. 221–243.

Spillers, Hortense. "Changing the letter: the yokes, the jokes of discourse, or, Mrs. Stowe, Mr. Reed." *Slavery and the Literary Imagination*. Ed. Deborah McDowell and Arnold Rampersad. Baltimore: Johns Hopkins University Press, 1989. 25–61.

Stern, Julia. "Spanish masquerade and the drama of racial identity in *Uncle Tom's Cabin*." *Passing and the Fictions of Identity*. Ed. Elaine K. Ginsberg. Durham: Duke University Press, 1996. 103–130.

Stoneley, Peter. "Sentimental emasculations: *Uncle Tom's Cabin* and black beauty." *Nineteenth-Century Literature* 54 (1999): 53–72.

Tonkovich, Nicole. "Writing in circles: Harriet Beecher Stowe, the Semi-Colon Club, and the construction of women's authorship." *Nineteenth-Century Women Learn to Write*. Ed. Catherine Hobbs. Charlottesville: University Press of Virginia, 1995. 145–175.

Wardley, Lynn. "Relic, fetish, femmage: the aesthetics of sentiment in the work of Stowe." *Yale Journal of Criticism* 5 (1992): 165–191.

Warner, Nicholas O. "Temperance, morality, and medicine in the fiction of Harriet Beecher Stowe." *The Serpent in the Cup: Temperance in American Literature*. Ed. David S. Reynolds and Debra J. Rosenthal. Amherst: University of Massachusetts Press, 1997. 136–152.

Whitney, Lisa. "In the shadow of *Uncle Tom's Cabin*: Stowe's vision of slavery from the Great Dismal Swamp." *New England Quarterly* 66 (1993): 552–569.

Zwarg, Christina. "Fathering and blackface in *Uncle Tom's Cabin*." *Novel* 22 (1989): 274–287.

Stowe/Uncle Tom's Cabin *in Popular Culture*

Birdoff, Harry. *The World's Greatest Hit: "Uncle Tom's Cabin" Illustrated with Old-time Playbills, Daguerreotypes, Vignettes, Music-Sheets, Poems, and Cartoons*. New York: S. F. Vanni, 1947.

Bogle, Donald. *Toms, Coons, Mulattoes, Mammies, and Bucks: An Interpretive History of Blacks in American Films*. New York: Continuum, 1994.

Fiedler, Leslie. *The Inadvertent Epic: From "Uncle Tom's Cabin" to "Roots"*. New York: Simon & Schuster, 1979.

Fisch, Audrey. *American Slaves in Victorian England: Abolitionist Politics in Popular Literature and Culture*. New York: Cambridge University Press, 2000. [*Uncle Tom's Cabin*]

Gossett, Thomas F. *Uncle Tom's Cabin and American Culture*. Dallas: Southern Methodist University Press, 1985.

Lott, Eric. *Love and Theft: Blackface Minstrelsy and the American Working Class*. New York: Oxford University Press, 1993.

Mason, Jeffrey D. *Melodrama and the Myth of America*. Bloomington: Indiana University Press, 1993.

Meer, Sarah. *Uncle Tom Mania: Slavery and Transatlantic Culture in the 1850s.* Atlanta: University of Georgia Press (forthcoming).

Railton, Stephen, director. *Uncle Tom's Cabin* and American Culture: A Multi-Media Archive. Website: www.iath.virginia.edu/utc.

Warhol, Robyn R. "'Ain't I De One Everybody Come to See?!': popular memories of *Uncle Tom's Cabin.*" *Hop on Pop: The Politics and Pleasures of Popular Culture.* Ed. Henry Jenkins, Tara McPherson, and Jane Shattuc. Durham: Duke University Press, 2002. 651–670.

Williams, Linda. *Playing the Race Card: Melodramas of Black and White from Uncle Tom to O. J. Simpson.* Princeton: Princeton University Press, 2001.

Wood, Marcus. *Blind Memory: Visual Representations of Slavery in England and America.* New York: Routledge, 2000.

INDEX

Adams, Bluford 130n
Adams, Nehemiah 42–43, 44
Alexander, Robert 15, 16–17, 19, 26
   I Ain't Yo' Uncle: The New Jack Revisionist Uncle Tom's Cabin 15–16, 17, 22, 23, 35
Althusser, Louis 164
Altick, Richard 98
American Colonization Society 176
American Renaissance 10, 58–60
Ammons, Elizabeth 8, 36n, 56n, 217n, 220
"An Affectionate and Christian Address" 109
Anthony, Susan B. 1
anti-slavery fiction 204–206
anti-slavery movement 13, 175–177, 185
   in England 97, 105–107
"anti-Tom" novels 10, 42–44, 45
Arac, Jonathan 230
Aristotle 77
Atlantic Monthly 132, 144, 187
Austin, Mary 149
Avery, Gillian 94n

Bailey, Gamaliel 4, 206
Baker, Jehu 159
Baldwin, James 13, 28, 34–35, 224–226, 228
   "Everybody's Protest Novel" 28, 224–226
   "Many Thousands Gone" 224, 226
Barclay, Alexander 75n
Bay, Mia 37n
Baym, Nina 201n
Beardslee, Karen E. 218n
Beecher, Catharine 1, 93n
Beecher, Henry Ward 1, 215, 216
Beecher, Lyman 1, 76n, 175
   Six Sermons on Intemperance 175

Behn, Aphra
   Oroonoko 101
Berlant, Lauren 220, 230, 231
Berry, Wendell 133
Best, Stephen 36n
Bible 34, 51, 54, 59–60, 70, 79–80, 87–89, 122, 164, 186
Bingham, John 159
Birdoff, Harry 100, 129n
Birney, James G. 177
Blackett, R. J. M. 110n
Bolton, H. Philip 130n
British–American relations 106–107
Brook Farm 174
Brooks, Cleanth 151n
Brougham, John 113, 126
Brown, Gillian 9, 10, 36n, 220
Brown, John 185
Brown, William Wells
   Clotel; or, The President's Daughter 208–209
Budick, Emily 201n
Buell, Lawrence 4, 9
Bunyan, John
   The Pilgrim's Progress 98, 99

Calvinism 141–142, 212, 213
Carpenter, Charles 94n
Carson, Rachel
   Silent Spring 13, 211
Cassell, John 100
Cather, Willa 214
   O, Pioneers! 214
Chase, Richard 7
Cherniavsky, Eva 76n
Chesnut, Mary Boykin 39, 56
Chesnutt, Charles 149
   The Conjure Woman 149

Child, Lydia Maria 25, 204
  anti-slavery stories 205
  An Appeal in Favor of that Class of
    Americans Called Africans 204
children 10, 77–93
  in American literature 82
  and reading 10, 77–93
Chopin, Kate 149
Christian Union 215
Civil War 1, 132, 135, 187, 188, 190,
  219–220
Cole, G. D. H. 111n
commercial popular culture 172–173
  and gender 172–173
Compromise of 1850 3
Constitution 156, 159–160, 167, 176
Conway, H. J. 125, 126, 127
Cooke, Rose Terry 149
Cooper, James Fenimore 10, 64–65, 190, 192
  The Last of the Mohicans 64–65, 162
Cowper, William 97, 105–106
Cox, James M. 135, 154, 201n
Crane, Gregg 12, 37n, 38n, 76n, 169n
Cruikshank, George 100

Davis, Rebecca Harding
  "Life in the Iron-Mills" 210–211
Declaration of Independence 34, 59, 156,
  176, 209
Defoe, Daniel
  Moll Flanders 191
  Robinson Crusoe 191
DeForest, John W. 12, 190–191, 197
  Miss Ravenel's Conversion from Secession
    to Loyalty 192
Delany, Martin 9, 13, 17–18
  Blake; or the Huts of America 163, 208,
  209
Derrida, Jacques 75n
Dickens, Charles 206
Donovan, Josephine 151n, 218n
Dos Passos, John
  USA trilogy 191
Douglas, Ann 7, 8, 93n
Douglass, Frederick 1, 3, 6, 16, 17–18, 25,
  45, 60, 72, 82, 98, 167, 181, 188, 206
  "The Heroic Slave" 208, 209
  Narrative of the Life of Frederick
    Douglass 16, 72
  "What to the Slave is the Fourth of July?"
    165
Du Bois, W. E. B. 83
Dunbar-Nelson, Alice 149

Eastman, Mary 43
  Aunt Phillis's Cabin 43
Eaton, Clement 74n
Edgeworth, Maria 151n
Edwards, Jonathan 26
Ellison, Mary 112n
Ellison, Ralph 17, 220
  Invisible Man 15, 219
  "The World and the Jug" 16
Elmer, Jonathan 76n
Equiano, Olaudah 97
Estlin, J. B., 99, 110n

Far, Sui Sin 149
Faulkner, William
  Light in August 192, 193
Feidelson, Charles 7
feminism 226–228, 230–231
Ferber, Edna
  Ice Palace 211
Ferguson, Robert A. 168n
Fetterley, Judith 134, 150n, 152n, 218n
Fiedler, Leslie 14n, 220, 221, 232–233
Fisch, Audrey 9, 11, 110n
Fisher, Philip 7, 36n, 75n, 95n, 220, 222,
  231–232
Fitzhugh, George 111n, 157, 162, 164–165
  Cannibals All! 157
Foster, Charles H. 144–145
Foucault, Michel 164
Fourier, Charles 174
Fourteenth Amendment 159
Franklin, Benjamin 173
Franklin, H. Bruce 218n
Frederickson, George 4, 19, 202n
Freeman, Mary Wilkins 2
Fugitive Slave Law 3, 6, 12, 60, 157, 158,
  159–160, 161, 164, 166, 175, 179,
  221, 222

Garrison, William Lloyd 3, 173, 176, 179,
  185, 206
gender
  inequality 136–137
  and legal status 178
  and masculinity 145–146
  women's movement 7, 215–216
Gilmore, Michael T. 9, 10
Glazener, Nancy 201n
Godey's Ladies' Book 173
Goodell, William 27
Gossett, Thomas F. 16, 111n, 202n, 216n,
  217n

Gougeon, Len 76n
"great American novel" 190–200
  and gender 193
Grimké, Sarah 176
Grossman, Allen 74n
Guillory, John 229

Hadley, Elaine 127
Hale, Sarah Josepha 30
  Northwood 192
Halttunen, Karen 76n
Hamand, Wendy F. 112n
Hamer, Mary 110n
Hamilton, Kendra 111n
Harper, Frances Ellen Watkins
  Iola Leroy; or, Shadows Uplifted 208, 209
Harris, George Washington 150n
Harris, Susan K. 141
Hawthorne, Nathaniel 2, 10, 58, 66–67,
     174, 190, 192
  The Blithedale Romance 174
  The Scarlet Letter 4, 5, 66–67
Hedrick, Joan D. 8, 37n, 75n, 93n, 94n,
     111n, 136, 169n, 189n, 217n
Henson, Josiah 13, 18, 25
Hentz, Caroline Lee 40, 50, 51, 56
  The Planter's Northern Bride 40, 45–50,
     192
Higashida, Cheryl 218n
Higginson, Thomas Wentworth 173
Hildreth, Richard 177
  The Slave, or Memoirs of Archy Moore
     177, 206
Hirsch, Stephen A. 102
Holmes, George Frederick 39, 45, 51, 52, 158
Holmes, Mary Jane 42
Hooker, Isabella Beecher 1, 229
Hooper, Johnson Jones 150n
Hopkins, Samuel 175, 183
Howard, Leon 201n
Howells, William Dean
  A Modern Instance 216

Irving, Washington 131–132, 190
  "The Legend of Sleepy Hollow" 131–132
  "Rip Van Winkle" 132

Jackson, Helen Hunt
  Ramona 211
Jacobs, Harriet 25
  Incidents in the Life of a Slave Girl 25
James, Henry
  The Bostonians 193, 216

James, Louis 98
James, William 73
Jefferson, Thomas 161, 209
Jewett, John P. 2, 41
Jewett, Sarah Orne 2, 149
  A Country Doctor 216
  The Country of the Pointed Firs 214
Johnson, Charles 20

Kalayjian, Patricia 212
Kansas–Nebraska Act 29
Kaplan, Amy 94n
Karcher, Carolyn L. 9, 13, 217n
King, Grace 149
Kinmont, Alexander 20
  Twelve Lectures on Man 194
Korobkin, Laura Hanft 168n

Larsen, Nella 83
law 12, 154–168
  and consensus 164–166
  and contract 163–164
  and sentiment 154–155
  and slavery 157–159
Lee, Debbie 110n
Lee, Harper
  To Kill a Mockingbird 94n, 155
Levine, Robert S. 14n, 36n, 37n, 209
The Liberator 175, 176, 177, 185,
     206
Lincoln, Abraham 1, 2, 58, 60, 155
linguistic agency 59, 64–74
Link, Eric Carl 201n
Lippman, Monroe 129n
literature of social change 203–216
local color writing 132–133
London, Jack 210, 211
Longfellow, Henry Wadsworth 33
Longstreet, Augustus Baldwin 150n
Lord Denman 157
Lorimer, Douglas A. 99
L'Ouverture, Toussaint 29
Lucas, Sam 177

Maine Law 173
Marsh, Jan 100–101
Martineau, Harriet 203
Mason, Jeffrey 124
Mather, Cotton 173
Matthiessen, F. O. 7
McCord, Louisa 43, 44, 51
McGuffey, William H. 93n
McIntosh, Maria J. 42

Melville, Herman 10, 29, 58, 66, 67–68,
191–192
"Bartleby, the Scrivener" 61, 68
"Benito Cereno" 68
The Confidence Man 29
Moby-Dick 4, 5–6, 67–68, 190
Typee 191–192
Meyer, Michael J. 36n, 202n
Michaels, Walter Benn 220
Miller, David C. 38n
Miller, William Lee 74n
Mintz, Steven 189n
Moss, Elizabeth 57n
Moynihan, Daniel Patrick
The Negro Family 27
Mullen, Harryette 38n
Murfree, Mary Noailles 149

National Era 2, 4, 17, 21, 160, 178, 206
Newman, Judie 9, 11, 37n, 130n
Noble, Marianne 75n
North American Review 187
novel 77, 190–192
Nye, Russel B. 74n

Oakes, Karen Kilcup 153n
O'Connell, Catherine E. 75n
Odum, Howard W. 151n
Olmstead, Frederick Law 43
Ong, Walter 94n
Otter, Samuel 9
Owen, Robert 174

Parker, Joel 178
Parsons, C. G. 42–43
Pateman, Carole 164
Pattee, Lewis 8
Pease, Donald 230
Phelps, Elizabeth Stuart 210–211
Doctor Zay 216
Phillips, Frederick 115–117, 121, 122
Pitcock, Jennifer Workman 129n
Plato 77
Poe, Edgar Allan 10, 58, 65–66, 74, 230
"The Fall of the House of Usher" 65–66,
74
Prince, Mary 97, 105–106
protest literature 13, 204
see also literature of social change
Pryse, Marjorie 9, 11, 150n, 218n

race 15–35
and civil rights 7, 227

Railton, Stephen 36n, 56n, 93n
Randolph, J. Thornton 51
reading 10–11, 77–93
in Victorian England 97–98
Reed, Ishmael 16–17, 19, 26
Flight to Canada 16, 18, 226, 227–228
reform 12, 171–188
failure of 186–187
and gender 173, 215–216
and moral suasion 175
and utopianism 174
see also literature of social change
regionalism 2, 11–12, 131–150, 204
formal features of 134
and gender 139
and social change 212–216
versus local color 134
Riss, Arthur 36n
Romero, Lora 36n
Roth, Phillip 59
Rowe, John Carlos 198
Rush, Caroline 43
*The North and South, or Slavery and its
Contrasts* 43–44

St. Augustine 195
Schultz, Nancy Lusignan 218n
Sedgwick, Catharine Maria 205, 212–213
The Linwoods 212
A New England Tale 212
Redwood 192, 205, 212
sentimentality 8, 77–78, 92–93, 178, 222,
224–226, 230–232
Seward, William 157, 160
Sewell, Anna
Black Beauty 211
Shakespeare, William 192
The Tempest 90–91, 137
Sherman, Alfonso 129n
Sherman, Sarah Way 36n
Silber, Nina 192
Sinclair, Upton
The Jungle 6, 210–211
slave narratives 11, 97, 98–99, 206
slavery 16
and British Romantic writers 97
defenses of 43–45, 50–53
and the law 26–27, 52, 157–159
and sexual abuse 25
Smith, Adam 93n
Smith, W. L. G. 4, 45
Southern Literary Messenger 39
Speaight, George 130n

Spillers, Hortense 27, 36n, 220, 227–228, 243
Spufford, Francis 93n
Stanton, Elizabeth Cady 1, 167, 215
Stanton, William 37n
Stephens, Marion 57n
Stepto, Robert B. 38n, 217n
Stowe, Calvin 1, 22, 136
Stowe, Charles Edward 37n, 216n
Stowe, Harriet Beecher:
  and British travels 109
  and family 3, 175
  and gender 39–40, 103, 144
  and religion 7
WORKS:
  Agnes of Sorrento 2, 7, 152n
  "Appeal to the Women of the Free States" 171
  Dred 2, 8, 9, 11, 12–13, 17, 19, 24, 25, 26, 27, 29–35, 154, 157, 162–163, 171, 178, 181–182, 185, 193, 204: as compared to *Uncle Tom's Cabin* 196–200: stage adaptations of 11, 113–128; British and American adaptations compared 115–116
  "The Drunkard Reclaimed" 175
  "The Freeman's Dream: A Parable" 160
  A Key to Uncle Tom's Cabin 2, 10, 12, 17, 21, 22, 23, 24–29, 32, 33, 34, 40, 154, 156, 178–179, 191, 204: as argument against slavery 50–56
  Lady Byron Vindicated 7, 9, 12, 154, 156, 167–168, 204
  "Love versus Law" 12, 154–155
  Men of our Times 156–157, 167
  My Wife and I 9, 13, 204, 212, 214–216
  The Minister's Wooing 2, 7, 8, 9, 11, 12, 13, 140–142, 171, 174–175, 177, 178, 183–184, 197, 204, 212–214
  "The Old Meeting-House" 11
  Oldtown Folks 9, 11, 132, 135, 140–141, 142–144, 204
  "Our Florida Plantation" 187
  Palmetto Leaves 7, 8, 11
  The Pearl of Orr's Island 2, 8, 9, 10, 11, 78–79, 86–93, 136–140, 204
  Pink and White Tyranny 204
  Poganuc People 7, 8, 204
  Sam Lawson's Oldtown Fireside Stories 132, 142, 144–149

"Uncle Enoch" 166
"Uncle Lot" ("A New England Sketch") 131–132, 212
Uncle Tom's Cabin 1–13, 18–24, 25, 26, 29, 31, 32, 33, 60–64, 77–85, 154, 171, 185, 193–196, 204: afterlife of 3–4, 13, 177, 219–233: as argument against slavery 44, 69, 84–85, 160–161, 177–178, 179–181, 206–208: British response to 11, 96–110: and Christianity 63–64, 70, 72–73, 83–84, 207, 208: critical response to 3, 6, 7–8, 13, 18, 58, 203, 220–223, 224–233: as "great American novel" 190–191: as model for American protest fiction 208–212: and names of characters 194–195, 207: and pedagogy 4–5: and practices of reading 79–86: publishing history of 79–86, 190: and race 3, 9, 19–20, 24, 85, 114: and "real presence" 60–64, 69–73, 221: and regionalism 134–136: southern responses to 10, 39–50: stage adaptations of 32, 101, 113, 203: and "Tom-mania" 11, 99–110
We and our Neighbors 204
Sumner, Charles 6, 29, 31, 59, 156–157, 158–159, 167, 181, 196–197
Sundquist, Eric J. 7, 36n, 38n, 94n, 220
Suter, W. E. 114, 120, 122
sympathy 8, 10, 21, 41, 43–56, 77–78, 161–162, 178, 192

Taylor, C. W. 122, 124
temperance movement 175
Thaxter, Celia 139, 149
Thomas, Brook 154
Thompson, G. R. 201n
Thompson, John R. 39
Thoreau, Henry David 10, 58, 68–69
  "Resistance to Civil Government" 62, 68–69
Tompkins, Jane 6, 7, 8, 36n, 74n, 93n, 220, 222, 229
Turner, Nat 29, 34
  Confessions 178
Twain, Mark 119, 229
  Pudd'nhead Wilson 119

Uncle Tom in England (anon.) 108–109
Upham, Thomas 160

Vesey, Denmark 29, 34, 181
Von Frank, Albert J. 76n
Von Suttner, Bertha
   Lay Down Your Arms! 211

Walker, Kara 16
Walters, Ronald G. 9, 12, 189n
Warren, Kenneth W. 9, 13
Warren, Robert Penn 151n
Warren, William 124
Washington, George 34
Waters, Hazel 101, 129n
Webb, Frank J. 30, 32
   The Garies and Their Friends 32, 171
     Stowe's preface to 171
Webb, Mary E. 101
Weinstein, Cindy 10, 37n, 93n, 110n, 216n
Weld, Angelina Grimké 176
Weld, Theodore Dwight 25, 168n, 176, 206
   American Slavery as It Is 176, 178, 206
Westra, Helen Petter 76n
Wharton, Edith
   The House of Mirth 216

Wheatley, Phillis 97
Whitney, Lisa 38n, 168n
Widdicomb, Henry 123
Wiegman, Robyn 230–231
Williams, Linda 36n, 113
Wilson, Edmund 219–220
Wilson, Forrest 110n
Winship, Michael 201n
Wishy, Bernard 94n
Wood, Marcus 99
Wright, D. G. 112n
Wright, Richard 13, 83, 223–224
   Native Son 223–224
   Uncle Tom's Children 208, 209–210,
     223

Yarborough, Richard 36n, 38n, 136, 152n,
   220, 226
Yellin, Jean Fagan 217n
Young, Elizabeth 200n

Zitkala-Ša 149
Zwarg, Christina 36n

CAMBRIDGE COMPANIONS TO LITERATURE

*The Cambridge Companion to
Greek Tragedy*
edited by P. E. Easterling

*The Cambridge Companion to Old English
Literature*
edited by Malcolm Godden and Michael
Lapidge

*The Cambridge Companion to Medieval
Women's Writing*
edited by Carolyn Dinshaw and David
Wallace

*The Cambridge Companion to Medieval
Romance*
edited by Roberta L. Krueger

*The Cambridge Companion to Medieval
English Theatre*
edited by Richard Beadle

*The Cambridge Companion to English
Renaissance Drama,*
second edition edited by A. R. Braunmuller
and Michael Hattaway

*The Cambridge Companion to Renaissance
Humanism*
edited by Jill Kraye

*The Cambridge Companion to English
Poetry, Donne to Marvell*
edited by Thomas N. Corns

*The Cambridge Companion to English
Literature, 1500–1600*
edited by Arthur F. Kinney

*The Cambridge Companion to English
Literature, 1650–1740*
edited by Steven N. Zwicker

*The Cambridge Companion to English
Literature, 1740–1830*
edited by Thomas Keymer and
Jon Mee

*The Cambridge Companion to Writing of
the English Revolution*
edited by N. H. Keeble

*The Cambridge Companion to English
Restoration Theatre*
edited by Deborah C. Payne Fisk

*The Cambridge Companion to British
Romanticism*
edited by Stuart Curran

*The Cambridge Companion to
Eighteenth-Century Poetry*
edited by John Sitter

*The Cambridge Companion to the
Eighteenth-Century Novel*
edited by John Richetti

The Cambridge Companion to Gothic Fiction
edited by Jerrold E. Hogle

*The Cambridge Companion to Victorian
Poetry*
edited by Joseph Bristow

*The Cambridge Companion to the Victorian
Novel*
edited by Deirdre David

The Cambridge Companion to Crime Fiction
edited by Martin Priestman

The Cambridge Companion to Science Fiction
edited by Edward James and Farah
Mendlesohn

The Cambridge Companion to Travel Writing
edited by Peter Hulme and Tim Youngs

*The Cambridge Companion to American
Realism and Naturalism*
edited by Donald Pizer

*The Cambridge Companion to
Nineteenth-Century American Women's
Writing*
edited by Dale M. Bauer and Philip Gould

*The Cambridge Companion to the Classic
Russian Novel*
edited by Malcolm V. Jones and Robin
Feuer Miller

*The Cambridge Companion to the French
Novel: from 1800 to the Present*
edited by Timothy Unwin

*The Cambridge Companion to the Spanish
Novel: from 1600 to the Present*
edited by Harriet Turner and Adelaida
López de Martínez

*The Cambridge Companion to the Italian
Novel*
edited by Peter Bondanella and Andrea
Ciccarelli

*The Cambridge Companion to the Modern
German Novel*
edited by Graham Bartram

The Cambridge Companion to Jewish American Literature
edited by Hana Wirth-Nesher and Michael P. Kramer

The Cambridge Companion to the African American Novel
edited by Maryemma Graham

The Cambridge Companion to Contemporary Irish Poetry
edited by Matthew Campbell

The Cambridge Companion to Modernism
edited by Michael Levenson

The Cambridge Companion to Postmodernism
edited by Steven Connor

The Cambridge Companion to Australian Literature
edited by Elizabeth Webby

The Cambridge Companion to American Women Playwrights
edited by Brenda Murphy

The Cambridge Companion to Modern British Women Playwrights
edited by Elaine Aston and Janelle Reinelt

The Cambridge Companion to Twentieth-Century Irish Drama
edited by Shaun Richards

The Cambridge Companion to Homer
edited by Robert Fowler

The Cambridge Companion to Virgil
edited by Charles Martindale

The Cambridge Companion to Ovid
edited by Philip Hardie

The Cambridge Companion to Dante
edited by Rachel Jacoff

The Cambridge Companion to Cervantes
edited by Anthony J. Cascardi

The Cambridge Companion to Goethe
edited by Lesley Sharpe

The Cambridge Companion to Dostoevskii
edited by W. J. Leatherbarrow

The Cambridge Companion to Tolstoy
edited by Donna Tussing Orwin

The Cambridge Companion to Chekhov
edited by Vera Gottlieb and Paul Allain

The Cambridge Companion to Ibsen
edited by James McFarlane

The Cambridge Companion to Proust
edited by Richard Bales

The Cambridge Companion to Thomas Mann
edited by Ritchie Robertson

The Cambridge Companion to Kafka
edited by Julian Preece

The Cambridge Companion to Brecht
edited by Peter Thomson and Glendyr Sacks

The Cambridge Companion to Walter Benjamin
edited by David S. Ferris

The Cambridge Companion to Lacan
edited by Jean-Michel Rabaté

The Cambridge Companion to Chaucer,
second edition edited by Piero Boitani and Jill Mann

The Cambridge Companion to Shakespeare
edited by Margareta de Grazia and Stanley Wells

The Cambridge Companion to Shakespeare on Film
edited by Russell Jackson

The Cambridge Companion to Shakespearean Comedy
edited by Alexander Leggatt

The Cambridge Companion to Shakespeare on Stage
edited by Stanley Wells and Sarah Stanton

The Cambridge Companion to Shakespeare's History Plays
edited by Michael Hattaway

The Cambridge Companion to Shakespearean Tragedy
edited by Claire McEachern

The Cambridge Companion to Christopher Marlowe
edited by Patrick Cheney

The Cambridge Companion to Spenser
edited by Andrew Hadfield

The Cambridge Companion to John Dryden
edited by Steven N. Zwicker

The Cambridge Companion to Ben Jonson
edited by Richard Harp and Stanley Stewart

The Cambridge Companion to Milton,
second edition edited by Dennis Danielson

The Cambridge Companion to Samuel Johnson
edited by Greg Clingham

The Cambridge Companion to Jonathan Swift
edited by Christopher Fox

*The Cambridge Companion to Mary
Wollstonecraft*
edited by Claudia L. Johnson

The Cambridge Companion to William Blake
edited by Morris Eaves

The Cambridge Companion to Wordsworth
edited by Stephen Gill

The Cambridge Companion to Coleridge
edited by Lucy Newlyn

The Cambridge Companion to Keats
edited by Susan J. Wolfson

The Cambridge Companion to Mary Shelley
edited by Esther Schor

The Cambridge Companion to Jane Austen
edited by Edward Copeland and
Juliet McMaster

The Cambridge Companion to the Brontës
edited by Heather Glen

*The Cambridge Companion to Charles
Dickens*
edited by John O. Jordan

The Cambridge Companion to George Eliot
edited by George Levine

*The Cambridge Companion to Thomas
Hardy*
edited by Dale Kramer

The Cambridge Companion to Oscar Wilde
edited by Peter Raby

*The Cambridge Companion to George
Bernard Shaw*
edited by Christopher Innes

The Cambridge Companion to Joseph Conrad
edited by J. H. Stape

*The Cambridge Companion to D. H.
Lawrence*
edited by Anne Fernihough

*The Cambridge Companion to Virginia
Woolf*
edited by Sue Roe and Susan Sellers

The Cambridge Companion to James Joyce,
second edition edited by Derek Attridge

The Cambridge Companion to T. S. Eliot
edited by A. David Moody

The Cambridge Companion to Ezra Pound
edited by Ira B. Nadel

The Cambridge Companion to Beckett
edited by John Pilling

*The Cambridge Companion to
Harold Pinter*
edited by Peter Raby

*The Cambridge Companion to
Tom Stoppard*
edited by Katherine E. Kelly

*The Cambridge Companion to
David Mamet*
edited by Christopher Bigsby

*The Cambridge Companion to Herman
Melville*
edited by Robert S. Levine

*The Cambridge Companion to Nathaniel
Hawthorne*
edited by Richard Millington

*The Cambridge Companion to Harriet
Beecher Stowe*
edited by Cindy Weinstein

*The Cambridge Companion to Theodore
Dreiser*
edited by Leonard Cassuto and
Claire Virginia Eby

*The Cambridge Companion to Edith
Wharton*
edited by Millicent Bell

The Cambridge Companion to Henry James
edited by Jonathan Freedman

The Cambridge Companion to Walt Whitman
edited by Ezra Greenspan

*The Cambridge Companion to Ralph Waldo
Emerson*
edited by Joel Porte and Saundra Morris

*The Cambridge Companion to Henry
David Thoreau*
edited by Joel Myerson

The Cambridge Companion to Mark Twain
edited by Forrest G. Robinson

*The Cambridge Companion to Edgar
Allan Poe*
edited by Kevin J. Hayes

*The Cambridge Companion to Emily
Dickinson*
edited by Wendy Martin

*The Cambridge Companion to William
Faulkner*
edited by Philip M. Weinstein

*The Cambridge Companion to Ernest
Hemingway*
edited by Scott Donaldson

*The Cambridge Companion to F. Scott
Fitzgerald*
edited by Ruth Prigozy

The Cambridge Companion to Robert Frost
edited by Robert Faggen

*The Cambridge Companion to Eugene
O'Neill*
edited by Michael Manheim

*The Cambridge Companion to Tennessee
Williams*
edited by Matthew C. Roudané

The Cambridge Companion to Arthur Miller
edited by Christopher Bigsby

*The Cambridge Companion to Sam
Shepard*
edited by Matthew C. Roudané

CAMBRIDGE COMPANIONS TO CULTURE

*The Cambridge Companion to Modern
German Culture*
edited by Eva Kolinsky and Wilfried
van der Will

*The Cambridge Companion to Modern
Russian Culture*
edited by Nicholas Rzhevsky

*The Cambridge Companion to Modern
Spanish Culture*
edited by David T. Gies

*The Cambridge Companion to Modern
Italian Culture*
edited by Zygmunt G. Barański and
Rebecca J. West

*The Cambridge Companion to Modern
French Culture*
edited by Nicholas Hewitt

*The Cambridge Companion to Modern
Latin American Literature*
edited by John King